T0140258

Human–Computer Interaction Series

Editors-in-Chief
Desney Tan, Microsoft Research, USA
Jean Vanderdonckt, Université catholique de Louvain, Belgium

HCI is a multidisciplinary field focused on human aspects of the development of computer technology. As computer-based technology becomes increasingly pervasive—not just in developed countries, but worldwide—the need to take a human-centered approach in the design and development of this technology becomes ever more important. For roughly 30 years now, researchers and practitioners in computational and behavioral sciences have worked to identify theory and practice that influences the direction of these technologies, and this diverse work makes up the field of human-computer interaction. Broadly speaking it includes the study of what technology might be able to do for people and how people might interact with the technology. The HCI series publishes books that advance the science and technology of developing systems which are both effective and satisfying for people in a wide variety of contexts. Titles focus on theoretical perspectives (such as formal approaches drawn from a variety of behavioral sciences), practical approaches (such as the techniques for effectively integrating user needs in system development), and social issues (such as the determinants of utility, usability and acceptability).

Titles published within the Human–Computer Interaction Series are included in Thomson Reuters' Book Citation Index, The DBLP Computer Science Bibliography and The HCI Bibliography.

For further volumes:
http://www.springer.com/series/6033

Regina Bernhaupt
Editor

Game User Experience Evaluation

 Springer

Editor
Regina Bernhaupt
Institut de Recherche en Informatique de
Toulouse (IRIT), ICS Group
Toulouse
France

ISSN 1571-5035
ISBN 978-3-319-36293-9   ISBN 978-3-319-15985-0 (eBook)
DOI 10.1007/978-3-319-15985-0

Springer Cham Heidelberg New York Dordrecht London
© Springer International Publishing Switzerland 2015
Softcover reprint of the hardcover 1st edition 2015

Printed on acid-free paper

Springer is part of Springer Science+Business Media (www.springer.com)

Contents

Contributors

Regina Bernhaupt   IRIT, ICS, Toulouse, France

Ruwido, Neumarkt, Austria

Nadia Bianchi-Berthouze   UCL Interaction Center University College London, London, WC, UK

Michael Brown   Horizon Digital Economy Research, University of Nottingham, Nottingham, UK

Paul Cairns   Computer Science Department, The University of York, York, UK

Eduardo H. Calvillo-Gámez   Innovation and Technology, San Luis Potosí, S.L.P., México

Anna L. Cox   UCL Interaction Centre, University College London, London, UK

Heather Desurvire   User Behavioristics, Inc., Marina del Rey, CA USA

Anders Drachen   Department of Communication, Aalborg University, Copenhagen SV, Denmark

Cornelia Graf   Center for Usability Research and Engineering, Vienna, Austria

Jukka Häkkinen   Psychology of Digital Life (PDL)/Psychology of Evolving Media and Technology (POEM), University of Helsinki, Helsinki, Finland

Christina Hochleitner   Innovation Systems Department, Business Unit Technology Experience, AIT Austrian Institute of Technology, Vienna, Austria

Wolfgang Hochleitner   Playful Interactive Environments, University of Applied Sciences Upper Austria, Hagenberg, Austria

Katherine Isbister   New York University, 2 Metrotech Center, Office 874, Brooklyn, NY, USA

Aidan Kehoe   Logitech, Cork, Ireland

Jurek Kirakowski   People and Technology Research Group, Department of Applied Psychology, University College Cork, Cork, Ireland

Michael Lankes Department of Digital Media, University of Applied Sciences Upper Austria, Hagenberg, Austria

Graham McAllister Player Research, Brighton, UK

Florian Mueller Exertion Games Lab, RMIT University, Melbourne, Australia

Lennart E. Nacke Faculty of Business and Information Technology, University of Ontario Institute of Technology, Ontario, Canada

Göte Nyman Psychology of Digital Life (PDL)/Psychology of Evolving Media and Technology (POEM), University of Helsinki, Helsinki, Finland

Ian Pitt IDEAS Research Group, Department of Computer Science, University College Cork, Cork, Ireland

Elena Márquez Segura Department of Informatics and Media, Uppsala University, Uppsala, Sweden

Jari Takatalo Psychology of Digital Life (PDL)/Psychology of Evolving Media and Technology (POEM), University of Helsinki, Helsinki, Finland

Manfred Tscheligi Innovation Systems Department, Business Unit Technology Experience, AIT Austrian Institute of Technology, Vienna, Austria

Center for Human-Computer Interaction, Christian Doppler Laboratory "Contextual Interfaces", Department of Computer Sciences, University of Salzburg, Salzburg, Austria

Gareth R. White University of Sussex, Brighton, UK

Charlotte Wiberg Umea University, Umea, Sweden

Chapter 1
User Experience Evaluation Methods
in the Games Development Life Cycle

Regina Bernhaupt

Abstract User Experience (UX) evaluation methods can be applied at any stage in the design and development life cycle. While the term user experience is still not well defined, this chapter gives an overview on a large number of UX related terms, dimensions, factors and concepts. It presents specialized UX evaluation methods classified in (a) user-oriented methods including focus groups, interviews, questionnaires, experiments, observation, bio-physiological measurements, (b) expert-oriented methods like heuristic evaluations, (c) automated methods like telemetry analysis and (d) specialized methods for the evaluation of social game play or exertion games. Summarizing the contributions in this book, a user-experience centered game development is presented, allowing readers to understand when in the life cycle to apply what kind of UX evaluation methods.

1.1 Introduction

Major goal for any game development is to have a game that is fun to play, that is entertaining, that provides surprises, enables gamers to be challenged and apply their skills, but also to provide aesthetically pleasing experiences, to support social connectedness or allow the player to identify with the game. There is a broad variety of game evaluation methods currently available that help game designers and developers, researchers and practitioners, but also the users—the players—themselves that start to design, develop and extend games. In the following the word user experience is used synonymously for player experience or gamer experience.

User experience evaluations in games and more general in interactive entertainment systems have been performed from early on in games development. Programmers of the first computing systems started to develop their games and simply tried them out themselves to see if they were fun. Today user experience evaluation methods have their roots in a variety of fields and areas, the two most prominent ones represented in this book are the area of game design and development and

R. Bernhaupt (✉)
Ruwido, Neumarkt, Austria
e-mail: Regina.Bernhaupt@ruwido.com

the area of human-computer interaction (HCI). In industry today a broad range of methods is deployed to understand the various contributing aspects of the overall gaming experience. The term user experience was only rarely used in the games industry (Federoff 2002), but became extremely prominent in the field of HCI. Today the communities of human-computer interaction and game research are starting to learn from each other (Bernhaupt et al. 2015). On the one hand, user experience evaluation methods from HCI are used during the game development to improve user experience, on the other side HCI is borrowing and investigating aspects of the gaming experience like immersion, fun or flow to better understand the concept of user experience and apply it to standard software design and development.

This introduction gives an overview on both aspects. First an overview on definitions of user experience in the area of HCI is given, followed by some basic terms that are currently used in the games industry like immersion, flow or playability. Then an overview on currently applied methods for the evaluation of user experience in games is given. This overview includes also all of the methods that are proposed, described, discussed and presented in the following chapters of the book. To allow an easy overview on the currently applied methods for user experience evaluation the most commonly used methods are presented. To help identify the applicability of the various user experience evaluation methods, the methods are presented following typical game design and development phases: initial conceptual and prototypical stage, early development stages (alpha), later development stage including localisation phase and post release phase.

1.2 Defining User Experience

User Experience (UX) still misses a clear definition especially when it comes to the fact to try to measure the concept or related constructs or dimensions (Law et al 2009). As of today the term user experience can be seen as an umbrella term used to stimulate research in HCI to focus on aspects which are beyond usability and its task-oriented instrumental values (Hassenzahl 2003). User experience (UX) is described as dynamic, time dependent (Karapanos et al 2010) and beyond the instrumental (Hassenzahl and Traktinsky 2006). From an HCI perspective the overall goal of UX is to understand the role of affect as an antecedent, a consequence and a mediator of technology. The concept of UX focuses rather on positive emotions and emotional outcomes such as joy, fun and pride (Hassenzahl and Traktinsky 2006).

There is a growing number of methods available to evaluate user experience in all stages of the development process. Surveys on these contributions are already available such Bargas-Avila and Hornbæk (2011) who present an overview on UX and UX evaluation methods or HCI researchers who have summarized UX evaluation methods in a website (allaboutUX 2015). Beyond that work on generic methods, contributions have been proposed for specific application domains, e.g. for interactive television (Bernhaupt and Pirker 2013) or for the evaluation of mobile devices like mobile phones (Roto et al. 2008). User experience does include a look on all the (qualitative) experience a user is making while interacting with a product

(McCarthy and Wright 2004), or on experiences made during interacting with a special type of product e.g. a mobile phone (Roto et al. 2008). The current ISO definition on user experience focuses on a person's perception and the responses resulting from the use or anticipated use of a product, system, or service. From a psychological perspective these responses are actively generated in a psychological evaluation process, and it has to be decided which concepts can best represent the psychological compartments to allow to measure the characteristics of user experience. It is necessary to understand, investigate and specify the dimensions or factors that are taken into account for the various application domains. Table 1.1 shows a summary of user experience dimensions that have been addressed by researchers in the domain of HCI and Games.

The *aesthetics* dimension describes how aesthetically pleasing or beautiful something is perceived. The visual/aesthetic experience deals with the pleasure gained from sensory perceptions (Hekkert 2006). It incorporates beauty (Hassenzahl 2004), as well as classic aesthetics (e.g. clear, symmetric) described by Lavie and Tractinsky (2004).

Emotion has been identified as a key factor of UX (Hassenzahl and Tractinsky 2006). For Desmet and Hekkert (2007), the emotional experience is one of the three main factors contributing to product experience, including feelings and emotions elicited. Additionally, the feeling of competence as a need fulfillment is covered within this dimension (Hassenzahl et al. 2010).

Table 1.1 Overview on selected literature identifying major user experience dimensions

	Aesthetic	Emotion/affect	Stimulation	Identification	Others
Hekkert (2006)	x	x			VM
Desmet and Hekkert (2007)	x	x		x	VM
Hassenzahl (2004)	x		x	x	SRC
Karapanos et al. (2010)			x		
Jordan (2000)	x		x	x	VM, SRC
Wright et al. (2003)	x	x			
Hassenzahl et al. (2010)		x	x	x	VM, SRC, DST
Jääskö and Mattelmäki (2003)	x		x	x	VM
Desmet et al. (2001); Mandryk et al. (2006); Norman (2004)		x			
Sheldon et al. (2001)		x	x	x	VM
Pirker et al. (2010)	x	x	x		VM, SRC
Lavie & Tractinsky (2004)	x	x	x		SQ
Jsselsteijn et al. (2008)	x	x			Flow, C

(*VM* value/meaning, *SRC* social/relatedness/co-experience; *C* challenge; *DST* dependability/security/trust; *SQ* service quality)

The *stimulation* dimension describes to what extent a product can support the human need for innovative and interesting functions, interactions and contents. Hassenzahl (2004) describes stimulation as a hedonic attribute of a product, which can lead to new impressions, opportunities and insights. Hedonic experiences were subsumed by Karapanos et al. (2010) under the term innovativeness to describe hedonic experiences and the ability of a product to excite the user through its novelty. In the area of games, Jääskö and Mattelmäki (2003) defined product novelty as one of the qualities of user experience.

The *identification* dimension indicates to what extent a certain product allows the user to identify with it. For Hassenzahl (2006), the identification dimension addresses the human need to express one's self through objects. Thus, using or owning a specific product is a way to reach a desired self-presentation. Identification can be seen as self-expression through an object to communicate identity.

Other factors include *Value and Meaning, Social Connectedness, Dependability, Security and Trust, Service Quality* and *Flow* (Csikszentmihalyi 1991). These dimensions are considered in the following chapters along with other constructs and factors like immersion, fun, presence involvement, engagement or play, playability and social play.

1.3   Methods to Evaluate UX in Games

A central question for UX evaluation methods for games is to what extend those (general) methods can be applied and provide meaningful and sufficiently precise insights? While there is some evidence general usability evaluation methods from HCI could be applied for game development, there is a number of approaches adapting these methods for the specifities of the domain. Due to the idiosyncratic nature of user experience that is situational, time dependent, and influenced by the technological context especially the type of system and functionality, and especially the specifities of games, the authors in this book tend to support the idea that there is a need to adapt, customize and validate specific UX evaluation methods for the games and entertainment domain.

Based on the various definitions and concepts used to evaluate user experience the following section will present an overview on methods that are currently used to evaluate user experience during the various game development phases. Game development can be structured in a set of development phases. Most of these phases are used in standard software development processes, other phases are special for game development.

Following Novak (2008) the following phases are used to structure the overview on methods for evaluating user experience in games:

- Concept: This phase is dedicated to the initial game idea and is devoted to producing a first concept document describing the game. The development team in this phase is typically small (e.g. consisting of designer, programmer, artist and producer).

- Pre-Production Phase: This phase includes the development of art style guides, production plans and first description of the game design and the technical design document.
- Prototype: Goal of this phase is a first working piece of software allowing to demonstrate key characteristics of the game and enabling to understand basic concepts related to the general user experience of the game ("Is the game fun to play?").
- Production: The production phase can range from few weeks development to years of programming. This phase can be structured additionally, following approaches like an increment to completion approach, a cascade approach or an "iterative- until you drop" approach (Irish 2005).
- Localization: an important phase for games that will be delivered to different markets (countries) is the localization phase. In this phase game-play can be adjusted to suit the tastes of the market, to allow language translation and modifications due to local regulatory authorities.
- Alpha-Phase: This is the phase when a game is playable from start to finish, allowing different evaluation methods to be applied to better understand aspects like fun, playability and user experience.
- Beta-Phase: Main goal during this phase is normally to fix bugs. In terms of user experience in this phase lots of fine-tuning is necessary to improve the overall user experience. The beta-phase includes steps like certification or submission (the hardware-manufacturer of the proprietary platform will test the game).
- Gold: In this phase the game is sent to be manufactured.
- Post-Production: In this phase subsequent versions of the game may be released (including patches and updated) and allows to improve the user experience of the game.

During the various development phases there is a set of UX evaluation methods that can be applied. To give an overview Table 1.2 provides a list of the various phases in games design and development and indicate applicability of each of the user experience methods.

UX evaluation methods can be classified in methods that involve the user, methods that are based on user data, but enable automated testing or analysis (Bernhaupt et al. 2008) and methods that are applied or conducted by experts. The following chapters give an overview and insights on each of the UX evaluation methods:

(1) user-oriented methods:

McAllister et al. lay the basis explaining how UX evaluation can be different, but also can be similar to traditional usability evaluation. Based on the typical game development phases they describe four case studies showing how UX evaluation is currently performed in industry, including focus groups, play testing and interviews.

Looking at various dimensions, factors or concept related to UX, Calvillo-Gamez and colleagues investigate the core elements of the gaming experience showing with the CEGE model and a validated questionnaire how to evaluate user experience with a focus enjoyment as key UX dimension.

Table 1.2 Game design and development phases and applicability of methods

	Concept	Prototype	Pre-production	Production (alpha, beta, gold)	Post-production
User-oriented methods					
Focus groups	x	x			
Interviews	x	x	x		
Observation (exertion games)		x		x	x
PIFF questionnaire		x		x	
CEGE questionnaire		x		x	
Play-testing (incl. social play-testing)			(x)	x	x
Physiological UX evaluation		x		x	x
Experiments (incl game controller evaluation)	x	x		x	x
Expert-oriented methods					
Heuristic based evaluations (GAP)		x		x	
Using video heuristics		x		x	
Other approaches					
Behavioral game telemetry		(x)		x	x

Nacke gives an overview of standard UX evaluation methods that are currently applied for games including Focus Groups, Interviews and Observation. Based on an analysis of advantages and limitations of these methods he introduces physiological oriented UX evaluation and explains how EEG, EMD, EDA and GSR can be used to enhance games.

Takatalo investigates other UX dimensions based on a detailed statistical analysis of games proposing the PIFF questionnaire enabling the evaluation of presence, involvement and flow. Lankes et al show how to use experiments to study the influence of game elements like avatars or non-player characters on a set of user experience dimensions.

(2) automated methods:

The chapter by Drachen introduces telemetry-based game evaluation as a second group of UX evaluation methods. These methods are based on user behavior but allow an analysis that is automated.

(3) expert-oriented methods:

Desuvire et al show how principles can be applied to help make games playable for certain user groups.

Koeffel et al show how video game heuristics can be applied at various stages of the development process to enhance game.

(4) games-specific approaches:

The multitude of games and how they are played have led to the development of special UX evaluation approaches.

Marquez-Segura et al. show how social play can be investigated, while Mueller et al investigate exertion games.

Finally Brown et al re-investigate the relationship between usability, user experience and the ability to control the game, helping to understand how user experience can be influenced by other (software) qualities.

To summarize, this book is an assembly of chapters dealing with user experience evaluation methods. My personal fundamental believe is that user experience is not just one construct, factor or dimension, but that this experience of the player is made up by various dimensions that influence each other. From my personal view a successful evaluation starts with the selection of a set of factors or dimensions that we want to evaluate. Even if the sum of these factors and dimensions can be a holistic experience that might be more than just the individual pieces, I argue it will be better to start with some few dimensions that can be carefully investigated and evaluated. In the end, what counts, is that the game is fun to be played.

Acknowledgements A special thank you goes to all the people who helped make this second edition come true: Ferdinand Maier, Philippe Palanque, the ICS group and my research teams in France and Austria.

References

allaboutUX (2015) www.allaboutUX.org. Accessed 13 Apr 2015

Bargas-Avila J, Hornbæk K (2011) Old wine in new bottles or novel challenges. Proc CHI'11. pp. 2689–2698

Bernhaupt R, Navarre D, Palanque P,Winckler M (2008) Model-based evaluation: A new way to support usability evaluation of multimodal interactive applications. In: Maturing usability, pp. 96–119. Springer London

Bernhaupt R, Pirker M (2013) Evaluating user experience for interactive television: Towards the development of a domain-specific user experience questionnaire. In: Human-Computer Interaction—INTERACT 2013 (pp. 642–659). Springer Berlin Heidelberg

Bernhaupt R, de Freitas S, Isbister K (2015) Introduction to the special issue on games and HCI. J HCI, to appear

Csikszentmihalyi M (1991) Flow: the psychology of optimal experience. Harper Perennial, N.Y

Desmet PMA, Hekkert P (2007) Framework of product experience. Int J Des 1(1):57–66

Desmet PMA, Overbeeke CJ, Tax SJET (2001) Designing products with added emotional value. Des J 4(1):32–47

Federoff MA (2002) Heuristics and usability guidelines for the creation and evaluation of fun in videogames. Master's thesis, Department of Telecommunications, Indiana University

Hassenzahl M (2003) The thing and I: understanding the relationship between user and product. In: Blythe MA, MOnk AF, Overbeeke K, Wright PC (eds) Funology: from usability to enjoyment. Kluwer Academic Publishers, Netherlands

Hassenzahl M (2004) The interplay of beauty, goodness, and usability in interactive products. J HCI 19(4):319–349

Hassenzahl M, Tractinsky N (2006) User experience—a research agenda. Behav Inf Technol 25(2):91–97

Hassenzahl M, Diefenbach S, Göritz A (2010) Needs, affect, and interactive products—facets of user experience. Interact Comput 22(5):353–362

Hekkert P (2006) Design aesthetics: principles of pleasure in product design. Psychol Sci 48(2):157–172

Irish D (2005) The game producer's handbook. Course Technology Press

Jääskö V, Mattelmäki T (2003) Observing and probing. In: Proceedings of the 2003 international conference on Designing pleasurable products and interfaces, pp. 126–131. ACM, New York

Jordan P (2000) Designing pleasurable products. Taylor & Francis, London

Jsselsteijn W, van den Hoogen, Klimmt C, de Kort Y, Lindley C, Mathiak K, ... Vorderer P (2008) Measuring the experience of digital game enjoyment. In: Proceedings of measuring behaviour (pp. 88–89). Maastricht, Netherlands

Karapanos E, Zimmerman J, Forlizzi J, Martens J-B (2010) Measuring the dynamics of remembered experience over time. Interact Comput 22(5):328–335

Lavie T, Tractinsky N (2004) Assessing dimensions of perceived visual aesthetics of web sites. Int Journ Hum Comput Studies 60(3):269–298

Law E, Roto V, Hassenzahl M, Vermeeren A, Kort J (2009) Understanding, scoping and defining user experience: a survey approach. Proceeding CHI 09. ACM, New York

Mandryk RL, Inkpen KM, Calvert TW (2006) Using psychophysiological techniques to measure user experience with entertainment technologies. Behav Inf Technol 25(2):141–158

McCarthy J, Wright P (2004) Technology as experience. MIT Press, Cambridge

Norman DA (2004) Emotional design: why we love (or hate) everyday things. Basic Books, New York

Novak J (2008) Game development essentials. Delmar Cengage Learning, Clifton Park, NY

Pirker M, Bernhaupt R, Mirlacher T (2010) Investigating usability and user experience as possible entry barriers for touch interaction in the living room. In: Proceeding of 8th international interactive conference on Interactive TV&Video, pp. 145–154. ACM, New York

Roto V, Ketola P, Huotari S (2008) User experience evaluation in Nokia. Now let's do it in practice: User experience evaluation methods for product development. www.research.nokia.com. Last accessed 15 June 2009

Sheldon KM, Elliot AJ, Kim Y, Kasser T (2001) What is satisfying about satisfying events? Testing 10 candidate psychological needs. J Person Soc Psychol 80(2):325–339

Wright P, McCarthy J, Meekison L (2003) Making sense of experience. In: Funology, pp. 43–53. Springer Netherlands

Part I
User Orientated Methods

Chapter 2
Video Game Development and User Experience

Graham McAllister and Gareth R. White

Abstract In order to design new methodologies for evaluating the user experience of video games, it is imperative to initially understand two core issues. Firstly, how are video games developed at present, including components such as processes, timescales and staff roles, and secondly, how do studios design and evaluate the user experience.

This chapter will discuss the video game development process and the practices that studios currently use to achieve the best possible user experience. It will present four case studies from game developers Disney Interactive (Black Rock Studio), Relentless, Zoe Mode, and HandCircus, each detailing their game development process and also how this integrates with the user experience evaluation. The case studies focus on different game genres, platforms, and target user groups, ensuring that this chapter represents a balanced view of current practices in evaluating user experience during the game development process.

2.1 Introduction

In order to design new methodologies for evaluating the usability and user experience of video games, it is imperative to initially understand two core issues. Firstly, how are video games developed at present, including aspects such as processes and time scales, and secondly, how do studios design and evaluate the user experience?

This chapter will discuss the video game development processes and practices that studios currently use to achieve the best possible user experience. It will present four case studies from AAA game developers Disney Interactive (Black Rock Studio), Zoë Mode, Relentless and mobile developer HandCircus, all based in the

G. McAllister (✉)
Player Research, Brighton, UK
e-mail: graham@playerresearch.com

G. R. White
University of Sussex, Brighton, UK

© Springer International Publishing Switzerland 2015
R. Bernhaupt (ed.), *Game User Experience Evaluation,*
Human-Computer Interaction Series, DOI 10.1007/978-3-319-15985-0_2

UK. Each case study will detail their game development process and also how this integrates with the user experience evaluation. In an attempt to represent a balanced view of state-of-the-art in game development practices, the games studios chosen focus on different game genres and target user groups.

Reader's take-away:

- Four concrete case studies of how video games are developed at world-leading studios.
- A clear understanding of the game development life cycle.
- Understanding of industry terminology, laying the foundations for a common language of user experience.
- An understanding of industry needs, both in terms of what they expect and require from usability and user experience evaluations.

In summary, the key contribution that this chapter makes to the games usability community is an understanding of the game development process and how these studios currently involve the end user.

2.2 Previous Work

Although the topic of evaluating video game user experience is gaining more attention from both academia and industry, it is not a particularly new area. One of the earliest papers (Malone 1981), discusses which features of video games makes them captivating and enjoyable to play. Today, this discussion still continues, and there is active research in determining which game features to evaluate and which approaches should be used.

Current approaches to evaluating the usability and user experience of video games have centred around themes such as mapping established HCI methods to video games, refining these methods, identifying guidelines and perhaps most importantly, evaluating the overall player experience. A summary of relevant literature will be discussed below.

2.2.1 Traditional HCI Approaches

Due to the generic nature of the majority of usability methods, researchers have analysed how existing usability methods can be applied to video games (Jørgensen 2004). Others such as Cornett have employed usability methods such as observations, questionnaires, think aloud and task completion rate, to determine if they would be successful in identifying usability issues in MMORPGs (Cornett 2004). Without much, if any, modification, there is evidence to support the claim that conventional usability techniques can be successfully applied to video game evaluation.

2.2.2   Refining Traditional Methods

Although established usability methods can be directly applied to games, Medlock and others at Microsoft Games Studios have developed a usability process which is specific to games (Medlock et al. 2002). Their approach is called the RITE (Rapid Iterative Testing and Evaluation) method and although it is very similar to a traditional usability study, there are two key differences. Firstly, the process is highly iterative, meaning that whenever a fault is found and a solution identified, it is immediately corrected and re-tested with the next participant. Secondly, the usability engineer and design team identify and classify each issue to determine if it can be resolved immediately, or if further data is needed before a solution can be found. This can be thought of as usability "triage".

2.2.3   Heuristics

Nielsen's usability heuristics (Nielsen 2007) have long served as general guidelines for creating usable applications or websites. However, various researchers (Federoff 2002; Desurvire 2005; Schaffer 2008; Laitinen 2006) have constructed sets of heuristics which are specific to video games, and compared their effectiveness to Nielsen's. They found that their heuristics are most useful during the early phases of game development. Despite the existence of specific game heuristics, questions remain about their specificity and utility (Schaffer 2008), and feedback from developers suggests that they are too generic to be of much use.

2.2.4   User Experience

According to Clanton, the overall deciding factor of a good game is game play (Clanton 1998). Trying to specify what makes a good game is not a straightforward task, and Larsen has tried to unpack this problem by examining how professional game reviewers rate games (Larsen 2008).

Others have addressed the key criticism of heuristics by wrapping them up in a unified process (Sweetster 2005). This process, which they call GameFlow, can be used to design, evaluate and understand enjoyment in games. Meanwhile, Jennet has conducted a series of experiments to measure and define the immersion in video games (Jennet 2008). The concepts of immersion and flow in games are often related to involvement or enjoyment, but they appear to have subjective and imprecise definitions, thus making them difficult to design for and measure. Furthermore flow seems to be only applicable to describing competitive gaming, despite other research pointing to the diversity of emotions a player can experience during play (Lazzaro 2007), and indeed the diversity of players and games (Schuurman et al. 2008).

2.2.5   Game Development

Most research in the area measures games towards the end of the development life cycle. Although this may be suitable for fixing small changes on time, it is not sufficient for altering key game mechanics. If new techniques are to be designed which can evaluate a game during its development cycle as well as the final product, then a better understanding of the development life cycle needs to be obtained.

One reason for the lack of tailored techniques which could be applicable to all stages of game development is that the game development process itself is not known in detail to the HCI community. Federoff work shadowed a game development team for five days and has reported some details of the development process (Federoff 2002). However, the main focus of this research was to construct game heuristics, not report on the development process per se.

The next section will discuss the general characteristics of game development including the development life cycle and relevant industry terminology.

2.3   Introduction to the Game Development Life Cycle

In the video game industry, it is nominally accepted that the development life cycle is constructed from the following phases, though in practice those occurring prior to production are often contracted or skipped entirely:

2.3.1   Concept

Game concepts can be initiated either from the publisher, who provides finance, or the development studio, who are responsible for the day-to-day production of the game. Once a general concept has been agreed between the two parties a small development team of perhaps 5 staff may spend 1–2 months producing an initial Game Design Document and visual representations such as still images or a movie to communicate the vision for the game. Additionally, a rough budget and plan is produced, including milestone agreements which define the production commitments of the developer, and the corresponding financial commitments of the publisher. This would normally represent a phased or iterative delivery of the product, where only a first-pass of each feature is completed prior to evaluation and feedback from the publisher. Later in the schedule a second delivery is made which is a more concrete implementation. Agreements made at this stage are still subject to adjustment at any future point.

2.3.2 Prototyping

During the early stages of development many different aspects of the game may be prototyped simultaneously and independently. These provide examples of features such as menus, physics and vehicle handling, or could be technical demos such as grass rendering or other components of the game or graphics engine. In order to define a visual benchmark, the art team may construct virtual dioramas, which are models of events that players will experience during the game. Some of these prototypes could be interactive, others could be non-interactive movies demonstrating an example from which the interface for this part of the game could be developed.

This initial phase can take between 3–6 months, by the end of which these prototypes and concepts are evaluated, and if the project is given a green-light it moves into pre-production.

2.3.3 Pre-Production

Following design approval, the game development team enters the important pre-production phase, during which time fundamental game mechanics are proven and problematic areas are identified. The purpose of this phase is to try out ideas quickly without getting bogged down in issues of final presentation quality, to identify risks and prove the important aspects of the game concept.

2.3.4 Production

During the main production phase the team will be scaled up to full size and would tend to spend in the order of 12 months producing all of the characters, levels, front end menus and other components of the game. Often during this stage the team will produce a "vertical slice", which is a high quality, 10–15 min demonstration of a small sample of the game.

In addition to the core team of programmers, artists, designers, and audio engineers, game developers also include a Quality Assurance (QA) group who are responsible for testing the game. This is essentially functional testing rather than usability or experiential testing. The QA team are keen gamers with a good understanding of the market and what to expect from a high quality game. As such, in addition to functional bugs which are entered into a database and addressed in a formal process, testers may also identify 'playability' issues which are informally discussed with the rest of the development team. Final issues of usability and playability are the responsibility of the producer and designers. QA teams are often only scaled up to full size toward the end of the production phase, through Alpha and Beta.

2.3.5   Alpha—Beta—Gold

Toward the end of production the game progresses through a series of statuses which indicate how close development is to completion.

In order to achieve Alpha status all content in the game should be represented, but not necessarily be of final quality. Placeholder content is common, but the game should exist as a coherent whole.

From Alpha a further 6 months would typically be spent advancing through Beta status until the game is finally available for release, with attention turned to bug fixing and finalising the quality throughout.

By Beta all content and features should effectively be finished, with all but final polishing still to take place. Nothing further will be added to the game, only tweaking and final adjustments. In particular this phase is focussed on bug fixing. After Beta the developer and publisher consider the game to be of a shippable quality and submit a Master candidate disc to the format holder (i.e., Microsoft, Nintendo or Sony) for approval.

Each game that is released on any of their consoles has to first be approved by the format holder's own QA team. Strict technical and presentation standards define how all games on the platform should deal with issues of brand-recognition as well as certain HCI guidelines. For example, which controller buttons to use for navigating dialog boxes, the format and content of messages to display to the player while saving games, or where to position important interface elements on the television screen.

The approval process usually takes 2 weeks, but in the event that the submission candidate fails, a further submission will have to be made once the development team have resolved all of the faults. How long this takes depends on the severity of the issues, but once the team have successfully dealt with them another 5–10 days will be required for the re-submission approval process. Conceivably, further submissions could be required until all issues have been resolved.

Once approval has been given, the publisher uses the Gold Master disc to begin manufacturing and distribution, which takes between 1–4 weeks. Typically a unified release date is agreed upon with all retail outlets, which requires an additional week to ensure stock is delivered from the distributors to all stores in time for simultaneous release. In the UK this results in retail outlets releasing games on a Friday.

2.4   Case Studies

This section presents four case studies from world-leading developers Black Rock Studio (part of Disney Interactive), Zoë Mode, Relentless and HandCircus. Each studio will discuss their development process, time scales and how they involve end-users.

Case Study 1—Black Rock Studio Black Rock Studio specialise in developing racing games for Xbox, PlayStation (PS) and PC. Their latest game, *Pure*, was released in September 2008 to critical acclaim. We interviewed Jason Avent, the Game Director of *Pure*, who attributes the high ratings to not only the talent of his team, but also the usability evaluations that were conducted during development.

2.4.1   Game Development at Black Rock Studio

Game development at Black Rock Studio typically takes between 18–24 months, with a phase breakdown as follows:

- Prototyping (3–6 months)
- Pre-production (6 months+)
- Production (6–12 months)
- Alpha, Beta, Submission, release (4–9 months)
- Testing by the format owner (10 days)
- Disc manufacture (2–4 weeks)

The total development time for *Pure* was approximately 20 months, which was at the lower end of the range of each phase. Delivering the product while keeping to the lower end of the range was attributed to the team's experience and their agile development process. Each of these phases will now be explained in more detail.

2.4.2   Prototyping

During the prototyping phase, the publisher's marketing team employed a recruitment agency who produced a detailed online questionnaire about the game concept and distributed it to approximately 100 people within the target demographic. Following the online survey, a focus group study was conducted with 3 groups of 4–5 participants to discuss the game concept. The study was run in a lounge environment, with two members of staff, one taking notes from behind a one-way mirror, and the other sitting with the participants to facilitate the discussion.

The team also decided to build a "Pre-Vis" (pre-visualisation) prototype for one of *Pure's* key features, player customised vehicles. This took the form of a non-interactive movie showing each part of the bike attaching to a central frame. This was not a technical demo, but rather just a visual benchmark or reference from which the interface for this part of the game could later be developed.

2.4.3   Pre-Production

Pure had originally been intended to just be an incremental advance on the previous title in the series, but over the course of 7 months the game concept evolved through several different designs. The initial idea was to make the most authentic quad bike racing game on the market, but this was abandoned in favour of a concept tentatively called *ATV Pure* which avoided realistic sports simulation in favour of informal, social, off-road racing. The final concept, called simply *Pure*, was only settled upon by the time the team were half-way through pre-production. Each of the preceding versions contributed some design features to the final game, but many were prioritised so low that they were never included in the released title. The design strategy for *Pure* was to focus on implementing a few core features to a very high standard, rather than attempt many features to a lesser standard.

By 12 months into the development cycle, the team had fixed their vision for the game and were only addressing issues that supported 4 key aspects: massive airborne tricks, customisable vehicles, 16 player online games, and so-called "FHMs" (which for the purposes of this paper we will describe as "Flying High" Moments). These FHMs represent the core experience of *Pure*: when the player drives round a corner at high speed, only to realise that what they thought was just a bump in the road turns out to be the edge of a cliff face, leaving them flying thousands of feet up in the air. This is not only a highly exciting part of the game, but also a key mechanic as it allows the player plenty of time to perform tricks in the air, which eventually results in a higher score and other rewards.

These concepts were graphically documented in a number of ways specific to Black Rock, but which have similar implementations in other studios. An important tool for summarising the concept of the game and keeping the team on track is the X-Movie, used by some of the world's largest games publishers such as Electronic Arts. The X-Movie for *Pure* was a video showing a bike rider on an off-road race track jumping high into the air. Black Rock maintained the idea of "X marks the spot" when it came to their "Core Idea Sheets". These were large display boards hung around the team's development area showing the 4 key game aspects superimposed onto a bull's-eye target. At the centre of the target was the FHM feature, as this was intended to represent the essence of the entire game. It is worth highlighting that this essentially puts the user experience (of excitement), as the single most important criteria for the game.

2.4.4 Alpha to Release

For *Pure*, Black Rock did not employ a QA team throughout the entirety of the project, instead they only used 1 or 2 testers in the month leading up to Alpha. From Alpha, this was increased to 5 staff to deal with both the Xbox 360 and PS3 versions of the game (which were simultaneously developed). Furthermore, the QA team was only concerned with addressing functional testing rather than questions of usability or user experience.

2.4.5   Post-Launch

The publisher's marketing team conducted studies after the game had been released and sold most of its units. The purpose of these studies was to identify what consumers liked or did not like about the game, and what made them purchase it. Similar themes were discussed with consumers who did not purchase the game.

After release of the game, some informal analysis was conducted of official reviews and user comments on forums. Avent asserts that with the exception of some aspects of the garage, few usability issues were mentioned in game reviews. Most user's comments related to features that were intentionally excluded by the team for practical reasons (such as the excessive technical overhead of including replays and split-screen multiplayer).

2.4.6   Understanding the User

Pure was the first title on which Black Rock employed usability tests. They began running tests with company staff, careful to choose people who were not on the development team. They then expanded to recruit other people who worked in the same building as them, but who were not part of their own company. Finally the most substantial tests began with members of the public, recruited directly from the streets and local universities. In total around 100 participants were involved over the course of 4 months, of which the final month was only concerned with quantitative analysis of the game's difficulty level and any issues that would prevent players from completing the game. The only requirements for recruitment were that participants were 14–24 years old, male, and owned at least one of the current generations of console, i.e. they were likely candidates to make a purchase. Tests were run in-house, in regular office space separated from the development teams. Up to 8 players would be present simultaneously, with 1 supervisor for every 2–3 players. One of the supervisors was responsible for taking notes, and no video data was captured as this was considered too difficult to analyse due to the very large volumes produced.

Black Rock conducted "blind testing" meaning that testers had never played the game before, and several different categories of testing were devised:

- Free Flow. This is an unguided test where the player is encouraged to play the game however they wish. This is particularly useful for giving an impression of how much fun the game is, because as soon as the game becomes boring they would be inclined to stop playing.
- Narrow Specific. In this mode the player would only play a single level, and they might play it multiple times in order to measure their improvement with familiarity. This appears to be similar to vertical prototype testing employed in usability evaluations.
- Broad Specific. Similar to the narrow specific test, but playing over many levels. This seems similar to horizontal prototype testing in usability evaluations.

Most of the development team also had visibility of the playtests, but generally it was only designers who observed the sessions. Avent reflects that it may have been helpful for more programmers and artists to also have been involved with observation earlier on.

Despite the absence of video data, one of the programmers on the team had implemented "instrumentation" for the usability tests. This is the process of recording quantitative data directly from the games console that describes the timings of events during the game session. This can be used to measure specific events such as lap times or how long it took to restart a game. Similar techniques have been employed by other studios such as Valve and Microsoft (Steam 2008; Thompson 2007).

At the start of a game *Pure* does not present the player with the traditional selections of Easy, Medium and Hard difficulty level, but rather dynamically adjusts the AI vehicles to suit the player's performance while they play. During the final 2 weeks of testing, the Black Rock team focused only on balancing this dynamic difficulty system. The team were able to approximate a learning or performance curve by comparing the player's finishing position after their initial and subsequent playthroughs of a given track. By tweaking the dynamic balance system they were able to adjust this difficulty curve to keep players challenged and engaged enough to replay races and improve their performance.

Avent strongly believes that these tests were crucially important in order to ensure a Metacritic score of 85 %, and that without them he felt that the game would have been reviewed at around 75 % instead. This is a strong recommendation for even simplistic and lo-fi usability testing.

However, reflecting on the quality of results, Avent does recognise some of the limitations with a principally quantitative approach. In particular he comments that even with a large dataset, results could be misleading or misinterpreted. For example, if the data shows that players consistently come last in a race, one response may be to reduce the AI vehicles performance to be more in line with that observed from the players. However, this may be inappropriate if the real cause lies not with the AI over performing per se, but perhaps with bugs in the vehicle physics system which bias in favour of computational rather than human control.

In order to identify such cases, Avent recognises that qualitative approaches would be beneficial and this is where more effort will be focused in the future. He hopes that future projects will take the agile development model even further, incorporating user testing throughout the development life cycle, including during prototyping and pre-production.

Furthermore, usability testing could begin as soon as the team has produces lo-fidelity prototypes. For example an HTML mockup of a front end menu; a 2D interactive demo of vehicle handling; a whitebox of a level where the visuals are of the minimum possible standard in order to test gameplay (i.e., typically without colour, and with purely blocky, geometric shapes). Indeed, while only a small amount of usability testing was carried out from the vertical slice, Avent believes that the team should be conducting at least 1 test per week from that point onward, with 2–3 play-tests per week by the time Alpha has been reached.

During *Pure*'s development, the key team member to be formally concerned about usability was Jason Avent, the Game Director. While individuals in the design team specialised on difficulty and tracks, Avent talks about the possibility of hiring an HCI specialist in the future who would be the team's user experience expert by the time a vertical slice is produced. Eventually he imagines multiple usability designers for different aspects of the game, one to specialise on track design, others for difficulty curve, vehicles, or avatar design (for more on this topic see Isbister 2006) While these may seem highly specific, the team already speak about a nomenclature for the design of tracks, a "track language" involved in the dialogue between game and player. An example of good communication in track language would be a vivid distinction between areas the player can drive on and areas they cannot. This 'language' must be clear and 'readable' to the player, otherwise their mental model of the game will be inaccurate. Of course, there are occasions when communication in this language is intentionally obfuscated, for example where there are secret shortcuts that should be indicated in a much more subtle way. Avent hopes that for future projects semiotic codes can be defined for each of these areas of game design.

2.4.7 Pure Development Summary

Off-road racing game for Xbox 360, PS3 and PC.
Target demographic: young, male console owners.
60–70 staff.
Agile development model.
20 month development lifecycle.
5 functional testers from Alpha.
100 playtesters.
Custom quantitative usability analysis.
Usability studies increased Metacritic score by 10 %.

Case Study 2—Zoë Mode In 2007 Zoë Mode rebranded itself as a casual games developer, with a mission to become the world's leader in music, party and social games. In general the company tends not to design for a specific age group, but rather hope to create games that anyone can pick up and play easily. Such a broad target can present obvious challenges, such as a development team who are largely in their 20s and 30s trying to design for consumers who could be 6–60 years old.

We spoke to Martin Newing, Executive Producer, Karl Fitzhugh, Design Director and Dan Chequer, Lead Designer about the studios recent games including *You're in the Movies*, *Rock Revolution* and a number of titles in the *EyeToy* and *SingStar* series of games.

2.4.8 Understanding the User

The studio head, Ed Daly, was the core driver for involving usability and quality control in the studio's development process, though a number of usability techniques came to Zoë Mode from outside the company, and Microsoft were a particularly strong influence. Despite CodeMasters being the publisher, Microsoft were involved in the testing of *You're in the Movies* as the game ran on their Xbox 360 platform. Fitzhugh comments that the quantification of results was particularly useful for the team, with Microsoft presenting data in the form X out of Y participants found this aspect of the game problematic. 12 groups of 4 participants were involved during the course of a week. Recognising that this is a small sample size, particularly given the intention to sell the game to millions of consumers, Fitzhugh would like to involve more people but does reflect on the difficulty of analysing a much greater volume of data. In particular he comments that participant selection is critical, so while the kind of ad-hoc testing they have performed with friends and families can be productive, formal testing should be of a much higher standard.

Some focus testing was also conducted with *EyeToy Play Sports*. Sessions were lead and run by the publisher, Sony, at a location in London rather than in the developer's studio. Newing is keen to point out, as have others in our case studies, that publisher interest in this kind of testing is very welcome but currently uncommon. Furthermore Newing is also aware that focus group testing can be misleading if the sample size is too small to draw general conclusions, or so wide that the results suggest the game be reduced to the lowest-common denominator. Chequer is also anxious about individual participants controlling focus group discussions by exerting their influence on other participants who may have valuable feedback which is never revealed. This is a concern for all focus group studies however, and we would argue that good moderation should be able to overcome this challenge and draw out all issues that any of the participants may have.

As with other studios in this series of case studies, Zoë Mode point out the problems of presenting pre-release games to focus groups. In particular Newing relates an anecdote about showing an early version of the game to personal friends and family who were simply too distracted by the poor quality of early artwork to want to play the game.

Zoë Mode's latest release, *Rock Revolution*, incorporated observational playtesting as a key part of the development process. Chequer argues that running these studies was essential for Jam Mode, a more freeform music making part of the game. Although the team already had some ideas about aspects that needed to be changed, observing real players struggle gave them the impetus to actually make the changes before release. Indeed the bulk of revisions came from focus group and playtesting, with Chequer mentioning two issues in particular: help text to explain what onscreen buttons do, and further encouragement for first-time players to just get in and start making music. Despite *Rock Revolution* being a challenging project with some poor reviews, and only one iteration for testing, the team were pleased that a GameSpot preview praised the game's Studio, in which Jam Mode takes place, saying "The most fun we found is in the jam session."

2.4.9 Game Language

Discussing the value of observing playtests, Newing and Chequer reflect on how easy it is for developers to overlook the simplest of things which can impede novice players from even starting to play. Like the other studios in this study the team are now aware of the problems associated with using traditional terminology for games that are intended to appeal to a broader demographic.

Newing referred to the distinction between "Challenge Mode" and "Story Mode", which are clear labels for the team who've discussed and created these different play modes, but for the player who's just interested in playing for the first time they can be a source of uncertainty. Newing goes on to discuss the difference between the traditional "Easy", "Medium" and "Hard" difficulty levels, commenting that typically these offer effectively the same game with more or less, and harder or weaker enemies. Critiquing the terminology of difficulty further, Newing also refers to *Brothers In Arms—Hell's Highway*, which offers "Casual", "Veteran" and an unlockable setting, "Authentic". However, the descriptive text for even the casual setting gives the impression that it is a challenging setting even for experienced players. The alternative he proposes is rather than varying the number and strength of the opposition, to vary the game mechanics. This way the easiest levels would accommodate only a simple subset of possible mechanics which could be opened up to the player at harder levels. A case in point is the Nintendo 64's *Golden Eye* where higher difficulty levels provided extra challenges by adding more demanding success criteria. Levels could be completed by beginners, but on the more advanced settings players would be required to complete additional goals.

The *EyeToy* series of games gave Zoë Mode a particular challenge due to their unique input mechanism. Players interact with these games primarily through their real-world movements which are seen by a camera attached to the console. For gamers and non-gamers alike this is a novel mode of interaction which introduces the potential for many problems.

Chequer remembers one particular scenario where the player was in-game, then the game cut to a non-interactive animation before returning to interactive play. During the observational sessions it became clear that the players did not understand the difference between the interactive and non-interactive sections, and were unclear when their physical movements in front of the camera would have an effect or not.

Fitzhugh likewise discusses some of the challenges of *You're in the Movies* and communicating technical instructions to the player. For this game there is a calibration process which requires the player to evaluate whether the game has successfully identified and separated the camera's image of the player from the background of the room they're playing in. The developers refer to this process as "segmentation", a technical term that comes from the field of image processing—a concept and term that's almost certainly alien to players of this casual game. Despite using everyday language both in voiceover and onscreen text, the team had to iterate through several different phrases during focus testing, for example "have you been successfully cut out from the background?" Unfortunately even this apparently straightforward question was inappropriate for the audience who were concentrating more on the fact that they appeared onscreen than on attending to the game's needs of identifying whether its algorithm had been successful or not. Finally the team settled on the presentation of images showing examples of what successful and unsuccessful results would look like, which is effectively a tutorial or training session for the player. This is particularly significant for casual games which are intended to be played by anyone, and especially people unwilling to invest much time and effort in learning how to effectively use them.

2.4.10   Game Complexity and Accessibility

Note that in the games industry the term 'accessibility' usually does not refer to disability as is often the case in the HCI community, but rather any player's initial contact with a game, and especially so for casual games (see also Desurvire and Wiberg 2008). Throughout our text here we keep to this meaning.

Newing is keen to point out that while games should be open to play without having to read through complex instructions or manuals, having a degree of hidden depth behind the scenes is still important for the longevity of the title. Chequer sums the issues up by stating that games should try to avoid any issues that would block the player from play, but should also provide interesting secondary systems and mechanics for advanced players. Fitzhugh goes on to point out the success of games like *Guitar Hero* which offer notoriously challenging difficulty levels for the most experienced players, but which also appeal to beginners on easy levels.

Chequer reflects that in retrospect some of the minigames in *EyeToy Play 3* required too much learning through trial and error before players could really experience them. In contrast, *EyeToy Play Sports*, which featured 101 minigames, lacked some of the depth but perhaps was more accessible to beginners. Finding the middle ground is where the art of balancing comes in, and we would suggest that usability and user experience testing provides a number of approaches to facilitate this.

Chequer points out that the most accessible games on the Wii are relatively instinctive and easy for beginners to play. This can be observed in *Wii Sports* where most of the games are based directly on real life actions that non-gamers are familiar with, such as swinging your arm for tennis, and which serve to give the impression of a transparent interface. The boxing minigame, however, is significantly less accessible due to its more abstract input mechanism which responds less well to natural movements.

Another example of accessibility is navigation flow through menus. Proficient gamers are used to a certain set of conventions for menu screens, such as where to find controller options, etc, but observing non-expert players can reveal that this is a learnt association that may be at odds with the assumptions novice players bring with them.

2.4.11   Usability Tests

During 2005 Sony employed a usability company to run tests for *EyeToy Play 3* with children and families, which were observed by Chequer and others from the team. The results of the sessions were encouraging for the team both as a morale boost to show real players having fun with their work, but also as a keen insight into some big design flaws they hadn't considered before. Unfortunately these sessions occurred late in development as the game approached Beta and so the team didn't have sufficient time to address some of the more significant issues. Newing mentions that the quality of reports from these sessions was very high, providing recommendations for the team in a non-prescriptive way. For the focus group sessions, reports also provided background on individual participants and interpretations for events during play as well as a description of the overall mood. Finally the large amount of video data gathered was invaluable for demonstrating and resolving problems with the game.

2.4.12   Changing Demographic

Chequer comments on the development of the industry as a whole, and points out that in earlier times the market was predominantly made of a small core of people who were experienced players, of which the game developers themselves were part. In those times it was relatively easy for developers to make games they liked and be more confident that they would appeal to the market, as the team represented that market (for more discussion of the background and effect of these "cultures of production", see Dovey and Kennedy 2006) Now with a broader market and games that are particularly intended to be played by less experienced players, the distance between the developers and market means that fewer assumptions can be made and more attention has to be paid to testing. Chequer describes observing his own mother playing a game (see also the "mum-factor" in the Relentless case-study), who wanted to stop playing but wasn't familiar with the convention that the "Start" button not only starts games but is also used to stop them. These kinds of conventions can clearly be confusing to the casual audience who may need additional assistance and explanation.

2.4.13   Studio-Wide Quality Review

Currently Zoë Mode do not have an official mandate to conduct usability studies, though a new initiative in the company does incorporate usability techniques as part of their new studio-wide quality review which also includes focus group testing and their standard postmortem of the development process itself. This is a relatively new initiative which was only begun around a year ago, and which is itself currently under review. Under this process qualitative comments about the development process are collated and summarised, then anonymously reported back to the team. Previously only senior management were involved in the process of deciding whether a game was of sufficient quality to ship, but a new model for this process additionally involves members of the team. These include senior staff such as the discipline leads, but some people from other teams in the company are also brought in for a fresh perspective. Newing points out that internal reviews can be problematic, whereas bringing in external reviewers helps to provide fresh, impartial and unbiased assessment. We would agree and further recommend considering feedback from players *external to the game development industry*.

2.4.14 Postmortem

Games finished in the previous 2–3 years have run postmortems but not in a standardised manner than would allow the team to quantify and compare their successes and failures with previous projects. The definition of a standardised postmortem template is one of the goals of the quality review process. Typically Zoë Mode's previous postmortems have been conducted 1–3 months after each game has been finished, and only circulated internally after 3–6 months, by which time some of the team may have moved on, and others may have simply forgotten important issues that arose during the 1–2 year development period.

The ability to quantify data is also considered important by the Zoë Mode team. For instance, the games industry is prone to underestimating the amount of time required for tools and technology production, so in that sense the same sort of issues commonly cause the same sort of scheduling problems. However, due to the R&D and creative endeavour involved, the specific instances of these problems are hard to estimate in advance. By taking an approach similar to that used in agile software development, comparing the amount of time initially estimated for a given task and the amount of time actually required, overall trends become apparent that could be used to plan future projects. Fitzhugh states that quantifiable measurements should allow the postmortem to identify 3–5 specific goals that should be addressed in the next project, and provide conditions by which to measure success.

2.4.15 Summary

Casual game developer.
Casual (non-technical/non-traditional) terminology.
12 months from pitch to release.
QA for functional bugtesting.
12 groups of 4 participants for playtesting.
Video data invaluable.
Usability & focus group testing around Beta.

Can anticipate future need for in-house usability expert.
Postmortem circulated 3–6 months after release.

Case Study 3—Relentless Software Relentless are an independently owned developer, working exclusively for Sony Computer Entertainment, manufacturers of the PlayStation series of games consoles.

Following the release of Relentless' first title, *DJ Decks and FX* for the PS2 in 2004, the creation of the *Buzz!* franchise began when Sony approached Relentless with the proposal to develop a music-based game. As a result, *Buzz! The Music Quiz* was released in October 2005. Their most recent title, *Buzz! Quiz TV*, was released in July 2008 and is a continuation of the *Buzz!* series. Casper Field, Senior Producer, discussed with us the process of designing a new game, and where user experience currently fits into their development strategy.

2.4.16 Internal Testing

In addition to the core team of programmers, artists, designers, and audio engineers Relentless have a QA group who are responsible for testing the game throughout production. This is essentially functional testing rather than usability or experiential testing. As an example, Field comments that network functionality is a perennial problem, and that their testers try to identify scenarios under which the current implementation will fail—such as how to handle a matchmaking case where one party loses connectivity.

Relentless have no formal procedures for dealing with these concerns, particularly toward the beginning of a project, rather relying on the skill of the producer to recognise what the audience want. Later on, when the game is of a sufficient standard that people external to the team are brought in for focus group testing, the producer's earlier decisions are put to the test.

2.4.17 Understanding Users

In addition to internal and external QA, the producers at Relentless decided to employ external focus group testing for *Buzz! Quiz TV*. This study was conducted during February 2008, 8 months prior to the game's eventual retail release date, which Field describes as being approximate 75% of the way through production. Based on data from previous games in the series, Sony's marketing team had identified 3 demographic groups, from which the focus group test company sourced 4 individuals each, totalling 12 participants:

1. Social players (mid-20s, the 'post pub crew')
2. Family players (mother, two children, family friend)
3. Gamers (students, late teens)

Field devised 64 questions for the focus test, which were grouped into the following 8 categories,

- Instructions in the intro sequence (4 questions)
- Using the game's menus (12 questions)
- News page (4 questions)
- First impressions (16 questions)
- The overall experience (14 questions)
- Enjoyment (5 questions)
- User created quizzes (5 questions)
- Future purchases (4 questions)

Each participant rated their response on a 4-point Likert scale, with an additional non-numerical code for no data. The responses were analysed as ordinal data and metrics were produced per question and per participant. In addition to this numeric analysis, mean responses were also presented back to the development team in bar graph form, whose value axis ranged from 1.00 to 4.00.

Focus group testing in the games industry is generally approached with a degree of trepidation. Most developers are sceptical about the quality of the processes, participants, their feedback and interpretation of data. Subsequently it can be hard to get buy-in from the development team, and most importantly from the senior members who have the authority to make decisions relating to them. Field's answer is to prove the quality of these issues to the major stakeholders in the team. For example, during their recent testing sessions the lead programmer and artist were actively involved, visited the testing site and gave their feedback about the research questions the study was intended to address.

Field praised the work of the focus group company, and despite commenting that it was an expensive process, would consider doubling the number of participants for their next game. In particular, he pointed out that all of the participants were already aware of *Buzz!*, so an additional control group who had never played before would be beneficial.

The identification of demographic groups does guide the development process, and Field points out the importance of understanding the context and manner in which the game will likely be played. Throughout the development life cycle the team try to bear in mind what Field calls "the mum-factor"; an informal persona-based approach where they try to imagine their own mothers holding the controllers and enjoying playing the game. Similarly, they have a "drunk factor" scenario, for groups of gamers who come home to play after a drinking session at the pub. Similar to Zoë Mode, it is acknowledged that the Relentless development team does not represent the typical consumer, and that features which individual developers might enjoy are not necessarily appropriate to include in the final game.

This attention to players permeates the whole design process to the extent that the designers try to use a more conversational language when addressing players, such as avoiding conventional game terms like "Loading". This terminology could potentially alienate players for whom *Buzz!* might be their first video game experience, so the team prefers to speak to the players informally with phrases like "How would you like to play this game?" instead of the terse but typical "Select Mode".

2.4.18 Post Launch

Not unlike the technique of instrumentation discussed earlier in the Black Rock case study, *Buzz! Quiz TV* captures data which allows the team to identify what, how, and when the game is played. However, rather than being captured and used only internally with pre-release versions of the game, Relentless capture telemetry data remotely from players of the final, released game as they play in their own homes. Sony's legal department understandably limits what kind of data can be collected, but clearly this still continually produces a vast quantity of data, and Field comments that this does make it difficult to filter and analyse.

Relentless also analysed the 50 or so reviews available after the game shipped in an attempt to identify problematic issues and incorporate this feedback into future developments. This process involved a frequency analysis of comments about specific individual areas such as menus systems and the user interface, but Field is more interested in whether reviewers understood the game generally. Additionally not all reviews are treated with the same significance. For the *Buzz!* series, reviews from casual or mainstream media like The Sun newspaper in the UK are considered more important than niche or hardcore gaming publications. However, once again the issue of historical context is pertinent—as *Buzz! The Music Quiz* was released during the early part of the PS3's life cycle, the market is more likely to be early-adopters who have paid more to purchase the console, and who have different interests and concerns than the more casual or mainstream market that typically adopts a platform later in its life cycle when the price point has reduced. As such, they are more likely to read website reviews and comment in online forums, so these sites are of more importance than they might be for future games released later in the console's life.

2.4.19 Relentless Software Typical Development Summary

12 months production.
3 months Alpha—Release.
Functional QA.
Target demographic: Social, Family, Gamers.
Everyday language in games.
Focus group test conducted 75 % through development.
3 groups of 4 focus group test participants.
Content analysis of reviews.

Case Study 4—HandCircus HandCircus is a London-based independent games studio, founded in 2008 and dedicated to creating bold, original, and playful games for the exciting world of digital distribution and emerging platforms.

Their first game, Rolando, a platform-puzzle-adventure for the iPhone and iPod Touch launched in December 2008 to universal critical acclaim. This was followed by the award winning Rolando 2: The Quest for the Golden Orchid in July 2009.

We interviewed HandCircus founder Simon Oliver on the unique challenges of mobile game development.

2.4.20   Background

In March 2008, Apple announced that the App Store was going to be open for business in July later that year. This method of digital distribution would allow developers to publish their games more easily and also reach a wide audience. Although lacking physical controls, which posed obvious restrictions from a game design perspective, Simon saw the iPhone as an opportunity to innovate in the game space.

Designing for revolutionary new platforms is a unique design challenge as there are often going to be a limited set of previous examples to draw upon. However, Simon was well positioned to cope with this challenge by having previous job roles as head of R&D at Random Media and interactive designer for Sony Computer Entertainment Europe. By applying his previous knowledge of designing new interactions, he was confident he could deliver a unique game for the iPhone which would result in a satisfying player experience.

2.4.21   Prototyping

An initial creative phase began by exploring the range of interactions possible with the new touch-based interface. For example, how would the player select an item, how would they move an item, the building blocks of any touch-based game. Simon strongly believes in this bottom-up approach to game development rather than top-down, after all, if the essential basic interactions are not intuitive and satisfying, then the game which comes on top is never going to feel right.

One of the early prototypes was of a ball which would be controlled by gesture. The user would have to click on a ball to select it, then flick right to tell it to roll right, tap on the ball to tell it to stop, or flick up to tell it to jump. This was the very earliest prototype for what was to become Rolando. This exploratory phase highlighted some immediate issues such as if the ball is moving it's actually quite difficult to tap it to stop. The solution for this issue was changing the interaction to drag to select, however this caused other issues and so the prototyping process would iterate.

Most of this early work took place on the iPhone simulator as it was not yet possible to run code on the actual iPhone. He was accepted onto iPhone SDK Beta around April 2008, and only then could the prototypes be tried on the physical device. Being able to show the prototypes running on an actual iPhone allowed for user testing with friends and family. This feedback revealed issues that the simulator could never capture, and the interactions would be further refined.

By the end of the prototyping phase, a strong concept was falling into place. By June 2008, Simon, who had been freelancing for IDEO, now dedicated two days a week to Rolando.

2.4.22   Development

Realising that the demo had strong potential, Simon began to look for an artist. He met Mikko Walamies on a T-shirt design site and liked his artwork. He sent through some screenshots of the game and Mikko agreed to work on the project (remotely from Finland).

By July 2008 they felt it was ready to show the world a glimpse of what they had been working on. They uploaded a teaser trailer to YouTube which received over 100,000 views over a period of just a few days [1]. As a result, ngmoco contacted HandCircus and become their publisher, offering QA, marketing, and more generally a good sounding board for ideas.

One of those ideas was to use the accelerometer to control the Rolando rather than gesture. Simon hadn't prototyped this interaction method as he thought it wouldn't work well in a mobile context (on public transport etc.), but thought he would give it a try as it would only take a few hours to get a demo up and running. After some tweaking, the interaction proved very successful, and stayed as the main control scheme. If you look at the early teaser trailer for Rolando on YouTube, you'll notice all the controls are touch-based, not using the accelerometer.

In July, with the support and partnership of ngmoco, Simon went full-time on Rolando. The publisher, ngmoco assigned an extra developer to help out, also producers Matt Roberts and Chris Plummer, and musician Mr Scruff was brought on board to write the music.

Rolando launched on the App Store in December 2008, and was one of the first three games published by ngmoco.

2.4.23   User Testing

Near the end of the project, ngmoco carried out two weeks of user testing and market research. Simon spent these 2 weeks in ngmoco's offices in San Francisco, to be on-site to react to any feedback.

During these playtests, many issues were tweaked:

- Selecting a Rolando caused confusion, the user did not know to look off-screen.
- General messaging and signposting.

- Flick to jump—Matt Roberts the producer noticed that the character jumped when the user's finger was released, but this didn't feel right. In the modified version, the jump happened once the user dragged more than a specified number of pixels, giving a more natural feeling.
- Selection tap radius was adjusted.
- Number of pixels before drag initiated was adjusted.

These changes were happening quickly and often between each playtest. As it was easy to change most threshold values, rapid testing could be conducted to establish the 'sweet spot'. Other insights were also valuable, such as how users were holding the device.

2.4.24 Release

Whereas many early iPhone games were criticized for having interfaces which were essentially shrunk down versions of PC/console games, Rolando was praised with comments such as, "the first game designed specifically for the iPhone". It was awarded 9.5 out of 10 by IGN and voted as best iPhone game of 2008 by Venturebeat.

2.4.25 Summary

9 months development (3 of those part-time).
iPhone/iPod Touch platform.
New platform, no real reference point for best-practice.
Evaluated interaction demos with friends and family from very early stages.
Accelerometer interaction method added near the end, with success.
Rapid user testing, made code changes between participants.
Very well received by critics and users.

2.5 Discussion

The single most important issue that has emerged from the case studies is that the studios are testing too late in the life cycle (sometimes as late as Beta). This means that any feedback they obtain from usability studies is unlikely to make it into the final game.

Fitzhugh discussed some of the problems with testing, in particular highlighting the apparent paradox of when to test. Testing later on in the life cycle ensures that the game is more representative of the final product, and hence improves the validity of test results, but from a production point of view this is the worst time to find out about problems. Newing also comments on the scope of testing, and mentions that for both *Rock Revolution* and *You're in the Movies*, only parts of the game were tested due to constraints on time and budget. We would suggest that a productive solution would be to embrace testing as part of an agile development process, whereby discrete aspects of the game are tested individually during prototyping, vertical slice, and throughout the remainder of development. To that end, by the time of release all aspects of the game should have been tested individually and in coordination as a whole—with the usual proviso that the finished game may have a tighter scope or size than originally intended in order to ensure that quality is maintained.

All studios agreed that they should be testing sooner, and approaches such as EA's method of using focus groups early on to decide on key game concepts, could easily be integrated into the development plan.

The vertical slice could be used as an approximate measure for dividing usability testing from user experience testing. All studios acknowledge that testing a game's overall user experience can only be measured once all the components are in place (final artwork, audio, game mechanics etc.), and the earliest that this can be achieved is at the vertical slice. During interview, Zoë Mode mentioned that they were considering writing mock reviews before a game is released, and we feel that the vertical slice is a useful point at which reasonably representative and hence valuable data could be generated early in the lifecycle.

If everything after the vertical slice is user experience oriented, then before that milestone the focus should be on usability issues. This would typically mean issues such as user interface layout, game controls or menu navigation.

However, the usability/user experience divide around the vertical slice is not so clear cut. Usability issues will still need to be evaluated after this point (such as game flow and pace), and it is possible to evaluate user experience before the vertical slice (such as game concept focus group test at the start of a project).

2.6 Future Challenges

Player enjoyment is currently understood by observing or asking participants for their reactions to a game. One of the key future challenges is to capture, measure and understand player's body data. Signals such as heart rate (EEG), skin conductance (GSR), facial muscle tension (EMG) or eye tracking, may become integrated into commercial game usability evaluations in the future. Indeed, studios such as Valve, have already expressed that bio-data could help them to better understand the gameplay experience (Newell 2008).

Extensive academic research has been conducted on psychophysiological metrics (Mandryk 2005; FUGA 2006; McAllister and Mirza-Babaei 2011), and excellent tools and techniques for the capturing and analysis of such data are available (Nacke et al. 2008). However the focus of these research projects has been on using biofeedback for automatic adaptation of game AI, rather than as a tool with which to iterate on the design of games prior to release. Furthermore such studies tend to analyse very short periods of gameplay with small numbers of participants. It remains to be demonstrated whether such approaches can scale to be applicable for games that may be played by millions of diverse players, and whether such techniques could be used for representative longitudinal studies of potentially many tens of hours.

In addition to gathering data from the player's body, the studios in our case studies have already begun to automatically capture player performance data directly from the game (such as *Pure's* Dynamic Competition Balancing). This makes it straightforward to capture an enormous amount of quantifiable metrics, making comparison across a large number of players easier.

This chapter has presented four case studies on how world class games are currently developed. Although studios are keen to integrate usability evaluations into their life cycle, they are not certain how this can best be achieved. As such, one of the main barriers to conducting usability evaluations is the lack of a formal process that studios can follow. However, traditional usability has a similar issue where there is no strict process that can be followed, rather there are a toolbox of methods that exist which practitioners can use when needed. Future work may involve moving towards a general framework of game usability, which would detail not only the usability techniques which can be used, but also where in the life cycle they should be ideally applied.

Acknowledgements The authors would like to thank interviewees Casper Field, Jason Avent, Martin Newing, Dan Chequer, Karl Fitzhugh and Simon Oliver, and additional feedback from Thaddaeus Frogley.

References

Cornett S (2004) The usability of massively multiplayer online roleplaying games: designing for new users. Proceedings of the SIGCHI conference on Human factors in computing systems . ACM, New York, pp 703–710. doi:10.1145/985692.985781

Desurvire H, Wiberg C (2008) Master of the game: assessing approachability in future game design. CHI '08 Extended Abstracts on Human Factors in Computing Systems

Desurvire H, Caplan M, Toth JA (2004) Using heuristics to evaluate the playability of games. CHI '04 Extended Abstracts on Human Factors in Computing Systems. doi:10.1145/985921.986102

Dovey J, Kennedy HW (2006) Game cultures: computer games as new media. Open University Press, Maidenhead

Federoff M (2002) Heuristics and guidelines for the creation and evaluation of fun in video games. Indiana University

FUGA (2006) Fun of gaming. http://project.hkkk.fi/fuga/. Accessed 13 Dec 2008

Isbister K (2006) Better game characters by design. Morgan Kauffman

Jørgensen AH (2004) Marrying HCI/usability and computer games: a preliminary look. Proceedings of NordiCHI 2004. doi:10.1145/1028014.1028078

Laitinen S (2006) Do usability expert evaluation and test provide novel and useful data for game development? J Usability Stud 2(1):64–75

Larsen JM (2008) Evaluating user experience—how game reviewers do it. CHI Workshop

Malone T (1981) Heuristics for designing enjoyable user interfaces: lessons from computer games. Proceedings of Conference on Human Factors in Computing Systems, pp 63–68

Mandryk RL (2005) Modeling user emotion in interactive play environments: a fuzzy physiological approach. Ph.D dissertation. Simon Fraser University, Burnaby, Canada

McAllister G, Mirza-Babaei P (2011) Player metrics: using behaviour and biometrics to analyse gameplay. Proceedings of Future and Reality of Gaming (FROG)

Medlock MC, Wixon D, Terrano M, Romero R, Fulton B (2002) Using the RITE Method to improve products: a definition and a case study. Usability Professionals Association. Orlando

Nacke L, Lindley C, Stellmach S (2008) Log who's playing: psychophysiological game analysis made easy through event logging. Proceedings of 2nd International Conference Fun and Games 2008, Eindhoven, The Netherlands

Newell G (2008) Gabe newell writes for edge. Edge online. http://www.edge-online.com/blogs/gabe-newell-writes-edge. Accessed 27 March 2009

Nielsen J (2005) Heuristics for user interface design. http://www.useit.com/papers/heuristic/heuristic_list.html. Accessed 13 Dec 2008

Schaffer N (2008) Heuristic evaluation of games. In: Isbister K, Schaffer N (eds) Game usability. Morgan Kaufmann, Burlington

Steam (2008) Game and player statistics. http://www.steampowered.com/v/index.php?area=stats. Accessed 13 Dec 2008

Sweetster P, Wyeth P (2005) GameFlow: a model for evaluating player enjoyment in games. ACM Comput Entertain 3(3)

Thompson C (2007) Halo 3: How Microsoft labs invented a new science of play. Wired Magazine 15.09. http://www.wired.com/gaming/virtualworlds/magazine/15-09/ff_halo. Accessed 13 Dec 2008

Chapter 3
Assessing the Core Elements of the Gaming Experience

Eduardo H. Calvillo-Gámez, Paul Cairns and Anna L. Cox

Abstract This chapter presents the theory of the Core Elements of the Gaming Experience (CEGE). The CEGE are the necessary but not sufficient conditions to provide a positive experience while playing video-games. This theory, formulated using qualitative methods, is presented with the aim of studying the gaming experience objectively. The theory is abstracted using a model and implemented in questionnaire. This chapter discusses the formulation of the theory, introduces the model, and shows the use of the questionnaire in an experiment to differentiate between two different experiences.

In loving memory of Samson Cairns

3.1 The Experience of Playing Video-Games

The experience of playing video-games is usually understood as the subjective relation between the user and the video-game beyond the actual implementation of the game. The implementation is bound by the speed of the microprocessors of the gaming console, the ergonomics of the controllers, and the usability of the interface. Experience is more than that, it is also considered as a personal relationship. Understanding this relationship as personal is problematic under a scientific scope. Personal and subjective knowledge does not allow a theory to be generalised or falsified (Popper 1994). In this chapter, we propose a theory for understanding the

E. H. Calvillo-Gámez (✉)
Innovation and Technology, City of San Luis Potosí, San Luis Potosí, S.L.P., México
e-mail: eduardo.calvillo@gmail.com

P. Cairns
Computer Science Department, The University of York, York, UK
e-mail: paul.cairns@york.ac.uk

A. L. Cox
UCL Interaction Centre, University College London, London, UK
e-mail: anna.cox@ucl.ac.uk

© Springer International Publishing Switzerland 2015
R. Bernhaupt (ed.), *Game User Experience Evaluation,*
Human-Computer Interaction Series, DOI 10.1007/978-3-319-15985-0_3

experience of playing video-games, or gaming experience, that can be used to assess and compare different experiences.

This section introduces the approach taken towards understanding the gaming experience under the aforementioned perspective. It begins by presenting an overview of video-games and user experience in order to familiarise the reader with such concepts. Last, the objective and overview of the whole chapter are presented.

3.1.1 Introduction to Video-Games

A video-game is, at its most basic level, the implementation of a game in a computer-based console that uses some type of video output. Providing a formal definition of a video-game was one of the first challenges that game studies faced. Since many things can be considered a game, the following definition is used:

> A game is a rule-based system with a variable and quantifiable outcome, where different outcomes are assigned different values, the player exerts effort in order to influence the outcome, the player feels emotionally attached to the outcome, and the consequences of the activity are negotiable (p. 36). (Juul 2005)

We extend the definition by specifying that the rules are covered by a story, as suggested by Koster (2005). The key part in the above definition is that the player "exerts effort". In other words, the user of the video-game has an active role in the interaction process. Thus, when discussing the experience of playing video-games we are referring to the process of interaction between player and video-game. Our focus is not on the creation, implementation or design of the video-game. Nor is it the motivation of the user to engage with a particular game or the psychological implications that the user may have after engaging with it. The focus is, as we have called it, the gaming experience; the experience of playing video-games on a one to one basis of the interaction between player and game. This concept will be untangled as we move forward within the chapter. First, in order to understand what we mean by experience, we proceed with a discussion of the concept of user experience.

3.1.2 Introduction to User Experience

The concept of user experience is understood as the subjective relationship between user and application (McCarthy and Wright 2004). It goes beyond the usability of the application, focusing on the personal outcome that the user gets from interacting with the application while performing a task. Considering user experience only as a personal or subjective outcome is problematic within the scope of scientific knowledge. Scientific knowledge allows us to generalise about our understanding of the world. If we identify the phenomenon being studied as personal, then it would not be possible to provide a general description of the phenomenon. For this reason, unlike video-games, we do not provide a current definition for user experience.

Rather, we will provide a definition which we build and use to understand the experience of playing videogames.

3.1.3 Overview of the Chapter

We divided the chapter in six sections. First we present a definition for user experience, and then we look at how user experience relates to the experience of playing video-games. We proceed by presenting a qualitative study for identifying a theory for the gaming experience. We then present a model and a questionnaire, which is included in the Appendix, based on the theory. Then, the theory is used in an example to differentiate among two different gaming experiences. Finally, we present concluding comments.

3.2 The Concept of User Experience

As we have discussed above, defining and understanding the concept of User Experience as only personal or subjective seems to be insufficient for providing a scientific approach. In this section, we present a definition of user experience that helps in bringing the concept of user experience towards an objective understanding. The discussion is grounded in different concepts about user experience, from the colloquial use, to the different uses within Human Computer Interaction and philosophy.

3.2.1 Understanding Experience

In our everyday life, we usually do not need further explanation when talking about experiences. In the Merriam-Webster's Collegiate Dictionary (Experience 2009), experience is defined as something intrinsic to human life. Every activity that a human performs constitutes and produces an experience; it is both constituent and product. Experience is the result of the individual interacting with the environment (Dewey 1938). In Human Computer Interaction (HCI), the term designing for experience is about considering the user, the task and the context when designing a computer application (Buxton 2007). But as experience is part of the human every-day life, evaluating experience is not as clear-cut as designing for experience appears to be. Experience is defined as personal and subjective, so evaluating experience is about evaluating a subjective appreciation of the user.

Evaluating experience places the emphasis on going beyond usability by looking at the relation of the user and the task. Usability is how an application is implemented to let the user perform a task effectively and efficiently; the main focus is productivity, to let the user do the tasks with good quality in an optimal time. Secondary goals are user preference and satisfaction (Bevan 1995). It is the evaluation of this relationship, of the user with task and context mediated by the application (Beaudouin-Lafon 2004). Preece et al. (2002) define experience as how the interaction *feels* to the users; an application taps into experience, when during the interaction process, factors such as fun, enjoyment, pleasure or aesthetics have an influence on the user. That is, the evaluation of experience is associated with evaluating enjoyment, fun, pleasure, etc. (Kaye 2007). To evaluate experience, HCI usually focuses in the end result of the experience. The user has a relationship with the object within a specific context (Hassenzahl 2003). From this interaction, the user can isolate or share the experience with more individuals (Forlizzi and Battarbee 2004). Or the experience is just personal and transitory, formed by a series of threads that the users mix together in order to make sense of it (McCarthy and Wright 2004). All these approaches require a close understanding of a user to understand how that particular experience was affected. The explanation can not be generalisable as it was dependent on an individual sense making process. The current methods that exist that look into the evaluating experience (Light 2006; Mahlke and Thüring 2007; Swallow et al. 2005), while they do offer insight to understand the experience, they do not generate objective knowledge out of it.

However, even if experience is personal, it is possible to share it and empathise with it among social groups. In the interaction process, the individual is not focusing on the application at hand, but on the task being done (Heidegger 1927). The actions performed by the individual using the application have resonance in the world (Winograd and Flores 1986), and even if this resonance is particular to the individual, the process of the interaction is common among many individuals.

3.2.2 Definition of User Experience

Experience is both the process and outcome of the interaction. And here we build on the theories discussed by Winograd and Flores (1986), Dourish (2001), and McCarthy and Wright (2004). During the interaction process the different elements that form the experience are blended to form a personal outcome. To formalise the discussion, we propose the following definition for experience, based on Dewey's definition of experience (Dewey 1938):

> Experience is both the process and outcome of the interaction of a user with the environment at a given time.

In the interaction process, the environment is formed by the goal to be achieved, the tool to be used, and the domain in which the interaction is taking place. The domain and tasks are selected by the user, e.g. the user can decide to write a document, this becomes the goal; the domain could be to write the document for college level class or to be published by a newspaper; the tool could be a personal computer or a PDA, or may even be a typewriter. In order for the user to focus on the task, we identify three properties that have to be present in the application: functional, usable and aesthetically pleasing. The functional quality is the ability of the tool to perform the desired task; e.g. a hammer can be used to nail something to the wall, and so can a shoe, but not a tomato. Usable relates to how well the properties of the tool match those of the user, using concepts such as effectiveness, efficiency and affordance; e.g. both a hammer and a shoe can be used to nail something to the wall, but a hammer is more usable than a shoe. The final property aesthetics is, in lay terms, how the tool looks; e.g. given enough options of identically usable hammers for the user to nail the object to the wall, the user would select the most appealing based on aesthetic value. These three properties allow to evaluate the application, and to the user to focus on the task at hand.

It is doing the task which would lead to a positive experience. By looking at the elements that form the process of this interaction between user and task we are able to understand the common elements of the experiences among many users. Even though the experience at the end is personal, there are common elements in the process of the experience that allow us to compare and share them with other users with similar experiences. User experience is in a feedback loop, as past experiences affect future experiences (Dewey 1938). The resulting experience can create changes in the mood of the person. This could be optimal experiences such as happiness or Flow (Csikszentmihalyi 1990), or at least a sense of satisfaction. Not satisfaction in the classic usability sense of comfort towards using the tool, but as a holistic approach in which the user is able to integrate all the elements of experience while doing a task. The user should feel that all the elements of the experience acted in symphony during the interaction producing a positive experience. So, evaluating the experience can be done by evaluating the elements that are present in the process of the interaction.

3.3   The Experience of Playing Video-Games

A video-game is a game played with the aid of the computer. The computer can take the role of a game companion, either foe or ally. Also, they can be used as a rule enforcer and to draw the story that covers them. The design of current video-games requires a big enterprise to pull together graphics experts, game designers and story tellers involved in a process of pre/post-productions (McCarthy et al. 2005). But even with all the complexities that are demanded for commercial video-games, they are still designed following the guidelines of the experts. Video-games, from the designer's point of view, are formed by a three tier structure: I/O, Program and Game (Crawford 1984; Rollings and Adams 2003). The I/O Structure defines the interaction between the user and the video-game. The program structure details how the game would be implemented at the code level. Game structure defines the objective and rules of the game. The program structure is not discussed in this chapter. The I/O structure is the interface of the program. Looking at the game as a computer interface does not offer any contradictions in terms of what it is expected to provide: an interface that lets the user perform a task efficiently, effectively and with a sense of satisfaction (Federoff 2002). Interfaces are just tools in order to do a task, so there was no reason to expect that this would differ from traditional interfaces.

To understand the relation between game and interface, the Mechanics, Dynamics and Aesthetics (MDA) model (Hunicke et al. 2004) tries to bridge what the designer is creating with what the player is expecting from the game. The mechanics describe the components of the game, such as representation and algorithm. Dynamics describes the behaviour of the mechanics as responses of the player's inputs. And Aesthetics is about the desirable emotional responses evoked in the player. For the designer, the game is built from the mechanics on; while for the player the game builds from the aesthetics on. The model explains this relationship in which dynamics are the bridge between aesthetics and mechanics; between player and designer. Considering only the player's perspective, the experience can be explained in terms of different immersions. Looking further at the relation between dynamics and aesthetic, the Sensory, Challenge-Based and Imaginative (SCI) immersions for the game-play experience model (Ermi and Mäyrä 2005) integrates the different aspects of game-play that have an effect on the experience. This model is based on what are considered the three different "immersions", sensory, challenge-based and imaginative, which occur, and interact, while playing video-games. The sensory immersion is about the player recognising how the implementation of the game influences his senses, either sound or video. Challenge-based immersion is "when one is able to achieve a satisfying balance of challenges and abilities" (p. 8). Finally, imaginative immersion is what allows the player to "use her imagination, empathise with the characters, or just enjoy the fantasy of the game" (p. 8). The intersection between the three senses of immersion is what provides the player with a fully immersive game-play experience. The sensory immersion is the link of the interface with the game, while challenge-based and imaginative immersions are the link of the player with the game. Both the MDA and SCI model make a clear differentiation between the game and the player. The MDA model proposes that it is the interface where the player establishes contact with the game, while the SCI argues is through challenge-based and imagination. Both models are in resonance by providing a separation of the "game" with the "play"; the implementation from the interaction. These models, however, include an element in which the interface is not only a series of widgets, but a series of realistic graphics which the player manipulates. The imagery produced in the interface is the story that covers the rules of the game; these were called the "aesthetics" in the MDA model and "imagination" and "sensory" in the SCI model. These models provide an understanding at the outcome of the experience. They explain how the different parts of the game are needed so the user can have a playing experience; however, they fail in provide an objective metric to understand the process that forms the overall experience.

3.3.1 Optimal and Sub-Optimal Experience in Video-Games

Playing games is supposed to produce a positive experience. They are usually associated with the term immersion (Brown and Cairns 2004). Besides immersion, other two terms try to describe these states: Flow (Csikszentmihalyi 1990) and Presence (Slater and Wilbur 1997). Flow is a state that an individual achieves after completing a series of steps while engaged in a task. Immersion is the sense of being away of the real world and Presence is the sense of being inside a virtual world. It has been suggested that Flow, the optimal experience, can be achieved by playing video-games (Sweetser and Wyeth 2005). The GameFlow model translates the stages needed to reach flow into a series of qualities that video-games offer. Flow was formulated as a model of the stages achieved by the individual, while GameFlow is being proposed as a series of characteristics that video-games possess. That is, this model only suggests that video-games might allow an individual to reach flow. On the other hand, immersion and presence do not automatically mean that the player is having an enjoyable activity, but it is assumed that they are valued but sub-optimal experiences. It is the activity which determines the degree of the experience. Playing video-games can produce an optimal experience, such as Flow, or sub-optimal, such as Immersion; a well implemented video-game might help the individual to reach a state of Presence.

3.3.2 The Need for a New Approach to Understand Experience in Video-Games

The experience is both process and outcome. While playing video-games, the ideal experience is for the player to have fun. In order to build that fun, a series of elements have to be amalgamated together. The MDA and SCI models try to understand the outcome of the experience by looking at the different elements that could form the process, but these elements are not measurable. Outcomes such as flow, immersion or presence, are only concerned with extreme experiences; ignoring the prosaic experience of playing. For example: playing for 5 min while using public transport, is overlooked in favour of the extreme experience, such as playing a game for hours and hours until the real world fades away.

In some sense, these theoretical approaches are top-down, applying large frameworks to the study of gaming experience. Our approach is, by contrast, bottom-up, approaching empirically the question of how the gaming experience feels in order to operationalise such concept within HCI. In order to measure or design for experience we should be able to look at those elements of the interaction process that are common among users.

3.4 Defining the Gaming Experience

We believe that by looking at the process of experience it is possible to study objectively and eventually generalize about experience. We are looking at the elements of the process of the interaction that build the basic experience; those elements without which the experience would be poor. These are the hygienic factors of the gaming experience (Herzberg 1968). We are deliberately leaving aside the social aspect of playing video-games. The social aspect of playing video-games has been documented (Lazzaro 2004), but this is a secondary aspect of playing, once the bond between the player and the game has been established. We are interested in looking as closely as possible at the process of playing video-games, not just from our own reckoning of what makes a good experience, but with the idea of grounding our results in qualitative data. We call this one to one relationship between player and video-game, the gaming experience.

The section is divided as follows: first we present an overview of the qualitative method that we used. Second, we present our analysis to formulate the grounded theory. Last, we present an overview of the theory.

3.4.1   A Grounded Theory Approach

The question driving this analysis is: what are the necessary conditions to procure a positive gaming experience? The nature of the question suggests that the route to finding the answer should be bounded by qualitative methodologies (Green and Thorogood 2004). In particular, we used Grounded Theory (Strauss and Corbin 1998) to propose a theory for the gaming experience. The intennt is to develop a better understanding of the process of experience that emerges from the data itself. The method to develop Grounded Theory is composed of a series of coding procedures. Firstly, the data is *open coded* in which quotes or words are selected and labelled; this process produces a set of labels, or codes, which can be related to each other producing a set of meta-codes or *axial codes*. These axial codes are the axis on which the forming theory stands. This process is done iteratively until no new codes emerge from the data. The codes are then *selectively coded* where each category is fully developed in order to produce the theory. The data that formulates the theory are different quotations presented throughout the discussion.

The data used for this analysis are game reviews. Game reviews are aimed at telling the general player the reasons that a certain games should be played. They do not tell the ending of the game, but just try to describe what it is like to be playing. Game reviews, in some sense, convey the experience of playing video-games. Four over-the-counter magazines from the month of August 2006 and three websites, all of them with a focus on video-games, were used as source data; see Table 3.1 for details of the sources. Besides game reviews, interviews and articles within the magazines were also used on a smaller scale.

The fact that the four magazines are from the same month and year should not hinder the results of the study. One reason is that Grounded Theory is robust enough to overcome the variances that are innate to commercial influences. The second reason is that the interest is in the common parts of the experience. The experience of playing the same video-game described by different magazines should still have the same common elements. Also, the use of websites adds some variance to the types of games reviewed, as well as the fact that two magazines specialised in console games and two in PC games. Since it has been suggested that using only magazines could bias the results of the study, five interviews were conducted once the Grounded Theory study was finished. One game designer, two game reviewers and two players took part in this process. The interviews were semi-structured,

Table 3.1 Sources of data for the qualitative study. The abbreviation within brackets is how that source is referred within the document. Magazines are quoted providing the page number from where the quotation was taken; Websites are quoted providing the name of the game from where the quotation was taken, as it is more manageable than providing the complete URL

Source	Material
PC-Gamer. 64, August 2006—{PCG}	24 reviews and 2 articles
PlayStation 2 Official Magazine, 75, August 2006—{PSO}	11 interviews and 1 editorial
Edge. 165 August 2006—{Edge}	31 reviews, 3 interviews and 7 articles
PC-Zone. 171, August 2006—{PCZ}	20 reviews and 3 articles
GameSpot—{GS} http://www.gamespot.com	3 reviews and rating system
GameFaqs—{GF} http://www.gamefaqs.com	3 reviews
ReviewsGameSpy—{GP} http://www.gamespy.com	3 reviews and rating system
Designer 1 {d1}	Interview
Reviewer 1{r1}	Interview
Reviewer 2 {r2}	Interview
Player 1 {p1}	Interview
Player 2 {p2}	Interview

transcribed and then analysed. The interviews asked the participants to explain what they focus on while playing/designing/reviewing a video-game, what makes a game enjoyable, and what factors made them stay playing a game. As the interviews were semi-structured, the questions that followed aimed at deepening the answers that the participants gave to the previous questions.

The objective of this study is to find the core elements of the process of the experience. Core elements are those necessary but not sufficient to ensure a positive experience; they can also be understood as *hygienic factors* (Herzberg 1968). Herzberg argues that the opposite of satisfaction is not dissatisfaction, but no-satisfaction; satisfaction and dissatisfaction are then two different concepts that are not necessarily related to each other. He argues that motivator factors are those that lead to satisfaction, and the lack of hygienic factors lead to dissatisfaction. With a similar concept in mind, this study looks for those elements that if missing they would mar the experience, but that their presence would not necessarily imply an optimal experience.

3.4.2 Defining the Core Elements

The Core Elements of the Gaming Experience (CEGE) incorporate the video-game itself and the interaction between it and the user, which we labelled "puppetry"; a full discussion of the selection of this label can be found elsewhere (Calvillo-Gámez and Cairns 2008).

3.4.2.1 About the Video-Game

The video-game is intrinsic to the experience, without it there would not be a gaming experience. The forming theory does not try to describe what makes a good video-game; rather, it focuses on how it is perceived in terms of the forming experience.

> **(PCZ, p. 20):** The premise, if you're not familiar with the multiplayer modes of *Pandora Tomorrow* and *Chaos Theory*, is one of spies versus mercenaries. Three spies must hack three security terminals, controlling from a standard *Splinter Cell* third-person viewpoint and using many of the main game's acrobatic tricks. Three mercs [sic] must prevent the spies from doing this, from a first-person viewpoint, using a gun and a flashlight. Sound familiar? Well it should, because it's based on the much-played ancient Egyptian sport of hide-and-seek, albeit on a far more deadly and technological level.

The preceding quote is the typical way in which a review refers to a video-game. The game being discussed, *"Splinter Cell: Double Agent"*, is related to others with similar story lines or rules. The story of the game is about "spies versus mercenaries", the reader of the review could have a better perception of that story in case of familiarity with the two games mentioned. The rules of the game are bounded by the classic play of hide and seek, two teams are playing each with three members. Each team has a different goal in the game, and, presumably, the player can select the team of his choice. This excerpt of the review also describes the basic environment of the game, "security terminals", and a third-person view point (the character is fully visible), or first person (the player can only see what the player sees).

The video-game is perceived by two elements: **game-play** and **environment**. The former can be thought of as the soul of the game while the latter as the body. Game-play defines what the game is about, its rules and scenario. Environment is the way the game is presented to player, the physical implementation into graphics and sounds.

The rules are somehow implicit within a game. This can be due to the fact that the numbers of rules in a video-game are many to be listed:

> **(Interview, p2):** I like games that challenge your intellect: strategy, politics, and so on.

Those types of comment refer to the rules, to the "do's and don'ts" that the player can do in the game. The story is the dressing of the rules, taking the abstraction of the rules into characters and scenarios. Sometimes the story of the game can be inferred with the title of the game:

> **(Edge, p.46):** Miami Vice opens with an option screen that says as much about gaming's potential as you wish fulfilment in four words as you could in 40,000.

The story is also presented

> **(Edge, p.42):** B-Boy. A dance-combat game that's not so much turn-based as headstand, toprock [sic] and spin based.

Those rules and scenarios are considered within the Game-play of the video-game. The video-game is also experienced in terms of the environment it creates. This is done by providing the game with graphics and sound. In the printed data, they use pictures as aids to describe the graphics, with usually one or two lines to help in the description:

(Edge, p.89): There is a huge amount of destructible scenery [...] rocks, however, seem to be made of polystyrene.

But not only are the graphics responsible for creating the environment, there are also sounds:

(PCZ, p.12): Sound is hugely important for creating atmosphere and character in games – can you imagine being as tense in *Counter Strike* without hearing 'the bomb has been planted'?

Both sound and graphics make the environment of the game. The environment describes then what the game looks and sound like:

(GameSpy, "Flatout2"): Car impacts are loud and violent, and never fail to be utterly satisfying.

Once the video-game has been defined in terms of the game-play and the environment, it is the turn of the player to take those elements to his disposal.

3.4.2.2 About Puppetry

The interaction of the player with the video-game is the puppetry. Puppetry describes how the player starts approaching the video-game until eventually the game being played is the outcome of the actions of the player. This process of interaction is affected by three conditions: **control, ownership** and **facilitators**. Control is formed by the actions and events that the game has available to the player. Once the player takes control of the game, by using the game's resources the player makes the game respond to his actions, he makes the game his own. Ownership is when the player takes responsibility for the actions of the game, he feels them as his because they are the result of his conscious actions and the game has acknowledged this by rewarding him. There are also external factors that have an impact the interaction process. These external factors relate to the player's subjectivities, such as previous experiences with similar games or aesthetic value. Even if the player fails to rapidly grasp control, these factors can facilitate the ownership of the game by the player.

Control is the player learning to manipulate the game. It is about the player learning how the objects in the game move, understanding the goals of the game, keeping the player occupied. It is also learning about the controllers, getting used to the objects and angles in which the objects are displayed and the ability of the player to memorise the relationship between controllers and the actions of the game. The first two elements of control, controllers and small actions, relate the basic actions that the characters in the game can do and the manipulation of the controller to make them do something. Without losing generality and to facilitate the discussion, the manipulable objects of the game would be called characters. The process of gaining control is formed by six members: goal, small actions, controllers, memory, something to do (S2D) and point of view (POV). Goal is the objective, the player has to understand what is the overall objective of the game, even if still not clear on the details. Small actions are the basic actions that the player can do on the characters, such as moving to the left or to the right. Controllers are the way through which the player can exercise the small actions, for example pressing a button makes the object move to the left. Memory is the ability of the player to recall the connection between small actions and controllers. S2D refers to the concept that the player must be kept busy, or doing something. Last, POV is the way that the player sees the environment of the game.

The *controllers* are the basic tools that the player needs to take control of the game. This is how the player starts to manipulate the different characters or objects on the screen.

(PCZ, p.53): Wave your mouse means wave your sword.

Controllers only refer to the player's manipulation of the physical tool, the set of actions that the character can perform are the *Small Actions*. These are the other side of the controllers. Small actions are the basic blocks that allow the player to get the character to do something on the screen. Pressing button "x" is part of the controller, the fact that the character jumps is a small action. Consider the following quote:

(PSO, p.32): By targeting civilian and pressing L2 to shout at them.

From this quote the player has to relate the act of pressing, with the act of shouting that the character can do. In order to make the character shout, then, the player has to press L2.

Memory is the element of control that gives the player the repertoire of actions to get into the game and that can be recalled at a given moment. After learning about the controller and the small actions, the player has to memorise the bindings between controllers and small actions.

(PCZ, p.47): 250 skills for you to master.
(Interview, r2): [...] you may find very hard to explain why you need to press that button to reload [...].

Point-of-view is how the information is displayed to the player. The player is able to see what is going on in the game from different angles, depending on the game. The reviews do tell the player what to expect from the point of view, and it is also used as a way to classify games:

(PCZ, p.52): First person makes a combat that actually works.

Point-of-view is not Environment, POV is how the environment affects the control of the game.

The *goal* is the overall objective of the game. That is, the player learning what is to do. It is the player grasping the game-play of the game:

(PCG, p.45): Village pillaging is hard work, get your posse of goblin minions to do it for you.

The goal is the top level objective of the game, as in the preceding quote, there are no details of what the player is exactly to do, but the player understands that the overall objective is to do village pillaging while directing an army of goblins. The player must be clear in what is the overall objective of the game in order to get control of the game.

The final element is *something to do*, that is, to keep the player busy doing something:

> **(Interview, r2):** Say an interesting example is going to be […] it is a driving game set in Hawaii, huge free space for you to drive around, but it is just roads like roads on an island, they are not race track roads they are not fake need for space curses they are just roads. And quite a lot of people who kind of sat with thought this just really boring just drive 40 miles and nothing happens and no one chases me and I don't have a gun and you know what is the point and it took all of us I think a while to adjust to this new experience is different kind of driven challenge, it is a different kind of experience the fun is in a different place where you are just used to looking for the game does do at all wrong it is just a genuinely new idea and it takes a while for your brain to adjust.

In the above quote, the player can identify the goal, however, the experience failed to become positive because the player got the sense that there were large spaces without things to do.

Once the player starts to grasp control of the game, the player gears the game with his own intentions in order to make it his. The process of ownership is about using the elements that give the player control in his favour to enjoy the game. The elements that influence ownership are big actions, personal goals, rewards, and you-but-not-you. Big actions are those actions that the player implements as strategies, by using a collection of small actions, in order to complete the goal of the game. The player can also draw his personal goals, and use big actions to complete them. This process of the player achieving the game and personal goals through his actions is the basis of the process of ownership. The game acknowledges the ownership of the player by providing rewards. Last, you-but-not-you refers to the idea that the player is engaging in activities that are alien to his everyday actions, which allows the player to create his personal goals.

> **(Interview, d1):** But also use tend to set their own challenges in their head, not to how much you script the challenge, or, they are actually really playing their own, you can tell them what to do, but they'll play it by themselves, they made their own mini-challenges subconsciously, they don't even know they are doing it half the time, but if you are playing a game [..], you may be on a mission to do something, but in their back of their heads they are oh, last time I did this bit, I did not this street, how did I get to here? Where am I going? some people are mapping the game in their backs of their heads, other people are searching for radio stations, others are concentrating in shooting civilians, everyone plays the game in their own little way, I think is were game-play comes from, as their own challenge. a lot of multiplayer games tend to take on because want that level of challenge that someone else brings, you have 30 people playing the same game at the same time but not one of them is playing quite the same game, they are all playing from their own viewpoint, from their own idea, and that is comes from.

This quote summarises the concept of ownership quite well. The player gets hold of all the elements of the experience and starts doing his own game. To gain ownership, the player starts implementing *big actions*. Big actions are the set of smaller actions that the player uses in order to achieve the goal of the game.

> **(PCZ, p.53):** Knock out a strut from a nearby shelf & barrels can tumble your foes.

Besides the objectives that the game imposes, the player also has *personal goals* while playing.

> **(Interview, p1):** On more recent games, sort of on the online games, I actually enjoy help-ing people, but to be able to help other people you usually have to achieve more than they have. So it is kind of self-fulfilling, the more you achieve the more you can help more people.

The personal goals can also appear while the player is engaging with the game, and decides to do something that has no influence on the outcome of the game, but rather just a personal goal:

> **(PCZ, p.53):** Giving you the option to ally yourself with the good or the ill without actually changing the trajectory of the story-arc.

Or it could also be to use the environment, game-play and controls that the game provides to create your own game:

> **(Interview, r1):** I'll take this as an example, is a game where you are a boy who lives just to wonder around the world which is instead of cars they have this little bumpy trucks they call walking mock machines and part of the game you can indulge in is to get your own mock, customize it, play around with it but also around town is this beautiful cartoonish kind of town, you can join a band you can start playing the harmonica in a street corner and people wouldn't listen until you get better, you can hang out with other people and you will group people to get a band and it is completely pointless and is just another way for you just to enjoy the game, you can play through the entire story with your big robot or you can become many other things as well but you can stay in the corner playing the harmonica people gather around clapping and you play a bump note and it just doesn't matter that it looks a bit rough and it sounds a bit cheap.

The game acknowledges the ownership of the player by providing *Rewards*.

> **(Interview, d1):** [Question: What do you think is the thing that keeps a player for the same game?] It is bit a dough and bullet, it has to be continuously rewarding, but I am not sure, continuously challenging, there is something always that you want to do, even though, there is always rewards given to you, as completing little micro bits, and also larger sections, so there is always a feeling of you moving forward, so you always feels the potential, you can feel this you know, there are more cool things around the corner or something you haven't seen before or just in the next screen, it comes down to I want to find out what is next, I want to find out if I press that button I am so engross that I cant stop now I have to keep going now, until I find a nice place to stop. is not you pushing the user to do more, is the user pushing themselves to do more, to discover what is around the corner, take the next turn, is that little intangibility of the more turn, or next door, or five more minutes.

These rewards can be achieved via sub-goals or by finishing missions:

> **(Interview, p1):** You fight a big boss at the end of may be 5 or 6, or several sub bosses and then a final big boss at the end with many characters over the final area, and then you share the loot and you go off and do something else.

Or a continuum of challenges to the player.

> **(Edge, p83):** We were fed up with games that if someone starts to win, it becomes easier for them to win outright.

Or could also be those actions that have no direct impact on the game development, but amuse the player:

> **(PSO, p.36):** Also funny is princess Leia's mêlée attack – a cheek-stinging slap.

(PCG, p.45): It's clearly wrong to run into an inn and cut [sic] decapitate the cook, but your heart melts when one of them puts the chef's hat on.

While the player is taking big actions and personal goals, the player engages in actions that would not necessarily do in real life, it is a *You-but-not-You* effect:

(PCZ, p.51): Before you offer them a quick painful smiting.

Most games would set the player in activities foreign to his everyday life

(Interview, p2): [Question: Why do you play video-games?] To have fun, to be some one else.

These activities can be seen as something that the player would be able to do:

(PSO, p.3): Movies and books use real life war as rich source material, so why shouldn't games? (Although you don't get to pull the trigger yourself in a movie).

Not only is the player able to do things otherwise illegal or alien to his own reality, but the player is also making the character grow under his control.

(PCZ, p.49): Who you meet, how you treat them and how you solve their problems determines what recruits you can gather.

This suggests players would take responsibility for their actions as if they themselves are to blame, and not the result of lack of control.

(Interview, p2): I don't like games where you get stuck because you can't do the button combination in the precise second to jump over the pitfall.

Ownership lets the player see the game as part of his daily life activities:

(PCZ, p.10): Well let's see. I can leave my house and wander around the streets of east London to witness filthy roads [...] or I can ride around Cyrodiil's beautiful forests on my horse, while slashing any potential thieves.

The last element of the theory to be discussed is the facilitators. Facilitators are the most subjective elements of the CEGE. It has been discussed so far that in order to have a positive experience the player should achieve ownership, and to do so the player must first get control of the game. However, it is possible for the player to achieve a level of ownership, then a positive experience, even if the player fails to get control. Also, the player may fail to achieve ownership even if getting control. This is done by the use of facilitators. These facilitators are time, aesthetic values and previous experiences. The amount of time that the player is willing to play, the previous experiences with similar games or other games, and the aesthetic values of the game.

The *aesthetic values* of the game are important in facilitating ownership. If the game looks attractive to the player, then he may be willing to try longer:

(PSO, p.3): How the increased graphical fidelity changes the way you feel about your action?

These values also influence the player, if the music is attractive:

(Edge, p.82): Locoroco is a nursery rhyme you can play.

Or it may be because they see something about the game that is just amusing to observe.

> **(PCZ, p.59):** There are also Indian naked female archers that'll have your men furiously polishing their spears.

The *previous experiences* of the player motivate the player to play longer and to assume the consequences, or benefits, of his actions while playing:

> **(PCZ, p.2):** I don't know about everyone else out there, but I'm really pining for a *Max Payne*. Fans are still churning out mods for the stylish fall of our hero. I'd love nothing more than to see a beautiful new incarnation to empty my clips at. Payne didn't look like he was going anywhere fun after the last game. Well, I say whatever it takes, we want him back. For all I care he can wake up from a cheesy *Dallas*-like dream and start all over again.

Previous experiences may not only be about similar video-games, but may just relate to a similar goal:

> (PCG, p.86): I've never lost the heady sense of excitement when I first read about Alexander, and I've been waiting for a game to bring his story to life ever since. Rome: Total war let me live out my fantasies of conquest.

The *time* facilitator is about the time the user is willing to dedicate to play. The time can be intrinsic to the type of game:

> **(PCG, p.87):** 30 cities in 100 turns is an alarming tight schedule, and it radically changes the way you play. You can't sit back, develop your economy, and gradually build up your mega-army: there isn't time.

Or just to the experience in that moment:

> **(Interview, d1):** [It] is that little intangibility of the more turn, or next door, or five more minutes.

The lack of those extra 5 min could make the player not want to play again, as there is an acknowledgment that without it, the game would not be enjoyed fully.

3.4.3 About the Theory

Both elements, video-game and puppetry, are part of the process of the experience. The theory states that if elements are missing, then the experience would be negative. But, if they are present, then the experience could be positive. Users first identify the game and then their relationship with it. Ownership is eventually the link that leads to enjoyment. Ownership is achieved when the player has control over the game; if the control is low, then the facilitators have to be high to allow the player to have a sense of ownership. The game is then used by the player to create his own story. The way the player starts making the game his own is by first applying his own actions toward playing the game. Those actions can be used to win the game, or accomplish the player's own goals. As the game progresses, the player starts to receive different types of rewards, which can be helpful toward winning the game, or just something that the player enjoys doing. It is also an opportunity so that the player can do something alien to his reality. The facilitators that influence puppetry

Table 3.2 The core elements of the gaming experience: The two guiding elements are puppetry and video-game, followed by control, ownership and facilitators

Puppetry			Video-Game	
Control	Ownership	Facilitators	Game-Play	Environment
Small actions	Big actions	Time	Rules	Graphics
Controllers	Personal goals	Aesthetic value	Scenario	Sound
Memory	You-but-not-you	Prev. experiences	–	–
Point-of-View	Rewards	–	–	–
Goal	–	–	–	–
Something-to-Do	–	–	–	–

are part of the subjective relationship of the player with the game: a previous experience with a similar game, the amount of time willing to play, or the aesthetic value that the player can perceive from the game. See Table 3.2 for a listing of all the core elements of the gaming experience in their corresponding categories.

3.5 Operationalising the Theory

Once we have formulated the theory, we proceeded to operationalise it. This was done in two ways: first we created a model for the theory and then an instrument, a questionnaire, to measure aspects of the model. The model provides an abstraction of the theory which shows the relationship among the different elements of the theory. It identifies the elements in two categories, those that can be directly measured versus those that are theoretical constructs. The former are known as observable variables and the latter as latent variables. The questionnaire is created using the observable variables, which allow us to understand the changes for the latent variables.

3.5.1 The CEGE Model

The theory can be summarised in the following three points:

1. A positive experience (enjoyment) while playing games is achieved by the player's perception of the video-game and the interaction with it. These are the Core Elements of the Gaming Experience: Video-game and Puppetry.
2. Puppetry, the player's interaction with the game is formed by the player's sense of control and ownership. Control produces ownership, which in turns produces enjoyment. Ownership is also produced by Facilitators to compensate the sense of control.
3. The player's perception of the video-game is formed by the environment and the game-play, which also produces enjoyment.

All the elements just mentioned are latent variables. In order to observe the change in the Facilitators, for example, we have to be able to observe the forming elements, namely, Aesthetic Value, Time and Previous Experiences (Table 3.2). Facilitators are a latent variable, while Aesthetic Value, Time and Previous Experiences are observable variables. These relationships among variables can be modelled graphical in the following way: latent variables are represented as circles and observable as rectangles. We draw an arrow from a causing variable to a receiving variable. In Fig. 3.1, we present the relationships among the different latent variables based on above statements.

All the latent variables depend on the observable variables. However, the observable variable is a consequence of the latent one. That is, the observable variable exists because it belongs to the construct specified by the latent variable (Nunnally and Bernstein 1994). See Fig. 3.2 for a graphical representation between latent and observable variables.

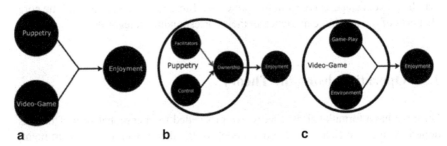

Fig. 3.1 The CEGE model: The figure depicts all the relationships among the latent variables. **a** Inside CEGE, video-game and puppetry produce enjoyment. **b** Inside puppetry, control, facilitators produces ownership, which produces enjoyment. **c** Inside video-game, game-play and environment produce enjoyment

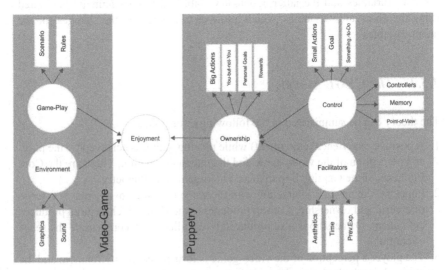

Fig. 3.2 The CEGE model: The figure depicts the relationships among observable (*rectangles*) and latent (*circles*) variables

Table 3.3 The items in the questionnaire belongs to different scales

Items	Scale 1	Scale 2
1, 4, 5	Enjoyment	–
2, 3	Frustration	–
6–38	CEGE	–
6–12, 38	Puppetry	Control
13–18	Puppetry	Facilitators
19–24	Puppetry	Ownership
25	Puppetry	Control/Ownership
26–31	Video-Game	Environment
32–37	Video-Game	Game-Play

3.5.2 A Questionnaire for the Gaming Experience

The CEGE Questionnaire (CEGEQ) was developed to measure the observable variables in order to understand the behaviour of the latent constructs. The questionnaire was developed using an iterative process following the usual psychometric guidance (Loewenthal 2001; Nunnally and Bernstein 1994). The questionnaire is presented in the Appendix.

Observable variables are considered as items in the questionnaire context and latent variables as scales. The questionnaire is created with 38 items and 10 scales. The scales are Enjoyment, Frustration, CEGE, Puppetry, Video-Game, Control, Facilitators, Ownership, Game-Play and Environment. The first two scales were included as a reference to see the relationships between CEGE and Enjoyment and Frustration. If the CEGE are present, then Frustration should be low and uncorrelated. The remaining scales are the latent variables produced from the theory. See Table 3.3 for a relationship between items and scales. Due to the hierarchical formulation of the theory, items may belong to more than one category. An item can belong to the Puppetry and Control scales, for example.

3.6 Examples of Using the Questionnaire

In this section we present an example of how to use the CEGE theory to differentiate among different experiences. The experiment explores the differences when two different input devices are used to play Tetris. The results of the experiment are discussed using the CEGE theory to differentiate among the different experiences.

3.6.1   Method

3.6.1.1   Design

The experiment used a within-subjects design. The independent variable was the type of controller used. Two types of controllers were used and the order in which the controllers were used was balanced. The dependent variable was the gaming experience, which was assessed using the CEGEQ.

3.6.1.2   Participants

Fifteen participants took part in the experiment. There were seven women and eight men. The age group of the participants was divided as follows: 4 were between 18 and 20; 2 between 21 and 25; 2 between 26 and 30; 2 between 31 and 35; 2 between 36 and 40; 1 between 41 and 45; and 1 above 51. Participants were recruited with emails to students within UCL and neighbouring colleges.

3.6.1.3   Apparatus and Materials

Tetris was installed in a PC using a shareware Java implemented version. This version of Tetris does not have sound. The input devices used were the standard QWERTY keyboard and a knob like device. Both devices can be used to play Tetris, the mappings of the devices are presented in Table 3.4.

The CEGEQ (see the Appendix) has 38 items with a 7-point Likert scale. It was modified by removing the four items that query about sound, leaving a total of 34 items. The questionnaire provides seven different scores: Enjoyment, Frustration, CEGE, Puppetry, Video-game, Control, Facilitators, Ownership, Environment and Game-play. A general survey asking about the participants' data, such as age and gender, was also used.

3.6.1.4   Procedure

Participants carried out the experiment individually. They started the experiment with a briefing of the experiment, verbally and written, after which they were asked

Table 3.4 Mappings of both input devices in order to play Tetris

Tetris	Keyboard	Knob
Drop	Down arrow	Push
Move left	Left arrow	Rotate counterclockwise
Move right	Rigth arrow	Rotate clockwise
Rotate counterclockwise	Up arrow	Push-Rotate counterclockwise
Rotate clockwise	Shift-Up	Push-Rotate clockwise

to sign a consent form and complete the general survey form. Participants were asked to try to forget they were in a lab and think they were in the place where they usually engaged with video-games.

The order in which the participants used the input device was randomised. Each participant was given an explanation of how to play the game with each device. Participants would play for approximately 15 min for each condition, and then they would complete the questionnaire and perform the second condition.

3.6.2   Results

A related samples t test was used to compare the mean of the enjoyment score for the Keyboard condition ($M=0.739$, $SD=0.176$) with the Knob condition ($M=0.568$, $SD=0.169$); as the keyboard provided a better experience. The alpha level was 0.01 two tailed. The test was found to be statistically significant, $t(14)=3.24$, $p=0.006$. Since there was significance in the results, we proceeded to look further into the CEGE scores. Comparing with a related samples t test the mean score for the Keyboard condition ($M=0.644$, $SD=0.051$) with the Knob condition ($M=0.610$, $SD=0.044$) using the same alpha level as before. The test was found to be statistically significant, $t(14)=3.08$, $p=0.008$.

Hence, we proceeded to look into the two major categories of CEGE: Video-game and Puppetry. The t test comparing the means of Video-game (Keyboard condition: $M=0.485$, $SD=0.056$; Knob condition: $M=0.484$, $SD=0.052$) resulted in a non significant result, $t(14)=0.20$, $p=0.840$. While the t test of the means of the Puppetry score (Keyboard condition: $M=0.735$, $SD=0.071$; Knob condition: $M=0.682$, $SD=0.063$) was found to be statistically significant, $t(14)=2.97$, $p=0.01$.

Pursuing further the variables that constitute Puppetry, it was found that comparing the Control scores of the Keyboard condition ($M=0.817$, $SD=0.118$) with the Knob condition ($M=0.728$, $SD=0.093$) was significant, $t(14)=3.28$, $p=0.005$. The other two variables, facilitators (Keyboard: $M=0.657$, $SD=0.118$; Knob: $M=0.628$, $SD=0.117$) and ownership (Keyboard: $M=0.690$, $SD=0.078$; Knob: $M=0.666$, $SD=0.081$) were not significant with the following t test respectively: $t(14)=1.545$ and $t(14)=1.221$.

Lastly, the score of Frustration (Keyboard: $M=0.476$, $SD=0.180$; Knob: $M=0.685$, $SD=0.196$), was also found to be statically significant higher for the knob condition, $t(14)=-3.55$, $p=0.003$.

3.6.3   Discussion

Using the CEGE questionnaire, it is possible to identify what produces the difference in both experiences. The CEGE theory provides a hierarchical approach to understand the gaming experience. This approach allows identifying that there is a significant difference in the level of enjoyment with each device. Methodically, it is identified that this difference is due to the sense of CEGE, the puppetry, specifically to the level of control that the participants had over the game. Participants experienced the video-game in similar way with both devices. This was to be expected as the graphics, rules and scenario of the game did not change. The low score for video-game could be explained by the fact that it had no sound, and the graphics were quite simple. Regarding puppetry, the main difference is in the sense of control. The sense of ownership and facilitators did not change between both games. That meant that players were still able to overcome the lack of control in order to concentrate on the game.

The difference of control did have a final impact on the level of enjoyment. Answering the original question, the difference between both input devices is that the keyboard gives the player better control of the experience. Even though both devices let users perceive the game equally while making it their own, it was the lack of control with the knob made the difference in the gaming experience. Further more, there was such a lack of control with the knob that it actually marred the experience. That is, one of the CEGE was missing thus providing a negative experience.

With this example we have shown how to use the CEGE theory to objectively study different gaming experiences. The theory provided an explanation of the outcome of the experience.

3.6.4 Other Examples

Schonauer et al. (2011) used the CEGEQ to evaluate the levels of enjoyment and frustration of players that used a Chronic Pain Rehabilitation Serious Game. Unlike the previous example, where the questionnaire was used to pursue a statistically significant comparison of means in order to differentiate experience, Schonauer et al. used the questionnaire just to establish a norm and to determine if a given game provides enjoyment or frustration.

Zaman (2011) used the principles behind CEGE to differentiate between the experiences of teenagers and pre-schoolers. She did not use the questionnaire to differentiate or assess the experiences, but just to provide a theoretical framework in which to build an understanding of gaming experience for a different type of users.

3.7 Summary

In this chapter we have presented a novel approach to User Experience. We have argued that by looking at the experience as a two fold phenomenon, process and outcome, and by studying the elements of the process it is possible to formulate an objective theory regarding experience. We acknowledged that experience is indeed a personal endeavour, but there are also common elements in the experience that allow it to be shareable among different users.

We presented the Core Elements of the Gaming Experience (CEGE) theory to understand the experience of playing video-games. The theory describes those elements that are necessary, but not sufficient, to provide a positive experience while playing video-games. The formulation of the theory using a grounded theory approach is presented. The theory can be summarised as follows: if the CEGE are present then there is no guarantee that the experience would be positive, but it will not be negative; if they are missing, then the experience would be negative. A model that abstracts the relationship of the CEGE and a questionnaire to assess them was also presented.

An example of using the theory to study two different experiences was also presented. Following a hierarchical approach to find the element of the process that affected the outcome of the experience we showed how to compare two different experiences. The results showed that in one case the lack of control produced a negative experience, while in the other example it produced a positive experience. The theory allowed to formulate and test an objective hypothesis regarding the user experience of playing video-games.

The CEGE theory can be used to evaluate different experiences. Future work can look at the theory to evaluate single instances of experience, instead of comparing two similar experiences. The CEGE theory can be used to assess experience in a objective way, it is not about assessing the game or the user, but the interaction of both of them. Further work can look at the elements that might be sufficient to obtain a positive experience, or that complement the CEGE.

Acknowledgments The authors wish to thank Dr. Sarah Faisal, Dr. Lidia Oshlyansky and Charlenne Jennett for valuable comments on this work. Eduardo H. Calvillo Gámez is sponsored by SEP-PROMEP.

Appendix

Core Elements of the Gaming Experience Questionnaire (CEGEQ)

Overview This questionnaire is used to assess the core elements of the gaming experience. Each item is rated with a 7-point Likert scale. The questionnaire is to be administered after the participant has finished playing with the game.

Scales There are eight scales in the questionnaire: CEGE, Video-Game, Puppetry, Game-Play, Environment, Control, Ownership and Facilitators.

Reliability The Cronbach alpha for the whole questionnaire is 0.794 and for the CEGE scale is 0.803.

Instructions Please read the following statements and answer by marking one of the numbers that best describes your experience.

1. I enjoyed playing the game
2. I was frustrated at the end of the game
3. I was frustrated whilst playing the game
4. I liked the game
5. I would play this game again
6. I was in control of the game
7. The controllers responded as I expected
8. I remember the actions the controllers performed
9. I was able to see in the screen everything I needed during the game
10. * The point of view of the game that I had spoiled my gaming
11. I knew what I was supposed to do to win the game
12. * There was time when I was doing nothing in the game
13. I liked the way the game look
14. The graphics of the game were plain
15. * I do not like this type of game
16. I like to spend a lot of time playing this game
17. * I got bored playing this time
18. * I usually do not choose this type of game
19. * I did not have a strategy to win the game
20. The game kept constantly motivating me to keep playing
21. I felt what was happening in the game was my own doing
22. I challenged myself even if the game did not require it
23. I played with my own rules
24. * I felt guilty for the actions in the game
25. I knew how to manipulate the game to move forward
26. The graphics were appropriate for the type of game
27. The sound effects of the game were appropriate
28. * I did not like the music of the game
29. The graphics of the game were related to the scenario
30. The graphics and sound effects of the game were related
31. The sound of the game affected the way I was playing
32. * The game was unfair
33. I understood the rules of the game
34. The game was challenging
35. The game was difficult
36. The scenario of the game was interesting
37. * I did not like the scenario of the game
38. I knew all the actions that could be performed in the game

* Denotes items that are negatively worded.

References

Beaudouin-Lafon M (2004) Designing interaction, not interfaces. In: AVI: Proceedings of the Working Conference on Advanced Visual Interfaces, ACM Press, New York

Bevan N (1995) Measuring usability as quality of use. Softw Qual J 4:115–130

Brown M, Cairns P (2004) A grounded investigation of game immersion. In CHI '04 Extended Abstracts on Human Factors in Computing Systems (CHI EA '04). ACM, New York, NY, USA, 1297-1300. DOI=10.1145/985921.986048 http://doi.acm.org/10.1145/985921.986048

Buxton B (2007) Sketching user experiences. Morgan Kaufmann, San Francisco

Calvillo-Gámez EH, Cairns P (2008) Pulling the strings: a theory of puppetry for the gaming experience. In: Günzel S, Liebe M, Mersch D (eds) Conference proceedings of the philosophy of computer games 2008, Potsdam University Press, Potsdam

Crawford C (1984) The art of computer game design. Osborne/McGraw-Hill, New York

Csikszentmihalyi M (1990) Flow: the psychology of optimal experience. Harper Perennial, New York

Dewey J (1938) Experience and education. Kappa Delta Pi (Reprinted version by Touchstone), New York

Dourish P (2001) Where the action is: the foundations of embodied interaction. MIT Press, Cambridge

Ermi L, Mäyrä F (2005) Fundamental components of the gameplay experience: analysing immersion. In: Proceedings of changing views: worlds in play, DiGRA Conference, Vancouver

Experience (2009) In: Merriam-Webster Online Dictionary. http://www.merriam-webster.com/dictionary/experience. Accessed March 2009

Federoff M (2002) Heuristics and usability guidelines for the creation and evaluation of fun in Video games. Master's thesis, Indiana University, Bloomington Indiana

Forlizzi J, Battarbee K (2004) Understanding experience in interactive systems. In: Proceedings of the 2004 conference on Designing interactive systems, ACM Press, New York

Green J, Thorogood N (2004) The orientations of qualitative research. Sage Publications, London

Hassenzahl M (2003) The thing and I: understanding the relationship between user and product. In: Blythe MA, Monk AF, Overbeeke K, Wright PC (eds) Funology: from usability to enjoyment, Kluwer Academic Publishers, Netherlands

Heidegger M (1927) Sein und Zeit (trans: Gaos J). Max Niemeyer Verlag, Tübingen

Herzberg F (1968) One more time: how do you motivate employees? Harv Bus Rev 46:53–62

Hunicke R, LeBlanc M, Zubek R (2004) MDA: a formal approach to game design and game research. In: Proceedings of AAAI Workshop on Challenges in Game AI

Juul J (2005) Half–real: video games between real rules and fictional worlds. MIT Press, Cambridge

Kaye JJ, Boehner K, Laaksolahti J, Anna Ståhl (2007) Evaluating experience-focused HCI. In CHI '07 Extended Abstracts on Human Factors in Computing Systems (CHI EA '07). ACM, New York, NY, USA, 2117-2120. DOI=10.1145/1240866.1240962 http://doi.acm.org/10.1145/1240866.1240962

Koster R (2005) A theory of fun for game design. Paraglyph Press, Arizona

Lazzaro N (2004) Why we play games: together: four keys to more emotion without story. In: Games Developer Conference

Light A (2006) Adding method to meaning: a technique for exploring peoples' experience with technology. Behav Inf Technol 25:91–97

Loewenthal KM (2001) An introduction to psychological tests and scales. Psychology Press, London

Mahlke S, Thüring M (2007) Studying antecedents of emotional experiences in interactive contexts. In: Proceedings of CHI 2007, ACM Press, New York

McCarthy J, Wright P (2004) Technology as experience. MIT Press, Cambridge

McCarthy D, Curran S, Byron S (2005) The complete guide to game development, art & design. Ilex, Cambridge

Nunnally JC, Bernstein IH (1994) Psychometric theory, 3rd edn. McGraw Hill, New York

Popper KR (1994) Knowledge and the body-mind problem. In defence of Interaction. Routledge, London

Preece J, Rogers Y, Sharp H (2002) Interaction design—beyond human computer interaction. Wiley, Danvers

Rollings A, Adams E (2003) On game design. New Riders, Berkeley

Schonauer C, Pintaric T, Kaufmann H, Jansen—Kosterink S, Vollenbroek-Hutten M (2011) Chronic pain rehabilitation with a serious game using multimodal input, In: Proceedings of International Conference of Virtual Rehabilitation (ICVR)

Slater M, Wilbur S (1997) Framework for immersive virtual environments (FIVE): speculations on the role of presence in virtual environments. Presence 6:603–616

Strauss A, Corbin J (1998) Basics of qualitative research: techniques and procedures for developing grounded theory, 2 edn. SAGE Publications, London

Swallow D, Blythe MA, Wright P (2005) Grounding experience: relating theory and method to evaluate the user experience of smartphones. In: Proceedings of the conference on European association of cognitive ergonomics, University of Athens

Sweetser P, Wyeth P (2005) Gameflow: a model for evaluating player enjoyment in games. Comput Entertain 3:3–3

Winograd T, Flores F (1986) Understanding computers and cognition. Addison Wesley, Norwood

Zaman B (2011). Laddering method with preschoolers: understanding preschoolers' user experience with digital media. PhD Thesis. Katholieke Universiteit Leuven

Chapter 4
Games User Research and Physiological Game Evaluation

Lennart E. Nacke

Abstract This chapter introduces physiological measures for game evaluation in the context of games user research (GUR). GUR consists of more than playtesting game; it comprises a collection of methods that allow designers to bring their creations closer to the initial vision of the player experience. With the prices of physiological sensors falling, and the advancement of research in this area, physiological evaluation will soon become a standard tool in GUR and game evaluation. Since mixed-method approaches are of increasingly prominent value, this chapter describes core GUR methods with a special focus on physiological evaluation, keeping in mind both benefits and limitations of the approach in academic and industrial applications.

4.1 Introduction

From the academic domains of human-computer interaction, human factors, and social psychology, robust and scientific user-testing approaches have been adopted in a game industry field called games user research (GUR) to ensure optimal quality of the user experience (UX) in games and virtual entertainment products. In the games industry, the domains of quality assurance (QA) and game testing are focusing on finding technical errors in the game code (i.e., bugs) and ensuring smooth execution of the game on a technical level. By contrast, GUR is concerned with evaluation through the observation and analysis of players. A game designer communicates their thoughts to the player using the game. In turn, the user researcher applies methods that are inspired by psychology and user-centered design to evaluate the player. The communication channel is mutual, and allows for interpretation of player reactions (and often questions) from the user researcher to inform the designer what features of the game could be improved. Figure 4.1 illustrates the flow of information resulting from communication channels at all stages of the game

L. E. Nacke (✉)
Faculty of Business and Information Technology, University of Ontario
Institute of Technology, Ontario, Canada
e-mail: lennart.nacke@acm.org; web: www.hcigames.com

© Springer International Publishing Switzerland 2015
R. Bernhaupt (ed.), *Game User Experience Evaluation,*
Human-Computer Interaction Series, DOI 10.1007/978-3-319-15985-0_4

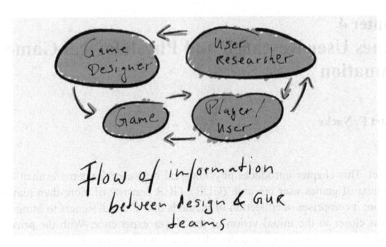

Fig. 4.1 Flow of information between game design and user research teams

creation and evaluation process. This allows for communication between player, designer, user researcher and the game (the designer's communication tool).

Notably, the focus of GUR in industry lies on experience analysis and understanding player interaction, with the objective of not simply testing the player, but improving the game's design. Seasoned GUR professionals describe their job as well done when they can provide game designers with an (often frustrating) moment of insight about how their designs are being interpreted by players. In this way, GUR can take inspiration from the scientific method as an approach of evaluating design hypotheses that are created during each development cycle in a game. Ultimately, GUR aims to allow designers to create more compelling gameplay experiences by identifying weaknesses in the design and structure of a game prototype. Some of the most advanced methods for GUR, such as physiological evaluation and methods using expensive recording and analysis equipment, are currently used primarily in a laboratory setting (Nacke 2013). They are likely to become more popular within the next years, because sensors are becoming more affordable as technology advances. In the context of these advanced GUR methods, this chapter will focus on the physiological evaluation of players, which takes inspiration from psychophysiological research.

Psychophysiology is a research area where body signals, or so-called "physiological responses", are measured to understand their underlying psychological processes, and the connections between those processes. I will refer to this as physiological evaluation in this chapter. Essentially, we are studying the signals that our body produces (the physiological part) to get an idea of what our mind was doing at that point (the psychological part). This makes physiological evaluation a useful method for evaluating arousal/excitement, emotion, or mental workload in games, although valid academic studies or experiments require much caution, as I will explain later. Most of our body signals or responses are spontaneous, which means that they are difficult to fake, making physiological measures highly objective. This lends the technique a comparatively low level of bias when analyzing a player's reactions to gameplay. They are also continuously recorded without interrupting a player's gameplay session. Physiological metrics consist of vast amounts of data that become meaningful only in the correct context (Mandryk 2008; Nacke 2009). For example, as game designers, we want to create meaningful decisions that involve some form of tradeoff in terms of game resources (e.g., resource trades, weighing risk against reward, and choosing an appropriate action) (Brathwaite and Schreiber 2008). Emotional decisions are one of the primary fun factors in playing games, because they add value to the outcomes of our decisions. In these decision situations, physiological metrics allow for an objective way to assess a player's emotional and cognitive response (in addition to the behavioral response, which can be observed or inferred from gameplay interaction logs). In the case of our example, this refers to whether the designers have succeeded in causing an emotional response in the player with the decision options that they have provided. For example, an experiment could compare whether it is more interesting (emotionally) to buy a powerful sword that does the same amount of damage and has the same price as a comparably effective attack scroll. However, one has to keep in mind that quantitative physiological data has to be interpreted to make correct design suggestions, which leaves room for interpretation bias on the part of the researcher.

If we were to roughly distinguish physiological games user research in industry and academia, we could craft a series of generalizations separating the two approaches. In the *game industry*, games user researchers are using psychophysiological methods to evaluate, for example, emotional and cognitive effects of game design (Ambinder 2011). In *academia*, human-computer interaction and psychology researchers are often using psychophysiological methods to study concepts of user interaction or effects of game content on player aggression (Carnagey et al. 2007). Academics emphasize using controlled experimental conditions and participant samples, place importance on statistical power, and carefully remove order effects by counterbalancing the design. Especially for experimental research psychologists, the game is a means to an end. It provides the virtual environment or engaging task that is used to study player behavior. From an experimental psychology viewpoint, one main difference between academic and professional approaches is that psychophysiological research is more concerned with experimental validity, underlying scientific questions, and controlled conditions, while GUR professionals are more interested in quick insights regarding game design or interface design that are immediately actionable. A new breed of GUR researchers in HCI is trying to combine the best of both worlds: Providing actionable and relevant results without sacrificing experimental validity. For example, if a think-aloud protocol is applied when recording physiological metrics, a researcher risks influencing heart rate and respiration considerably. External physical activity can create a physiological response in similar ways as internal physiological activity; this can lead to environmental effects influencing results.

It has to be emphasized here that physiological data is volatile, variable, and difficult to interpret without a high level of experimental control. When interpreting physiological metrics, it is also important to understand the relationship between psychological effect and physiological response. I am using the term physiological response to refer to different physiological response signals (e.g., brainwaves, muscle activity, or skin conductance). The most common relationship in physiological evaluation is the many-to-one relationship, where one physiological response may be associated with many psychological effects (Cacioppo et al. 2007). Therefore, it is important to keep in mind that a direct mapping of an emotional state to a psychological effect is not possible, and physiological responses must be understood as elements of sets with fuzzy boundaries. When we measure physiological signals, we are measuring essentially the operation and activity of muscles, nerve cells, and glands (Stern et al. 2001).

4.2   Games User Research Methods

Before we focus on physiological evaluation, let us have a look at the currently common non-physiological GUR methods: behavioral observation, think-aloud protocol, interviews, heuristic evaluation, focus groups, surveys and questionnaires, and game metrics. While these traditional methods are still the industry standard, some newer methods are being developed currently that combine traditional approaches of user testing (Mirza-Babaei et al. 2013).

4.2.1   Behavioral Observation

This technique can be as simple as looking over the shoulders of individuals when they are playing a game, or as complex as high-definition video recording of players from different angles in a natural gaming environment, such as a living room. Because of its relative simplicity and the actionable results that it produces, behavioral observation is often regarded as the most valuable GUR technique. Direct observation is especially valuable to the designers of a game. Seeing how players deal with the game's challenges, or where they get stuck or frustrated in the game level, can lead to profound insights regarding the gameplay experience for game designers. However, some inference is required on the designer's part, since observation only tells them *what* is happening when players play their game; it does not answer *why* something is happening to a player, or how the player felt when it was happening. Another valuable observation is players' body language and facial expressions while they play the game. It is important to note that during observation, the researcher should only take notes of the things that are being observed, without including any premature inferences. This is why there should always be a GUR experimenter[1] present when designers are observing players. It is not until discussion with the GUR professional after the observation that points of improvement

---

[1] Note that we use the term "experimenter" here to refer to a trained GUR professional or physiological researcher in charge of running the experiment.

Table 4.1 An example protocol for behavioral observation

1	*Design the experimental session.* Decide what parts of the game and the player you want to observe. This has to be a small and modifiable part of your game.
2	*Write an experimental script.* Following a script in general allows a formalization of this test approach (and is necessary in many other methods as well). The script needs to explain where the starting point for the player is, since a session needs clearly defined start and end points. Make sure you have software or a notebook ready for recording your observations.
3	*Think about what behaviors could be expected.* It helps to label reoccurring behaviors, and makes conversation with other observers easier. In behavioral observation this catalogue of common nomenclature is called an *Ethogram* (van Abeelen 1964).
4	*Test the script and setting in a pilot run-through.* Make sure to get feedback from a team member regarding the clarity of your instructions.
5	*Define your target demographic and start recruiting.* It helps to have a narrowly defined target group of players for your test. Once the limiting parameters of this demographic have been defined, it is time to recruit people.
6	*Run the session.* Make sure to sit outside the field of view of your players and record the gaming session. Make detailed notes (even if you are using recording software, since it is always good to have a backup of observations), not only about what the players are doing, but at what time of your session this behavior occurred. Be sure to only write the observation down and not the interpretation (e.g., "the player is sighing and frowning" instead of "the player is frustrated"). It is also important to log all the performance measures the game gives you (e.g., time taken for a level, high score). Especially if you are not using metrics logging, this information is invaluable for your analysis.
7	*End of session protocol.* You should have a procedure in place to thank players for their time, and give them some more information about the session if required. However, this information must be neutral in tone, without any value judgments about a player's performance.
8	*Schedule for break time.* In case there are multiple sessions scheduled in your day, make sure to allow for breaks in between your sessions to reset everything and ensure a relaxed mindset and comfortable environment for the next participant.

can be clearly identified. It is best to have one or two observers focusing on a single player, so that neither player nor observer is distracted during the process. During observation, communication and any interruption of gameplay should be avoided (if necessary, only neutral communication should occur between experimenter and player). This requires skill and patience on the observer's part, for example, not to influence the player when they get stuck (Table 4.1).

Becoming a good observer takes time and practice, so even though the observation method is easy to use, there is some training time involved. Like any subjective interpretation method, there is some bias arising from the experimenter's interpretation of observational data (which some might argue is stronger when interpreting observational vs. numeric data). Finally, most of the time, there are actionable results to be gathered from behavioral observation, especially when a game designer is present to discuss the next iteration steps together with the user researcher.

While behavioral observation is most often used in an industry setting, one could use the same method to investigate an academic hypothesis. A research question would likely be targeted to explore how participants react to the events that the game presents. An analysis would need to investigate the occurrence and quality of the behavioral cues observed.

4.2.2 Think-Aloud Protocol

The think-aloud protocol was developed in usability testing for products (Lewis 1982) and later made its way from interaction design to GUR. It could be seen as a natural expansion of behavioral observation, because it introduces player narrative to the observations. Players are asked to talk about what they are thinking as they play through the game. This voice over is often (and ideally) recorded, so that later in the analysis, the researcher can draw conclusions not only based on behavior, but also on player descriptions. Similar to behavioral observation, it is important to let the player speak and not interrupt the train of thought. It is also important that the speaking is natural, so that the players know that they do not have to talk and think about what to say. The analysis of the narrative has to happen after the session.

This method requires some skill from the player (for unskilled think-aloud participants, a moderator might need to be present to trigger player reporting, which could influence the natural flow of information). The better the player is at commenting their own behavior in the game, the more insights this method is likely to yield for the GUR professional. Talking about what one is doing is not natural for many people, and will likely require some practice, so that it is useful to make a note of which players have been particularly good at commenting, and inviting them again when another game is being tested. A skilled moderator can encourage players to speak freely, but adds another person to the testing session (since the GUR professional should only observe and make notes of the behavior), which adds some overhead on the planning side.

4.2.3 Interviews

Interviews are a common method of qualitative subjective inquiry, providing direct insight into the player experience. Much of the quality of the data collected during an interview session depends on the skill of the interviewer. Interviews allow a greater degree of depth when analyzing player opinions, emotions, and reactions. However, data collection and analysis can be time-consuming.

Interviews are a classic GUR method allowing for rich data collection if done correctly, providing the opportunity to increase the specificity and accuracy of data with follow-up questions. However, the analysis procedure is time-consuming, and might not produce patterns in responses that can be categorized into common themes. These common themes can help quantify the responses from multiple individuals to produce more reliable conclusions from interviews. Since human memory is limited, sometimes a gameplay video (recorded during the play session) is used

Table 4.2 An example of an interview session

1	*Set up a calm environment.* To get the most out of interview data, it is important that you and the person you are interviewing can focus on the questions at hand. Therefore, try to find a comfortable and distraction-free setting to conduct the interview.
2	*Get recording aid.* While it is possible to conduct the interview with just you and your interviewee while you are taking notes, you might lose interesting data, since it is impossible to capture everything that is being said in your notes. It is highly recommended to use at least an audio recorder for an interview. This way you can focus on the interview, and do not have to worry about what to write down. Like any other discussion with players, it is important that you make sure it is understood that the game is being analyzed and not the players.
3	*Prepare your questions and interview script.* Like any other experimental GUR method, a script will help you executing your interviews more smoothly. At the very least, you should have a set of questions prepared for the interview session. Writing non-biased questions is another skill that takes some time to develop. Ideally, the questions should aim at the how and why of player actions to get the most insight out of an interview. For simple yes or no questions, a questionnaire might be the more appropriate method.
4	*Conduct the interview.* Start with an easy question to establish a good atmosphere, and then drill deeper regarding certain behaviors that you are interested in. It is important to acknowledge that you understand and listen to what is being said, so that the interviewee feels good about talking to you. At the very end of an interview, it is good to allow for some general questions about the process, or to ask the players to add anything they feel strongly about or that they would really like to talk about.
5	*Transcribe your interview.* This will be time consuming, as you have to revisit all the audio that you have recorded and find patterns in the answers of different interviewees. Software can help a lot in this process, but it is ultimately up to the researcher to find common themes.

as a recall aid to trigger the memory of a player's experience (Table 4.2). Finally, interviews are a subjective GUR method, since they allow for interpretation and answer biases.

4.2.4 Questionnaires

Questionnaires or surveys are a common GUR method, because they allow collecting large volumes of self-report data simultaneously from many different players. Surveys are usually used to get insights into value judgments about gameplay moments. Again, this book provides two excellent chapters about survey construction: Cavillo-Gamez et al.'s Chap. 3 about the core elements of the gaming experience, and Takatalo et al.'s Chap. 5 about presence, involvement, and flow.

A questionnaire can be delivered to players directly after a gameplay event (e.g., making a choice in the game) or after a gameplay session, so that experience is still present in memory. This is arguably less biased than, for example, recalling an experience during an interview session post-gameplay. Often, gameplay questionnaires feature a Likert-scale (Likert 1932) rating type of a gameplay interaction item. Surveys can also facilitate the understanding of a player demographic or psychological type (Eysenck et al. 1985; Carver and White 1994; Buss and Perry 1992; John and Srivastava 1999) and can be delivered before a play session to assess a gamer type (Bartle 1996; Nacke et al. 2014). Some of the more popular surveys used within GUR evaluations are focused on immersion (Jennett et al. 2008), emotion (Lang 1995), and game engagement (Brockmyer et al. 2009). Surveys allow the construction of subjective metrics, which can be valuable for improving insights into biometric and game metric data. While questionnaires provide a quick way to obtain quantitative insights into player feelings and attitudes, they lack the depth of an interview or the objectivity of metrical measures. They also work most reliably when a large number of people are available for testing.

4.2.5 Focus Groups

Focus groups are another method of qualitative inquiry, where a group of players is gathered to talk about their opinions, beliefs, and attitudes towards the game (Poels et al. 2007). The group has complete freedom to talk about their likes and dislikes, but usually a moderator is present to facilitate the discussion and lead the group toward a topic of interest. Again, I will not go into depth about focus group methodology here, since Poels et al. (2010) describe a focus group study about qualitative insights into postgame experiences, which is an excellent overview of the methodology.

Since focus groups are an easy way to gather opinions and feedback on ideas, they can be used early on in development, even after a game prototype session or an initial design presentation. While focus groups allow feedback from crowds rather than individuals (somewhat seeming like an extension of the interview technique), they have the disadvantage that once an opinion is present in the crowd, others may pick up on this opinion and the results may become biased. Imagine, for example, that only a couple of strong voices dominate a focus group. This can lead to group pressure, preventing other individuals in the group from voicing their own opinions about their gameplay experience. Sometimes, focus groups skew toward the discussion of a particular solution rather than focusing on issues regarding player experience. In the end, this method might not be as useful as other GUR methods, due to the limited actionability of pure opinions, as opposed to the more complete data offered by methods involving observation or standardized metrics. A GUR professional is usually more interested in what players are actually doing when playing the game (not so much in what they think they want to do in the game).

4.2.6 Heuristic Evaluation

Heuristic evaluation is a method stemming from usability research (Nielsen and Molich 1990). In this context, the evaluation consists of judging how an interface complies with recognized usability principles, which are called "heuristics". It is known as a discount usability method, because it is cheap to conduct and can yield significant actionable results for a game. The method includes GUR experts playing a game and evaluating it based on a set of criteria. So, in a way, a heuristic evaluation can be likened to a tightly structured game review. After the expert has played the game, they give feedback on whether the game fits a certain playability guideline, or "heuristic", and what problems might arise from non-compliance. Several different heuristics have been proposed by researchers (Korhonen and Koivisto 2006; Korhonen and Koivisto 2007; Jegers 2008; Koeffel et al. 2010; Pinelle et al. 2008a) and practitioners (Desurvire et al. 2004; Desurvire and Wiberg 2008). We will not get into details about game heuristics here, because Chaps. 8 and 9, Part III of this book by Desurvire and Wiberg as well as Hochleitner et al. already cover much in-depth information about the topic.

In general, a heuristic might be more powerful if it fits a certain game platform (e.g., mobile) or genre. While there is no commonly agreed upon set of heuristics, certain overlaps exist, such as the game having a clear goal and an understandable control scheme. Other heuristics might concern the difficulty level, fair outcomes, learning curves, and repetitiveness. These guidelines may seem like common sense, but often they are not followed, and using written rules for the structural evaluation of games makes the evaluation process easier. It is important to note some useful modifications to traditional heuristic approaches that we have seen in recent years, especially the genre weightings proposed by Pinelle et al. (2008b) and the critic proofing approach developed by Livingston et al. (2010), which produces a list of heuristic violations (taking into account a problem's frequency, impact, persistence, the heuristic it violates, and a game's genre).

A definitive advantage of heuristic evaluations is that only a small number of experts are needed for evaluating the game. However, the selection of these experts can already pose a problem, since each person needs to have expertise relevant to the game at hand, and should use heuristics that are directly applicable to the game being evaluated. Another issue is the subjective bias of the evaluators, which has been shown to cause low agreement in the issues and causes detected by evaluators (White et al. 2011). In some cases, an expert might still miss a problem that is relevant for a novice player. Ideally, this method is combined with the observation of novice players, to extend the feedback gathered from the experts.

4.2.7 Game Metrics

Game analytics and metrics are undeniably a recent trend within the GUR community (Seif El-Nasr et al. 2013). Chapter 7 by Drachen in this book focuses on game metrics or more specifically on a part of game metrics that is also referred to as game telemetry (because data are often collected after delivery of the game and not always during testing). The term "game metrics" generally refers to the process of logging player interactions, positions in the game world, camera angles, and all data that relates to the gameplay interaction process in the game. To do this, a programmer has to define appropriate hooks in the game engine that allow the logging of all this data. A huge advantage of metrics is the large amount of data being collected. This can also prove detrimental, as this data has to be analyzed quickly and accurately, which often means that a GUR professional has to use visualization software to make sense of such vast collections of data. The potential of this GUR methodology is promising, because it can measure key gameplay events (e.g., player deaths) and their surrounding circumstances in detail. By integrating these log files with synchronized physiological sensor data, we can craft a more complete picture of player experience.

4.3 Physiological Game Evaluation

Quantitative data is not only available from in-game logging, but can also be acquired directly from players. For a deeper understanding of the complex physiological processes involved in decision-making in games or emotional processing of game events, we can use physiological measures to evaluate user experience (UX) aspects of games. It has to be understood—before we start—that physiological measures do not measure UX itself, but tap into parts of UX that include measurable physiological components (Kivikangas et al. 2010). Various physiological measures are not covered in this chapter, such as respiratory sensors, eye trackers, temperature sensors, and several brain imaging techniques. A part of this introduction to physiological measures has previously appeared in Nacke (2013).

4.3.1 Introduction

Physiological signals are small energy measures gathered from the surface of our body. We need to understand how our body operates on a neurobiological level to better understand the meaning of these signals. On a macro level, the human nervous system controls the operations of the body. This is split into two parts: the central nervous system (CNS) and the peripheral nervous system (PNS). The CNS manages any information received from the whole body, coordinating activity accordingly. The skull and spine bones protect the CNS, which also makes it difficult to access outside of the body. The PNS includes all nerve cells outside of the CNS, and it connects the CNS to the rest of our body.

The PNS transmits most of our physical sensations. This exposes it to measurements on our skin. Consequently, the skin surface is the location from where physiological sensors commonly get their signal. The PNS is further divided into the somatic and autonomic nervous system. The somatic nervous system regulates body activity that we have under conscious control, such as deliberate muscle activity. The autonomic nervous system (ANS) controls our unconscious, visceral responses. We have two opposing players in the ANS, the sympathetic nervous system (which triggers fight or flight reactions in emergency situations) and the parasympathetic nervous system (which controls our relaxation, resting, and digestion). It is important to keep those two systems in mind when we measure emotions with physiological sensors.

Physiological and mental processes contribute equally to the formation of emotions (LeDoux 1998). We associate emotions with feelings, behaviours, and thoughts. Recent research supports a strong connection between affective and cognitive processes as a foundation for emotions (Pessoa 2008; Damasio 1994). A popular emotion model currently used in psychophysiological research is Russell's circumplex model (Russell 1980) that suggests two emotional dimensions (see also (Larsen et al. 2001; Larsen and Diener 1992)), pleasant/unpleasant emotion (or valence) and high/low stimulation (or arousal, excitement). When we are trying to measure stimulation or arousal, the PNS is more reliable than when we are trying to measure emotional valence. However, by using measurement techniques that detect muscular movement in the face (e.g., an activation of the cheek or the brow muscle), we can measure emotion based on facial expressions. According to the psychological literature, negative emotion manifests in a frowning facial expression and positive emotion is displayed as a smiling face (Cacioppo et al. 1990). As games user researchers, we are interested in feelings (or how players interpret their emotions in context), and player experience. Therefore, currently we cannot solely rely on physiological metrics for player testing; we have to accompany these methods with other GUR techniques (e.g., the techniques discussed at the beginning of this chapter) to fully understand player experience. However, the basic tenet of physiological experimentation still holds true: we measure the physiological response (in addition to other subject responses) while manipulating a behavioural factor, often an element of gameplay. To have a better understanding what physiological metrics are capable of, we are going to discuss the most common ones in the following sections. Since the experimental procedure for physiological evaluation in a laboratory setting can be similar, I am giving a sample overview of an experimental protocol here (see Table 4.3).

4.3.2 Electromyography (EMG)

EMG measures whether or not our muscles are active. Therefore, an EMG electrode attached to the surface above a muscle is able to sense even the slightest activation of this muscle (Bradley et al. 2001; Lang 1995). Whenever we flex a muscle on our body, this produces a difference in electrical activity or isometric tension which is measurable by EMG. EMG is all about measuring PNS activation, in contrast to other techniques focused on CNS activation (such as EEG, which measures brainwave activity). Since most muscles can be directly controlled, EMG is a measure of high interest for interacting with computers in a more natural way (Nacke et al. 2011b). The most prevalent use of this technique in evaluating games is through facial EMG (Fridlund and Cacioppo 1986), which measures the activation of specific facial muscles responsible for displaying our positive or negative reactions to an emotional moment in a game (Hazlett 2006). In particular, physiological game research has focused on using brow muscles (corrugator supercilii) to indicate negative emotion and cheek muscles (zygomaticus major) to indicate positive emotion (Mandryk et al. 2006) or even fun and flow in a game (Nacke and Lindley 2008).

Table 4.3 An sample experimental protocol for physiological evaluation

1	*Check lab inventory.* It is a good idea to have a lab inventory set up for physiological experimentation, since these experiments usually require disposable items to be used in every session (e.g., pre-gelled electrodes, surgical tape, electrode paste). The inventory should always be up to date (and checked) at least a week before experiments start, so that missing items can be ordered in. Most physiological systems operate with batteries, so it has to be checked that the physiological recording unit is fully charged before the experiment.
2	*Prepare informed consent forms.* These should be required for any kind of experimentation, but are most valuable for physiological experimentation, to inform the participants that they will not be harmed by the measures and that they can opt out at any time. These forms often fulfill the role of both ethical documentation and participant education (no mind-reading or graphical access to thoughts). Participants need to be informed before participation that they should not consume substances that influence physiological responses (e.g., coffee, energy drinks, candy).
3	*Prepare and attach the electrodes.* The differences between physiological recording systems will require different preparations. In general, it is good to keep in mind that pre-gelled and dry electrodes are generally much easier to handle (and will decrease the total time needed for your experiment) than electrodes that require paste. If EEG is being used, a cap will facilitate the proper alignment of electrodes. It is good practice to mark the channel names (usually numbers), so that it is easy to identify electrode locations for multichannel systems. (For example, which EMG electrodes were measuring what muscle site.)
4	*Check for noise and start recording.* Often it is quite easy to identify the noise in physiological signals, as they will look jittery in the recording software or exhibit unnatural spikes. Many factors can influence this; some of the common culprits are cable issues (broken or bent), electrolyte bridges (too much gel), and lack of skin contact (not enough gel). It is good practice to check for a couple of potential causes and repeat the attachment procedure until the error disappears. At the start of the recording, participants should sit in an eyes-open and calm position, so that a baseline can be recorded (which is necessary for the later normalization of data). Depending on the software used, recording files may differ, but it is good practice to have a numbering scheme that allows sorting and comparison of the data that is being recorded.
5	*Run experiment, follow up with additional measures.* After recording is set in place, the regular experiment can be run. Ideally, the participant's behavior should be observed, and markers put in place when the observer notices too much movement from the participant (which can lead to movement artifacts in the physiological recording). Surveys can provide a good addition (just like any other GUR method discussed in this chapter) to the physiological data, and are often administered after the session.
6	*Debrief and back up data.* After the experiment is over, participants are generally thanked and debriefed about the study. Given that physiological files are generally large and will grow over time as more data is being collected, it is a good idea to back up the data after the experiment is over.

For longer term evaluation (say over a few minutes of gameplay), the eye muscle (orbicularis oculi) has also proven helpful in registering high arousal pleasant emotions (Ravaja et al. 2008).

Similar to EEG, EMG uses silver-silver chloride electrodes (see Fig. 4.4) because they have only a small measurement error, little drift potential, and minimal polarization. EMG electrodes are applied to the surface of the skin and will also need a reference (if part of a larger system, this reference can be on head or close to the actual electrodes, which are often arranged in a triangular patch). The risk of facial EMG is the presence of considerable muscle activity that you possibly do not want to measure (e.g., experimental participants cannot chew gum, laugh, or talk during facial EMG, because this will introduce large artifacts into your data). Since muscular signals are again amplified from microvolts, careful signal processing has to be done on EMG data before it is interpreted (e.g., a log normalization or a Butterworth low-pass filter).

Emotions are usually interpreted on a two-dimensional model (Russell 1980). We find that by measuring facial muscles, we are able to get an idea of pleasant or unpleasant emotions. This is called valence assessment, as we are able to say whether an emotion was evaluated by a player as pleasant or unpleasant. The other dimension of emotional measurement, arousal, serves as an indicator of player excitement. While facial recognition software or direct observation would also allow the analysis of facial expressions and therefore the mapping of emotions, the software or the observer often miss less salient expressions, which are picked up by physiological measures. The analysis of EMG signals is pretty straightforward, as usually after application of a notch filter, we are already able to compare the signals. However, these measures require the attachment of electrodes to the player's face, which make this method somewhat intrusive, although often the electrodes and cables can be easily taped to the player's head to remove discomfort and reduce movement artifacts. Since just by feeling the electrode on their face, players might be feeling the need to elicit more pronounced muscle movements, this might lead to unnatural signals, which could make data interpretation more difficult.

4.3.3   Electrodermal Activity (EDA) and Galvanic Skin Response (GSR)

When measuring the level of skin conductance over time, we refer to this as measuring the EDA of the skin, but when measuring the direct response to a stimulus, we refer to this as galvanic skin response (Boucsein 1992). In any case, EDA measures changes in the passive electrical conductivity of the skin, relating to increases or decreases in sweat gland activity.

Most of us have seen EDA measures in movies, branded as lie detector tests. EDA measures are attached to the fingers, palms or toes because the sweat glands in those body areas are more likely to react to changes in the PNS (sympathetic vs. parasympathetic activity). Since we are measuring the differences in conductivity, we only need two electrodes, which make EDA a very easy physiological measure to prepare and apply. EDA electrodes are prone to movement artifacts just like other psychophysiological measures, but because of their location (hand or feet), special care has to be taken in the preparation of steering controls for the game. If a regular game controller is used, and the EDA sensor is applied on the palm of the hand, movement artifacts are likely to occur, so using the feet or fingers of the non-dominant hand would be a better location (or the side of the palm of the hand). EDA is also very easy to interpret, since it almost has a one-to-one relationship with physical arousal. Similar to the EMG analysis, EDA values need to be normalized to allow for a meaningful statistical comparison between participants in your study. EDA can be normalized by calculating each sample as a percentage of its entire span, using the min and max values over all samples for one participant (Mandryk 2008; Lykken and Venables 1971).

Another benefit of this measure is the inexpensive hardware that usually comes at a fraction of the cost of a research-grade EEG setup. Many modern EDA systems use dry electrodes, and some EDA setups even allow easy attachment of the electrodes to the little and ring fingers with a Velcro strap.

A benefit of EDA is that analysis can be done in a macro (over larger chunks of playtime) or micro fashion (related to events). When analyzing the response to a direct event, one needs to take into account that EDA is a relatively noisy signal that also has some latency in response to a stimulus (often around 5 seconds, see Fig. 4.5). After a galvanic skin response is registered, there is also a decay or recovery time during which no further event responses will be registered (or the responses are registered together). While it is pretty clear that EDA indicates physical arousal, there is still some interpretation effort required as to the source of the initial stimulation (e.g., caused by a game event, or influenced by non-game environmental factors). This is why planning and controlling physiological experiments is very important. Since EDA also has large individual variations in baseline and responsiveness of the signal, it is very important to clean up the raw data with baseline corrections and other filtering techniques.

4.3.4 Cardiovascular Measures

There are many cardiovascular measures available for physiological evaluation, and all of them relate to the heart rhythm, its changes, and how this influences one's physiological state. The most common measures are electrocardiography (ECG), heart rate (HR), Interbeat Interval (IBI), heart rate variability (HRV), blood volume pulse (BVP), and blood pressure (BP). However, blood pressure is not a real-time measure, and, while useful in medical contexts, has not shown relevance in games, user research. For all other relevant measures, physiological electrodes are required to collect the necessary data.

ECG measures the electrical activity caused by the heart pumping blood and is measured usually with three electrodes or leads, which are positive, negative, and neutral and are usually applied to the upper body.

Heart rate is understood as the number of heart beats per time unit (usually measured in beats per minute). The IBI, or time between heart beats, is also of interest. If IBI decreases, HR obviously increases, and this has been tied to increased information processing and emotional arousal. So, IBI and HR are two related measures. However, HR variability is a more complicated measure (with a complex analysis procedure) as it relies on the spectral analysis of sinus arrhythmia. In plain English, we are looking at frequency changes and differences in the IBI over time. In general, we need to keep in mind that cardiovascular measures are intrusive to measure accurately, and that they are affected by many things, such as physical activity.

4.3.5   Electroencephalography (EEG)

It is fascinating to see a computer plot out the frequencies and amplitudes of one's brainwaves in real time. While some relationships between EEG activity and behavior have been established, there is still much left to be researched, especially with complex stimuli like video games. Participants unfamiliar with EEG might assume that an experimental researcher is able to find out exactly what they are thinking, or obtain graphical representations of their thoughts. Recent research has investigated the latter (i.e., reconstructing visuals from brain activity using magnetic resonance imaging [MRI]) (Nishimoto et al. 2011). However, the reality of EEG measures is a little more abstract. EEG, which uses electromagnetic measurement, can be considered less invasive and easier to use compared to other CNS response analyses, such as functional MRI, which analyses brain function based on hemodynamic response[2], or positron emission tomography (PET) scans, which use metabolic response to display brain function. A major advantage of EEG for brain activity measurement over these other techniques is its temporal resolution, which allows processing EEG responses in millisecond accuracy. One disadvantage of EEG to the other approaches is its spatial resolution, which is constrained, for example, by a low signal-to-noise ratio and limited spatial sampling. In addition, while EEG electrodes record the signal from a particular scalp location, it is not guaranteed that the signals originate precisely from the measured areas of the skull. EEG signals may originate from overlapping areas of the brain. This can be problematic when researchers want to investigate signals originating from the lower brain, such as the basal ganglia.

In EEG, a series of electrodes are placed on a participant's scalp. The location of these electrodes and their alignment is standardized in the 10–20 system or map of electrode placement (Jasper 1958) (see Fig. 4.2, and also the 10–10 EEG sensor placement system (Chatrian et al. 1988)), which is a reference map used to align electrodes to scalp locations corresponding to brain lobe areas. Often an electrode cap makes the placement on the head easier. EEG measures slight electrical activity, such as the signals generated by neural activity in the brain (Pizzagalli 2007). There are a variety of different measurement devices available for this type of physiological measure, ranging from more sophisticated medical grade headcap setups with high-density electrode arrays (from 32 to 256 electrodes) to simpler devices that have fewer electrodes and less spatial accuracy, but similar temporal signal accura-

---

[2] In the context of brain activity, the hemodynamic response consists of delivering blood to active brain tissues. The blood delivers oxygen and glucose, which are needed for brain tissue to function.

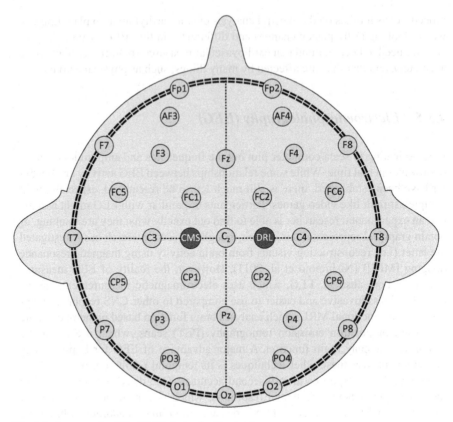

Fig. 4.2 An example of the 10–20 electrode placement

cy. The 10-20 system indicates brain areas at scalp locations by lettering (Stern et al. 2001). For example, C is at the central, O is at the occipital, P is at the parietal, T is at the temporal, and F is at the frontal lobe site of the scalp. Additionally, the system uses numbers to indicate laterality (e.g., odd numbers of the left side, even numbers on the right side) and subscripts to indicate placement in relation to the midline.

EEG measures oscillations of inhibitory and excitatory brain activity (Pizzagalli 2007; Stern et al. 2001)[3]. This means that EEG lets us record electrical activity on the scalp that relates to brain activity. We usually distinguish brain activity by using the amplitude and frequency of the signal, which is what we can see in the graphical plots of brainwaves with which many readers are familiar. Amplitude describes the size of the signal, while frequency refers to the speed of signal cycles. Lower frequencies measure large synchronized amplitudes of neural activity, and higher

---

[3] The electrical potential of a neuron in the brain is influenced by neurotransmitters that either increase (e.g., excitatory signal) or decrease (e.g., inhibitory signal) the probability of producing an action potential (e.g., a short neural event during which a cell's electrical potential briefly rises and falls) in a connecting cell.

Fig. 4.3 EEG, EMG, and GSR electrode setup shown on a study participant

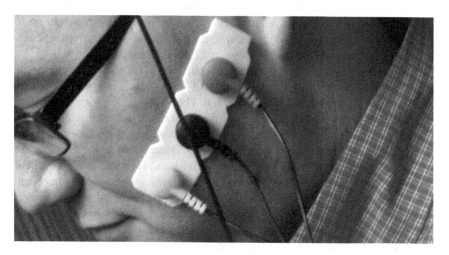

Fig. 4.4 Example of EMG electrodes (silver-silver chloride) attached to the face of a player

Fig. 4.5 An example of log-normalized EDA measurement. See also the study in Nacke (2013)

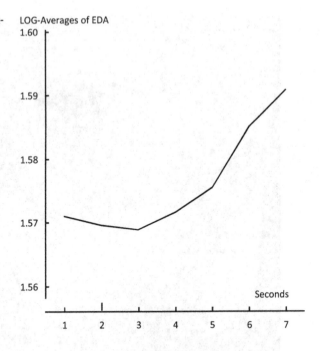

frequencies show smaller, desynchronized amplitudes of neural activity. EEG measures the amplitude of this activity in dimensions of a few microvolts (µV), usually between 10 and 100 µV. This measurement consists of amplifying a differential signal between two electrodes, one at the location of measurement and others at a location of reference. Common reference points are the nose, scalp center, or mastoids. Alternatively, the average signal can be calculated as a global reference. Each electrode's electrical activity is then subtracted from the reference point.

Research-grade EEG devices compute brain waves in different frequency bands, such as alpha (e.g. 8–13 Hz), beta (e.g. 13–30 Hz), theta (e.g. 4–8 Hz), delta (1–4 Hz), and sometimes gamma (30–50 Hz)[4]. The following are some rough distinctions of frequency bands according to some of the recent literature. Alpha activity indicates a drowsy or relaxed state, and a lack of active cognitive processes; it has also been tied to information and visual processing. Beta activity has been discussed as replacing alpha rhythms during cognitive activity and is related to alertness, attention, vigilance, and excitatory problem solving activities. Theta activity has been related to decreased alertness and lower information processing. However, frontal midline theta activity in the anterior cingulate cortex scalp area is linked to mental effort, attention, and stimulus processing. This means that there are two types of theta activity: Low alertness (leading to sleep) and selective cognitive inactivity because of automated processing. Delta is most prominent during sleep, relaxation

---

[4] Another way of analysing EEG is through Event-Related Potentials, which I do not cover in this chapter. A more in-depth discussion of this can be found in Wehbe et al. (2013).

or fatigue, and is diminished with increasing age. Gamma activity is still largely unexplored (although recent studies relate it to the creation of meaning from separate pieces). While it has to be noted that most of these findings come from research in the medical and psychological domain, some of these simplified interpretations might make it easier to evaluate a game based on the brainwave activity revealed by EEG. For example, if increased beta activity is prevalent during gaming, it could be linked to player attention and increased arousal during a focused task. More studies are needed in this area to investigate a possible relation between this phenomenon and meaningful decision-making in games.

EEG is rather prone to artifacts, especially caused by head movement (the electrodes might move on the scalp while the player is moving). Therefore, some games are less suited for this type of evaluation (e.g., Guitar Hero, Kinect, or Wii Games that involve much movement) than others. Movement artifacts are a problem of all physiological measures, but are especially problematic with EEG, as we are interpreting very low-level electromagnetic activity. Researcher often remove artifacts by visual inspection, during which the data is inspected for irregular signals, peaks, rectangular patterns associated with lateral eye movements, or other patterns.

In addition, as with all physiological measures, EEG measures should be recorded with a preceding baseline, meaning a neutral moment (where the player does nothing but stare at a cross on a grey background, for example). This will allow any filtering procedure or algorithm applied for the analysis to filter out the signal noise that individuals naturally produce when not engaged in an activity. Since we all have different physiological activity due to natural physical differences, it is important to correct for these individual differences and focus on the changes from the normal activity in any following analysis. A final major problem with EEG as a measurement method is the difficult interpretation of the data. Similar to many physiological measures, this is called the one-to-many relationship between physiologically visible signals and the underlying psychological causes. For example, when delta activity is increased during a playing session, do we argue that the game is relaxing, or that it is boring and fatigue-inducing? It is quite important to keep one's game design goals in mind when doing this type of evaluation, and even then the process of triangulating this data with other measures is paramount for a solid interpretation.

In Fig. 4.3, an example physiological participant setup is shown. The EEG cap has all electrodes placed in locations around the scalp. Since EMG and EEG are fed through the same system, this acts as reference for the EMG electrodes as well, which allows for very small EMG sensors to be attached to the participant's face. Some additional surgical tape is used to make sure that the electrode cables do not move around too much, to mitigate movement artifacts in the physiological data.

4.3.6 Ten ways in Which Physiological Evaluation is Valuable to the Games Industry

With the wealth of techniques and approaches available, it is important to understand the specific benefits of physiological evaluation and games user research in the game development industry. Fairclough (2011) suggested a thought experiment, where he outlines ten suggestions for improving the use of physiological metrics in games user research. Many of these suggestions are necessary to be implemented by games user researchers for physiological metrics to work effectively in an industry setting.

1. Physiological metrics can be recorded continuously during a games user research session without interrupting play. This makes these methods less obtrusive than subjective measures that either break the experience (by interrupting and prompting with questions) or introduce memory bias (by asking questions about the game in retrospect). The only downside of physiological metrics is that the player has to wear sensors, and that some might find this intrusive (although based on personal experience, many players forget that they are wearing sensors a few minutes into the game).

2. A games user researcher interested in physiological assessment of players needs to be well-informed about what each sensor type measures. Company executives and the marketing department need to understand that this is no emotion quantifier or thought printer. Sensors measure electrical activity that can be elicited from motor, skin, or brain activity, and depending on the area of application, provide some measurement and insight as to the activity of the body area being measured. This also means that we need an experience vocabulary working from a high-level psychological concept (engagement) toward the low-level body response (sympathetic activation higher heart rate). Inferences made from low-level body responses to high-level concepts in comparison always face challenges in withstanding closer scientific inspection.

3. For capturing player experience, a hypothesis-driven approach is suggested, where only one particular aspect of experience (ideally, one that is well-defined in the literature) is under investigation. For example, we may choose to investigate only the positive and negative emotional responses to a certain game event or game area, or the cognitive workload experienced during a game tutorial.

4. To establish a link between ideal player experience and the corresponding physiological responses, we should investigate responses to key aspects when naïve participants play the most successful games of the industry (in terms of financial and critical success). If we could find out which at physiological responses relate to the player experiences that drive the success of these games, we could work towards establishing a physiological success metric.

5. In every aspect of physiological experimentation, we need to be aware that the human body is still present in the real world while playing a video game.

Our nervous system, therefore, also responds to stimuli in this world as well as internal cognitive processes that we might have given our current environmental/living situation. These contextual influences (that may be nascent during the screening of a participant) may result in changes in emotion or motivation during the experiment. Influences such as room temperature, movement, drugs, chemicals, noise, and many more can also introduce contextual bias into our interpretation of physiological activity. In the end, it is important to keep in mind how sensitive our nervous system really is when interpreting physiological metrics.

6. Physiological metrics do not distinguish between physical activity and psychological events. Three components are involved in recording physiological metrics: external physical activity, internal emotional activity, and internal cognitive activity (Stemmler et al. 2007).

7. Given what we now know about physiological responses, we will always have a certain signal-to-noise ratio in our physiological metrics. We can counteract the amount of noise by enforcing a strict experimental protocol in a very controlled environment, or by recording all possible confounds with additional sensors (e.g., temperature, noise, light) to remove their influence during analysis.

8. Before testing players, it is important to carefully record their demographic background, including their skill level and past game preferences and experiences. Novelty and habituation can impact physiological responses considerably.

9. It is important to create the different experimental conditions carefully within a systematically manipulated environment (e.g., a game engine). Ideally, only change one variable at a time (although this is often not possible in an industry environment).

10. Other gameplay tracking metrics can be considered overt behavior markers in the game world, as they are visible instantly, whereas physiological metrics are covert measures that are not always visible directly. Both metrics should be tracked together, and a possible relationship between them should be explored using statistical analyses. Subjective responses should be recorded before and after, rather than during, physiological measurement.

We can conclude that psychophysiological measures in games should not be used alone, but always in conjunction with other measures to establish relationships between player experience facets and physiological responses. Much work remains to be done in this area before it becomes part of the everyday testing practices of games user researchers, but given recent advances by sensor manufacturers, this technology will soon become common in games user research. When using these technologies, we must be careful to remember the associated contextual influences and sensitivities, ensuring that data is obtained and analyzed in the most accurate way possible. Through precise application and exploration of this technology, we can strive to improve not only our own games, but the very state of the art in games user research.

Acknowledgements This research was supported by the Network of Centres of Excellence (NCE), Graphics, Animation and New Media (GRAND) and NSERC. Dr. Nacke thanks Samantha Stahlke and Rina Wehbe for proofreading the final manuscript.

References

Ambinder M (2011) Biofeedback in gameplay: how valve measures physiology to enhance gaming experience. Paper presented at the game developers conference

Bartle R (1996) Hearts, clubs, diamonds, spades: players who suit MUDs. J MUD Res 1(1) 19 pages. http://mud.co.uk/richard/hcds.htm

Boucsein W (1992) Electrodermal activity. Plenum Press, New York

Bradley MM, Codispoti M, Cuthbert BN, Lang PJ (2001) Emotion and motivation I: defensive and appetitive reactions in picture processing. Emotion 1(3):276–298

Brathwaite B, Schreiber I (2008) Challenges for game designers. Charles River Media, Boston

Brockmyer JH, Fox CM, Curtiss KA, McBroom E, Burkhart KM, Pidruzny JN (2009) The development of the game engagement questionnaire: a measure of engagement in video game-playing. J Exp Soc Psychol 45(4):624–634. doi:10.1016/j.jesp.2009.02.016

Buss AH, Perry MP (1992) The aggression questionnaire. J Pers Soc Psychol 63(3):452–459

Cacioppo JT, Tassinary LG, Fridlund AJ (1990) The skeletomotor system. In: Cacioppo JT, Tassinary LG (eds) Principles of psychophysiology: physical, social, and inferential elements (pp 325–384). Cambridge University Press, New York, xiii, 914 pp.

Cacioppo JT, Tassinary LG, Berntson GG (2007) Psychophysiological science. In: Cacioppo JT, Tassinary LG, Berntson GG (eds) Handbook of psychophysiology. pp 3–26. Cambridge University Press. 3rd Edition. ISBN: 0521844711

Carnagey NL, Anderson CA, Bushman BJ (2007) The effect of video game violence on physiological desensitization to real-life violence. J Exp Soc Psychol 43(3):489–496

Carver CS, White TL (1994) Behavioral inhibition, behavioral activation, and affective responses to impending reward and punishment: the BIS/BAS scales. J Pers Soc Psychol 67(2):319–333

Chatrian GE, Lettich E, Nelson PL (1988) Modified nomenclature for the "10%" electrode system. J Clin Neurophysiol: Off Publ Am Electroencephalogr Soc 5(2):183–186

Damasio AR (1994) Descartes' error. G.P. Putnam, New York

Desurvire H, Wiberg C (2008) Master of the game: assessing approachability in future game design. In: CHI '08 extended abstracts on human factors in computing systems, Florence, Italy, April 5–10, 2008. ACM, New York, pp 3177–3182. doi:10.1145/1358628.1358827.

Desurvire H, Caplan M, Toth JA (2004) Using heuristics to evaluate the playability of games. In: CHI '04 extended abstracts on Human factors in computing systems, Vienna, Austria, 2004. ACM, pp 1509–1512. doi:10.1145/985921.986102

Duchowski AT (2007) Eye tracking methodology: theory and practice, 2nd edn. Springer, New York

Eysenck SBG, Eysenck HJ, Barrett P (1985) A revised version of the psychoticism scale. Pers Individ Differ 6(1):21–29

Fairclough SH (2011) Biometrics and evaluation of gaming experience part two: a thought experiment. http://www.physiologicalcomputing.net/?p=1760. Last accessed 20 Oct 2012

Fridlund AJ, Cacioppo JT (1986) Guidelines for human electromyographic research. Psychophysiology 23(5):567–589. doi:10.1111/j.1469-8986.1986.tb00676.x

Hazlett RL (2006) Measuring emotional valence during interactive experiences: boys at video game play. Paper presented at the Proceedings of the SIGCHI conference on Human Factors in computing systems, Montréal, Québec, Canada. doi:10.1145/1124772.1124925

Jasper HH (1958) Report of the committee on methods of clinical examination in electroencephalography. Electroencephalography and Clinical Neurophysiology 10

Jegers K (2008) Investigating the Applicability of Usability and Playability Heuristics for Evaluation of Pervasive Games. In: Internet and Web Applications and Services, 2008. ICIW '08. Third International Conference on, 2008. pp 656–661. doi:10.1109/ICIW.2008.54.

Jennett C, Cox AL, Cairns P, Dhoparee S, Epps A, Tijs T, Walton A (2008) Measuring and defining the experience of immersion in games. Int J Hum Comput Stud 66:641–661. doi:10.1016/j.ijhcs.2008.04.004

John OP, Srivastava S (1999) The big five trait taxonomy: history, measurement, and theoretical perspectives. In: Pervin LA, John OP (eds) Handbook of personality: theory and research. 2nd edn. Guilford Press, New York, pp 102–138

Kivikangas JM, Ekman I, Chanel G, Järvelä S, Salminen M, Cowley B, Henttonen P, Ravaja N (2010) Review on psychophysiological methods in game research. Paper presented at the Proceedings of 1st Nordic DiGRA

Koeffel C, Hochleitner W, Leitner J, Haller M, Geven A, Tscheligi M (2010) Using heuristics to evaluate the overall user experience of video games and advanced interaction games evaluating user experience in games. In: Bernhaupt R (ed). Human–computer interaction series. Springer, London, pp 233–256. doi:10.1007/978-1-84882-963-313

Korhonen H, Koivisto EMI (2006) Playability heuristics for mobile games. In: Proceedings of the 8th conference on Human-computer interaction with mobile devices and services, Espoo, Finland, 2006. ACM, pp 9–16. doi:10.1145/1306813.1306828.

Korhonen H, Koivisto EMI (2007) Playability Heuristics for Mobile Multi-player Games. In: International conference on Digital interactive media in entertainment and arts (DIMEA), Perth, Australia, 2007. ACM, pp 28–35 doi:10.1145/1306813.1306828

Lang PJ (1995) The emotion probe. Studies of motivation and attention. Am Psychol 50:372–385

Larsen RJ, Diener E (1992) Promises and problems with the circumplex model of emotion. Rev pers soc psychol 13:25–59

Larsen JT, McGraw AP, Cacioppo JT (2001) Can people feel happy and sad at the same time? J Pers Soc Psychol 81(4):684–696. doi:10.1037/0022-3514.81.4.684

LeDoux J (1998) The emotional brain. Orion Publishing Group, London

Lewis C (1982) Using the thinking-aloud method in cognitive interface design. Vol technical report. IBM TJ Watson Research Center, Yorktown Heights

Likert R (1932) A technique for the measurement of attitudes. Arch Psychol 22(140):1–55

Livingston IJ, Mandryk RL, Stanley KG (2010) Critic-proofing: how using critic reviews and game genres can refine heuristic evaluations. Paper presented at the Proceedings of the International Academic Conference on the Future of Game Design and Technology, Vancouver, British Columbia, Canada doi:10.1145/1920778.1920786

Lykken DT, Venables PH (1971) Direct measurement of skin conductance: a proposal for standardization. Psychophysiology 8(5):656–672. doi:10.1111/j.1469-8986.1971.tb00501.x

Mandryk R (2008) Physiological measures for game evaluation. In: Isbister K, Schaffer N (eds) Game usability: advice from the experts for advancing the player experience. Morgan Kaufmann, Burlington, pp 207–235

Mandryk RL, Inkpen KM, Calvert TW (2006) using psychophysiological techniques to measure user experience with entertainment technologies. Behav Inform Technol 25(2):141–158. doi:10.1080/01449290500331156

Mirza-Babaei P, Nacke LE, Gregory J, Collins N, Fitzpatrick G (2013) How does it play better?: exploring user testing and biometric storyboards in games user research. In: Proceedings of the SIGCHI Conference on Human Factors in Computing Systems (CHI '13). ACM, New York, NY, USA, 1499–1508. doi:10.1145/2470654.2466200. http://doi.acm.org/10.1145/2470654.2466200

Nacke L (2009) Affective ludology: scientific measurement of user experience in interactive entertainment. Ph. D. thesis, Blekinge Institute of Technology, Karlskrona

Nacke L (2010) Wiimote vs. Controller: Electroencephalographic Measurement of Affective Gameplay Interaction. Paper presented at the Proceedings of Future Play 2010, Vancouver, BC

Nacke L, Lindley CA (2008) Flow and Immersion in First-Person Shooters: Measuring the player's gameplay experience. Paper presented at the Proceedings of the 2008 Conference on Future Play: Research, Play, Share, Toronto, Canada, November 3–5 doi:10.1145/1496984.1496998

Nacke LE, Bateman C, Mandryk RL (2014) BrainHex: A Neurobiological Gamer Typology Survey. Entertain Comput 5:55–62. doi:10.1016/j.entcom.2013.06.002

Nacke LE, Kalyn M, Lough C, Mandryk RL (2011) Biofeedback game design: using direct and indirect physiological control to enhance game interaction. Paper presented at the CHI 2011, Vancouver, BC, Canada. doi:10.1145/1978942.1978958

Nacke LE (2013) An introduction to physiological player metrics for evaluating games. In: Seif El-Nasr M, Drachen A, Canossa A (eds) Game Analytics - Maximizing the Value of Player Data. Springer London, 585–619. doi:10.1007/978-1-4471-4769-5_26

Nielsen J, Molich R (1990) Heuristic evaluation of user interfaces. Paper presented at the Proceedings of the SIGCHI conference on Human factors in computing systems: Empowering people, Seattle, Washington, United States doi:10.1145/97243.97281

Nishimoto S, Vu AT, Naselaris T, Benjamini Y, Yu B, Gallant Jack L (2011) Reconstructing visual experiences from brain activity evoked by natural movies. Curr Biol CB 21(19): 1641–1646 doi:10.1016/j.cub.2011.08.031

Pessoa L (2008) On the relationship between emotion and cognition. Nat Rev Neurosci 9(2):148–158 doi:10.1038/nrn2317

Pinelle D, Wong N, Stach T (2008a) Heuristic evaluation for games: usability principles for video game design. In: The 26th annual CHI conference on human factors in computing systems, Florence, Italy. ACM, pp 1453–1462 doi:10.1145/1357054.1357282

Pinelle D, Wong N, Stach T (2008b) Using genres to customize usability evaluations of video games. In: 2008 Conference on future play: research, play, share, Toronto, Ontario, Canada. ACM, pp 129–136 doi:10.1145/1496984.1497006

Pizzagalli DA (2007) Electroencephalography and high-density electrophysiological source localization. In: Cacioppo JT, Tassinary LG, Berntson GG (eds) Handbook of psychophysiology, 3rd edn. Cambridge University Press, New York, pp 56–84

Poels K, et al. (2010) Digital games, the Aftermath: qualitative insights into postgame experiences. Evaluating user experience in games. Springer London, 149–163. doi:10.1007/978-1-84882-963-3_9

Ravaja N, Turpeinen M, Saari T, Puttonen S, Keltikangas-Järvinen L (2008) The psychophysiology of James Bond: phasic emotional responses to violent video game events. Emotion 8(1):114–120. doi:10.1037/1528-3542.8.1.114

Russell JA (1980) A circumplex model of affect. J Pers Soc Psychol 39(6):1161–1178. doi:10.1037/h0077714

El-Nasr M, Drachen A, Canossa A (2013) Game analytics: Maximizing the value of player data. Springer London. doi:10.1007/978-1-4471-4769-5

Stemmler G, Aue T, Wacker J (2007) Anger and fear: separable effects of emotion and motivational direction on somatovisceral responses. Int J Psychophysiol 66(2):141–153. doi:10.1016/j.ijpsycho.2007.03.019

Stern RM, Ray WJ, Quigley KS (2001) Psychophysiological recording, 2nd edn. Oxford University Press, New York

van Abeelen JHF (1964) Mouse mutants studied by means of ethological methods. Genetica 34(1):79–94. doi:10.1007/bf01664181

Wehbe RR, Nacke LE (2013) An introduction to EEG analysis techniques and brain-computer interfaces for games user researchers. Proceedings of DiGRA 2013. DiGRA, Atlanta, GA, United States, pp 1–16

White GR, Mirza-Babaei P, McAllister G, Good J (2011) Weak inter-rater reliability in heuristic evaluation of video games. Paper presented at the Proceedings of CHI EA 2011, Vancouver, BC, Canada doi:10.1145/1979742.1979788

Chapter 5
Understanding Presence, Involvement, and Flow in Digital Games

Jari Takatalo, Jukka Häkkinen and Göte Nyman

Abstract Digital games elicit rich and meaningful experiences for the gamers. This makes games hard to study solely with usability methods that are used in the field of human–computer interaction. Here is presented a candidate framework to analyze multidimensional user experience (UX) in games. Theoretically the framework is grounded both on previous game studies as well as relevant psychological theories. Methodologically it relies on multivariate data analysis of approximately 320 games ($n=2182$), with the aim of revealing the subcomponents of UX in games. The framework captures the essential psychological determinants of UX, namely, its quality, intensity, meaning, value, and extensity. Mapping these determinants to the game mechanics, the narrative and the interface offers a rich view to UX in games and provides added value to those who want to understand why games are experienced in certain ways and how these experiences shape the numerous consequences related to games.

5.1 Introduction

Entertainment computer and video games, that is, digital games, elicit rich and personally meaningful experiences for the gamers. This makes games hard to study solely with methods that are used to analyze the functionality or productivity of software in the field of human–computer interaction (HCI). The emergence of research into user experience (UX) in HCI has opened new ways of evaluating digital games. The critical criteria in making these evaluations are psychological in nature. Thus, there is a need for a relevant research framework that concerns both technical game components and user psychology in UX that evolves from game playing. Here we present a theoretical and methodological background of a candidate empirical framework for analyzing UX in games. Theoretically our psychologically-based

J. Takatalo (✉) · J. Häkkinen · G. Nyman
Psychology of Digital Life (PDL)/Psychology of Evolving Media and Technology (POEM),
University of Helsinki, Helsinki, Finland
e-mail: Jari.Takatalo@helsinki.fi

© Springer International Publishing Switzerland 2015
R. Bernhaupt (ed.), *Game User Experience Evaluation,*
Human-Computer Interaction Series, DOI 10.1007/978-3-319-15985-0_5

and content-oriented framework is grounded both on previous game studies as well as on relevant psychological theories (Takatalo 2011). Methodologically it relies on multivariate data analysis of approximately 320 games ($n=2182$), with the aim of revealing the subcomponents of UX in games. We emphasize the multidimensional approach in both the analysis of the game and the gamer. This enables capturing the essential psychological determinants of UX, namely, its quality, intensity, meaning, value, and extensity. These basic determinants have already been outlined in the early days of psychology (James 1890; Wundt 1897) and they still provide relevant metrics to evaluate such rich psychological experiences.

The proposed framework is applied and demonstrated here with two different cases to disclose the holistic UX. Firstly, it is used to analyze the differences between two different games. The results are then related to expert reviewer's critics (METASCORE®) and user ratings provided by the Metacritic.com (Metacritic.com 2009). Secondly, we show how the framework can be utilized in an individual-level analysis of evaluated difficulty of playing and skill development during the first hour of play. Performance analysis and qualitative interview of the gamers are integrated into this case. The examples demonstrate the multifaceted nature of UX and show how it is related to technical game components. In both cases, the utilization of the framework in different phases of the game development life-cycle is discussed.

5.1.1 Games and Playing

Any digital game can be considered a system that can be controlled and tuned by its designers. The available technology, their designing skills and desired end-user UX are typical constraints on designers. The components of the game system can be broadly described as the mechanics, the narrative and the interface included in Winn's "Design/Play/Experience" framework for designing digital games (Winn 2008). Game mechanics include the goals of the game, the rules and rewards of action, and the choices provided the gamers. The narrative creates the game world, setting the stage for the storyline. Closest to the gamers is the interface, that is, what the gamers actually see, hear, perhaps even feel, and how they interact with the game (e.g., control system). Although the designer may have a clear idea of the UX that the game system should provide, this experience will not necessarily be the gamers' experience. The UX is founded on the above components of the game system, but it evolves from the game play.

When games are played, the game dynamics emerge from the mechanics (Hunicke et al. 2004; Winn 2008). Meaningful game goals direct gamers' actions. Within the game rules and choices, gamers pursue these goals, earn rewards and achievements, make decisions, and face challenging situations. Gamers consistently evaluate, consciously or unconsciously, their performance in the game; are they reaching the desired goals and do they have the abilities to meet the challenges? When they reach the goals after overcoming obstacles, positive feelings and a sense of competence emerge. Game narrative turns into storytelling, in which the gamer has an active role. Curious places in spaces draw the gamers' focus to the game world and provide escape from the real world. The gamers become engaged in their role with the events in the game. The creation of the game world is also supported by the interface, which sets limits on both physical and social interactions in the game. The interface provides an environment to explore, discover, and collect new things. There gamers autonomously interact with other agents and adapt and become drawn deeper into the game world. All this is inseparably accompanied by rich emotions, which are an essential part of playing games. But how can we measure the UX in such a rich interaction?

Many authors have presented different motivating aspects of game play, such as challenges, sensations and feelings, other gamers, and narrative that encourage gamers to play and elicit fun experiences (Hunicke et al. 2004; Lazzaro 2004; Sherry et al. 2006). Motivation to play is also explained by rewards and achievements. Seeking game rewards is believed to reinforce playing chiefly in order to obtain more rewards (Ducheneaut et al. 2006). The above studies show clearly what playing affords the gamers, and they provide a useful list of game-relevant issues. But to help designers in their efforts to offer gamers the chance to "think clever thoughts and feel profound emotions" (Pagulayan et al. 2003, p. 891), an analysis of the UX that goes beyond fun, gratification, and the behaviouristic reward cycle is needed. Understanding games is approaching a phase where it is close to understanding the psychology of individual life experiences in general.

5.1.2 Psychology of User Experience

There is no one unified and general definition of the UX, but there have been serious attempts to achieve such a definition. Current research on the UX concentrates on a person's perceptions and responses resulting from the use or anticipated use of a product, system, or service (ISO 9241-210:2008 2008). Here, both "perceptions and responses" are considered psychological in nature. According to this view, for example, the perception of a reward by the gamer will not simply lead to an impulsive response to play more. Even if both "perception and response" are considered psychologically, the perceived reward will not lead to fun either. Responses are actively generated in an evaluation process that includes basic psychological compartments, which form our psychological base. For example, we perceive and focus our attention on stimuli that motivate and interest us (James 1890). Only those perceptions that are interesting and meaningful enough to us will be evaluated in our consciousness and will form a part of our inner world. Some perceptions are evaluated subconsciously, whereas others are evaluated in awareness. Awareness can best be understood through the concept of trilogy of mind, namely, the psychological set consisting of thinking, feeling, and will (Hilgard 1980). Over decades this trilogy has concerned human cognition, emotion, and motivation (Mayer 2001).

As the research paradigms in psychology have changed from the stimulus-response paradigms to information processing paradigms this traditional trilogy has been cut to pieces and studied separately (Lubart and Getz 1998). However, for example, cognitions and emotions are so intimately connected that studying emotions without cognitions makes a little sense (Lazarus 1991a). When we look at the UX by integrating cognition, emotion, and motivation with perception and attention, we obtain a realistic set of psychological compartments that make an analysis of "person's perceptions and responses" relevant and valid in any given context. Naturally, our past experiences (memories) and attitudes have an impact on this experiential process (Särkelä et al. 2004).

Although the foundations of these psychological compartments can be traced back to the history of psychology, they have not changed significantly. An excellent example of this is that such compartments are present when today's gamers spontaneously describe their experiences: they report emotional feelings (e.g., enjoyment), cognitive evaluations (e.g., game challenge), and motivations (e.g., curiosity) while playing games (Komulainen et al. 2008). Thus, the content we are dealing with orients our psychological base along the above psychological compartments. If we are able to recognize how these psychological compartments are shaped by the game and represented in the game play we can achieve many advantages for evaluating the UX. Measuring gamers' cognition, emotion, motivation, perception, and attention will reveal relevant determinants of the UX, such as its quality, intensity, meaning, value, and extensity (i.e., voluminous or vastness, a spatial attribute). Taken together, these determinants allow the profiling of experiences and give them their special and distinctive characteristics. Although the determinants have also been outlined already in the beginning of the psychology (James 1890; Wundt 1897), their importance in understanding any mental phenomena and human behaviour should not be overlooked.

Together with the external game components the internal psychological base help us to understand different aspects of the multidimensional UX in games. The experiential cycle (Fig. 5.1) describes the UX process between a gamer and a game (Takatalo 2011). By using the psychological base as a lens through which we observe the gamers' inner world, we can consider the game achievements and rewards discussed earlier in a new light. Because not all rewards motivate gamers equally to continue playing, it is likely that there is a deeper psychological evaluation process underlying human motivation. A reward will be evaluated based on how relevant it is, how challenging it was to achieve, whether it required the use of special skills and abilities, and how enjoyable and satisfying it was to achieve. Such an evaluation assigns a particular reward its intrinsic value. If some specific behavior pattern in a game has no intrinsic value but is done because of an external reward (e.g., one gets paid), then it is said to be extrinsically motivating (Atkinson 1964). In general, intrinsically rewarding behaviors are experienced as more enjoyable and are more likely to be repeated (Csikszentmihalyi 1975). Whether some rewards are intrinsically or extrinsically rewarding is difficult or even impossible to know by looking at the outer behavior only. Evaluating UX from the outer behavior possess its own

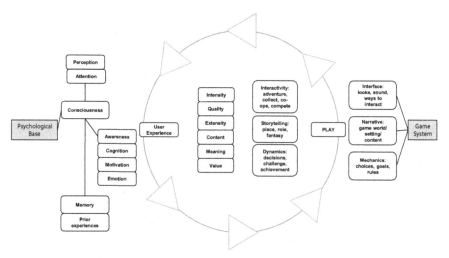

Fig. 5.1 The game system, that is, the content can be affected by the game designer. The psychological base is oriented by the game system in play, when the user interacts with a game. This interaction creates an experiential cycle (Takatalo 2011), in which UX characteristics evolve. Experiential cycle is affected by the user background as well

challenges as well. But what are the relevant game-related concepts that best represent the psychological compartments in games and could enable us to measure the true characteristics of the UX?

5.1.3   User Experience in Games

Numerous candidate concepts, such as, immersion, fun, presence, involvement, engagement, and flow have been used to describe the UX in games (Brown and Cairns 2004; IJsselsteijn et al. 2007; McMahan 2003; Nakatsu et al. 2005; Sweetser and Wyeth 2005). Often these concepts are defined quite broadly; for instance, presence is "the sense of being there", while flow describes "an optimal experience." Various psychological compartments are attached to these concepts; for example, concentration, emotions, and cognitive evaluations of the game's challenges are each referred to as immersion (McMahan 2003). Thus, there is a great overlap among the concepts and as a consequence, numerous challenges to understanding and actually measuring them. For instance, considering flow as an "optimal experience" by definition (Csikszentmihalyi 1975) and restricting it to extreme situations only (Jennett et al. 2008) would diminish its applicability to the analysis of the UX in typical games. The subcomponents of flow, such as, skills and challenges (Csikszentmihalyi 1975) provide psychologically valid metrics to evaluate games, even if the gamers would never reach the actual "optimal experience". Concentrating on the subcomponents instead of the concept that has a complex underlying structure itself has other advantages as well. We have shown, for example, how equally high "meta-presence" scores in four different games actually hide clear experiential differences between the games found in five measured presence subcomponents (e.g., physical presence, attention, co-presence) (Takatalo et al. 2006a).

There is empirical user-centered data that provide evidence for potential subcomponents of the UX in games across the concepts. Jennett et al. (2008) studied immersion in games. They extracted five experiential subcomponents in a principal component analysis ($n=260$) and named them as *cognitive involvement* (curiosity and interest), *real-world dissociation* (attention, temporal dissociation), *challenge*, *emotional involvement* (empathy, enjoyment), and *control* (ease of controls, interacting with a game). Similarly, Ermi and Mäyrä (2005) studied immersion. Although their model is based on the interviews of children who played the games with their parents, the model was further supported by a factor analysis of a sample ($n=234$) collected from grown-up gamers. Their three extracted subcomponents were: *sensory immersion* (e.g., "The sounds of game overran the other sounds from the environment"), *challenge-based immersion* (challenges and abilities), and *imaginative immersion* (use of imagination, empathy, fantasy)

Sherry et al. (2006) used factor analysis ($n=550$) to extract uses and gratifications dimensions. They named the six extracted motivations to play as *competition*, *challenges*, *social interaction*, *diversion* ("I play instead of other thing I should do"), *fantasy* (to be someone else), and *arousal* (excited, adrenaline). Lazzaro (2004) found four main motivations to play from the qualitative and quantitative analysis of 15 gamers and 15 non-gamers. Included were *hard fun* (meaningful challenges), *easy fun* (excitement and curiosity of exploring new adventures), *altered states* (emotions inside), and *people factor* (compete and co-ops with others). Likewise, Ryan et al.'s (2006) Player Experience in Need Satisfaction (PENS) – framework deals with the reasons that keep gamers playing the games. Measures in this framework are composed of summed scales that have been used in previous studies: *in game competence* (capable and effective), *in game autonomy* (free to do things that interests), *presence* (physical, emotional, narrative), and *intuitive controls* (easy to remember). In addition to PENS measures, *subjective vitality* (energy and aliveness), *self-esteem, mood, game enjoyment, preference for future play*, and *continued play behaviour* were measured. Sweetser and Johnson (2004) investigated, which issues in games impact player enjoyment. Their principal components analysis ($n=455$) resulted five subcomponents, *physics* (gravity, life-like graphics), *sound* (effects and soundtrack), *narrative, intuitiveness* (interaction with objects), and *the freedom of expression* (many different as well as unique ways of using objects).

Pagulayan et al.'s (2003) four important factors in game evaluation were *overall quality* (e.g., fun), *ease of use* (controls, interface), *challenge*, and *pace* (the rate of new challenges) are based on strong empirical data gathered in various studies conducted in Microsoft Game Studios. Poels et al. (2007) study revealed nine relevant subcomponents that were based on both qualitative gamer interviews and expert evaluations. Included were *enjoyment* (fun, pleasure, relaxation), *flow* (concentration, absorption), *imaginative immersion* (story, empathy), *sensory immersion* (presence), *suspense* (challenge, tension, pressure), *negative affect* (disappointment, frustration), *control* (autonomy, power), *social presence* (being connected with others, empathy), and *competence* (pride, euphoria). An overview of the ten general UX subcomponents found in the above empirical studies is presented in Table 5.1. There is conceptual overlapping between the subcomponents depending on both the scope and the methodology of the approach. However, common to majority of the studies is some kind of a reference to both emotions and challenges. We have developed the Presence-Involvement-Flow Framework (PIFF) (Takatalo et al. 2004) in order to integrate the vast amount of relevant UX subcomponents into one framework and to study the UX in games as multidimensional and psychological in nature.

5.1.4 Presence-Involvement-Flow Framework (PIFF)

PIFF is a psychological research framework to study experiences in digital games. It has been constructed on the basis of the extensive concepts of the sense of presence, involvement, and flow. They represent the psychological compartments in digital games well: presence (Lombard and Ditton 1997) describes the perception of and attention to the game world and both spatial- and social cognitions in game play, involvement (Zaichkowsky 1985) is considered a measure of gamer motivation, and flow (Csikszentmihalyi 1975) refers to the subjective, cognitive-emotional evaluation of the game. Each concept includes subcomponents that are relevant to both technical game components and psychological determinants of the UX.

5.1.4.1 Presence and Involvement

Gamers often mention realistic high-quality graphical interface and an engaging narrative as central game components responsible for various game-related feeling (Sweetser and Johnson 2004; Wood et al. 2004). The feeling of being in a realistic place with others is indeed the core idea of the concept of presence (Lombard and Ditton 1997). Presence has been studied in a variety of different media, for instance, in virtual environments, movies and television (Schuemie et al. 2001). Unlike many other concepts around games, the concept of presence has extensive theoretical and empirical foundation; over 1800 publications currently make up the presence literature (Lombard and Jones 2007). Hence, it provides valid and tested metrics to study experiences in games (Pinchbeck and Stevens 2005). The subcomponents of presence are proven to be especially useful when the intensity and extensity of the UX is evaluated (Takatalo et al. 2006a).

The following three subcomponents of presence have been used to study the "sense of being there" or spatial presence in mediated environments: attention (psychological immersion), perceptual realness (naturalness), and spatial awareness (engagement) (Lombard and Ditton 1997). This threefold construct has also been

Table 5.1 A summary of game-related studies introducing potential empirically derived UX subcomponents. Marked x indicates that the authors have considered that subcomponent. The main scopes (e.g. motivation to play, immersion) and the methodologies used (e.g., qualitative, quantitative) vary across the studies

	Skill, competence	Challenge	Emotions	Control, autonomy, freedom	Focus, concentration	Physical presence	Involveent, meaning, curiosity	Story, drama, fantasy	Social interaction	Interactivity, controls, usability
Jennett et al. 2008	–	x	x	–	X	–	x	–	–	x
Poels et al. 2007	x	x	x	x	X	X	–	x	x	–
Ryan et al. 2006	x	–	x	x	–	X	–	x	–	x
Sherry et al. 2006	–	x	x	–	–	–	–	x	x	–
Ermi and Myyrä 2005	–	x	–	–	–	X	–	x	–	–
Lazzaro 2004	–	x	x	–	–	–	x	–	x	–
Sweetser and Johnson 2004	–	–	–	x	–	X	–	x	–	x
Takatalo et al. 2004	x	x	x	x	X	X	x	x	x	x
Pagulayan et al 2003	–	x	x	–	–	–	–	–	–	x

reliably extracted in empirical studies (Lessiter et al. 2001; Schubert et al. 2001). Additionally, the level of arousal and the range and consistency of the physical interaction are integral parts of spatial presence (Lombard and Ditton 1997). Social content is a significant factor in many games and it elicits the sense of social presence. In Lombard and Ditton's (1997) explication, social presence was composed of social richness, social realism, and co-presence (shared space). These aspects correspond well to the social features found in digital games, such as, narrative and the engagement with one's own role in a story. Social richness refers to the extent to which a game is perceived as personal and intimate. Social realism refers to the sense of similarity between real-world and game-world objects, people and events. Co-presence is the feeling of being and acting in a game together with other agents.

We have found out a clear distinction between presence and the motivational concept of involvement (Takatalo et al. 2006b). Psychologically, involvement is defined as a motivational continuum toward a particular object or situation (Rothschild 1984). Involvement concerns the level of relevance based on inherent needs, values, and interests attached to that situation or an object (Zaichkowsky 1985). Thus, involvement determines the meaning and value of the UX. The main interest here is not in what motivates gamers to play, but in understanding the meaning and personal relevance of the game. Whether we want to understand UX in a high-end technological set-up or mobile device in a rush-hour subway meaning plays always a key role. Involvement is a central and well-established concept both in the fields of buyer behavior (Brennan and Mavondo 2000) as well as in mass communication and mass media (Roser 1990). It includes two distinct but closely related dimensions: importance and interest (McQuarrie and Munson 1992). Importance is dominantly a cognitive dimension concerning the meaning and relevance of the stimulus, whereas interest is composed of emotional and value-related valences (Schiefele 1991). This makes importance similar to the cognitive involvement subcomponent that was extracted by Jennett et al. (2008). On the other hand, interest is close to Lazzaro's (2004) curiosity and the will to find out something new in a game. Curiously enough, we have found out that first-person shooters are less involving compared to third person role-playing games (Takatalo et al. 2006a), but it is difficult to point out exactly which game components affect involvement the most.

Taken together, presence and involvement indicate the switch between the real world and a game, namely, the way gamers willingly form a relationship with the physical and social features of the game.

5.1.4.2 Flow

The concept of flow in PIFF describes the subjective, qualitative direction of the UX. In psychological terms, it explains the cognitive evaluation and emotional outcomes of the game play. The cognitive evaluation is often related to game mechanics. In PIFF the cognitive evaluation of the game concerns, for example, game challenges and gamer skills. These evaluations are related to a number of emotional outcomes (e.g., enjoyment, boredom). This way of looking at the subcomponents of flow is based on different flow-channel models, such as the four-channel flow model (Csikszentmihalyi 1975). The flow-channel models share the idea that there are certain cognitions that are followed by emotions. In an ideal situation where skills and challenges are high and in balance, an optimal state of flow occurs. Such a close coupling of cognitions and emotions is widely acknowledged in psychology in cognitive theories of emotion (Lazarus 1991b). Cognitive evaluations by the gamers and the related emotional outcomes provide useful subcomponents for analyzing the UX from the first hour of play to the full completion of the game.

In addition to describing the subjective evaluations of challenge and skill, the flow theory (Csikszentmihalyi 1975) considers clear goals and instant feedback as important features that are evaluated cognitively in a given situation. The theory also includes the sense of control, the level of arousal, concentration, time distortion, the loss of self-consciousness, and the merging of action and awareness as prerequisites or correlates of the flow experience. In PIFF, the level of arousal, concentration, and time distortion are included as subcomponents of presence. This theoretical overlap between flow and presence supports the findings of presence being a prerequisite of flow (Novak et al. 2000). Losing self-consciousness and merging action and awareness have been difficult for respondents to recognize in previous studies (Rettie 2001). The actual state of flow is often characterized as ease of doing, enjoyment and positive valence (pleasure) as well as the absence of boredom and anxiety (Csikszentmihalyi 1975). Previously, flow has been related to playfulness (e.g., cognitive spontaneity) (Webster and Martocchio 1992) and the sense of control (Ghani and Deshpande 1994; Novak et al. 2000). In addition to these, a wide variety of other emotional feelings has been reported in games, such as, pleasantness, strength, and impressiveness of the experience, amazement, and excitement (Lazzaro 2004; Schubert et al. 2001).

Although all the above PIFF subcomponents have a strong theoretical foundation, we have studied them psychometrically in a large empirical data-set. Psychometric inspection reveals the structure of each larger concept in digital games context and provides reliable metrics for their measurement.

5.2 PIFF: Methodological Background

PIFF is based on the quantitative data gathered with the Experimental Virtual Environment Experience Questionnaire-Game Pitkä (i.e., long) (EVEQ-GP). EVEQ-GP is composed of approximately 180 items presented in previous studies concerning the sense of presence (Kim and Biocca 1997; Lessiter et al. 2001; Lombard et al. 2000; Schubert et al. 2001; Usoh et al. 2000; Witmer and Singer 1998), involvement (McQuarrie and Munson 1992), and flow prerequisites and correlates (Della Fave and Massimini 1988; Fontaine 1992; Ghani and Deshpande 1994; Mehrabian and Russell 1974; Novak et al. 2000; Webster and Martocchio 1992). All the items were translated into Finnish and transformed either into a seven-point Likert-scale (1 = Strongly Disagree to 7 = Strongly Agree) or into seven-point semantic differentials. The items were modified so that they were assessing experiences received from one game playing session. EVEQ-GP is administered to an individual gamer after a playing session. The gamers who fill in the questionnaire are encouraged to reflect on their subjective experiences of the game they just played. The method enables the participants to report, within the boundaries of the 180 items, how they experienced that particular game. In the field of behavioral sciences the use of questionnaires has proved to be a valid way of assessing various mental phenomena (Rust and Golombok 1999).

The first version of the PIFF was based on two smaller data sets ($n=68$ & $n=164$). Of the 180 EVEQ-GP items 146 were used to form 23 subcomponents measuring the UX in games (Takatalo et al. 2004). Thereafter, a heterogeneous data from 2182 Finnish gamers who filled in the questionnaire were collected. Data from laboratory experiments and an Internet survey are included in the data set. The data include approximately 320 different games, various displays (HMD, TV, CRT), and contexts of play (online, offline, home, laboratory), giving a broad scope to the UX in games. This data enabled more advanced statistical analyses of the PIFF subcomponents. As a result of these analyses a refined version of the framework, i.e., PIFF^2 was developed.

Methodologically, PIFF^2 is grounded on two separate multivariate measurement models (Tarkkonen and Vehkalahti 2005), which assessed presence and involvement as well as flow (Fig. 5.2). In psychometrics, measurement models include latent variables (i.e., those difficult to measure straightforwardly), which are measured with observed variables such as questionnaire items. These observed variables are analyzed with multivariate methods to form subcomponents (i.e., measurement scales). These subcomponents thus formed can then be used to assess latent variables.

We used principal axis factor analysis (PFA) with an oblique direct Oblimin rotation (delta=0) independently in both measurement models to compress a large number of questionnaire items into the subcomponents. Of the 180 EVEQ-GP items, 163 measure presence, involvement, and flow. The rest of the EVEQ-GP items assess background information and game-related issues. After a series of PFA's in both the measurement models including the 163 items, 15 theoretically meaningful subcomponents could be reliably formed out of the 139 highest loading items (Takatalo 2011). Next, a short description of both the measurement models and each of the subcomponents forming them is given. The number of items forming a subcomponent and an estimation of the reliability of a subcomponent is given in parenthesis. Reliabilities were estimated with Tarkkonen's rho (ρ) (Vehkalahti et al. 2006). Rho was used instead of a popular Cronbach's alpha, because alpha has a build-in assumption of one-dimensionality of a measure and a tendency to underestimate the measures (Tarkkonen and Vehkalahti 2005; Vehkalahti et al. 2009). This may lead to biased conclusions and discarding of suitable items or even subcomponents (Vehkalahti et al. 2006). Tarkkonen's rho is interpreted the same way as the Cronbach's alpha: values above .70 indicate that the items forming a subcomponent measure the same phenomenon.

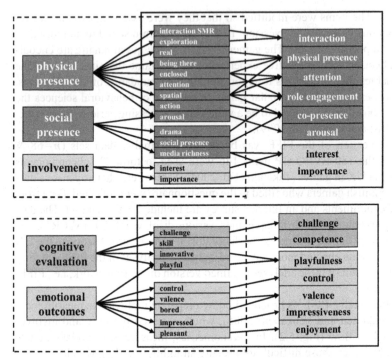

Fig. 5.2 The two measurement models that form the PIFF[2]. On the *left*, measured latent variables in five boxes, in the *middle*, 139 measured questionnaire items (observed variables) represented in 23 boxes. On the *right*, 15 factor-analytically (PFA) extracted subcomponents of UX in games

5.2.1 Presence and Involvement

Of 93 EVEQ-GP items forming the presence and involvement measurement model, 83 highest loading ones are those that form the eight extracted subcomponents (Fig. 5.2). This solution explained 41.67 % of the total variance in the final PFA (Appendix A). The *physical presence* subcomponent ($\rho=0.82/17$ items) describes the feeling of being in a real and vivid place. Items included, for example, "In the game world everything seemed real and vivid". The third presence dimension in Lombard and Ditton's (1997) description, *attention*, that is, time distortion, focus on the game world instead of the real world, formed a subcomponent of its own ($\rho=0.88/12$). Included were items, such as, "My vision was totally engaged in the game world" and "I was not aware of my "real" environment". Two subcomponents for different aspects of social presence were also extracted. *Co-presence* ($\rho=0.89/14$) includes the feeling of sharing a place with others and being active there (e.g., "I felt that I was in the game world with other persons"). *Role engagement* ($\rho=0.80/12$) describes being transported into the story: how captivated gamers were by the role provided in the narrative (e.g., "I felt that I was one of the characters in the story of the game"). Two more subcomponents measuring emotional *arousal* ($\rho=0.70/5$ items, e.g., active, stimulated vs. passive, unaroused) and game world's interactivity were extracted. *Interaction* subcomponent ($\rho = 0.72/9$) was composed of items assessing, for example, speed, range, mapping, exploration, and predictability of one's own actions in the game world (e.g., "The game responded quickly to my actions"). In our further analysis (Takatalo et al. 2006b), the *interaction* subcomponent did not fit with the rest of the subcomponents extracted in the presence and involvement measurement model. This empirical finding has also received theoretical support (Wirth et al. 2007). One explanation could be the nature of the interaction subcomponent: it is more of a cognitive evaluation of a range of game interactivity, such as reciprocity and feedback from one's actions, rather than a subjective perceptual experience, such as being in a game as pointed out by Shubert et al. (2001). Similarly, Jennett et al. (2008) considered their control subcomponent (i.e., "using the controls as travelling somewhere and interacting with the world") as a game factor instead of a person factor. Thus, we have analyzed interaction among the other cognitive game evaluations extracted in our flow measurement model.

In the same PFA the two theoretical subcomponents of involvement, namely, importance and interest, were extracted. *Interest* ($\rho = 0.72/6$) is composed of emotional and value-related valences, such as, "the game was exciting". *Importance* ($\rho = 0.89/8$) is dominantly a cognitive dimension showing how meaningful, relevant, and personal the game was (e.g., "the game mattered to me"). More details of the extraction and utilization of the eight presence and involvement subcomponents can be found in our previous studies (Takatalo et al. 2006a, b; Takatalo 2011; Takatalo et al. 2011).

5.2.2 Flow

Of the 70 EVEQ-GP items forming the flow measurement model, 56 highest loading ones are those that form the seven extracted subcomponents (Fig. 5.2). This solution explained 41.30% of the total variance in the final PFA (Appendix B). The *challenge* subcomponent ($\rho = 0.76/5$ items) assesses the degree to which abilities were required to play the game as well as how challenging the gamer felt it was to play (e.g., "playing the game felt challenging"). *Competence* ($\rho = 0.86/11$) combined measures of user skills and positive feelings of effectiveness. It also included items, which assessed clear goals and items that evaluated both demand and competence (e.g., "I felt I could meet the demands of the playing situation"). Furthermore, five subcomponents with emotional content were extracted. Hedonic *valence* ($\rho = 0.77/10$) is the bipolar subcomponent having pleasure on one end and displeasure on the other. It was composed of semantic differentials, such as, "I felt happy/ I felt sad"). The *enjoyment* subcomponent ($\rho = 0.74/7$) included aspects such as pleasantness and enjoyment. Playing was also somehow special (e.g.," I will recommend it to my friends" and "I had peak experiences while playing"). Items forming the original *playfulness* scale (Webster and Martocchio 1992) (e.g., "I felt innovative" and "I felt original") formed a subcomponent of their own ($\rho = 0.78/9$). Items measuring actual feelings of flow, such as ease of doing, loaded on the playfulness subcomponent as well. *Control*, that is, being dominant and independent, formed one subcomponent ($\rho=0.74/5$) composed of semantic differentials, such as, "I was dominant/I was submissive". Feelings of being amazed and astonished formed the *impressiveness* subcomponent ($\rho=0.79/9$), which included items, such as, "I was astonished and surprised at the game world" and "I felt something dramatic in the game world". For more details of the extraction and utilization of the seven flow subcomponents, see our previous studies (Takatalo et al. 2010; Takatalo 2011).

Factor scores with Bartlett's method (Tabachnick and Fidell 2001) were computed from the 15 PIFF^2 subcomponents. Next, these subcomponents are used to analyze different aspects of the UX in games.

5.3 PIFF^2 in Practice

We have demonstrated here the multidimensional and psychological nature of the UX in games. The rest of the chapter presents two distinct practical examples of how to utilize the mapping of PIFF^2 subcomponents in different phases of the game development life-cycle. First, all the subcomponents are used to compare groups of expert gamers in two different games. Psychological profile provided by the PIFF^2 is compared against METASCORE® and user ratings provided by the Metacritic. com (Metacritic.com 2009). However, sometimes more detailed information about a specific game feature is needed as quickly and efficiently as possible. Using only selected PIFF^2 subcomponents in a more qualitative manner would then be a better choice. Our second case deals with an individual-level analysis of experienced game difficulty and learning of skills during the first hour of play. Analysis of game mechanics and qualitative interview are integrated into this case. However, the use of complete subscales with several participants guarantees more extensive and reliable results.

5.3.1 Between Groups: PIFF^2 in Two Different Games

A standard way of using PIFF^2 is to gather post-game experiences with an EVEQ-GP questionnaire. This would be most beneficial, for example, in the production phase when all content can be represented, but there is still time and possibility to introduce changes before releasing the game. If used as a post-launch study, a PIFF^2 analysis can provide useful information and facilitate evaluation of the released product. Moreover, a PIFF^2 profile adds subjective and qualitative meaning for the other measures collected, e.g., diaries or behavioral logs. Here we conduct such a post-launch analysis to two first-person shooters (FPS) and compare PIFF^2 profiles with the METASCORE® and the user ratings of these games. Both these numeric values are provided by the Metacritic.com (Metacritic.com 2009). METASCORE® is based on a weighted average of various scores assigned by expert critics to that game. The user ratings are means of all the ratings given to a game by the users.

Metacritic.com provides the amount of users that have rated a particular game. This comparison will demonstrate the added value of the psychological and multidimensional analysis of the UX based on gamers' own reflections from the game.

The data included 109 expert male gamers, who played either Valve's *Half-Life 2* (*HL2*; $n=62$) or *Counter Strike: Source* (*CS*; $n=47$), which both run by the same Source® game engine. This makes the interface in studied games exactly the same. After they finish playing either *HL2* or *CS*, each gamer filled in the EVEQ-GP in our Internet survey. *HL2* is described as "it opens the door to a world where the player's presence affects everything around him, from the physical environment to the behaviors even the emotions of both friends and enemies. The player again picks up the crowbar of research scientist Gordon Freeman, who finds himself on an alien-infested Earth being picked to the bone, its resources depleted, its populace dwindling" (Half-Life 2 2004). In *CS*, gamers can "engage in an incredibly realistic brand of terrorist warfare in this wildly popular team-based game" (Counter-Strike: Source 2004). In addition, "*CS* modifies the multiplayer aspects of "*Half-Life*" to bring it a more team-oriented game-play. *CS* provides the player with an experience that a trained counter-terrorist unit or terrorist unit experiences" (Metacritic.com 2009). Thus, there were such differences in game mechanics and narrative between *HL2* and *CS* that should be able to be measured and analyzed.

HL2 has received a METASCORE® of 96/100 based on 81 reviews and *CS* 88/100 based on nine reviews. A METASCORE® between 90–100 is considered as an "Universal Acclaim" and between 75–89 a "Generally favorable reviews" (Metacritic.com 2009). The users rated *HL2* 9,3[9,2]/10 (3487 [4773] votes) and *CS* 9,2[9,0]/10 (7532 [9199] votes) (situation in March 2009 [updated April 2012]). Although the background of the players rating the games was not standardized in any ways (e.g., skill, gender), this variation between scores and ratings gives an interesting starting point for the analysis of the added value of the PIFF^2 profiles. Two distinct between-subjects multivariate analyses of variance (MANOVA) were conducted for both presence and involvement as well as flow subcomponents. Significant differences in MANOVA's were further studied in univariate analyses. The UX determinants are included in bold face.

Figure 5.3 shows that the levels of both *presence* and *involvement* differed between the games (Wilk's Lambda$=0.70$, $F(8,100)=5.46$, $p<0.001$, $\eta2=0.30$). *HL2* was considered more *interesting* (**value**) than *CS* (one-way ANOVA, $F(1, 4,05)=4.10$, $p<0.05$, $\eta^2=0.04$). The presence profiles of the games were also quite different. *CS* was high in *co-presence* ($F(1, 5,46)=5,93$, $p<0.05$, $\eta^2=0.05$), *attention* (NS), and *arousal* ($F(1, 5,90)=4.23$, $p<0.05$, $\eta^2=0.04$), whereas characteristic for *HL2* was quite steady scores in each of the subcomponents. Especially high it was in *role engagement* ($F(1, 16,38)=14.89$, $p<0.001$, $\eta^2=0.12$) and *physical presence* ($F(1, 8,08)=5.41$, $p<0.05$, $\eta^2=0.05$) compared to *CS*. Both the games were considered equally *important* and *attentive*. These differences show, quite simply, how the narrative affects the UX: *HL2* builds on of the realistic game-world, the city seven (**extensity**), and provides the role of the Gordon Freeman to an individual gamer (**meaning**). With a similar interface, *CS* provides team-work and **intensive** performance. Naturally, the difference in game narrative is linked to the game mechanics, which was studied with the flow subcomponents.

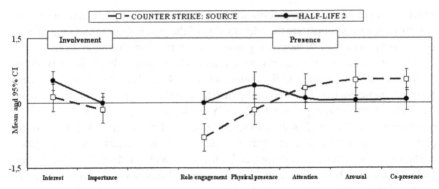

Fig. 5.3 Group means in involvement and presence subcomponents in *Half-Life 2* and *Counter Strike: Source*. The error bars represent a 95% confidence interval. An overlap by half the average arm length of the error bar indicates a statistical difference between the groups ($p \approx 0.05$). If the tips of the error bars just touch, then the difference is $p \approx 0.01$. A gap between the error bars indicates $p < 0.001$

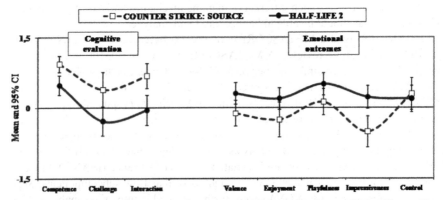

Fig. 5.4 Group means in flow subcomponents in *Half-Life 2* and *Counter Strike: Source*. The error bars represent a 95% confidence interval. An overlap by half the average arm length of the error bar indicates a statistical difference between the groups ($p \approx 0.05$). If the tips of the error bars just touch, then the difference is $p \approx 0.01$. A gap between the error bars indicates $p < 0.001$

Figure 5.4 shows that the cognitive-emotional flow subcomponents in both games were significantly different (Wilk's Lambda$=0.59$, $F(7,101)=10.10$, $p < 0.001$, $\eta2 = 0.41$). Especially in cognitive evaluations the games were quite different. Gamers evaluated *CS* more *challenging* ($F(1, 12,13)=4.04$, $p < 0.01$, $\eta^2 = 0.07$), *interactive* ($F(1, 14,35)=11.64, p < 0.01, \eta^2 = 0.10$), and themselves more *competent* to play ($F(1, 5,50)=10.58$, $p < 0.01$, $\eta^2 = 0.09$). However, the emotional **quality** of their UX was somewhat "thinner" compared to *HL2*. *HL2* was more positive in *valence* (pleasure) ($F(1, 4,80)=5.68, p < 0.05, \eta^2 = 0.05$), *enjoyable* ($F(1, 5,38)=4.64, p < 0.05, \eta^2 = 0.04$), *playful* ($F(1, 3,40)=4.40, p < 0.05, \eta^2 = 0.04$), and *impressive* ($F(1, 14,44)=13.60, p < 0.001, \eta^2 = 0.11$). There was no difference between the games in the sense of *control*. Game mechanics providing competition and co-operative performance are the most likely cause for the flattened emotional profile in *CS*. However, it should be emphasized that the UX in *CS* is still far from being negative or boring. Heightened attention and arousal and highly evaluated cognitive and social features in the game are enough to keep gamers in *CS* for hours. Notably, the competence-challenge ratio in both games indicates that the gamers experienced mastering the game instead of coping with its demands. This seems to be an ideal ratio when prolonged use of games is considered.

Both the PIFF^2 analysis and a METASCORE® found the differences between *HL2* and *CS*. A well prepared narrative combined with good AI-based action seems to be engaging and heart-touching compared to extreme challenge and action with live comrades. The advantage of the PIFF^2 is its potential use in any phase of the game development cycle: stimulating, supporting thinking and giving ideas for the UX goals in concept phase and providing a facilitative tool to evaluate these goals in beta versions in a production phase, as it was show here. Relating PIFF^2 to user ratings provides a good demonstration of our psychologically-based and content oriented approach in media psychology in general. In order to understand the true meaning of the user rating, one needs to understand both the content and the psychology involved. Gamers rated both *HL2* and *CS* as about equally high, but clearly for different reasons, which were out of the reach of the single rating grade given. However, these nuances could be disclosed by a multidimensional psychological profile of PIFF^2. The analysis of the profile indicated that the two games were equally interesting and attentive, which could explain the similar ratings given by the gamers. It is an old psychological fact that we perceive and focus our attention on stimuli that motivate and interest us (James 1890). This part of the UX cannot be reached by an outside observer, thus a measure which considers meaning and personal relevance in that particular game is needed. As presented in this example, the involvement concept fits well into this purpose.

5.3.2 Between Users: Competence and Challenge in the First Hour

In the previous example, games were evaluated by groups of gamers at a general level. User ratings and PIFF^2 profiles were based on hours of playing. However, sometimes a finer detail, such as, a particular game feature, a piece of new downloadable content, or user group needs to be investigated. Critical issues in production phase are often related to playability and game mechanics, and could include, for example, evaluating the learning curve or adjustment of the difficulty level. Usually, such issues take place in the first hour of play, which should convince the gamer to keep on playing instead of suffocating an evolving enthusiasm (Davis et al. 2005). To study these, a large data and a heavy questionnaire are not the best option. It is enough to (1) define the investigated problem well, (2) know what to measure, and (3) how to measure. Here we give an example where the focus is on understanding how competence develops and game challenges are evaluated during the first hour of play. The cognitive-emotional flow subcomponents provided by

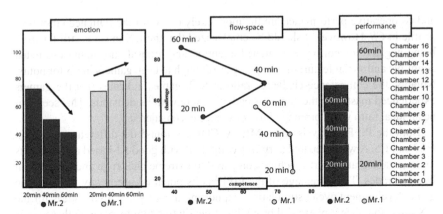

Fig. 5.5 **a** Composite measure of emotions of the two gamers during the first hour of play. **b** Flow-space and evaluations of challenge and competence of the two gamers during the first hour of play. **c** The number of chambers finished by the two gamers during the first hour of play. Each measure was taken after 20, 40 and 60 min of playing

PIFF[2] serve this purpose well, disclosing both the cognitive game evaluations and the quality of UX. In addition, a lighter way of utilizing PIFF[2] dimensionality is introduced and PIFF[2] findings are integrated into other measures collected, that is, gamer interviews and the observed performance in the game.

Evaluations of challenge and competence by two male gamers' (Mr. 1 and Mr. 2) were analyzed during their first hour playing Valve's *Portal*. *Portal* is a single player game, in which "Players must solve physical puzzles and challenges by opening portals to maneuvering objects, and themselves, through space". *Portal* has been called "one of the most innovative new games on the horizon and will offer gamers hours of unique game-play" (Portal 2007). *Portal* provides game mechanics with clearly distinguished levels (i.e., chambers) that enable study of the process that gives the UX its quality. This process was captured by suitably interrupting the gamers twice during the one hour of play. The breaks were timed so that the gamers were in "the elevator" between the chambers. The third evaluation was made after 60 min of playing. The gamers were in the laboratory by themselves, and the interruptions were made as natural as possible. During the breaks the gamers rated one item in each of the selected PIFF[2] subcomponents in the touch-screen next to them. Thus, the method was called PIFF[2]-in-breaks analysis. The first page on the touch-screen included a flow-space (Fig. 5.5b). The flow-space is formed from the *challenge* and *competence* subcomponents. The idea of the flow-space was to evaluate both competences and challenges together in each game period. So, during each break the gamers marked the point in the flow-space that best corresponded to their evaluations in that particular game period. Flow-space is based on the flow-channel models, such as the four-channel model (Csikszentmihalyi 1975) and the flow-grid (W. IJsselsteijn & K. Poels, personal communication, April 24, 2008). The second page of the touch-screen presented one question in each of the emotional subcomponents (*pleasure/valence, control, enjoyment, impressiveness, playfulness*). These five individual scores were summed and used as a composite measure of emotional outcomes in this example (Fig. 5.5a). Gamers could not see their previous evaluations when using the touch-screen. While using the touch-screen, the instructor interviewed the gamers in order to deepen their answers. This qualitative-quantitative data collection procedure during each break took app. 2–3 min. The performance in the game was evaluated based on how many chambers the gamers finished in each of the approximately 20-min game periods (Fig. 5.5c). Although both gamers fulfilled the prerequisite for participating in the experiment, namely, that they had no prior experience on *Portal*, there were other background differences between them.

Mr. 1 is 21 years old and plays games on average for 300 min at a time. He considers that "*I have played games for a long time…My little brother has told me that this is an easy one.*" Mr. 2 is 30 years old and plays games on average 60 min at a time. He thinks that "*I have not played this kind of game before. I'm not an expert at these games.*" Although both play games equally often (50 % or more of days), Mr. 1, being younger, invests more time in playing. He seems to be a more experienced gamer and more confident when starting a game. This difference in the gamers' backgrounds is seen both in their cognitive evaluation shown in the flow-space (Fig. 5.5b) and in their performance (Fig. 5.5c) after the first 20 min of play. They began their cognitive evaluation at different points, Mr. 2 being more challenged and less competent. Consequently, Mr. 2 completed only four chambers compared to Mr. 1's ten chambers. However, the composite measure of the two users' emotions was on the same level after 20 min of playing. This shows the complexity of measuring the UX. Gamers have the same level of emotions for different reasons. That is why, for example, measuring only fun or emotional valence in games is not enough; multidimensional measures are needed to uncover the underlying experiential subcomponents.

The shape and magnitude of the two gamers' flow-space profiles disclose the evaluation process that took place during the first hour. After 40 min of play, Mr. 1 had completed only four chambers more, shown in the flow space as increased challenge and stagnation in competence. However, Mr. 1's positive feelings kept increasing. Mr. 2 did essentially the same number of chambers as in his first 20 min. He considered himself competent and the game more challenging. Although his competence increased after 40 min, his feelings dropped dramatically. In the interview he said: "*(the level of) arousal decreased and I felt tired;*" "*The game doesn't feel novel any more; I have become numb,*"; "*It has become more demanding…so many things should be used and considered.*" This indicates a clear mental collapse, which is seen in his cognitive evaluation of the last period. During the last 20-min period, he reached Chamber 11, never finished it, and experienced a dramatic decrease in competence. At the end he described his UX: "*My skills decreased; I lost the logic. It is frustrating because I cannot proceed and do not understand what is going on…I lost concentration and started to try solutions randomly. The Portals were confusing; there were so many things that I could not control.*" Clearly, after an hour of play, Mr. 2 was giving up. The choices and challenges provided by the game were too overwhelming. He was not ready to commit himself to the game and work to meet its demands. By contrast, Mr. 1 was just getting warmed up. In the last period he managed to do only two more chambers, but he considered the game to be challenging: *"Clearly more challenging. I needed to really think of what to do. The feeling of skill is getting stronger when I learned what I can do...I'm becoming more and more impressed with it."* Although his evaluations of competence dropped somewhat in the last period, he was learning to play the game and was confident about continuing.

This simple example shows what kind of information can be obtained with the PIFF^2 subcomponents to support a specific design problem concerning, for example, the game mechanics. Cognitive-emotional flow subcomponents show how the learning curve, difficulty of the game, and the quality of the UX evolves and changes during the critical first hour of play. PIFF^2 -in-breaks method utilizes reliable measures drawn form a large data more efficiently. This example shows one way of utilizing the PIFF^2 -in-breaks method. If the interest is in the analysis of the interface or narrative, then the presence and involvement subcomponents could be included in the PIFF^2-in-breaks analysis. It can also be accompanied by other measures (e.g., usability, behavioral logs) in order to analyze design goals at particular game levels, game features, or user groups. The touch-screen can be used at home as well as in the laboratory and the time period evaluated can range from minutes to days, depending on the scope of the study.

5.4   Contributions and Future Challenges

Numerous concepts have been proposed to describe and explain the UX in games. Clearly, there is no one concept alone, but rather a wide and multidimensional array of psychologically relevant subcomponents that can capture the experiential richness provided by digital games. PIFF^2 provides one way of integrating such subcomponents into a single framework. Although it is based on the wider concepts of presence, involvement, and flow, PIFF^2 aims at understanding the subcomponents of "being there" and "optimal experience", for example, when playing games. Theoretically PIFF^2 is founded on previous studies conducted in the field of game research, while it takes into consideration the way the game content, that is, fundamental game components (i.e., the mechanics, the narrative, and the interface) orient the basic psychological base. Methodologically it is based on a large multivariate data set that is psychometrically analyzed in order to establish a reliable and valid set of subcomponents. These analyses have provided 15 subcomponents for analyzing the UX in games. These subcomponents disclose the content, quality, meaning, value, intensity, and extensity of the UX.

It was shown here how PIFF^2 can be utilized to analyze the UX in a group and individual contexts. Because in PIFF^2 gamers are considered to be in a game world instead of merely using a game, this framework enables consideration of a broad range of psychological phenomena occurring in games. This is beneficial for basic research in games. As it was shown in the two cases presented, PIFF^2 metrics can be incorporated into different phases of the game development cycle. In the concept and prototyping phases, a multidimensional framework will be helpful in determining the desired psychological attributes for the UX. Designers can use the psychological information as inspiration and support for their own thoughts when creating new and added value for their games. In the production phase, quality assurance professionals and those evaluating beta versions of the games appreciate efficient, validated and reliable tools when evaluating the UX alongside game usability.

Although EVEQ-GP seems to work well in the research settings, future work will involve condensing it into a more convenient tool to be used in various experimental settings. It will then be used to collect multicultural data to support the current framework. The use of the individual PIFF^2 subcomponents for the study of specific game design problems will also be considered in more detail. This will include studying the relationships between different PIFF^2 subcomponents and the game components. In future we will deepen the social and story-related subcomponents of the PIFF^2 in order to deal with socially rich game contents, such as massively multiplayer online role-playing games. The current multidimensional structure of PIFF^2 provides a firm foundation for these future goals.

Acknowledgments We thank prof. Takashi Kawai, Antti Hulsi, Heikki Särkelä, Jeppe Komulainen, Miikka Lehtonen, Maija Pekkola, Jaakko Sipari and Jari Lipsanen for help in collecting and analyzing the data and sharing thoughts. This work has been supported by the User Centered Information Technology graduate school, Oskar Öflund's Foundation and the Kone Foundation. The work in this edition has been supported by the Emil Aaltonen's Foundation and Ella and Georg Ehrnrooth's Foundation.

Appendix A: The Final PFA of the Presence and Involvement Measurement Model (Table A.1)

Table A.1 Total variance explained

Factor	Initial eigenvalues			Extraction sums of squared loadings			Rotation
	Total	% of variance	Cumulative %	Total	% of variance	Cumulative %	Total
Role engagement	19,650	23,674	23,674	19,125	23,042	23,042	9,382
Attention	6,189	7,456	31,130	5,657	6,816	29,858	8,350
Interest	3,394	4,089	35,220	2,811	3,387	33,245	4,235
Importance	2,715	3,271	38,491	2,204	2,646	35,900	10,179
Co-presence	2,025	2,439	40,930	1,496	1,803	37,703	11,823
Interaction	1,803	2,172	43,103	1,193	1,438	39,141	5,613
Arousal	1,782	2,148	45,250	1,147	1,382	40,523	4,498
Physical presence	1,485	1,789	47,040	0.954	1,150	41,673	11,537

Extraction method: principal axis factoring

Appendix B: The Final PFA of the Flow Measurement Model (Table A.2)

Table A.2 Total variance explained

Factor	Initial eigenvalues			Extraction sums of squared loadings			Rotation
	Total	% of variance	Cumulative %	Total	% of variance	Cumulative %	Total
Valence	13,279	23,713	23,713	12,762	22,788	22,788	7,543
Impressiveness	4,055	7,241	30,955	3,458	6,175	28,963	4,573
Competence	2,540	4,535	35,490	2,020	3,608	32,571	7,453
Challenge	2,013	3,594	39,084	1,445	2,581	35,152	3,272
Enjoyment	1,888	3,371	42,454	1,261	2,252	37,404	4,848
Playfulness	1,695	3,027	45,481	1,140	2,036	39,440	6,707
Control	1,627	2,906	48,387	1,041	1,860	41,299	4,628

Extraction method: principal axis factoring

References

Atkinson JW (1964) An introduction to motivation. D. Van Nostrand Company, New York

Brennan L, Mavondo F (2000) Involvement: an unfinished story? Proceedings of ANZMAZ 2000, pp 132–137

Brown E, Cairns P (2004) A grounded investigation of game immersion. Proceedings of CHI 2004, ACM, pp 1297–1300

Counter-Strike: Source (2004). http://store.steampowered.com/app/240/. Accessed 22 March 2009

Csikszentmihalyi M (1975) Beyond boredom and anxiety. Jossey-Bass, San Francisco

Davis JP, Steury K, Pagulayan R (2005) A survey method for assessing perceptions of a game: the consumer playtest in game design. Game Studies 5

Della Fave A, Massimini F (1988) Modernization and the changing context of flow in work and leisure. In: Csikszentmihalyi I, Csikszentmihalyi M (eds) Optimal experience: psychological studies of flow in consciousness. Cambridge University Press, Cambridge

Ducheneaut N, Yee N, Nickell E, Moore RJ (2006) Alone together? Exploring the social dynamics of massively multiplayer online games. Proceedings of CHI 2006. ACM, New York, pp 407–416

Ermi L, Mäyrä F (2005) Fundamental components of the gameplay experience: analysing immersion. Proceedings of DiGRA 2005

Fontaine G (1992) The experience of a sense of presence in intercultural and international encounters. Presence: Teleoper Virtual Environ 1:482–490

Ghani JA, Deshpande SP (1994) Task characteristics and the experience of optimal flow in human-computer interaction. J Psychol 128:381–391

Half-Life 2 (2004) http://www.half-life.com/overview.html. Accessed 22 March 2009

Hilgard ER (1980) The trilogy of mind: cognition, affection, and conation. J Hist Behav Sci 16:107–117

Hunicke R, LeBlanc M, Zubek R (2004) MDA: a formal approach to game design and game research. Proceedings of AAAI workshop on challenges in game AI, p 4

IJsselsteijn W, de Kort Y, Poels K, Jurgelionis A, Bellotti F (2007) Characterising and measuring user experiences in digital games. Proceedings of ACE 2007

ISO 9241-210:2008 (2008) Ergonomics of human system interaction—part 210: human-centred design for interactive systems (formerly known as 13407). International Standardization Organization (ISO)

James W (1890) The principles of psychology. H. Holt and company, Cambridge

Jennett C, Cox AL, Cairns P, Dhoparee S, Epps A, Tijs T, Walton A (2008) Measuring and defining the experience of immersion in games. Int J Hum Comput Stud 66:641–661

Kim T, Biocca F (1997) Telepresence via television: two dimensions of telepresence may have different connections to memory and persuasion. J Comput Mediat Commun 3

Komulainen J, Takatalo J, Lehtonen M, Nyman G (2008) Psychologically structured approach to user experience in games. Proceedings of NordiCHI 2008. ACM, New York, pp 487–490

Lazarus RS (1991a) Cognition and motivation in emotion. Am Psychol 46:352–367

Lazarus RS (1991b) Progress on a cognitive-motivational-relational theory of emotion. Am Psychol 46:819–834

Lazzaro N (2004) Why we play games: four keys to more emotion without story. http://www.xeodesign.com/whyweplaygames/xeodesign_whyweplaygames.pdf. Accessed November 2007

Lessiter J, Freeman J, Keogh E, Davidoff J (2001) A cross-media presence questionnaire: the ITC-sense of presence inventory. Presence: Teleoper Virtual Environ 10:282–297

Lombard M, Ditton T (1997) At the heart of it all: the concept of presence. J Comput Mediat Commun 3:20

Lombard M, Ditton TB, Crane D, Davis B (2000) Measuring presence: a literature-based approach to the development of a standardized paper-and-pencil instrument. Proceedings of presence 2000

Lombard M, Jones MT (2007) Identifying the (tele) presence literature. PsychNol J 5:197–206

Lubart TI, Getz I (1998) The influence of heuristics on psychological science: a case study of research on creativity. J Theory Soc Behav 28:435–457

Mayer JD (2001) Primary divisions of personality and their scientific contributions: from the trilogy-of-mind to the systems set. J Theory Soc Behav 31:449–477

McMahan A (2003) Immersion, engagement and presence: a method for analyzing 3-D video games. In: Wolf MJP, Perron B (eds) The video game theory reader. Routledge, New York

McQuarrie EF, Munson JM (1992) A revised product involvement inventory: improved usability and validity. Adv Consum Res 19:108–115

Mehrabian A, Russell JA (1974) An approach to environmental psychology. MIT Press. Cambridge

Metacritic.com (2009) http://www.metacritic.com/games/. Accessed 22 March 2009

Nakatsu R, Rauterberg M, Vorderer P (2005) A new framework for entertainment computing: from passive to active experience. Proceedings of ICEC 2005, IFIP, pp 1–12

Novak TP, Hoffman DL, Yung YF (2000) Measuring the customer experience in online environments: a structural modeling approach. Marketing Sci 19:22–42

Pagulayan RJ, Keeker K, Wixon D, Romero RL, Fuller T (2003) User-centered design in games. In: Jacko JA, Sears A (eds) The human-computer interaction handbook: fundamentals, evolving technologies and emerging applications. Human Factors and Ergonomics Society, Hillsdale

Pinchbeck D, Stevens B (2005) Schemata, narrative and presence. Proceedings of presence 2005, pp 221–226

Poels K, de Kort YAW, IJsselsteijnWA (2007) "It is always a lot of fun!" Exploring dimensions of digital game experience using focus group methodology. Proceedings of FuturePlay 2007, pp 83–89

Portal (2007) http://orange.half-life2.com/portal.html. Accessed 22 March 2009

Rettie R (2001) An exploration of flow during Internet use. Internet Res.: Electron Netw Appl Policy 11:103–113

Roser C (1990) Involvement, attention and perceptions of message relevance in the response to persuasive appeals. Commun Res 17:571

110 J. Takatalo et al.

Rothschild ML (1984) Perspectives on involvement: current problems and future directions. Adv Consum Res 11:216–217

Rust J, Golombok S (1999) Modern psychometrics: the science of psychological assessment. Routledge, London

Ryan R, Rigby C, Przybylski A (2006) The motivational pull of video games: a self-determination theory approach. Motiv Emot 30:344–360

Särkelä H, Takatalo J, Komulainen J, Nyman G, Häkkinen J (2004) Attitudes to new technology and experiential dimensions of two different digital games. Proceedings of NordiCHI 2004. ACM, New York, pp 349–352

Schiefele U (1991) Interest, learning, and motivation. Educ Psychol 26:299–323

Schubert T, Friedmann F, Regenbrecht H (2001) The experience of presence: factor analytic insights. Presence: Teleoper Virtual Environ 10:266–281

Schuemie MJ, van der Straaten P, Krijn M, van der Mast CAPG (2001) Research on presence in virtual reality: a survey. CyberPsychol Behav 4:183–201

Sherry JL, Lucas K, Greenberg BS, Lachlan K (2006) Video game uses and gratifications as predictors of use and game preference. In: Vorderer P, Bryant J (eds) Playing video games: motives, responses, and consequences. Lawrence Erlbaum, Mahawa

Sweetser P, Johnson D (2004) Player-centred game environments: assessing player opinions, experiences and issues. Proceedings of ICEC 2004. Springer, pp 321–332

Sweetser P, Wyeth P (2005) GameFlow: a model for evaluating player enjoyment in games. Computers in Entertainment 3: Article 3a

Tabachnick BG, Fidell LS (2001) Using multivariate statistics. Allyn & Bacon, Needham Heights

Takatalo J (2011) Psychologically-based and content-oriented experience in entertainment virtual environments. Doctoral dissertation, University of Helsinki, Unigrafia

Takatalo J, Häkkinen J, Särkelä H, Komulainen J, Nyman G (2004) The experiential dimensions of two different digital games. Proceeding of Presence 2004, UPV, pp 274–278

Takatalo J, Häkkinen J, Kaistinen J, Komulainen J, Särkelä H, Nyman G (2006a) Adaptation into a game: involvement and presence in four different PC-games. Proceeding of FuturePlay 2006

Takatalo J, Häkkinen J, Särkelä H, Komulainen J, Nyman G (2006b) Involvement and presence in digital gaming. Proceedings of NordiCHI 2006, ACM Press, Norway, pp 393–396

Takatalo J, Häkkinen J, Kaistinen J, Nyman G (2010) User experience in digital games: differences between laboratory and home. Simulat Gaming 42:657–674

Takatalo J, Kawai T, Kaistinen J, Nyman G, Häkkinen J (2011) User experience in 3D stereoscopic games. Media Psychol 14:387–414

Tarkkonen L, Vehkalahti K (2005) Measurement errors in multivariate measurement scales. J Multivar Anal 96:172–189

Usoh M, Catena E, Arman S, Slater M (2000) Using presence questionnaires in reality. Presence: Teleoper Virtual Environ 9:497–503

Vehkalahti K, Puntanen S, Tarkkonen L (2006) Estimation of reliability: A better alternative for Cronbach's alpha. Reports on Mathematics, Preprint 430, Department of Mathematics and Statistics, University of Helsinki, Finland. http://mathstat.helsinki.fi/reports/Preprint430.pdf. Accessed March 2009

Vehkalahti K, Puntanen S, Tarkkonen L (2009) Implications of dimensionality on measurement reliability. In: Schipp B, Kräer W (eds) Statistical inference, econometric analysis and matrix algebra. Springer

Webster J, Martocchio JJ (1992) Microcomputer playfulness: development of a measure with workplace implications. MIS Quart 16:201–226

Winn BM (2008) The design, play and experience framework. In: Ferdig RE (ed) Handbook of research on effective electronic gaming in education. Information Science Reference, Hershey

Wirth W, Hartmann T, Böcking S, Vorderer P, Klimmt C, Schramm H, et al. (2007) A process model of the formation of spatial presence experiences. Media Psychol 9:493–525

Witmer B, Singer M (1998) Measuring presence in virtual environments: a presence questionnaire. Presence: Teleoper Virtual Environ 7:225–240

Wood RTA, Griffiths MD, Chappell D, Davies MNO (2004) The structural characteristics of video games: a psycho-structural analysis. Cyber Psychol Behav 7:1–10

Wundt WM (1897) Outlines of psychology [C.H. Judd, Trans.] http://psychclassics.yorku.ca/Wundt/Outlines/. Accessed April 2002

Zaichkowsky JL (1985) Measuring the involvement construct. J Consum Res 12:341–352

Chapter 6
Evaluating User Experience Factors using Experiments: Expressive Artificial Faces Embedded in Contexts

Michael Lankes, Regina Bernhaupt and Manfred Tscheligi

Abstract There is an ongoing debate on what kind of factors contribute to the general positive user experience (UX) while playing a game. The following chapter introduces an experimental setting to measure UX aroused by facial expression of embodied conversational agents (ECAs). The experimental setup enables to measure the implications of ECAs in three contextual settings called "still," "animated," and "interaction." Within the experiment, artificially generated facial expressions are combined with emotion-eliciting situations and are presented via different presentation platforms. Stimuli (facial expressions/emotion-eliciting situations) are assembled in either consonant (for example, facial expression: "joy," emotion-eliciting situation: "joy") or dissonant (for example, facial expression: "joy," emotion-eliciting situation: "anger") constellations. The contextual setting called "interaction" is derived from the video games domain, granting an interactive experience of a given emotional situation. The aim of the study is to establish a comparative experimental framework to analyze subjects' UX on emotional stimuli in different context dimensions. This comparative experimental framework utilizes theoretical models of emotion theory along with approaches from human–computer interaction to close a gap in the intersection of affective computing and research on facial expressions. Results showed that the interaction situation is rated as providing a better UX, independent of showing consonant or dissonant contextual descriptions. The "still" setting is given a higher UX rating than the "animated" setting.

M. Lankes (✉)
Department of Digital Media, University of Applied Sciences Upper Austria,
Hagenberg, Austria
e-mail: michael.lankes@fh-hagenberg.at

R. Bernhaupt
ICS Group, Institut de Recherche en Informatique de Toulouse (IRIT), Toulouse, France
e-mail: Regina.Bernhaupt@irit.fr

M. Tscheligi
Center for Human-Computer Interaction, Christian Doppler Laboratory "Contextual Interfaces",
Department of Computer Sciences, University of Salzburg, Salzburg, Austria
e-mail: Manfred.Tscheligi@sbg.ac.at

© Springer International Publishing Switzerland 2015
R. Bernhaupt (ed.), *Game User Experience Evaluation,*
Human-Computer Interaction Series, DOI 10.1007/978-3-319-15985-0_6

6.1 Introduction

Various methods and new methodological developments have been proposed to evaluate UX in application domains ranging from UX evaluation of mobile phones (Roto and Rautava 2008) to UX for interactive TV (Bernhaupt et al. 2008b, Pirker et al. 2010) and several others (e.g. Law et al. 2007). Most of them did not take into consideration recent developments in the area of gaming, such as game play between thousands of players, multiplayer audio channels and the use of novel input devices to encourage physical activity (Bernhaupt et al. 2008a). Digital games constitute a tremendously varied set of applications, with a wide range of associated player experiences, defying a one-size-fits-all approach to their conceptualization and measurement. One of the main challenges facing the gaming research community is a lack of a coherent and fine-grained set of methods and tools that enable the measurement of entertainment experiences in a sensitive, reliable, and valid manner. Taking a factor-structure approach to characterize UX, terms like fun, flow, and playability are most often used to explain UX in game design. However, there is an open discussion to include other factors which might have relevance for games. Emotion is often cited as a key element of UX (e.g., Hassenzahl and Tractinsky 2006; Agarwal and Meyer 2009). On the other hand, the quality of the display of emotions portrayed by embodied conversational agents (ECAs) has a relevant influence on the UX (Lee and Marsella 2006; Dimas et al. 2011). The following chapter is looking in detail on the relation of UX and emotions that are expressed by ECAs. It shall provide some insights concerning the relation between emotions displayed in a game (through the characters) in conjunction with emotion-eliciting situations in regard to the UX. Results of this study are a first step in a series of experiments investigating the relationship between UX and interaction with ECAs. The chapter is organized as follows: Based on an overview on currently used models in emotion theory, the usage of emotional (factor) models in games is explained and how the modeling of nonplayer characters (NPCs)—a field of application of ECAs—is representing these emotional (factor) models. It shall be investigated how the display of emotions (still, animated, or interactive) in various contexts (either with a consonant or with a dissonant context description) is affecting the UX (measured with a questionnaire). The section on the experimental study describes in detail three prestudies for selecting stimuli and material followed by the main study on the relation of displaying emotion in games via ECAs and perceived UX. The conclusion shows how the findings can be used in game development in terms of designing positive UX.

6.2 Related Work

Incorporating emotional expressions for NPCs in games is seen as an appropriate way to improve the gamers' experiences. The research area of emotions is a central topic in human–computer interaction and is approached from various perspectives.

Subsequently, some of these perspectives, and their relation to current developments in UX research, are presented. First, we look at how emotions can be integrated, seen either as part of the computing system or as part of the overall UX. Second, we look on how emotions can be measured, and third, we present some related work on how emotions are integrated into ECAs and how we measure the user experiencing in regard to the emotional expressions performed by ECAs in conjunction with emotion-eliciting situations.

6.2.1 General Description on Emotion

The implementation of emotional factors in systems received an increased interest by the human–computer interaction (HCI) community as researchers within this field aim to develop machines that are focused on human needs (Branco 2003). Emotions play a crucial role in our everyday life with computers (Crane et al. 2007) and have a significant impact on UX as they influence actions, expectations, and future evaluations (Picard 1997). Technological advancements enable machines to perceive, interpret, express, and respond to emotional information. Traditionally, emotional factors were neglected as designers focused on usability aspects and developed systems with the aim to increase efficiency of required tasks (Picard et al. 2002). Although it might be argued that machines should be treated as mere tools that do not (or should not) require any emotions, results of Reeves and Nass (2003) showed that people tend to exhibit social and emotional behaviors toward machines. Picard et al. (2002) also note that interaction with machines is emotional even if the system was not designed to incorporate emotional aspects. Users should be enabled to utilize familiar communication mechanisms when interacting with computational systems. The human–machine interaction process should be designed to resemble human interpersonal interactions, in order to rely on skills obtained from human–human communication. Systems get easier to use if the interaction between human–machine is similar to human–human interaction (Bernhaupt et al. 2007a).

When dealing with the various objectives within HCI research in the field of emotion, we can choose from a tremendous amount of research approaches. Mahlke (2005) provides a taxonomy dividing emotion in HCI into affective computing and emotional design. The concept of affective computing postulates to develop systems that are able to perceive the emotional state of the user, interpret the affective state, adapt to the user's state, and generate an expressed emotion (Minge 2005). Emotional design claims that emotion is considered as an important factor of the user's experience with interactive systems and it is aimed to incorporate emotional aspects in the interactive system design process (Norman 2002). From the perspective of UX research, emotions are investigated to understand their role as antecedent, as a consequence and a mediator of technology use (Hassenzahl and Tractinsky 2006). Researchers in the field of UX evaluation thus try to concentrate on integrating emotional processes of the UX into the evaluation procedure of the interactive systems.

Our experiment addresses the factor emotion concerning UX by raising the questions how emotional stimuli (facial expressions by ECAs and emotion-eliciting situations) in interactive system affect the (more general) UX? Concerning the factor emotion, there are two major research foci: the assessment of emotional dispositions aroused by games and the incorporation of emotion into the game world (see the following two sections).

6.2.2 Games and User Experience

Several tools are available to investigate the factor emotion: the Self Assessment Mannequin (SAM) (Fischer et al. 2002), Emoticons (Desmet and Hekkert 2002), or Affective Grid (Russell and Fernandez-Dols 1997) are just a few examples. Until now, no commonly accepted method for measuring emotions is available.

Ravaja et al. (2006) presented 37 subjects different types of computer games (Tetris, James Bond, Nightfire, and others). To measure emotional response patterns they employed categorical (fear, joy, etc.) and dimensional measurement methods (arousal and valence dimensions). They conclude that different types of games elicit different types of emotional dispositions. Furthermore, the researchers believe that developers will increase the commercial success of a game by incorporating emotional aspects while testing different computer game concepts. Pleasant emotional episodes during game play are deemed to be an indicator to provide positive (and desirable) UX (Ermi and Mäyrä 2005).

To understand the overall UX, we decided to focus on a general perception instead of only looking at the elicited emotion. UX in games is evaluated using a large variety of approaches (Fierly and Engl 2010) ranging from questionnaires to physical measurements (Mandryk et al. 2006, Drachen et al. 2010). Nacke and Lindley (2008), for instance, investigated flow in first-person shooters. They carried out a study based on three Half-Life two mods using subjective and objective measures to investigate different traits of gameplay experience. According to the authors the method employed shows the potential for providing real-time emotional profiles of gameplay.

As we wanted to have a simple and flexible to use measurement, we decided to measure UX with the AttrakDiff questionnaire (www.attrakdiff.de) that has been used in various studies to investigate pragmatic and hedonic quality of users interacting with a system. The AttrakDiff questionnaire was developed to measure implications of attractiveness of a product. Users indicate their impression of a given product by bipolar terms that reflect four dimensions. The first dimensions, the pragmatic quality (PQ), describes traditional usability aspects, while the dimension Hedonic Quality-Stimulation (HQ-S) refers to the need of people for further development concerning themselves. By supporting this aspect, products can offer new insights and interesting experiences. Hedonic Quality-Identification (HQ-I) allows to measure the amount of identification a user has toward a product. Pragmatic and hedonic dimensions are independent from each other and share a balanced impact on the overall judgment. The two aspects contribute equally to the overall judgment of the situation/product and is referred to as hedonic quality (HQ). Attractiveness (ATT) resembles an overall judgment based on the perceived quality.

6.2.3 Embodied Conversational Agents

According to Bartneck (2000), computer games were one of the first applications that incorporated interactive virtual characters. One main driving force in the games industry is innovation in computer technology, which enables the development of more visually elaborated game entities (here: characters). As video game systems have become more powerful from a technical point of perspective, the gaming community has demanded games that push the technical capabilities of the platforms (Pruett 2008). At the beginning of video game, history game elements were displayed as very abstract and simple forms, while nowadays players are confronted with rather highly realistic virtual actors inhabiting complex virtual worlds. A lot of effort is put in the creation of NPCs by game companies. NPCs can include capabilities of verbal and nonverbal communication and may aid the player in a gaming situation. Players may encounter NPCs as enemies that try to interfere to reach game goals, or as characters that serve them as tutors or supporters. Isbister introduces in her book "Better Game Characters by Design" (Isbister 2006) a classification of NPCs based on their social roles within the game.

NPCs can be seen as a field of application regarding ECAs. In general terms, an ECA can be understood as a specific type of agent whose behaviors are executed by some type of perceivable digital representation (Bailenson 2008). Lieberman (1997) describes agents, in contrast to traditional interfaces, as any program that serves as an assistant or helper to aid users during the interaction process. Bates (1994) adds emotional aspects when defining ECAs. Nonverbal signals form an essential part in the communication process, which incorporate the portraying of emotional dispositions via facial expressions, gestures, voice, etc. With the implementation of emotional aspects, agents are more attractive to users because they communicate in ways we are used to (Elliott and Brzezinski 1998). Agents containing knowledge about the conversational process and capabilities to perceive and express emotional signals can be summarized under the term ECAs. They are characters that visually incorporate, or embody, knowledge about the conversational process (Prendinger and Ishizuka 2004). ECAs are virtual humans able to perform conversations with humans by both understanding and producing speech and nonverbal signals (Cassell 2008). They form a type of multimodal interface where the modalities are the natural communication channels of human conversation. The visual representation of ECAs of interacting is intrinsic to its function, meaning that visual information (for example, display of facial expressions) is crucial in the process (Bickmore and Cassell 2001). Nonverbal channels are necessary for both conveying information and regulating the communication process (Bickmore and Cassell 2001). They can be utilized to provide social cues as attentiveness, positive affect, and attraction. Nonverbal expressions also play an important role in regard to emotional contagion, which is the process through which a person's emotional state is in influenced by other people's emotions (Dimas et al. 2011). For investigating the effect of displayed emotions on the users (players) experience, the definition by Mancini et al. (2004, p. 1) shall serve as the basis: "ECAs are virtual embodied representations of humans that communicate multimodal with the user (or other agents) through voice, facial expression, gaze, gesture, and body movement."

6.2.4   Facial Expressions performed by Embodied Conversational Agents

Emotion theory offers a variety of approaches including perspectives of social constructivism, cognition, or theories based on the work of William James or Charles Darwin (Cornelius 1996). The "Darwinian approach" focuses on facial expressions and propagates a limited number of basic, fundamental, or discrete emotions that are directly linked to the motivational system (Scherer et al. 2004). Followers of this tradition assume that specific eliciting conditions would automatically trigger a pattern of reactions such as peripheral physiological responses. It is postulated that mechanisms of emotion mixing or blending occur, which lead to a great variability of facial expressions. Russell and Fernandez-Dols (1997) summarized the discrete emotion approach to outline basic assumptions. First, there is a small set of basic (or fundamental) emotions that are genetically determined and discrete. Each of these emotional states is composed of behavioral patterns like the portrayal of specific facial expressions. The encoding and decoding of emotional signals developed based on adoption processes. States that are not linked to facial signals are not considered as basic emotions. Evidence is present for the basic emotions happiness, surprise, anger, contempt (some uncertainty), disgust, sadness, and fear. These emotions are recognized by all humans (innate) independent from their cultural background. Emotions that share nonfundamental states are considered to be blends (mixtures) of basic emotions. Cultural restrictions may inhibit or mask certain behavioral patterns called display rules.

Based on these assumptions, Ekman and Friesen (1972) developed Facial Action Coding System (FACS). It serves as a high-level description of motions by feature points (Jaimes and Sebe 2007). Each facial muscle is assigned a numeric value that is modified when muscles move. Thus, facial expressions could be synthesized by relating to FACS codes. FACS allows measuring facial expressions objectively, which enables the synthesis of specific expressions by applying the required FACS codes. Movement of individual facial muscles sections lead to observable alternations within the overall appearance of the face. Fernandez-Dols and Carroll (1997) emphasized the importance of context, claiming that the perception of emotional signals is significantly influenced by situational factors and vice versa. Wallbott (1990) also supports this position by noting that subjects were confronted with isolated stimuli to indicate their perception of the presented emotion. He propagated the explicit incorporation of context-related information in the investigation of facial expression. Without context, subjects are forced to simulate (or construct) the missing information, which inevitably will lead to invalid research results. According to Wallbott (1990), three factors are relevant when judging the emotional quality: the stimulus (for example, photos showing facial expressions), the background (or context), and the emotional disposition of the observer. Contextual aspects are not only embedded in emotions, but also the cause for emotional dispositions. Context in facial expression can be subdivided into a situation-related context (modification of the current emotion), a comparative context (the relation of one nonverbal communication channel between others), the static context (captured via photos), and the dynamic context (involved channels in a given time frame).

To summarize the findings of Wallbott (1990), person-related aspects (here: facial expressions) have more influence on emotion judgments than situational components. However, the analyzed data revealed that (although visual stimuli are dominating the perception) descriptions of emotion-eliciting situations will gain importance if the constellation of stimuli is dissonant. Furthermore, subjects employ different strategies when being confronted with different types of stimuli constellations. Person-related aspects do not completely dominate situational factors, as they are always integrated into the judgment of emotional stimuli. An important factor that determines the importance of components is the type of presentation medium. The increase of visualization in regard to situational aspects leads to a shift of dominance. The more visualized a situation is presented, the more it will influence the judgment on emotion. Wallbott (1990) assumes that dynamic stimuli material (descriptions of emotion-eliciting situations) in "still" settings (presentation of facial expressions via film clips) grants more clear information on a given situation than static presentations (presentation of facial expressions via photos).

The following proposal for evaluating UX in the context of ECAs will build on these findings as it tries to extend the framework by employing a new (interactive) presentation medium. The relative importance of information channels shall not be addressed, but a novel experimental setting to investigate the perceived UX in regard to facial expressions and their relation to contextual aspects shall be presented. The introduced theoretical considerations on emotion should serve as a foundation, as well as to provide some insights into this multidimensional research topic. It should have been pointed out that situational aspects have to be considered when investigating the perception of facial expressions as they determine the quality of the interpretation process.

6.3   Evaluation

The goal of this experiment was to understand the influence of emotional facial expressions of ECAs and descriptions of emotion-eliciting situations in three interaction conditions (still, animated, or interactive) on the UX. We see UX as a concept that is best described as a property of the human interacting with the game. The overall UX during game play is consisting of some key components. Emotions are the most prominent component together with immersion, playability, or flow. As we only wanted to understand how changes in the emotional expression of an ECA and emotion-eliciting situations might influence the general perception, we decided to focus on a general measurement of UX, based on the AttrakDiff questionnaire.

6.3.1 Methodological Considerations

To investigate UX in games, a set of methods has been developed. Following traditional HCI approaches of classifying evaluation, methods can be grouped in expert- and user-oriented evaluations (Dix et al. 2004), other classifications are based on development cycles or more social science-oriented approaches (Bernhaupt et al. 2007b). How emotional expressions of ECAs and emotion-eliciting situations affect the UX in a game can be evaluated using several of these methods. But what the relationship between these methodologies is stays rather unclear. To understand the influence of emotional expressions of ECAs and the influence of emotion-eliciting' situations on UX, a more rigid approach is necessary. An experiment (including three prestudies) was set up to investigate the relationship between emotional expressions of ECAs and emotion-eliciting situations in interactive settings compared to still and animated settings. The main study investigates how a given emotional facial expression and an emotion-eliciting situation combined in either a consonant (for example, facial expression: "joy," emotion-eliciting situation: "joy") or a dissonant (for example, facial expression: "joy," emotion-eliciting situation: "anger") constellations presented in either a still, animated or an interactive format is influencing the overall UX. The goal was to investigate the influences on the overall UX to understand how the design of ECAs influences the game play.

6.3.2 Prestudy 1: Evaluation of Emotion-Eliciting Situations

The goal of prestudy 1 was to identify and validate emotion-eliciting situations. The purpose was to identify emotion-eliciting situations with "pure" emotions (weak or no presence of other emotions) and high intensity that will be utilized in the main study. As emotion descriptions set up by the researchers influence heavily the outcome (Wallbott 1990, p. 37), a categorized and standardized emotion-eliciting situation experienced in real life was used. Projects (for example, Summerfield and Green 1986, Scherer et al. 2004) were carried out for years in different cultures to identify emotion-eliciting situations that are culturally independent from their meaning. The "International Survey on Emotion Antecedents And Reactions" (IS-EAR) database (ISEAR 2008), which was made freely available for researchers interested in this field, contains data files and explanations for a major crossculturally comparative study on the cognitive antecedents of emotion (based on appraisal notions) and the reaction patterns reported for seven basic emotions (joy, fear, anger, sadness, disgust, shame, and guilt) by close to 3000 respondents in 37 countries.

We used 200 randomly chosen database entries as a basis and then removed descriptions that did not refer to the emotion categories of Summerfield and Green (1986). Within prestudy 1, the applicable descriptions were filtered using three criteria. Criterion 1 identify the dominating emotions by analyzing the intensity of all six basic emotions. The second criterion should reveal the presence of "pure" (one emotion present) and "blended" (mixture of emotions) emotions, as the questionnaire allowed multiple choice answers. Only pure emotions are considered applicable to the main experiment. The purpose of criterion 3 is to filter out pure emotions that have a fairly low intensity. Descriptions that are employed in the main experiment have to fulfill all three criteria.

Thirty participants (15 male, 15 female) aged 22 to 61 took part in the study. To validate the experimental descriptions based on the three criteria, a simple questionnaire was used. Participants rated the evoked emotion (joy, fear, anger, sadness, disgust, and surprise) and the dominance for each description (scale from zero to eight [emotion not present at all, emotion intensively present]). Based on the ratings of the participants, 11 descriptions are applicable for the main experiment. For criteria 1, the dominating emotion was analyzed (see Table 6.1), followed by criteria 3 selecting only emotion-eliciting situations that were rated on average higher than 4.75 (on the scale from zero to eight) and finally excluding blended emotions (ratings of two emotions that were higher than two on average).

Based on these criteria, finally 11 situations were showing pure emotions. For the following prestudies, we used two situations for each of the four emotions from the

Table 6.1 Selection of stimulus material based on pre-study 1, Critera 1. The mean values are shown for each emotion type

Stimulus	Joy	Fear	Anger	Sadness	Disgust	Surprise	Dominance
Aa1	5.76	0.76	0.00	0.10	0.06	1.26	Joy
Aa4	7.10	0.00	0.00	0.00	0.00	0.17	Joy
Ab1	6.16	0.00	0.00	0.00	0.00	0.93	Joy
Ab3	7.20	0.00	0.00	0.00	0.00	0.26	Joy
Bb1	0.00	0.86	0.26	4.76	0.06	1.73	Sadness
Bb2	0.00	0.13	1.13	7.33	0.00	0.43	Sadness
Bb3	0.00	0.33	0.63	7.50	0.00	0.80	Sadness
Bb4	0.00	0.03	0.66	7.26	0.00	0.33	Sadness
Ca4	0.06	3.40	0.00	0.80	0.23	1.86	Fear
Cb1	0.30	4.90	0.26	0.00	0.00	0.10	Fear
Cb3	0.00	6.66	0.86	0.13	0.13	1.33	Fear
Da1	0.00	0.03	5.46	0.63	0.00	1.16	Anger
Da2	0.20	0.00	3.83	0.93	0.96	1.00	Anger
Da4	0.00	0.33	6.40	0.76	0.06	1.20	Anger
Db1	0.00	0.03	6.20	0.93	0.00	1.13	Anger
Db4	0.00	0.00	6.73	0.80	1.66	0.70	Anger

Table 6.2 Descriptions selected based on prestudy 1

Stimuli	Description
Aa4	My girlfriend was arriving back from overseas and I picked her up from the airport. She finally appeared from customs and we came into contact again
Ab3	I went back home after a long trip and met beloved people and close friends
Bb3	A close friend was involved in an accident and passed away instantly. He had gone to buy a new car and had asked me to wait at his house so that I could see his new car
Bb4	I hear about the death of somebody I liked very much and I was not present either to see that person or to try to share my emotions with other friends
Cb1	At about midnight I had to go by bike through the city alone. On the whole it was a distance of several kilometers. A car followed me through the streets. Only when I went into a one-way street the car disappeared
Cb3	I was living with my brother and one day he went away on business. I was left alone to look after the house and the property. At night thieves came and wanted to break into the house
Da1	I had arranged with a friend to go with him to the city by car. We had arranged a place where to meet. I was a bit late and my friend had left already. I had no money to go by train. It was very important for me to go to the city
Db1	The headmaster of the job appointment committee in charge explained me that teacher (of the opposite gender) was more suitable for a particular post. I had more years of service than the male/female

category of Summerfield and Green (1986): sadness, joy, anger, and fear. Table 6.2 shows these eight situations that were used in the following steps of the experiment.

6.3.3 Prestudy 2: Evaluation of Artificial Facial Expressions

It proved to be a difficult undertaking to find appropriate stimuli material mainly due to license or quality issues of available virtual actors. Since no appropriate stimuli material was at hand, it was decided to create the actors and facial expressions. Constructing six ECAs performing four basic emotions along with a neutral one leads to a total number of 30 stimuli images.

After selecting the emotion-eliciting situations in prestudy 1, it was necessary to construct and investigate facial expressions performed by the constructed ECAs. The stimuli should be presented to subjects without any additional information and should communicate one of the four chosen basic emotions (joy, fear, anger, and sadness). The constructed expressions should convey pure emotions with a rather high intensity. As in the previous study, participants of prestudy 2 rated stimuli by answering via a multiple-choice questionnaire containing the six basic emotions and were rating the emotional intensity on a scale from zero to eight (emotion not present at all, emotion intensively present).

In contrast to prestudy 1, the questionnaire was not printed out on paper, but was shown via an LCD display to match the presentation as close as possible in regard to the main experiment. Therefore, a tablet PC was utilized in order to resemble study 1 as close as possible and to grant a certain amount of mobility. With the aid of the lime survey or application (Lime 2008), an online questionnaire tool, the questionnaire was set up and images were implemented along with emotion type and intensity scales. The application also enabled the scrambling of picture order. The evaluation of facial expressions is carried out by applying the three criteria from prestudy 2. This step was necessary to verify if constructed facial expressions are perceived as intended.

Thirty participants took part in prestudy 2 (16 male, 14 female), age ranging from 20 to 63. The filling out of the questionnaire via the tablet PC took about 15–20 min. Material was selected based on the same criteria as in prestudy 1. All stimuli were perceived as intended (criterion 1: most intensive emotion), the rates for perceiving blended emotions followed the reported recognition rates of emotions in faces (Ekman and Friesen 1972). For criterion 3, the intensity of the emotion was over 4.75 for all presented stimuli. The constructed material thus fulfilled the intended purpose. Figure 6.1 shows examples of female and male ECAs showing different emotions.

Fig. 6.1 Female and male ECAs showing the emotions joy, sadness, anger and a neutral face

6.3.4 Prestudy 3: Evaluation of Settings and Text Fragments

Prestudy 3 deals with the assessment of virtual settings mainly utilized in interactive condition of the main experiment. The virtual settings should indicate the physical context in which emotion-eliciting situations are embedded. The step of creating virtual settings is necessary as conversations in real life take place in physical contexts. The introduction of a physical context layer may cause unwanted artifacts. The interpretation of facial expressions and emotion-eliciting situations may be influenced by the color of settings. The work of Suk (2006), who investigated emotional responses to color to analyze the relationship between color attribute and emotional dimensions (dimensional approach), helped to overcome this issue. He found out that emotional responses to color vary more strongly with regard to tone than to hue categories. The overall color of settings and its lightness are slightly toned down to avoid affective-related influence. The blue prints for the construction of virtual settings are derived from the situations of study 1. Most descriptions of prestudy 1 indicate a physical context by containing words such as "airport," "home," or "town." We thus constructed eight contextual settings, one airport setting, two town settings, and five home settings for the eight emotion-eliciting situations. Eight settings were available as text (for the still images), and eight virtual settings were additionally constructed for the interactive setting of the main experiment.

Similar to study 1, the fragments of emotion-eliciting situations should be judged by presenting the six basic emotions, and intensity was rated on a scale from 1 to 8. Thirty participants (14 male, 16 female) aged 22–57 took part in the evaluation. The evaluation of text fragments and virtual settings led to a total number of 16 stimuli (eight images of virtual settings plus eight split up emotioneliciting situations). As in prestudy 2, the questionnaire presents stimuli via an LCD display to match the presentation as close as possible in regard to the main experiment. Table 6.3 presents the emotion ratings for the eight text fragments describing the context of the eight emotion-eliciting situations (see again Table 6.2) and the rating of the emotional judgment of the eight virtual scenarios (which should not influence the experiment, thus ratings should be below 2.00 on average).

6.3.5 Experiment: Facial Expression and User Experience

The goal of the main experiment was to evaluate the impact emotion-eliciting situations and facial expressions on the overall UX. We manipulated two conditions: condition one was the influence of a consonant/dissonant contextual descriptions. Condition two was the influence of either a "still" situation (frame), the "animated" (animation clips) situation, or the "interactive" situation (game environment).

The following hypotheses are related to the general research question on how emotional facial expressions of ECAs and emotion-eliciting situations influence the UX:

Table 6.3 Ratings of the stimuli for the emotion eliciting situations and ratings for the virtual settings showing that the design does not influence the emotion elicitation

Stimulus	Joy	Fear	Anger	Sadness	Disgust	Surprise	Stimulus	Joy	Fear	Anger	Sadness	Disgust	Surprise
T_Aa4	6.87	0.40	0.17	0.03	0.70	0.00	V_Aa4	0.53	0.80	0.17	0.63	0.43	0.13
T_Ab3	6.73	0.17	0.20	0.40	1.33	0.20	V_Ab3	1.30	0.23	0.23	0.23	0.63	0.37
T_Bb3	0.80	0.90	0.63	6.57	1.37	0.30	V_Bb3	1.03	0.27	0.07	0.10	0.53	0.10
T_Bb4	0.17	1.03	1.37	6.93	1.37	0.33	V_Bb4	0.37	1.17	0.20	0.33	0.27	0.17
T_Cb1	0.13	5.97	1.23	0.23	0.87	0.27	V_Cb1	1.30	0.23	0.10	0.17	0.77	0.13
T_Cb3	0.10	0.47	5.80	1.27	1.63	0.00	V_Cb3	1.67	0.20	0.17	0.07	0.80	0.10
T_Da1	0.10	0.47	5.80	1.27	1.63	0.00	V_Da1	1.10	0.03	0.23	0.03	0.37	0.03
T_Db1	0.03	0.40	6.83	1.50	1.53	0.83	V_Db1	1.57	0.47	0.23	0.10	1.23	0.27

- (H1) The overall UX in the interactive situation is rated higher than the UX in animation scenario and the still scenario.
- (H2) The animation scenario in terms of UX is rated higher than the still scenario.
- (H3) The perceived UX will be the higher for consonant settings than for settings with dissonant stimuli.

The experiment is based on 576 possible stimuli. Four consonant scenarios presenting the four selected basic emotions (joy, fear, anger, and sadness) and 12 dissonant settings, each performed by one out of six possible virtual actors, embedded in eight different emotion-eliciting situations. Since the experimental setup consists of three different scenarios, 192 constellations have to be multiplied by 3, resulting in 576 stimuli. Out of these 576, six scenarios are randomly chosen for each subject. Subjects have to indicate the perceived UX via the AttrakDiff (Hassenzahl et al. 2003) questionnaire. In order to avoid material effects caused by repeated measurements, items of the AttrakDiff were randomized result in six different versions of the AttrakDiff questionnaire. Furthermore, each participant received the six generated AttrakDiff questionnaires in a randomized order when providing information on their impression concerning UX factors.

For the experiment, each participant was presented three scenarios (still/animated/interactive) two times (one consonant/one discrepant). Each ECA appeared only one time for each participant. Repetition of consonant and dissonant emotion constellations was avoided and none of the emotion-eliciting situations was repeated for a participant. Concerning scenario 1 (still), a picture was shown containing a facial expression performed by a virtual actor (evaluated in prestudy 2), along with descriptions of the emotion-eliciting situations (evaluated in prestudy 1). An image of a virtual setting, referenced to the emotion-eliciting situation, is also displayed in the background. After subjects indicated that they were finished with their observations, the experimenter handed out the AttrakDiff questionnaires. Scenario 2 was structured similar to scenario 1, as facial expressions are presented along with emotion-eliciting situations. In contrast to scenario 1, the faces of virtual actors were animated by performing eye-blinking animations, slight head rotations, and minor changes of emotion intensity to grant a vivid impression.

The emotion-eliciting situations were presented in three information chunks (see study 3) along with an animated background showing one of the eight virtual settings. The animation of background contained short clips with camera tilts. Each sequence played in looped cycles and lasted 20 s. The animation is stopped when participants finished their observation task during the experiment. Scenario 3 involved the assessment of UX in an interactive setting. At the beginning of the experiment, subjects had the possibility to get used to the input controls (Wii-controller) by carrying out a tutorial. The tutorial contained an example scene made up of one ECA and three hotspots conveying dummy information. By performing the basic controls with the Wii-controller, the experimenter showed interaction possibilities. Afterward, participants were asked to maneuver within the scenery by themselves. They were told of the structure of interactive scenes and the purpose of information hotspots. Next, the stimulus was initialized by loading the required scenery.

The scenery contained one ECA showing one out of four basic emotions, and three information hotspots incorporating descriptions of an emotion-eliciting situation divided into three information chunks (study 3). Participants observed the facial expressions and entered hotspot areas to read the situation-related information. As in scenarios 1 and 2, the experimenter handed out the AttrakDiff to subjects after the observation task. Twenty participants took part in the study, 9 female and 11 male aged between 21 and 54 years (M=31.8).

6.4 Results

We present the findings according to the three hypotheses:

(H1) The overall UX in the interactive situation is higher than the UX in animation scenario and the still scenario.

The evaluation of how users experience the various emotional stimuli in the varying conditions showed that the overall UX in the interactive situation is rated at a higher level by users than in the animation scenario and still scenario (see Fig. 6.2). Comparing the overall judgment on the hedonic quality (HQ) of the users with a factor analysis shows that users rate the interactive scenarios presenting emotions as higher (M=0.81, SD=0.95) than for the still (M=0.24, SD=0.78) and the animated scenarios (M=0.29, SD=0.89). The post hoc analysis shows that the HQ is significantly different for the interactive scenario compared to the still scenario (LSD=0.51, $p=0.01$) and the animated scenario (LSD=0.57, $p=0.04$). We

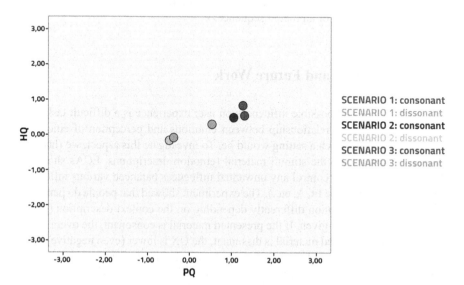

Fig. 6.2 Results of the AttrakDiff: Overview of values concerning the hedonic and pragmatic quality of the three employed scenarios (consonant/dissonant)

can conclude that emotions that are presented in an interactive setting lead to a higher UX.

(H2) The animation scenario in terms of UX is rated higher than the still scenario.

Comparing still and animated scenario, no significant difference could be found. The animated scenario is thus not contributing to a positive UX in the setting. The employment of animation in stimuli did not have the anticipated positive effect on UX.

(H3) The perceived UX will be higher for consonant settings than for settings with dissonant stimuli.

Overall, the perceived UX is rated different for consonant and dissonant settings. The ANOVA performed showed significant differences for consonant and dissonant settings ($F = 13.6$, $p < 0.000$). Looking into the differences in more detail, a second ANOVA showed that all scenarios were rated significantly different in terms of hedonic quality (HQ) ($F = 5.25$, $p < 0.000$), as well as for attractiveness ($F = 9.16$, $p < 0.000$) and pragmatic quality ($F = 14.23$, $p < 0.000$). Figure 6.2 shows these results in more detail: showing higher ratings for consonant scenarios (upper right) and lower ratings for dissonant scenarios (lower left). The interactive scenario is rated best in both conditions.

The type of the presentation medium is heavily influencing the overall UX in which an emotional stimulus is shown (in this case, a facial expressions of an ECA). For research on emotional aspects in psychology, it can be concluded that the context description can have a significant influence on how an emotion is perceived, as well as the scenario the stimuli are presented in. For the games industry, the UX in terms of facial expression of ECAs can be enhanced by providing consonant stimuli (consonant facial expression and description) and allowing direct interaction with the ECA (not only still or animated sequences).

6.5   Conclusions and Future Work

Investigating UX and possible influences on user experience is a difficult task. We were interested in the relationship between emotions and perception of emotions and how the UX for such a setting would be. To investigate this aspect, we (had to) carefully construct(ed) the stimuli material (emotion descriptions, ECAs showing these emotions) and to control any unwanted influences balanced various influencing factors (female/male ECA, etc.). The experiment showed that people do perceive ECAs that display emotion differently depending on the context description (emotion-eliciting situation) given. If the presented material is consonant, the overall UX is higher, if the presented material is dissonant, the UX is lower (even negative). UX can thus be influenced (and can be designed positively in a game) giving congruent information in form of (written) scenario and presented emotions of the ECA. Second, UX is not higher for semi-animated facial expressions. In general, UX is higher for interactive settings. The implications of this first results show that investment in small animations (for improving still images presenting emotions) is not improving the UX, except the user is allowed to interact with the ECA. Creators in the games domain are interested in establishing an entertaining and intense gaming experience for their audience. A lot of production time is spent on creating realistic characters in detailed environments. Most situational aspects are defined without any theoretical foundation by focusing on artistic procedures. The work should show the necessity to relate to character-based communication channels (such as facial expression) with the current event the player confronts.

From the methodological perspective on how to evaluate UX in games, we can summarize that experiments are one way to better understand the more general aspects of UX in games. As UX is consisting of a wide variety of factors, it is difficult to find an experimental setup limiting the possible influencing experimental components. A careful experimental setup (including many prestudies) is thus a long process, and results for influencing factors on UX are not immediately available. In general, experiments are a necessary means to understand the scientific basics of UX, for an industrial context this kind of methodology might not be applicable. On a long-term basis, we see this kind of experiments as a necessary means to lay the foundations for understanding UX.

References

Agarwal A, Meyer A (2009) Beyond usability: evaluating emotional response as an integral part of the user experience. Proceedings of the 27th international conference extended abstracts on Human factors in computing systems (CHI EA '09). ACM, New York, NY, USA, 2919–2930

Bailenson JN (2008) Avatars. http://www.stanford.edu/"bailenso/papers/avatars.pdf. Accessed 22 May 2008

Bartneck C (2000) Affective expressions of machines. Master's Thesis, Stan Ackerman Institute –III, Eindhoven, Netherlands

Bates J (1994) The role of emotion in believable agents. Commun ACM 37(7):122–125

Bernhaupt R, Boldt A, Mirlacher T et al (2007a) Using emotion in games: emotional flowers. Proceedings of ACE 2007. ACM, New York, pp 41–48

Bernhaupt R, Palanque P, Winkler M, Navarre D (2007b) Model-based evaluation: A new way to support usability evaluation of multimodal interactive applications. In: Law E et al. (eds) Maturing usability: quality in software, interaction and value. Springer, London, pp 95–127

Bernhaupt R, Ijsselsteijn W, Mueller F, Tscheligi M, Wixon D (2008a) Evaluating user experiences in games. Proceedings of CHI 2008. ACM, New York, pp 3905–3908

Bernhaupt R, Sloo D, Migos C, Darnell M (2008b) Towards new forms of iTV user experience. Workshop During EuroiTV 2008, 2nd July 2008, Adjunct Proceedings of EuroiTV 2008

Bickmore T, Cassell J (2001) Relational agents: a model and implementation of building user trust. Proceedings of CHI 2001. ACM Press, New York

Branco P (2003) Emotional interaction. Proceedings of CHI 2003. ACM, New York, pp 676–677

Cassell J (2008) Justin cassell: research. http://www.soc.northwestern.edu/justine/jc_research. htm. Accessed 8 May 2008

Cornelius RR (1996) The science of emotion: research and tradition in the psychology of emotions. Prentice Hall, Upper Saddle River

Crane EA, Shami NS, Peter C (2007) Let's get emotional: Emotion research in human computer interaction. Proceedings of CHI 2007. ACM, New York, pp 2101–2104

Desmet P, Hekkert P (2002) Pleasure with products, beyond usability, chapter: the basis of product emotions. Taylor Francis, London, pp 60–68

Dimas J, Pereira G, Santos PA, Prada R, Paiva A (2011) I'm happy if you are happy.: a model for emotional contagion in game characters. Proceedings of the 8th International Conference on Advances in Computer Entertainment Technology, ACE '11. ACM, New York, pp 2:1–2:7

Dix A, Finlay J, Abowd G, Beale R (2004) Human–Computer interaction. Prentice Hall, Essex

Drachen A, Nacke L, Yannakakis G, Pedersen A (2010) Correlation between heart rate, electrodermal activity and player experience in first-person shooter games. Proceedings of the 5th ACM SIGGRAPH Symposium on Video Games (Sandbox '10), Stephen N. Spencer (Ed.). ACM, New York, pp 49–54

Ekman P, Friesen W (1972) Emotion in the human face: guidelines for research and an integration of findings. Pergamon Press, New York

Elliott C, Brzezinski J (1998) Autonomous agents as synthetic characters. AI Mag 19(2):13–30

Ermi L, Mäyrä F (2005) Challenges for pervasive mobile game design: Examining players' emotional responses. Proceedings of ACE 2005. ACM, New York, pp 371–372

Fernandez-Dols JM, Carroll JM (1997) Is the meaning perceived in facial expression independent from its context. In: Russell JA, Fernandez-Dols JM (eds) The psychology of facial expression (studies in emotion and social interaction). Cambridge University Press, New York, pp 275–295

Fierley R, Engl S (2010) User experience methods and games: lessons learned. Proceedings of the 24th BCS Interaction Specialist Group Conference (BCS '10). British Computer Society, Swinton, pp 204–210

Fischer L, Brauns D, Belschak F (2002) Zur Messung von Emotionen in der angewandten Forschung: Analysen mit den SAMs: Self-Assessment-Manikin. Pabst Science Publishers, Göttingen

Hassenzahl M, Tractinsky N (2006) User experience—a research agenda. Behav Inf Technol 25(2):91–97

Hassenzahl M, Burmester M, Koller F (2003) AttrakDiff: Ein Fragebogen zur Messung wahrgenommener hedonischer und pragmatischer Qualität. In: Ziegler J, Szwillus G (eds) Mensch & Computer 2003. Interaktion in Bewegung. BG Teubner, Stuttgart, pp 187–196

ISEAR (2008) http://www.unige.ch/fapse/emotion/databanks/isear.html. Accessed 4 April 2009

Isbister K (2006) Better game characters by design: a psychological approach (the Morgan Kaufmann series in interactive 3d technology). Morgan Kaufmann Publisher, San Francisco

Jaimes A, Sebe N (2007) Multimodal human-computer interaction: a survey. Comput Vis Image Underst 108(1–2):116–134

Law EL, Vermeeren AP, Hassenzahl M, Blythe M (2007) Towards a UX manifesto. Proceedings of the 21st British HCI group annual conference on HCI 2008: people and computers Xxi: Hci. But Not As We know It-Volume 2 (University of Lancaster, United Kingdom, September 03–07, 2007). British Computer Society Conference on Human-Computer Interaction. British Computer Society, Swinton, pp 205–206

Lee J, Marsella S (2006) Nonverbal behavior generator for embodied conversational agents. In: Lecture Notes in Computer Science: Intelligent Virtual Agents. Springer, Berlin, pp 243–255

Lieberman H (1997) Autonomous interface agents. Proceedings of CHI 1997. ACM, New York, pp 67–74

Lime (2008) Lime surveyor. http://www.limesurvey.org. Accessed 27 September 2008

Mahlke S (2005) Studying affect and emotions as important parts of the user experience. http://www.emotion-inhci.net/workshopHCI2005/Mahlke_StudyingAffectAndEmotionsAsImportantPartsOfTheUserExperience.pdf. Accessed 28 February 2008

Mancini M, Hartmann B, Pelachaud C (2004) Non-verbal behaviors expressivity and their representation. http://pfstar.itc.it/public/doc/deliverables/pelachaud_tech_rep3.pdf. Accessed 10 February 2007

Mandryk RL, Atkins MS, Inkpen KM (2006) A continuous and objective evaluation of emotional experience with interactive play environments. Proceedings of CHI 2006. ACM, New York, pp 1027–1036

Minge M (2005) Methoden zur Erhebung emotionaler Aspekte bei der Interaktion mit technischen Systemen. Master's Thesis, FREIE UNIVERSITÄT BERLIN Fachbereich Erziehungswissenschaften und Psychologie

Norman D (2002) Emotion and design: attractive things work better. Interactions 9(4):36–42

Nacke L, Lindley C (2008) Flow and immersion in first-person shooters: measuring the player's gameplay experience. Proceedings of the 2008 Conference on Future Play: Research, Play, Share (Future Play '08). ACM, New York, pp 81–88

Picard RW (1997) Affective computing. MIT Press, Cambridge

Picard RW, Wexelblatt A, Nass CI (2002) Future interfaces: social and emotional. Proceedings of CHI 2002. ACM, New York, pp 698–699

Pirker M, Bernhaupt R, Mirlacher T (2010) Investigating usability and user experience as possible entry barriers for touch interaction in the living room. Proceedings of Euroitv 2010. ACM, pp 145–154

Prendinger H, Ishizuka M (2004) Life-like characters: tools, affective functions, and applications. Springer, Heidelberg

Pruett C (2008) The evolution of videogames. http://bcis.pacificu.edu/journal/2003/07/pruett.php. Accessed 5 April 2008

Ravaja N, Saari T, Turpeinen M, Laarni J, Salminen M, Kivikangas M (2006) Spatial presence and emotions during video game playing: does it matter with whom you play? Presence Teleoperators Virtual Environ 15(4):381–392

Reeves B, Nass C (2003) The media equation. The University of Chicago Press, Chicago

Roto V, Rautava M (2008) User experience elements and brand promise. http://research.nokia.com/files/UXelements-v2.pdf. Accessed 5 April 2009

Russell JA, Fernandez-Dols JM (1997) What does facial expressions mean. In: JA Russell, JM Fernandez-Dols (eds) Psychology of facial expression (studies in emotion and social interaction), chapter introduction. Cambridge University Press, New York, pp 3–31

Scherer KR, Wranik T, Sangsue J et al (2004) Emotions in everyday life: probability of occurrence, risk factors, appraisal and reaction patterns. Soc Sci Inf 43(4):499–570

Suk HJ (2006) Color and emotion: a study on the affective judgment of color across media and in relation to visual stimuli. PhD Thesis, Sozialwissenschaften der Universität, Mannheim

Summerfield A, Green EJ (1986) Experiencing emotion: a cross-cultural study. Cambridge University Press, Cambridge

Wallbott HG (1990) Mimik im Kontext. Verlag für Psychologie, Dr. C. J. Hogrefe, Göttingen

Part II
Automated Methods

Chapter 7
Behavioral Telemetry in Games User Research

Anders Drachen

Abstract Within the past few years the adoption of business analytics has provided powerful new tools to the interactive entertainment industry, giving rise to
the field of game analytics. Where traditionally user testing was limited to samples,
it is today possible to obtain behavioral telemetry data from entire populations of
players, and to map second-by-second interactions in the user testing lab. In this
chapter, the focus is on the behavioral side of user experience in games, rather than
user experience itself. The chapter outlines what behavioral telemetry is and its role
in game user research from an introductory, top-down perspective. The chapter also
introduces data mining as a toolbox that is available for analyzing large or small
telemetry datasets. Finally, several case studies are used to showcase examples of
how behavioral telemetry data can be used to evaluate game design in order to optimize the user experience.

7.1 The Magic Measure of Play Experience

Digital games are complex pieces of software that give rise to a diversity of potential play experiences (PX) (Nacke and Drachen 2011), i.e. user experience
(Hassenzahl and Tractinsky 2006) in the context of play. User experience in games
is affected by a multitude of factors, not the least the psychological makeup of
the player, the specific mechanics and aesthetics of the game, the context of play,
the time and duration and play, etc. (Nacke and Drachen 2011). As other chapters
in this book highlights, this means that it is challenging to know precisely what
the experience of a given user will be when playing a computer game, and at any
given instance of the playing activity. As there are no generally, widely accepted
models for how games create experience, nor for how specific elements of games,
or specific types of games, are related to specific components of game experience,

A. Drachen (✉)
Department of Communication, Aalborg University, A. C. Meyers Vænge 15,
2450 Copenhagen SV, Denmark
e-mail: andersdrachen@gmail.com

The Pagonis Network

developers are therefore faced with a demanding challenge when developing as well as when user-testing games (Pagulayan et al. 2003; Nacke and Drachen 2011; Drachen et al. 2009).

Taking a step back from the general problem of user experience evaluation in games, imagine it was possible to *measure* play experience. With a snap of our fingers, instant and easily interpretable numbers across all possible factors of the user experience were readily available, with a magic aggregate score that allow us to rate the experience of playing the game—for any interval of time—and thus evaluate whether the game generates enjoyable experiences. Such a measure would be incredibly useful, albeit probably not feasible, but unfortunately only solve half of a very complicated problem.

Measuring play experience (whatever it is) in games is an important challenge in advancing the usefulness of game user research methods (Kim et al. 2008; Nacke and Drachen 2011; Isbister and Schaffer 2008); however, from the perspective of industrial game development, such measures are essentially useless unless they can be connected to the game—ideally at highly granular levels so design can be evaluated in detail. Imagine having run a playtest, where after an hour the participants come out and feel energized, happy and report having had a very engaging experience, but where their activities during that hour are effectively a black box because the session was not properly monitored and/or recorded.

Even with a magic PX measurement method providing second-by-second values, this need to be related to the second-by-second behavior of the player—i.e. the interaction between the player and the game. In basic HCI terminology, PX is focused on the user side, not the system side (Dix et al. 2007). To take an example, if running a think-aloud, observational usability test of a game we find that the testers become frustrated, we need to find out why. Traditionally this is done by asking them, but interviewing is a resource-demanding exercise and virtually impossible to perform at the large-scale (unless resources for this are present). Additionally, the information obtained from the testers about why e.g. frustration occurred can be biased, unspecific and difficult to relate to the design of the game (Medlock et al. 2002; Pagulayan et al. 2003; Pagulayan and Keeker 2007; Nacke and Drachen 2011).

This is where game telemetry comes in, or more specifically player behavior telemetry, and the relatively new domain of **game analytics** (Seif El-Nasr et al. 2013). Game analytics has been rapidly adopted in the game industry within the past few years, notably within the mobile and social online segments.

While there is no unified definition of game analytics, the term fundamentally refers to the application of business intelligence processes to the specific context of games. The fundamental goal of game analytics is to inform and support decision-making at all levels and all areas of an organization—from design to programming, marketing to management, art to user research. Depending on how mature a given company's adoption of analytics practices is, the degree of integration of analytics processes can vary across teams or departments.

Game analytics is directed at both the analysis of the *game as a product*, e.g. whether it provides a good user experience (Law et al. 2007; Nacke and Drachen 2011) and the *game as a project*, e.g. the process of developing the game, including comparison with other games (benchmarking). The sources of data being worked with varies immensely, including market data, consumer data, supply chain information, production information and more, but the most widely utilized source of data in game analytics is game telemetry.

Game telemetry is data logged from clients or servers about how players play games, or conversely about how the game client itself responds to player behavior. Another important source of telemetry data is server logs, e.g. from multi-player games and MMOGs (Mellon 2009). The specific type of game telemetry that deals with player behavior is here referred to as behavioral game telemetry (Seif El-Nasr et al. 2013). What behavior telemetry offers is access to objective, real-time data about how people play games, including all actions and interactions taking place.

This means that if we had the magic PX measure, we would be able to pinpoint that at the time when a user or tester experienced X, they were doing Y in the game. For example, if we knew a player was feeling a positive sense of arousal (Ravaja et al. 2006; Mandryk 2008; Nacke 2009) during a specific time interval, e.g. 10 s, and that the player during that interval engaged in four rapid combats against a specific enemy, using a new ability just learned, we know that the combat sequence works as intended for that player (if a positive sense of arousal was the design goal of course).

While Game Analytics and Game User Research are recognized as individual domains of work, there is a large degree of overlap between them as the main focus of much work in Game Analytics is on the players, or users (Seif El-Nasr et al. 2013) (Fig. 7.1). Game Analytics also deals with e.g. project planning and supply chain management, which is outside the traditional domain of Game User Research, and similarly, the deep qualitative studies employed in Game User Research are rarely seen in Game Analytics. The difference nebulous, however, and opinions vary on the issue.

In theory, the combination of player behavior telemetry and PX measures is intuitive to understand the benefits of, but in practice the application of this theory to the reality of game development and game user research, whether in an industry or academic context, is not straight forward (Seif El-Nasr et al. 2013).

In this chapter, the focus is on the telemetry side of the PX-evaluation equation. Enabling the tracking, logging, storage, analysis and visualization of behavioral telemetry in the evaluation of game design, is one of the first steps on the way to merging PX-measures with game design. We will specifically avoid talking about

Fig. 7.1 While Game Analytics and Game User Research are recognized as individual domains of work, there is a large degree of overlap between them as the main focus of much work in Game Analytics is on the players, or users

what PX is in any detail, apart from noting that the goal from the perspective of commercial game development is to design and develop games that people will play, and ideally pay for, irrespective of the type of PX they obtain from the playing activity, and irrespective of how the actual payment is handled, e.g. retail vs. In-App Purchases (IAPs) (Fields and Cotton 2011). This topic is complicated by the fact that players can be valuable to a company along a variety of vectors, e.g. be strong recruiting factor in a MMORPG, and that payment can also occur via advertising of various kinds, serving to keep the game Free-to-Play (F2P), but this is a discussion that will not be covered in further detail here. See e.g. Luton (2013) for an introduction to F2P games and their design, and different monetization strategies. Similarly, Williams (2014, 2015) includes perspective on different ways players can have value to game companies.

The chapter will deliver the following:

- Describing the connection between play experience and player behavior.
- Introduce game analytics and its role in game user research.
- Describe the fundamental approaches used in the game industry when working with behavioral game telemetry.
- Introduce game data mining as the toolbox available for analyzing large-scale behavioral telemetry datasets.
- Walkthrough of case studies where behavioral telemetry has been used to evaluate game design and play experience.

We here adopt a general industry perspective, evaluating different aspects of behavioral game telemetry from the perspective of practical applicability, but will provide references along the way to more theoretical and broader academic work for those readers interested. The chapter is intended as an introduction to behavioral game telemetry work, and thus adopts a top-down view on the topics presented. The references used provide additional insights into specific topics, e.g. datatypes, algorithms, visualizations etc.

The chapter is fully based on previously published knowledge, and a lot of it is available publicly though online sites, articles in open-access or books which can be ordered through any university library. In a few cases research articles in the digital libraries of major publishers are used, however these will similarly be accessible from university libraries.

7.2 Player Behavior and Play Experience

The combination of player behavior telemetry and PX measures is challenging for a number of reasons, one of the obvious ones being that the magic PX measure has not been developed yet. A substantial amount of research has been put into the question of user experience evaluation in games (this book being a prime example), and recent years have seen valuable knowledge emerge on the topic, exploring models for describing PX, and the factors affecting it, as well as practical applications and frameworks, e.g. RITE and TRUE (Medlock et al. 2002; Kim et al. 2008; Isbister and Schaffer 2008). However, there remains many gaps in the knowledge available about how to link PX measures with behavioral game telemetry (i.e. with game design) at the highly granular level that behavioral telemetry can operate at. The game industry has been working with the problem for years (Pagulayan et al. 2003; Southey et al. 2005; DeRosa 2007; Ramero 2008; Kim et al. 2008; Drachen and Canossa 2009; Zoeller 2011), and some work has found that relying on relative simple measures of PX, e.g. a pop-up survey during playtesting asking people to rate their experience along a few carefully chosen parameters (Thompson 2007; Kim et al. 2008; Leone 2012), works fine for getting an overall idea of PX, despite the inherent limits of this kind of measurement strategy. In addition, it is a fast and in a cost-benefit perspective effective way of performing certain types of lab-based playtests (Pagulayan et al. 2003; Marsh et al. 2006; Pagulayan and Medlock 2007; Isbister and Schaffer 2008; Kim et al. 2008; Drachen et al. 2010). However, baring a few papers, online articles and presentations at industry events, there is very little knowledge available on the topic of telemetry-based evaluation, nor on how game telemetry and other user research methods can be merged. The lack of knowledge is partially due to the relative recent introduction of telemetry-based user behavior evaluation, but perhaps more importantly because telemetry data are typically confidential in nature (Drachen et al. 2009; Drachen and Canossa 2011; Weber et al. 2011). That being said, the topic of , merging behavioral telemetry analysis and PX measures is a topic that is seeing some interest in the recent years (Mandryk et al. 2006; Marsh et al. 2006; Kim et al. 2008; Drachen et al. 2010; Canossa et al. 2011), but is still very much in its infancy, and there are very few large-scale studies or – results, or work that tries to investigate behavior and experience across games (Seif El-Nasr et al. 2013; Sifa et al. 2014).

An alternative strategy, instead of tying together behavioral measures and PX measures is to use the behavioral measures to *infer* PX. This approach has been discussed by multiple authors, some of the oldest accounts being Lazzaro and Mellon (2005) and Southey et al. (2005), as well as in game AI research (Yannakakis 2012). Essentially, gameplay metrics do not inform what gender a player has, what kind of experience they get from playing the game, etc.—gameplay metrics cannot provide any contextual data. However, it may be possible to draw inferences about the reasons for observed behavior. For example, if players are observed having trouble progressing through a level in *Halo 2*, and dropping out of the game as a consequence, it could be argued that their PX is negatively affected, and the situation is indicative of a problem needing to be fixed (Thompson 2007; Kim et al. 2008; Romero 2008; Fields and Cotton 2011; Luton 2013; Seif El-Nasr et al. 2013).

Towards this end, Lazzaro and Mellon (2005) proposed the use of "fun meters". These are collections of specifically selected behavioral metrics, which are indicative of whether or not the players are enjoying the game. The gameplay metrics will often be game-specific (but see below). The essence of the argument of Lazzaro and Mellon (2005) is that the experience of the player is having (with the additional social factor) is represented in their behavior. For example, looking at what people spend their money on in *The Sims Online* as an indicator of what entertains them in the game, or evaluating death events to detect situations where players are feeling frustrated (Canossa et al. 2011). Similarly, if it can be observed from behavioral data from a game that a player keeps dying over and over, and spends several minutes in vain trying to progress through a game level, probably that player is not enjoying the experience (Pruett 2011).

The process of ensuring good PX in games was termed "gameplay management" by Southey et al. (2005), who noted that it is difficult to characterize the gameplay management task precisely as it involves human judgment, and enjoyment in a playing experience is essentially impossible to quantify. However, they argue that an integral but complex part of PX is the gameplay offered, highlighting difficulty as one of main features of gameplay that can be evaluated via behavioral telemetry: *"A game that is too hard is frustrating, while too little challenge can be boring. In multi-player games, it is important that the game be fair, offering no player an intrinsic advantage. Internal consistency in the game world is also important. Even in fictional worlds, players expect some sort of logic to apply"* (Southey et al. 2005).

Inferring PX from behavioral telemetry can however be prone to errors, as it is fundamentally not possible to verify whether conclusions drawn from behavioral analysis are correct unless a second measure is employed which maps the player experience, for example using post-session interviews or surveys (Medlock et al. 2002; Pagulayan et al. 2003; Kim et al. 2008) Towards this end, Lazzaro and Mellon (2005) noted that many features in games affect enjoyment (PX), and that each of these needs a "fun meter" (i.e. a data-driven measure). These meters in turn require a data source that is applicable to the over-arching question being asked. Finding the right data source for different measures can be challenging, with two fundamental pathways: **Indirect** (asking players) and **direct** (observing players) (Pagulayan et al. 2003). Lazzaro and Mellon (2005) highlighted that triangulating and correlating between data sources, whether all quantitative or mixed quantitative/qualitative, improves the validity and applicability of results.

Play experience data generated during playtesting or usability testing of games are generally obtained using qualitative or semi-quantitative methods, such as observation, interviews or surveys. Notably attitudinal data (users expressing their opinion about something, e.g. how much fun they are having, which elements of the game that are too hard, etc.) are commonly collected, across any of these methods. (Pagulayan et al. 2003; Pagulayan and Keeker 2007; Isbister and Schaffer 2008; Romero 2008). In comparison, analysis of behavioral telemetry data offers insights into how the users are actually playing the games being tested, but only by inference play experience. As mentioned above, this makes telemetry testing an ideal candidate for triangulation with usability/playtesting.

Towards this end, Kim et al. (2008) and Romero (2008) presented the TRUE-solution of Microsoft Studios Research. The system is capable of recording screen capture, video footage, behavioral and survey-data in one coherent framework, synchronizing the different data streams. The TRUE system uses e.g. small pop-up surveys that activate during timed intervals to quickly assess the play experience of the player, recording simultaneously the position of the player character in the game environment. The fundamental approach of this method has since then been adopted widely among the larger publishers in the game industry, and the triangulation of behavioral telemetry with other measures of user experience or user behavior, has been adopted in academic research as well, e.g. in AI (Drachen et al. 2010; Yannakakis 2012; Drachen and Schubert 2013).

The problem with this approach to measuring PX is that the interaction flow between player and game is interrupted. In addition, the evaluation of play experience is limited to one or a few dimensions, as pop-up surveys need to be kept short to keep the interruption to interaction flow to a minimum. An alternative approach, combining metrics with psycho-physiological measures (Mandryk et al. 2006; Mandryk 2008; Ravaja et al. 2006; Nacke 2009), has been explored and is increasingly being applied in industrial contexts, notably eye-tracking. The approach is promising because psycho-physiological measures can be obtained relatively unobtrusively and at high frequencies (e.g. second-by-second), making it possible to relate PX measures with player behavior. However, in practice, psycho-physiological measures of PX come with a range of challenges, notably the extensive resource demand and requirement of expert knowledge in applying them, which has so far prevented their wide-spread adoption in the game industry and associated academia (Seif El-Nasr et al. 2013).

In summary, the experience from industry-based game user research indicate that in practice, and especially with experience, it is possible to go a long way towards debugging the playing experience of a game just by analyzing behavioral telemetry data. However, the available knowledge also strongly highlights the acute benefits of combining or triangulating methods, e.g. obtaining both a PX measure and behavioral telemetry (Isbister and Schaffer 2008; Kim et al. 2008; Canossa et al. 2011; Drachen and Canossa 2011). Currently all major publishers and development houses in the Western game industry collect, store and analyze telemetry data, and presentations at big industry events like the yearly Game Developers Conference, Casual Connect and the Gaming Analytics Summits indicate that triangulation of methods is becoming commonplace (Ramero 2008; Zoeller 2011; Seif El-Nasr et al. 2013).

7.3 Behavioral Game Telemetry

Game telemetry is more than just quantitative data about player-game interaction (Mellon 2009; Drachen and Canossa 2011).

Fundamentally, telemetry is a term used for any technology that allows measurements to be made over a distance—irrespective of how long that distance is. Common examples include radio wave transmission from a remote sensor or transmission and reception of information via an IP network. Telemetry is generally used to refer to wireless data transfer, but also covers cable-based communication.

From the perspective of the game industry, telemetry is data collected about any process or aspect of game development, including information about the operations of technical infrastructure, game production and –processes, post-launch management of games, quality assurance and perhaps most importantly: behavior of users playing the game.

Game telemetry data are thus the raw units of data that are derived remotely, e.g. from an installed game client. In the case of behavioral data, code embedded in the game client transmits data to a collection server; or the data are collected from game servers (as used in e.g. online multi-player games like *Fragile Alliance, Quake* and *Battlefield*) (Derosa 2007; Kim et al. 2008; Canossa and Drachen 2009). Raw telemetry data can be stored in various database formats, which are ordered in such a way that it is possible to transform the data into various interpretable measures, e.g. average completion time as a function of individual game levels. These are called **game metrics.** Game metrics are interpretable measures of something, whereas telemetry is the raw data that we work with. The term game metrics is often used as a synonym for game telemetry data, but to be precise, metrics represent telemetry data that have been transformed somehow (see below).

As mentioned in the introduction, the vast majority of the work being done in the industry and game research using game metrics has been focused on the users, from the dual perspective of players being:

a) **Customers:** users as sources of revenue, e.g. churn analysis, average revenue per user, micro-transactions/IAPs.
b) **Players:** users who behave in a particular way when playing games (e.g. playtime, time-spent analysis, asset use evaluation, path (trajectory) analysis).

Less emphasis has been placed on game metrics as a source of information on the production process itself, i.e. technical, infrastructure, support and production metrics, although this appears to be changing (Mellon 2009; Seif el-Nasr et al. 2013).

As noted by Drachen et al. (2011), any action the player undertakes while playing can be tracked: every time a chest is opened, a weapon is fired or a level completed, a telemetry tracking system can register where and when that event took place. Behavioral game metrics form the basis for telemetry-driven PX evaluations, forming measures of player behavior, e.g. navigation, item- and ability use—any action the players perform inside the virtual environment of a game (whether 2D or 3D). Another term commonly used for these kinds of game metrics is **gameplay metrics,** denoting that they specifically relate to measures of user behavior. Any measure of player behavior inside the game environment, e.g. object interaction, object trade, navigation, player-player interaction etc., is a gameplay metric.

Gameplay metrics are the most important form of game telemetry when the purpose is to evaluate PX and game design in general (notably for "debugging" the playing experience), but are also furthest from the traditional perspective of the revenue chain in game development, and hence are sometimes under-prioritized in the industry, with some notable exceptions in the AAA sector and F2P (Pagulayan et al. 2003; Pagulayan and Keeker 2007; Isbister and Schaffer 2008; Kim et al. 2008; Drachen and Canossa 2009; Field and Cotton 2011; Luton 2013).

While there are some gameplay metrics that are universally useful to track and analyze in terms of evaluating games—such as time spent playing, session length, inter-session length etc. (see e.g. Fields and Cotton 2011; Luton 2013; Hadiji et al.

2014; Runge et al. 2014)—the choice of which features (behavioral variables) to log and how to log them (e.g. frequency of sampling Southey et al. 2005; Drachen and Canossa 2011; Hadiji et al. 2014; Runge et al. 2014) is highly varied across games and specific features such as whether or not the game features a persistent world, is single- or multiplayer, etc. This makes it challenging to generalize specific solutions across publishers, studios, and games, and it poses two inevitable questions, to which there is no simple answer as they are context dependent: (1) How should we work with the data? (2) What behaviors should we track?

7.4 Working with Behavioral Telemetry

The literature and information available on telemetry-driven (or *data*-driven) analytics from not only games, but also the older and much more mature field of web analytics, supply chain management, insurance, finance and other sectors, shows that there are a number of ways to approach the kind of detailed user behavior analysis that gameplay metrics permit (Davenport and Harris 2007; Davenport 2012; Minelli et al. 2013). Gameplay metrics form the "bread and butter" telemetry data when evaluating game designs, but how do you work with them?

Gameplay metrics form the basic pieces of information for working with telemetry data from a game design angle, and it is often in the gameplay metrics that we find the root causes for observed player behaviors (Kim et al. 2008; Ramero 2008; Zoeller 2011; Drachen et al. 2009; Seif el-Nasr et al. 2013). For example, that a specific level segment is to lethal and causes players to quit the game, that a specific item is not being used by the players, that the Omega Gun is overpowered and unbalances a class in a shooter game; or that aspecific curve is causing too many crashes in a racing game, or that players do not visit an otherwise important quest hub in a role-playing game.

Drachen et al. (2013c) provides an overview of the fundamental approaches to working with behavioral game telemetry that will be described here: The authors, writing from experience with fielding telemetry analysis at IO Interactive and Crystal Dynamics, noted behavioral analysis is typically either performed via **analysis** or **synthesis**—both classic empirical scientific methods. They are different, but in practice this difference can be subtle and they often go hand in hand: **Analysis** is when we break down a complex whole into parts or components. For example, when we break down the action-sequences of the players in a time spent analysis. **Synthesis** is the opposite procedure, i.e. combining separate elements or components in order to form a coherent and complex whole. For example a chart showing the number of daily active users (DAU) is a synthesis of time, number of users, date, etc. The system suggested by Drachen et al. (2013c) provide a structure provides guidance on planning how to answer particular problems—e.g. considering whether a problem is best solved analytically or using simple synthesis, whether we already have an idea about what the answer is and should test it, or not—and so forth.

Both analysis and synthesis can be initiated by fairly open-ended (do our players cheat?) or specific questions (does that player cheat by using the inverse-shield duping method?), roughly correlating with the concepts of explorative vs. hypothesis driven research from scientific theory (Bordens and Abbott 2013). What this means is that the analytical methods we use to find the answers to questions are either of a type where we are looking to confirm some idea we have and are looking for confirmation, or have a pretty good idea about the possible answers (hypothesis-driven); or alternatively more open, where we are not sure what the answer to a given question is, or have a hard time predicting the possible answers (explorative analysis). Both synthesis and analysis can be applied to explorative work (where we look for patterns in data) or hypothesis-driven work (where we have an idea what the answer is and need to confirm or reject the idea). Both types of analysis are in practice often iterative—an analysis may lead to new or more specific questions/problems.

Explorative work is when the possible answers cannot be, or are hard to predict from looking at the game design. For example, finding which set of 2000 virtual items that are the most important drivers for converting non-paying users to paying users in a social online game. Or the most effective build order in an RTS like StarCraft. A common data-driven method for explorative research is the drill-down analysis, where you examine the gameplay metrics data at more and more detailed levels until an answer is found. **Hypothesis**-driven work is when we are looking to confirming conclusions or ideas, or when we can predict the answer. For example, we may think that Zombies are way too powerful on level 10, and perform a statistical analysis in order to confirm this suspicion, finding that either we are right or wrong in our hypothesis (wrong in the case of the only zombie in the level being legless and suffering from bad eyesight).

Alternatively, a hypothesis could state that the amounts of player deaths on a certain map correlates to the perceived difficulty level of the map. Checking metrics data on player death events with feedback from research study participants can either lead to confirmation or rejection of the hypothesis, possibly leading to the formulation of a new hypothesis.

A commonly applied method in game data mining to answer these kinds of questions are prediction analysis—the application of specific algorithms to predict something, e.g. which users that will convert to paying users, or when a person will stop playing (Han et al. 2005; Williams 2014; 2015; Drachen et al. 2013d). In practice, as soon as you move outside of the kind of questions that can be answered with synthesis, a quick analysis or standard algorithms, e.g. "what is the number of active users today?" or "what is the average playtime for level 22?"; you often end up mixing hypothesis-driven and explorative work.

The explorative questions are usually more time-consuming to answer and more often requires analysis than the hypothesis-driven, specific questions, which can more often be handled using synthesis (or very simple statistical analysis) of the relevant data. Purely explorative questions are rare—a game developer usually does not have the luxury of throwing a dataset at some people and tasking them to see what interesting stuff they can find. This is not to say that purely explorative analysis of gameplay metrics data cannot be useful, but it is often a kind of "blue sky research" that companies can have a hard time justifying the expenditure of.

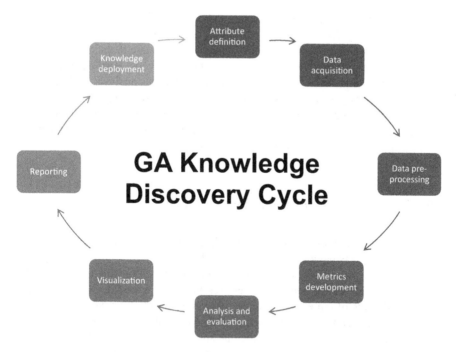

Fig. 7.2 The phases of the standard knowledge discovery process adapted to the context of game analytics. (Modified from Drachen et al. 2013d)

The description of explorative/hypothesis-driven methods is only descriptive in terms of the fundamental approaches to working with behavioral game telemetry. These methods are set in the broader contexts of the game development process, and notably game user research. The reader is referred to (Isbister and Schaffer 2008) for detailed information on this topic, but in brief, the application of behavioral telemetry to solve a problem follows the standard process for knowledge discovery in data (Berry and Linoff 1999; Larose 2004), which refers to the overall process of discovering useful knowledge from data. The knowledge discovery process can briefly be summarized to include the following phases (adopted from Drachen et al. 2013) (Fig. 7.2):

1. **Define objective:** Defining the objective and requirements. Southey et al. (2005) notes that during this phase it is decided metrics to collect and measure. An important step in this phase for behavioral analysis in games is deciding on acceptable values, e.g. it may be the goal that a game should take a maximum of 20 h to play;
2. **Collect data:** Collecting and evaluating the quality of the behavioral telemetry data;
3. **Prepare data:** Preparing data for analysis, selecting cases and features, and finally pre-processing;
4. **Generate model:** Selecting and applying the data mining technique desired and generating a model of the result;

5. **Evaluate result:** Evaluating the result and checking that it reaches the desired objective and finally:
6. **Deploy knowledge:** Deploying the discovered knowledge to the relevant stakeholder, e.g. visualizing the results in a meaningful way to a level designer, in an understandable fashion. Given the results of the metrics analysis, and the goals of the game design, adjustments may need to be made to the game to achieve the goals of the design. Traditionally, this process has been carried out by hand, but with the rise of the Free-to-Play (F2P) genre, semi-automation of this process is seeing increased use (Fields and Cotton 2011).

7.5   Finding the Right Behaviors to Track

One of the key questions when working with game telemetry is deciding what aspects of the player behavior that should be tracked.

It is nigh-on impossible to provide specific guidelines on this topic, because games do not fall within neat design classes but share a vast design space. Additionally, the rate of innovation is high, and would essentially mean that any specific recommendations would risk being outdated by the time this book is printed. According to Drachen et al. (2013), the one approach is to develop frameworks of behaviors to track from the top down, to ensure comprehensive coverage in data collection, and from the core out, starting from the main mechanics driving the PX (for helping inform game design) and monetization (for ensuring financial viability of the game). Another approach dictates to focus initially on features that all games share, or at least those shared within the specific type or genre of games, plus those that relate to the core of your gameplay or business. Logging more data is definitely useful, but it is the core behavioral data that will probably provide the most direct value. There are a specific set of metrics that are usually tracked in F2P games and those adopting IAP-based business models which are also seeing widespread use, for example Daily Active Users and Life Time Value (for an extended introduction please consult: Fields and Cotton 2011; Luton 2013; Seufert 2014).

There is a basic **cost-benefit relationship** in game telemetry: If selected correctly, the first variables will provide a lot of insights into player behavior and system performance, but as more variables is tracked, the return value becomes mainly additional nuance to existing metrics (Drachen et al. 2013).

Given an infinite number of resources, it is possible to track every single user-initiated event, every single time a player moves a tiny fraction in a virtual environment, all the server-side system information, every keystroke, etc.—the bandwidth from the game client to the collection layer may not like it but it is possible (Drachen and Canossa 2011). However, this type of brute-force approach typically leads to very large datasets, which in kind leads to huge resource requirements on the analysis side (Han et al. 2005; Kim et al. 2008; Drachen et al. 2009).

These resources are rarely available in the game industry (or anywhere else), which means that we need another approach: maximizing the bang we get for the buck (Mellon 2009). This means identifying the smallest possible feature set (number of variables) which provides the maximum benefit in terms of actionable insights for design, with the least frequency of recording possible—e.g. we may not need to track every single time someone fires a gun, but perhaps only 1 % of these events.

Another commonly reported problem is that instrumentation of games, i.e. the process on embedding hooks in the games' code which transmits data to a collection server from the game client, usually takes a few tries to get right. Most initial instrumentation of analytics generates false numbers or has gaps in the tracking stream (see e.g. Drachen et al. 2009, for a discussion relating to Tomb Raider: Underworld). Two common reasons for faulty implementations is the lack of database expertise with small and medium-size developers, and perhaps more commonly because games are complex information systems which can have bugs that can corrupt transmitted datasets. This is why data pre-processing is an important step in the GA knowledge discovery cycle (Fig. 7.2).

Identifying the key features that provide the maximal value is a highly game-dependent exercise. Games vary across a range of design gradients, and this means that what works in terms of analytics in one game will not work for all games. For games that share design features, e.g. F2P social online games for *Facebook*, metrics related to the shared features will likely be useful across these games—but not necessarily outside of them.

Gameplay metrics can be divided into three categories, depending on how broadly applicable they are across games:

1. **Generic gameplay metrics:** There are some features that are shared among all games, generally high-level user information such as total playing time, number of times a game has been played, the real-world time that has elapsed from a game was started until it finished, the ratio of players completing the game vs. those who gave up, playing time per level/segment of the game, total number of player actions, etc. These types of gameplay metrics are typically not useful for detailed gameplay analysis, but excellent for aggregated summaries of player activity. These form the starting point for selecting what features to record from the game client (we are here ignoring system telemetry, from servers). These include but are not limited to:

   - Player
   - Timestamps (playtime)
   - Session and inter-session intervals
   - Player location (via IP)
   - What was played (e.g. level 1 and start/completion time for this level)
   - Install language
   - Crashes (did the game client crash and at what point in the game?)
   - Version (or build)
   - Level/game area completed or not
   - The core telemetry data provide the starting point, and we can calculate a lot of useful metrics based on these, for example average session length, average completion time per level, stability (crashes/session) etc. But as mentioned, they do not give us any in-depth evaluation of the design of a game. A typical

addition to this core feature set is hardware information for quality assurance evaluation.

2. **Genre specific gameplay metrics:** Although the term "genre" is nebulous at best within a digital game context, it is however widely used in both industry and academia, to describe sets of games that share specific design features—not fictional setting as in literature. Irrespective of how digital games with shared feature sets are grouped, the advantage in terms of behavior analysis is that these potentially can carry over between games within the group. For example, there are a number of gameplay mechanics shared between *Tomb Raider: Underworld, Just Cause 2* and *Gears of War,* e.g. 3rd person camera, character-driven gameplay, and a mission-based story progression design. As an example, Tychsen and Canossa (2008) defined five categories of gameplay metrics relevant to character-based games like the ones mentioned above:

1. Navigation metrics: Covers navigation of the character in the game environment
2. Interaction metrics: Covers interactions with objects and entities of the game, initiated by the player via the character.
3. Narrative metrics: Covers navigation through a game storyline, for example quest completion data or navigation through story branches.
4. Interface metrics: Covers all interactions with the game interface, either while playing the game or during periods spent interacting with other interfaces of the game (e.g. game setup).
5. Non-player metrics: Covers all behaviors initiated by the game client, not the player, e.g. the actions of NPCs, activation of cut-scenes, or similar.

3. **Game specific gameplay metrics:** These are associated with the unique features of the specific game. In essence, the unique features lead to game-specific questions associated with user-testing. For example, in a game such as *Batman: Arkham Asylum*, the usage pattern of the main character's abilities could be of interest, e.g. for evaluating if there are abilities that are over- or under-used.

A good way to start defining these for a specific game is to look at the **core gameplay**. Is your game a platformer where the main challenge is timing jumps? Then tracking where a player jumps, and whether the jump is successful or not, will provide valuable feedback for locating trouble spots. Racing game? Tracking car selection, track completion times and crash locations/types will inform about the attractiveness of different cars, and whether tracks are balanced or too hard/easy.

To take an example, if the game is an action game, which are generally focused on quick reflexes, accuracy, timing, etc., then the key telemetry data to log is anything that relates to the reflex-based mechanics. If the action game is a First-Person Shooter like *Quake*, these include metrics focusing on weapon choice, weapon use, accuracy, map lethality (heatmaps), AI-enemy damage inflicted, and possibly even trajectory tracking of player, bots and projectiles. Is the game multi-player with strategic elements? Then include team scores, strategic point captures/losses, powerups use, object activation etc. Design teams are typically highly aware of which features that form the unique selling points of the game they are building, and tagging these up to get the associated telemetry data, is a good place to start. A final recommendation: involve the consideration of which gameplay metrics to track as early as possible. The earlier that designers and analysts/user researchers sit down together and figure out what information to track, the better (Kim et al. 2008; Drachen et al. 2013; Seif El-Nasr et al. 2013). It is worth noting that when performing user-oriented analytics, we are dealing with human behavior. This means that predicting which features to track is challenging, as predicting how humans will interact with an interactive system is difficult. This emphasizes the need for both hypothesis-driven and explorative approaches in game analytics.

7.6 Game Data Mining

Game data mining is the umbrella term for the methods employed when working with behavioral game telemetry data. Without it the knowledge that can be obtained from game telemetry is limited to simple aggregates (e.g. average playtime). Game data mining is about exploring the properties of and finding patterns in, game telemetry datasets. Applied right, game data mining is a powerful tool covering a range of scenarios, from evaluating how players play a game and find the weak spots in the design that impacts negatively on their play experience (Kennerly 2003; Canossa et al. 2011) to interpretation of larger scale structures like guilds in massively multiplayer online games (Thurau and Bauckhage 2010). For an overview of game data mining, see Drachen et al. (2013). Due to space, we will here only provide the briefest of overviews of this broad field of investigation.

Games can generate massive amounts of behavioral telemetry data (Drachen et al. 2013). This recent "data revolution" requires analysis methods that scale to massive data sizes, and which provide interesting, useful and intuitively accessible results. Unfortunately, when datasets become large, many traditional methods used on small datasets break down, and this has led to an increased focus on developing algorithms for large scale data mining over the past decade (Drachen et al. 2013d; Medler 2012; Bohannon 2010; Zoeller 2011; Drachen et al. 2014; Sifa et al. 2014).

Drachen et al. (2013d) noted that in games, some of the typical problems include **high dimensionality** (e.g. tracking the purchases of 750 different in-game items), **time-dependency** (e.g. if one player finds a bug that permits gold duplication in an MMOG, the news will spread fast and we need to react fast) and the focus in games on **PX** (e.g. evaluating whether specific player behaviors lead to good or bad user experiences).

Data mining methods are generally divided according to one of two systems: descriptive/prescriptive or unsupervised/supervised learning. Depending on the field of research, one of these two systems will be used. They are not completely identical, however: Predictive/descriptive data mining are **concepts**, and supervised/unsupervised learning are concrete groups of **methods** (and not the only ones used for data mining). For example, methods such as correlation are also used in descriptive data mining without being unsupervised learning techniques, and methods such as interpolation used in predictive data mining without being supervised learning techniques (Han et al. 2005). This difference is useful to be aware of as it helps identifying the type of approach needed to solve a given problem.

Descriptive data mining is used to describe the general properties of existing data in a concise way. This includes presenting any notable characteristics in the data, without having a pre-defined target. For example, exploring the number of daily users in a social online game like Farmville, and noting that there is a sharp increase in the number of active players during weekends (Field and Cotton 2011).

Predictive data mining is used to forecast explicit values, based on patterns determined from known data, i.e. attempting to predict something based on inference from the data available. For example, predicting how many players that will convert from a free account to a paid account in a Free-to-Play game, or predicting when people will stop playing a game based on their early play behavior (Mahlman et al. 2010).

Supervised learning originates in the field of machine learning. This is a branch of artificial intelligence that is focused on algorithms that permit computers to evolve behaviors based on input data. When performing supervised learning, the available data are divided into two sets: the "training data", and the main dataset. A supervised learning algorithm uses the training data to capture characteristics of interest of the underlying, unknown probability distribution of data and make intelligent decisions based on their properties. The output from the algorithm can be a continuous value, as in the case of regression analysis, or a prediction of a class label of the input variables, as in classification analysis. The learning algorithm, having seen the training data and calculated a result from these (e.g. a set of behavioral classes), then proceeds to predict the value of the function for the remaining data. In order to be able to do this, the supervised learning algorithm has to generalize from the training data to unknown situations in a way that is reasonable. In games, supervised learning can be used to forecast when a player will stop playing, if a player will convert from a non-paying to a paying user, what types of items players will purchase, classify player behavior, etc.

Unsupervised learning also originates in machine learning, and also focuses on fitting a model to observations. Unsupervised learning differentiates from supervised learning in that there is no pre-determined (a priori) output—for example, no pre-defined classes of player behavior. Instead, the input objects (variables) are treated as random variables, and a density model build for the dataset. For example, if the goal of an analysis was to find out if there were any patterns in the behavior of people in a first-person shooter like *Crysis*, but had no prior idea about what kind of behaviors that emerged in the gameplay, unsupervised learning techniques could be used. In this case, a cluster algorithm could look for players exhibiting similar behavior across a range of behavioral variables (movement speed, use of different weapons, accuracy, use of cover, etc.), and find players with similar behavior for these variables, i.e. behavioral classes (Drachen et al. 2009). Supervised learning would be applied when previous cluster analysis had been run, e.g. during an earlier playtest, and the goal is to find out whether new player fit into the defined classes of behavior.

Case Studies

In this section a series of brief examples are presented which show how behavioral game telemetry data can be employed to detect and/or solve problems with play experience in a game (directly or indirectly). The case studies all focus on computationally simple techniques for evaluating gameplay, and ignores the rapidly growing body of knowledge on the use of data mining and machine learning techniques on behavioral telemetry data from games (e.g. Thawonmas and Iizuka 2008; Thawonmas et al. 2008; Drachen et al. 2009; Mahlman et al. 2010; Thurau and Bauckhage 2010; Weber et al. 2011; Yannakikis 2012), because these remain much less widely used outside academia. This pattern is changing with the rapid adoption of behavioral analytics in the industry, and perhaps notably the increasing popularity of the Free-to-Play genre, where data mining and machine learning techniques such as prediction analysis and classification are proving highly useful, e.g. to test game features or identity players who generate large amounts of revenue (Fields and Cotton 2011; Luton 2013; Seif El-Nasr et al. 2013). The case studies selected also focus on detecting problems with gameplay, which either was shown or could lead to frustration among the players, presenting different strategies for detecting and solving these gameplay design issues. Frustration is generally characterized as an unwanted component of PX (Amsel 1990; Kiel et al. 2004), however, frustration forms a recognized component of the experience people can obtain from playing digital games (Pagulayan et al. 2003).

Evaluating Multi-Player Levels in Halo 3

Thompson (2007)'s article in *Wired Magazine* has become one of the seminal pieces in behavioral game telemetry evaluation, as it brought to the broader world the groundbreaking work being performed at *Microsoft Studios Research* (formerly Microsoft Games User Research) in the early-mid 2000s on behavioral evaluation and game user research (Kim et al. 2008; Ramero 2008). One of the examples mentioned is the *Valhalla* multi-player map in *Halo 3*, one of the best-selling first-person shooter game series in the world. Ramero (2008) noted that the map contained a specific building type, Towers, which are places where the player spawns into the game. Vehicles are found nearby for easy transport, and a pair of transport devices that will teleport players into the environment, the latter intended to be objects of contention between the two player teams (Fig. 7.3). The user research team developed heatmaps of the *Valhalla* level (heatmaps are commonly generated by dividing the game area under scrutiny into a grid of cells, and sum up the number of events that occur within the area covered by each cell. Adding a color ramp (e.g. green to red) allows easy interpretation of the density of the event, e.g. player deaths), showing where lethality was highest on the map. The map revealed however that players were not using the top half of the map, with resulting issues in the game balance. This was solved by changing the direction the teleporters would send players, so they experience the entire map and play it as intended by the design.

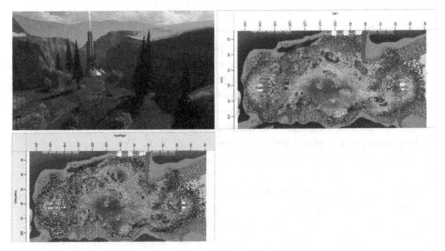

Fig. 7.3 (*left*): A Tower in the Halo 3 multi-player map *Valhalla. (right)*: A heat map of the Valhalla map generated during alpha testing at *Microsoft Studios User Research* (the deeper the shading, the more death events in the grid cell). The tower is near the deeper shaded area to the right of the map. *(bottom)* heat map from the adjusted level—players are now using the entire map. (© Microsoft, courtesy of Microsoft, reproduced from: Romero 2008)

Deadly Brutes in Halo 2

Another example from *Microsoft Studios Research* was described by Kim et al. (2008) (Fig. 7.4). The goal of the research was to identify and address problem areas participants encountered while playing *Halo 2*, with a specific focus on unintended increases in difficulty. *Halo 2,* like the other games in the series, is a first-person shooter. There are 12 missions in the single-player campaign, taking roughly 10–12 h to complete, and all linear in the progression design that can be broken down in "encounters" (10–30 encounters per level). In order to evaluate whether there were trouble spots in the design where the game was too difficult, Kim et al. (2008) collected behavioral metrics such as player deaths, time of death, cause of death and how the death events occurred. In addition, they collected attitudinal data through a survey (one item, 3 min interval).

Initially, the average numbers of death events per encounter, summed for each of the 12 missions, were examined. This revealed that the 10th mission in the game had much higher death rates than any other level. A closer inspection of the same death rates for each of the ten encounters in the mission revealed that the 3rd encounter comprises the vast majority of the death events in the entire mission. This information explained why the 10th mission had such a high death rate, and approximately where the problem occurred, but now why. The encounter sees players fighting successive waves of enemies, and one of them, Brutes, accounted for 85 % of all player deaths in its own right. Kim et al. (2008) further noted that there were three ways that Brutes can kill player characters: Melee attacks (27 %), Plasma grenades attach (the

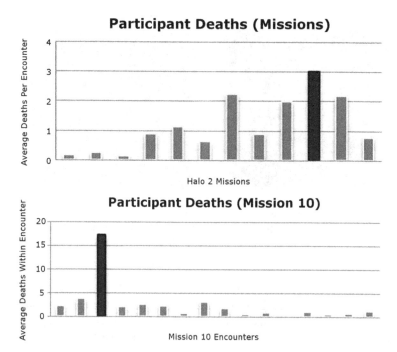

Fig. 7.4 (*left*) The first level of analysis for *Halo 2*. Data represent the average number of times a player died per encounter for each mission. *Red bar* highlights mission 10 as having unusually high rates of death events per encounter. (*right*) The 10th mission in *Halo 2* broken up into the component encounters. It can be seen that the third encounter (*red bar*) comprises the majority of the death events in the mission. (Source: Kim et al. 2008)

grenade sticks to the player) (22%) and plasma grenade explosions (19%). The designers modified the ways Brutes operate so they would not throw grenades, thus lowering the difficulty (the number of enemies was also reduced). In a similar situation described by Ramero (2008) during the user testing of Halo 3, players were during the first boss fight (a combat with an unusually strong opponent) not dying from the boss' attacks, but rather from a much less lethal minion of the boss, the Grunts. Being killed by Grunts had adverse effects on the enjoyment the playtesters experienced while playing through the encounter. Further investigating the causes of death, Ramero (2008) was able to find out that the problem was caused by a bug: the Grunts AI was reset to maximum during the encounter, dramatically increasing the difficulty. The bug was fixed and retesting showed the problem had been eliminated.

Overlay Analysis in Star Wars Knights of the Old Republic and Transformers: War for Cybertron
Zoeller (2011) reported an example of gameplay analysis from the MMORPG *Star Wars: The Old Republic* (developed at *Bioware*) (Fig. 7.5). The analysis was instigated by several dozen complaints on the games' forums, noting that

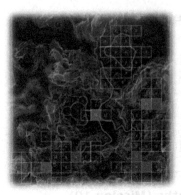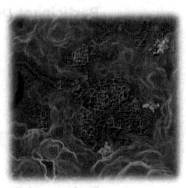

Fig. 7.5 (*left*) Heat map of death events from the *Tython* playfield *(Star Wars: The Old Republic)*. (Source: Zoeller 2011). *(right)* map of level differences in combats between players and Fleshraiders *(Star Wars: The Old Republic)*. (© Bioware, courtesy of Bioware, reprinted from Zoeller 2011)

a particular type of enemy, Fleshraiders, on the playfield (game area) *Tython*, were overtly lethal, causing frustration among the players. In order to find out what caused the problem, the locations of player death events were imported and overlain on a map of *Tython*. Associated features, such as player level, were also included in the analysis.

Overlay analysis is a spatial analysis and visualization method where two or more maps—or layers—registered to a common coordinate system are superimposed on top of each other (Demers 2008). The purpose is to visualize and analyze the relationship between features occupying the same space, e.g. a map of a game level, a grid-based heatmap of player death events, and the presence of Fleshraiders.

The heatmaps generated at *Bioware* revealed several trouble spots where player death events were frequent. Using drill-down analysis on a range of different possible causes for the high amount of death events, it was discovered that there was a level gap between the Fleshraiders and player characters in the playfield. The level curve for the area was modified, and this eliminated the problem—and the forum complaints stopped.

Using overlay analysis to solve these kinds of spatial problems is similar to the analysis presented by Drachen and Canossa (2011), who also used overlay analysis to evaluate the distribution of different causes of death in the *Valaskjalf* map of *Tomb Raider: Underworld* (developed by *Crystal Dynamics*). Unlike the example from Zoeller (2011), which was hypothesis-driven (players die due to Fleshraiders being overpowered), the analysis of Drachen and Canossa (2011) was explorative: It was not known whether there were any imbalances in the *Valaskjalf* map, as no player feedback had been gathered. However, overlaying heatmaps of locations where players had died from different causes (traps, enemies, environmental effects etc.), indicated several areas where the sheer diversity of threats drove the difficulty level up.

These correlated with locations of high death rates, indicating that these areas needed further user research to evaluate if the high difficulty impacted negatively on the playing experience. This is an example of behavioral telemetry analysis and playtesting feeding into one another.

An example with similar goals of gameplay analysis was presented by Houghton (2011) (Fig. 7.6) who combined heatmaps of player death locations and locations where players killed other players, to develop balance heatmaps for the *Molten* level of *Transformers: War for Cybertron*, based on a dataset of 30 million rows collected from public team deathmatch games (Fig. 7.6) The balance heatmaps were generated by subtracting the death heatmap from the kill heatmap, thus resulting in a map that displays the most deadly areas in the map. The results indicated that the most dangerous places in the game were wall areas, possibly due to restricted movement. The central bridge in the map was also highly lethal—fortunately this was also the intention of the level design.

Engagement Analysis in MonsterWorld

Monster World is one of the most successful titles of Wooga, a mobile game developer, with 71 million players as of March 2015, and at its peak over 2 million DAU (Daily Active Users), and a runtime of more than 3 years - and the game is still running. As of August 2013, more than 1.1 million players have invested over 200 hours in the game.

In *Monster World*, players are tasked with growing a variety of plants in a garden populated by monsters. Players gradually gain access to new crop types and level up, unlocking additional gameplay options, continuing the cycle of progression over the long term. The game has since its launch received a number of upgrades, including story missions to provide a different set of goals apart from planting and unlocking new crop types. Factories and WooGoo introduced a new layers of crafting, and in 2012 Wooga introduced timed missions (Fig. 7.7) (Shaul 2013; Wooga 2013).

Fig. 7.6 Example of overlay analysis. *(left)*: heat map from the Molten map of the game *Transformers: War for Cybertron. (middle)*: heat map showing the positions of players at the time they killed another player. *(right)*: A balance heat map generated using overlay analysis. Areas with negative values *(red/darker shading)* indicate dangerous areas. Areas with positive values *(blue/lighter shading)* indicate areas that are safer. (© Sean Houghton, courtesy of Sean Houghton, reprinted from: Houghton 2011)

Fig. 7.7 An example of a player garden in Monster World. (© Wooga, courtesy of Wooga)

Kaiser (2013) reported on the initial growing pains of *Monster World* (Fig. 7.8), which did not become a hit directly after launch. Wooga therefore launched a series of telemetry-based investigations and –tests in order to evaluate the connection between design features and user engagement.

The approach is a typical example of the integration between behavioral telemetry and user experience evaluation in social/mobile games, notably in the F2P domain where retention and monetization is crucial (Fields and Cotton 2011; Seif El-Nasr et al. 2013; Luton 2013).

In the example of *Monster World*, Wooga identified a series of Key Performance Indicators (KPIs) such as 1, 3 and 7-day retention of the users (essentially Monthly Active Users divided by Daily Active Users, or the MAU/DAU ratio), and the tutorial of *Monster World* was analyzed through funnel analysis, to investigate how effective the games initial moments were at retaining players. A/B tests were also performed. These are also called split-level tests, and in a game context refers to the practice of releasing multiple different versions of specific features to limited samples of live players. For example, varying the amount of virtual currency awarded to new players, to examine how this impacts on user engagement and churn rates. By analyzing the relevant performance indicators afterwards, we are deciding to continue developing one of the tested versions.

In the current example, Kaiser (2011) tested a version of the games tutorial that forced players to perform specific actions, vs. another sample of users that were given the decision to follow directions open to them. The engagement metrics employed showed that more players got to the end of the tutorial when they were guided through it. Wooga subsequently selected to have the enforced option for all new players (Fig. 7.9).

Fig. 7.8 Wooga used A/B testing to evaluate different versions of the tutorial for *Monster World*. A/B testing sees the release of multiple versions of the same game, or features of the game, to different audiences. Engagement metrics (and/or similar proxies for player experience) are then used to evaluate which version that works best. In this example, the version of the game to the *left* forces players to follow the action noted by the tutorial character, the one to the *right* received the same instructions but it was up to the player to follow the directions given. (© Wooga, courtesy of Wooga, reprinted from: Kaiser 2013)

It is important to note that mobile/social online games adopting F2P business models do not operate on behavioral telemetry alone. While it is vital for these types of games to keep an eye on how the game is played during the post-launch phase, because this is when the game provides income to the developer, development and maintenance does not occur without lab-based usability testing. Kaiser (2013) notes that usability testing is performed from the beginning of development, and post-launch *Monster World* is tested every 2 weeks, with staff in attendance. Test results are merged with behavioral telemetry data from the game, and the information goes into the next development cycle.

Frustration in Kane and Lynch: Dog Days
Kane and Lynch: Dog Days is a third-person shooter (developed by IO Interactive), which in terms of gameplay is a typical example of the genre, i.e. the player controls a single character and mainly has to worry about staying alive, eliminate enemies and solve specific tasks. This case study, reported by Canossa et al. (2011), focused on frustration, and was instigated by a playtest run at IO Interactive. During the playtest, a tester became vocally and physically frustrated, the user research team needed to find out why this occurred. Evaluating detailed behavioral telemetry data from the test session, Canossa et al. (2011) observed a pattern where the player repeatedly dies due to a malfunctioning checkpoint in the game. This problem cause the player to be required to progress substantially through the game level in order to not be pushed back a long way. As the players repeatedly failed in progressing, the behavior of the players changed dramatically in a number of ways with each attempt, including: (1) The number of enemies killed decreased considerably

in each play trough (five total). (3) The pace of the player became considerably faster in each play through, i.e. the player began running through the level, without taking care to use cover, and repeats the same route with no variation. (4) The player exhibited progressively less presence of special events such as triggering environment explosions or picking up weapons dropped by enemies. (5) The player makes less progress with each attempt. The fourth playthrough was the most unsuccessful, lasting a few seconds, and basically showed the player rushing into enemies and being almost instantly killed. Following this death, the player regained control, slowed the pace of movement and tried a new (leftward turn), killing a considerable amount of enemies and taking the time to pick up dropped weapons. A second situation where the same playtester exhibited signs of frustration during a test was also examined. In this case, the player needed nine attempts to get through the level segment with the malfunctioning checkpoint. This case study is an example of how questions can arise via user-testing in an industrial development (or empirical research) context, which can be answered using behavioural telemetry analysis, i.e. in this case finding out a waypoint was malfunctioning. Canossa et al. (2011) eventually extended this work to generate and test a model that was able to detect similar cases of frustration in the game, with frustration being defined as *"repeated failure to overcome challenges"* following e.g. Amsel (1990). Unfortunately it has not been possible to obtain permission to reproduce any of the figures from Canossa et al. (2011) here, but readers are directed to Fig. 7.3 in that publication.

Conclusions

Behavior analysis via gameplay metrics analysis addresses one of the major challenges to game user research, namely that of tracking and analyzing user behavior when interacting with the very complex systems that contemporary computer games represent. As a user-oriented approach, it complements existing methods utilized in the industry, providing detailed and quantitative data to supplement qualitative and semi-quantitative data from other user research methods on the quality of the play experience (Lazzaro and Mellon 2005; Kim et al. 2008; Isbister and Schaffer 2008; Drachen and Canossa 2011; Seif El-Nasr et al. 2013). Alternatively, behavior analysis can be used as a method for inferring player experience, although care need to be taken when doing so and secondary validation is recommended (Lazzaro and Mellon 2005; Marsh et al. 2006; Nacke and Drachen 2011; Drachen and Canossa 2011).

There are many ways to work with and utilize behavioral telemetry data, during production and post-launch, and it can be challenging to generate systematic overviews of methods and principles: The choice of approach is influenced by the available resources for telemetry logging, user research and not the least the game design. For example, traditional boxed, fire-and-forget games are different from persistent world massively multi-player online games and social online games, where an important focus is analysis and synthesis directed at monitoring the player population, tuning game design on a running basis, continually optimizing the play experience to tune game design on a running basis, and calculating business-oriented game metrics such as the average revenue per user and churn rate (Fields and Cotton 2011). Even within the confines of a single type of game, e.g. first-person shooters, there is a substantial space for developing approaches to working with gameplay metrics. On top of this come the problems in correlating behavioral data with robust and broadly applicable measures of play experience (Kim et al. 2008). Despite these challenges, there is a general consensus forming in the game industry and game academia that telemetry-driven behavior analysis mesh well with other user-oriented approaches for evaluating and testing games (Kim et al. 2008; Zoeller 2011; Seif El-Nasr et al. 2013; Luton 2013; Seufert 2014). Game analytics is here to stay.

Box 1: Drill-Down Analysis

The first analyses done on gameplay telemetry are typically high-level analyses and descriptive statistics, meant to provide an overview of how the game is doing. For example, looking at the number of player entering and leaving the game (if a live game), or the amount of time spent across different levels. These types of high-level views on datasets from pre-launch playtesting or post-launch live games provides one of the early means for detecting potential problems. However, they rarely show why specific problems occur. For example, when players are spending twice as much time on level 5 as intended, something we did not plan for is happening. To find out why, it is necessary to dive down into the data and find the root causes of player behavior. This process is known as drill-down analysis" and is a core method in data mining (Larose 2004; Han et al. 2005; Drachen et al. 2012).

Drill-down analysis is one of the most common forms of operations carried out in game analytics, and the term is commonly heard in game data mining contexts.

This is because the root causes of behavioral patterns are often nested at deeper levels of the behavioral data than what is apparent at high-level aggregate analyses. For example, a specific checkpoint malfunctioning for 25 % of the players, or only on some platforms. Drill down analysis, as a data mining operation, basically means moving from summary/aggregate information to detailed data via a particular focus. For example, noticing that a group of players have suspiciously high gold income rates in an MMORPG, and working down through the summary data to investigate the raw data of these particular player, to figure out if cheating is happening or not. When performing drill-down, we are essentially performing analysis on the parent attribute (e.g. gold income rate), via investigating child attributes (e.g. time spent playing, sources of gold income). At the lowest level of a drill-down analysis are the raw data

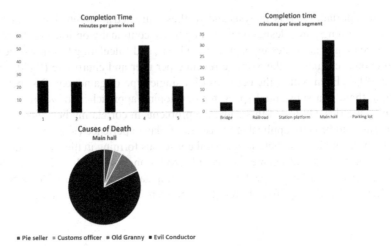

Fig. 7.9 An example of drill-down navigation from a fictive game. See text for explanation. (Modified from: Drachen et al. 2013)

In practice, when using business intelligence applications, drilling down is performed by selecting and querying data. This can be as simple as clicking a bar in a bar chart and getting the underlying data, to running queries in a relational database or writing scripts for a particular drill-down path. How far drill-down analysis can be taken depends on data granularity.

To take an example (Fig. 7.9) consider a simple breakdown of data consisting of a few variables is considered, e.g. average completion times for the levels of a game. At this top level, it may be noticed that a level appears to take longer to complete than others (see graphic). In order to explore why, the underlying data need to be exposed, in this case a breakdown of the completion times for individual components of the level. In this more detailed view of the data, it may be noticed that a specific sector of the level is where the players spend a lot of time (Main Hall). Drilling down further into the metrics data captured from the level, it may be found that the root cause is that players have trouble beating a specific type of enemy and keep dying (Evil Conductors), whose difficulty can be adjusted to accommodate.

If the cause of the observed pattern is not obvious from looking at the data, it can be useful to consider the actual game environment, as in the Halo cases mentioned in this chapter. This is about the closest we can get to the actual experience of playing the game, for example via mapping player telemetry directly into the virtual environment (Drachen and Canossa 2011).

Box 2: Managing the Allure of Numbers

For people working with game user research, behavioral telemetry is usually valuable. They form potentially highly detailed data about player behavior, and can be obtained from very large groups of people. Quantitative data take the form of numbers, and many popular metrics calculated in the game industry and –academia are intuitively understandable, e.g. Monthly Active Users (MAU) (Luton 2013; Fields and Cotton 2011; Seif El-Nasr et al. 2013). It can therefore be tempting to rely on behavioral telemetry alone following the launch of a game, and ignore lab- or field-based user research (see e.g.: Pagulayan et al. 2003; Isbister and Schaffer 2008). However, this is dangerous because behavioral telemetry does not permit analysis of e.g. user experience beyond what can be inferred from the telemetry trails themselves.

In game analytics, is it important to keep in mind that data can only say something about the data themselves, not about what other data that should be collected, or factors existing outside the dataset, which impact the results being generated. Furthermore, any measures of human behavior cannot include all the factors that influence the behavior. Assumptions therefore need to be made when working with behavioral telemetry in GUR just like for any other data source on human behavior and PX in games.

Strong knowledge of the principles for empirical research and knowledge acquisition are essential to the successful deployment of behavioral game telemetry in game user research.

Many common KPIs used in the game industry require contextual information to be used to drive decision making. For example, knowing that the number of Daily Active Users (DAU) increased 20 % last week, does not explain why this increase occurred, or whether it is sustainable, and it can even hide a problem—for example that the increase is due to a new feature, which however removes a key motivator for IAPs, thus reducing the Life Time Value (LTV) of the player base in the same period of time, endangering the financial survival of the game.

As noted by Drachen et al. (2012) critical thinking should always be applied when evaluating player behavior—sometimes the analysis will show one thing through a red color on a heat map or another suspicious pattern in the data, but the problem may actually rest in a minor design detail somewhere else. Small design changes in one area of a game can cause changes in behaviors in an entirely different section. Just because something looks good does not mean it is true, and this is why careful analysis is needed when suspicious or problematic patterns are detected in behavioral data. Heat maps and graphs are often intuitively understandable and travel better in organizations than two pages of text with detailed explanation of a specific finding from a comprehensive user test. However, data visualizations also make it easy to ignore other factors that could potentially hold an impact on whatever is being investigated, but which is not included in the metrics-based analysis in question. Metrics analysis, data mining, etc. all requires a human element—the numbers do not make things right, human interpretation does (Han et al. 2005). The key lesson here is that game analytics is not design (Fields and Cotton 2011; Seif El-Nasr et al. 2013), but can be an incredibly help to design, providing hard evidence on how design decisions are affecting player behavior. Just like any other method for game user research, good research practices should inform game analytics. (© Game Analytics, used with permission, www.gameanalytics.com)

References

Amsel A (1990) Arousal, suppression, and persistence: frustration theory, attention, and its disorders. Cognit Emot 4:239–268 (Psychology Press)

Berry M, Linoff G (1999) Mastering data mining: the art and science of customer relationship management. Wiley, New York

Bohannon J (2010) Game-miners grapple with massive data. Science 330(6000):30–31

Bordens K, Abbott BB (2013) Research design and methods: a process approach. McGraw-Hill, New York (Humanities/Social Sciences/Languages)

Canossa A, Drachen A (2009) Patterns of play: play-personas in user-centered game development. In: Proceedings of DIGRA 2009, (London, United Kingdom), DiGRA Publishers, DIGRA Digital Library: http://www.digra.org/dl/display_html?chid= http://www.digra.org/dl/db/09287.49165.pdf. Accessed 1 April 2015

Canossa A, Drachen A, Rau Møller Sørensen J (2011) Arrgghh!!!—blending quantitative and qualitative methods to detect player frustration. In: Proceedings of the 2011 Foundations of Digital Games Conference (Bordeaux, France), ACM Publishers

Davenport TH (2012) Enterprise analytics: optimize performance, process and decisions through big data. Pearson FT Press, Boston

Davenport TH, Harris JG (2007) Competing on analytics: the new science of winning. Harvards Business Review, Boston

Demers MN (2008) Fundamentals of geographical information systems. Wiley, New York

DeRosa P (2007) Tracking player feedback to improve game design. Gamasutra, August 7 (2007). http://www.gamasutra.com/view/feature/1546/tracking_player_feedback_to_.php. Accessed 1 April 2015

Dix A, Finlay JE, Abowd GD, Beale R (2007). Human-computer interaction, 3rd edn. Prentice Hall Publishers, Upper Saddle River

Drachen A, Canossa A (2009) Towards gameplay analysis via gameplay metrics. In: Proceedings of the 13th MindTrek 2009 (Tampere, Finland), ACM-SIGCHI Publishers, pp 202–209

Drachen A, Canossa A (2011) Evaluating motion. Spatial user behavior in virtual environments. Int J Arts Technol 4(3):294–314

Drachen A, Schubert M (2013) Spatial game analytics and visualization. In: Proceedings of IEEE Computational Intelligence in Games, pp 1–8. doi:10.1109/CIG.2013.6633629

Drachen A, Yannakakis GN, Canossa A, Togelius J (2009) Player Modeling using Self-Organization in Tomb Raider: Underworld. In: Proceedings of IEEE Computational Intelligence in Games

Drachen A, Nacke L, Yannakakis G, Pedersen AL (2010) Correlation between heart rate, electrodermal activity and player experience in First-Person Shooter games. In: Proceedings of the 5th ACM SIGGRAPH, ACM-SIGGRAPH Publishers, pp 49–54. doi:10.1145/1836135.1836143

Drachen A, Sifa R, Bauckhage C, Thurau C (2012) Guns, swords and data: clustering of player behavior in computer games in the wild. In: Proceedings of IEEE Computational Intelligence in Games, pp 163–170. doi:10.1109/CIG.2012.6374152

Drachen A, Canossa A, Sørensen JR (2013a) Gameplay metrics in games user research: examples from the trenches. In: Seif-El Nasr M, Drachen A, Canossa A (eds) Game analytics. Springer, London

Drachen A, Seif El Nasr M, Canossa A (2013b) Introduction to user analytics. May 2013, Game Developer Magazine (feature, later published on Gamasutra). http://www.gamasutra.com/view/feature/193241/intro_to_user_analytics.php

Drachen A, Seif El-Nasr M, Canossa A (2013c) Game analytics—the basics. In: Seif El-Nasr M, Drachen A, Canossa A (eds) Game analytics—maximizing the value of player data. Springer, London, pp 13–40 (http://www.springer.com/computer/hci/book/978-1-4471-4768-8)

Drachen A, Thurau C, Yannakakis G, Togelius J, Bauckhage C (2013d) Game data mining. In: Seif El-Nasr M, Drachen A, Canossa A (eds) Game analytics—maximizing the value of player data. Springer, London, pp 205–253 (http://www.springer.com/computer/hci/book/978-1-4471-4768-8)

Drachen A, Baskin S, Riley J, Klabjan D (2014) Going out of business: auction house behavior in the massively multi-player online game glitch. J Entertain Comput 5:20–31. doi:10.1016/j.entcom.2014.02.001 ([SJR H-index=5], Elsevier Publishers)

Field T, Cotton B (2011) Social game design: monetization methods and mechanics. Morgan Kauffman Publishers, Burlington

Hadiji F, Sifa S, Drachen A, Thurau C (2014) Predicting player churn in the wild. In: Proceedings of the IEEE Computational Intelligence in Games, pp 131–139

Han J, Kamber M, Pei J (2005) Data mining: concepts and techniques, 2nd edn. Morgan Kaufmann, Amsterdam

Hassenzahl M, Tractinsky N (2006) User experience—a research agenda. Behav Inf Technol 25(2):91–97

Houghton S (2011) Balance and Flow Maps. AltDevBlogADay Newssite. http://altdevblogaday.com/2011/06/01/balance-and-flow-maps-2/. Accessed 1 April 2015

Isbister K, Schaffer N (2008) Game usability: advancing the player experience. Morgan Kaufman Publishers, Massachusetts

Kaiser S (2013) Wooga: building a successful social game by combining metrics with emotion Social Times, July 20, 2011. http://www.adweek.com/socialtimes/wooga-building-a-successful-social-game-by-combining-metrics-with-emotion/585918

Kennerly D (2003) Better game design through data mining. Gamasutra, 15th August 2003. http://www.gamasutra.com/view/feature/2816/better_game_design_through_data_.php. Accessed 1 April 2015

Kiel M, Gilleade KM, Dix A (2004) Using frustration in the design of adaptive videogames. In: Proceeding of the 2004 ACM SIGCHI International Conference on Advances in computer entertainment technology, ACM New York, NY, USA

Kim JH, Gunn DV, Phillips BC, Pagulayan RJ, Wixon D (2008) Tracking real-time user experience (TRUE): a comprehensive instrumentation solution for complex systems. In: Proceedings of the twenty-sixth annual SIGCHI conference on Human factors in computing systems, CHI'08

Larose DT (2004) Discovering knowledge in data: an introduction to data mining. Wiley, Hoboken

Law E, Vermeeren APOS, Hassenzahl M, Blythe M (2007) Towards a UX manifesto. In Proceedings of the 21st British HCI Group Annual Conference on HCI 2008: People and Computers XXI: HCI...but not as we know it - Volume 2 (Swinton, UK, September 3–7). British Computer Society, pp 205–206

Lazzaro N, Mellon L (2005) Fun meters for games. Presentation at the 2005 Austin Game Developers Conference

Leone M (2012) Data entry, risk management and tacos: inside Halo 4's playtest labs. Polygon, October 24th 2012. http://www.polygon.com/2012/10/24/3538296/data-entry-risk-management-and-tacos-inside-halo-4s-playtest-labs. Accessed 1 April 2015

Luton W (2013) Free-to-play: making money from games you give away. New Riders, California

Mahlman T, Drachen A, Canossa A, Togelius J, Yannakakis GN (2010) Predicting player behavior in tomb raider: Underworld. In: Proceedings of the International Conference on Computational Intelligence and Games, CIG'10

Mandryk RL (2008) Physiological measures for game evaluation. In: Isbister K, Schaffer N (eds) Game usability: advice from the experts for advancing the player experience. Morgan Kaufman Publishers, Burlington, pp 207–235

Mandryk RL, Atkins MS, Inkpen KM (2006) A continuous and objective evaluation of emotional experience with interactive play environments. In: Proceedings of CHI 2006: Novel methods: Emotions, Gestures, Events, ACM Press

Marsh T, Smith SP, Yang K, Shahabi C (2006) Continuous and unobtrusive capture of user-player behavior and experience to assess and inform game design and development. In: Proceedings of Fun and Games, pp 76–86

Medler B (2012) Play with data—an exploration of play analytics and its effect on player experiences, Ph.D. dissertation. Georgia Institute of Technology

Medlock MC, Wixon D, Terrano M, Romero RL, Fulton B (2002) Using the RITE method to improve products: a definition and a case study. Usability Professionals Association, Orlando

Mellon L (2009) Applying metrics driven development to mmo costs and risks. Versant Corporation, Redwood City

Minelli M, Chambers M, Dhiraj A (2013) Big data, big analytics: emerging business intelligence and analytic trends for today's businesses. Wiley, Hoboken

Nacke L (2009) Affective ludology: scientific measurement of user experience in interactive entertainment. Ph. D. Thesis, BTH, Karlskrona

Nacke L, Drachen A (2011) Towards a framework of player experience research. In: Proceedings of the EPEX 11' Workshop (Bordeaux, France)

Pagulayan RJ, Keeker K (2007) Measuring pleasure and fun: playtesting. In: Wilson C (ed) Handbook of formal and informal interaction design methods. Morgan Kaufmann Publishers, Massachusetts

Pagulayan RJ, Keeker K, Wixon D, Romero RL, Fuller T (2003) User-centered design in games. In: Jacko J, Sears A (eds) The HCI Handbook. Lawrence Erlbaum Associates, Mahwah

Pruett C (2011) Hot failure: tuning gameplay with simple player metrics. Game developer magazine, September 2010. http://www.gamasutra.com/view/feature/6155/hot_failure_tuning_gameplay _with_.php?print=1. Accessed 1 April 2015

Ravaja N, Saari T, Turpeinen M, Laarni J, Salminen M, Kivikangas M (2006) Spatial presence and emotions during video game playing: does it matter with whom you play? Presence 15(4):381–392. (Teleoperators and Virtual Environments)

Romero R (2008) Successful instrumentation. Tracking attitudes and behaviors to improve games. Presentation at the Game Developers Conference

Runge J, Gao P, Garcin F, Faltings B (2014) Churn prediction for high-value players in casual social games. In: Proceedings of the Computational Intelligence in Games Conference 2014, IEEE Publishers

Seif El-Nasr M, Drachen A, Canossa A (2013) Game analytics. Springer, 800 pp, ISBN: 978-1-4471-4769-5. http://www.springer.com/computer/hci/book/978-1-4471-4768-8

Seufert EB (2014) Freemium economics: leveraging analytics and user segmentation to drive revenue. Morgan Kaufmann Publishers, Waltham

Shaul B (2013) Monster world developer Wooga looks back at three years of success on facebook. SocialTimes, August 14, 2013. http://www.adweek.com/socialtimes/monster-world-developer-wooga-looks-back-at-three-years-of-success-on-facebook/608648. Accessed 1 April 2015

Sifa R, Bauckhage C, Drachen A (2014) The playtime principle: large-scale cross-games interest modeling. In: Proceedings of the IEEE Computational Intelligence in Games, pp 365–373

Southey F, Xiao G, Holte RC, Trommelen M, Buchanan J (2005) Semi-Automated gameplay analysis by machine learning. In: Proceedings of AIIDE

Thawonmas R, Iizuka K (2008) Visualization of online-game players based on their action behaviors. Int J Comput Games Technol. doi:10.1155/2008/906931

Thawonmas R, Kashifuji Y, Chen KT (2008) Design of MMORPG Bots Based on Behavior Analysis. In: Proceedings of the 2008 International Conference on Advances in Computer Entertainment Technology, ACE'08

Thompson C (2007) Halo 3: how Microsoft labs invented a new science of play. Wired Magazine

Thurau C, Bauckhage C (2010) Analyzing the evolution of social groups in world of Warcraft. In: Proceedings of the International Conference on Computational Intelligence and Games, IEEE, CIG'10

Tychsen A, Canossa A (2008) Defining personas in games using metrics. In: Proceedings of FUTURE PLAY 2008 (Toronto, Canada), ACM Publishers, pp 73–80. doi:10.1145/1496984.1496995

Weber BGM, Mateas JM, Jhala A (2011) Modeling player retention in madden NFL 11. In: Proceedings of IAAI

Williams D (2014) Zombie epidemics and you, Gamasutra, 3rd February 2014, Gamasutra. http://www.gamasutra.com/blogs/DmitriWilliams/20140203/209921/Zombie_Epidemics_and_You.php. Accessed 1 April 2015

Williams D (2015) Prediction in the gaming industry, Part 2: prediction and gaming (Or, How to Know Your Players), Gamasutra, 2nd April 2015. http://www.gamasutra.com/blogs/DmitriWilliams/20150204/235660/Prediction_in_the_Gaming_Industry_Part_2_Prediction_and_Gaming_Or_How_to_Know_Your_Players.php. Accessed 1 April 2015

Wooga (2013) Monster world: keeping players engaged for more than 3 years, August 2013. http://www.wooga.com/2013/08/monster-world-keeping-players-engaged-for-more-than-3-years/. Accessed 1 April 2015

Yannakakis GN (2012) Game AI revisited. In: Proceedings of ACM Computing Frontiers Conference

Zoeller G (2011) MMO rapid content iteration. Presentation at Game Developers Conference 2011. http://gdc.gulbsoft.org/. Accessed 1 April 2015

Part III
Expert Orientated Methods

Chapter 8
User Experience Design for Inexperienced Gamers: GAP—Game Approachability Principles

Heather Desurvire and Charlotte Wiberg

Abstract Game Approachability Principles (GAP) is a set of useful guidelines for game designers to create better tutorials, and new player experiences—especially for the casual gamer. Developing better first learning levels can be a key step to ease the casual gamer into play and to do so proactively—at the conceptual design phase before it is too costly or cumbersome to restructure the tutorials as would be the case later in the development cycle. Thus, Game Approachability, in the context of game development, is defined as making games initially more friendly, fun, immersive, and accessible for those players who have the desire to play, yet do not always follow-through to actually playing the game. GAP has evolved through a series of stages assessing accessibility (NB Approachability and Accessibility are used interchangeably throughout this chapter) as a stand-alone, heuristic-based approach versus one-on-one User Testing. Outcomes suggest potential for GAP as an (1) effective Heuristic Evaluation, (2) adjunct to User Testing, and (3) as a proactive checklist of principles in to conceptually design the new player experience and/or tutorial to increase Game Approachability—for all levels of gamers.

8.1 Introduction

User Experience (UX), in general, has become one of the most central concepts in the research of interaction design (Benyon 2005). In general, it focuses on the high quality use of some kind of interactive technology. (cf. Forlizzi and Battarbee 2004; Hassenzahl and Tractinsky 2006; Hassenzahl et al. 2006; McCarthy and Wright 2004) User experience design in the context of computer games is likewise highly relevant (Pagulayan et al. 2003). The relevance is high due to, at least, two reasons;

H. Desurvire (✉)
User Behavioristics, Inc., Marina del Rey, CA USA
e-mail: Heather3d@gmail.com

C. Wiberg
Umea University, Umea, Sweden
e-mail: charlotte.wiberg@umu.se

© Springer International Publishing Switzerland 2015   169
R. Bernhaupt (ed.), *Game User Experience Evaluation,*
Human-Computer Interaction Series, DOI 10.1007/978-3-319-15985-0_8

(1) Games of all kinds are artifacts used by an enormous amount of people and therefore important to consider in itself because of this, and (2) interaction patterns and techniques seen, used and developed in games are spread into other digital artifacts and media, which intensify the potential of its relevance. Simply, if we gain knowledge in User Experience (UX) in gaming we give guidance in a large number of design projects—both inside and outside of the game industry (Wiberg 2003).

In order to understand UX in gaming it is important to pinpoint the specifics in this domain. Research in Human-Computer Interaction (HCI) and Interaction Design (ID) has throughout the years developed a number of concepts, theories and frameworks both in how to understand gaming as well as how to normatively and intelligently talk about it. It also allows us to have a common language (Vanderheiden 2003). Some concepts in the context of gaming research are, for instance, Flow (cf. Csikszentmihalyi 2008) as well as more narrow concepts specifically for use in gaming—GameFlow (Sweetser and Wyeth 2005; Jegers 2007). The concept of Flow by Csikszentmihalyi, has been used as a framework to describe how people attain experience by combining motivation and the level of what they (earlier) could achieve (Yee 2007). Overall the work shows great potential in UX in general and UX in gaming as well. However, the work was not necessarily intended to give specific guidance for designers but merely to describe and understand the loose notion of experience. The latter concept, Game Flow, loosely based on the work of Csikszentmihalyi, was further developed into frameworks of normative principles for evaluation and design (ibid.), thus with the intention to give guidance in game design. Methodologically, the approach of normative lists, for example as a list of heuristics, is highly influenced by early works in traditional usability research. For instance, it is noteworthy that the first published article of usability and heuristics in the field of Human Computer Interaction (HCI) was about Computer Games and Learning (Malone 1982). However, perhaps the most famous work here was the design of the method of Heuristic Evaluation by Nielsen (1993) was found to be efficacious as an adjunct and better than a 'best guess' method, (Desurvire et al. 1994). In general, research tradition and method when it comes to usability in HCI and ID tends to be more normative than descriptive in its' nature. The reasons may vary, but overall it can be said that many researchers in HCI focusing on usability issues are either somehow connected to or collaborating with industry, or see the great need to guide in design. The same could be said about game user research. Here the reasons are similar to usability research.

Historically, the game design industry evaluated mostly functional aspects on the code bug level for QA. This is still done, often by large crews of young people connected to game companies. However, nowadays, as a much more mature industry, game design also includes a focus on elements of traditional usability such as creating clear terminology and a non-intrusive easy-to-use user interface, but also on game mechanics, and among others, game play aspects such as fun and immersion. As the interaction domain of games and gaming matures, the research and methods also becomes more repetitive, longitudinal and thorough, thus more genuinely informative for industry.

When it comes to game user research, a small number of studies have been published, addressing issues regarding usability related issues in gaming. Other principles specific to games include pace and adequate challenge, i.e. offering a game that is neither too difficult nor too easy (cf. Desurvire and Chen 2006; Desurvire & Wiberg 2007); Federoff 2002, 2003; Kohnnen and Elina 2006). The boundaries between what is addressed as 'usability' and what is labeled UX are to some extent blurred when it comes to gaming. It is clear that the UX for games includes principles beyond usability that make games fun, immersive, challenging, and frankly, addictive, such as collections found in the 400 Project (Falstein and Barwood), and HEP and PLAY (Desurvire et al. 2004, 2009). The aspects of focus in games are not only many more than in other interaction domains, they also are highly interrelated and sometimes even contradictory, i.e. sometimes, if combined they amplify one another and sometimes they tend to cancel out each other. Nevertheless, this makes the analysis as well as the design of games seductive but extremely complex.

The history of who the game industry serves is long. From the 1970s and forward, games were designed mainly for an audience very similar to the game designer, i.e. they were designing for themselves. Later, as the industry grew, from late 1980s and forward, more subcultures could be found in the audience and the designers had to be more observant on how future players would react. Still, so called, hard core gamers could be seen as the priority group to target. However, over the last period, and recently, video game designers and publishers have been shifting their focus from meeting the desires of hardcore gamers to serving the less savvy and sophisticated casual gamer. The trend is clear, as more non gamer types are playing games on mobile, tablet, console and certainly more platforms in development and to be developed—the crowd of gamers is becoming more heterogeneous. The focus is no longer only on hardcore gamers. There is a distinct shift towards a world where the general player is an inexperienced gamer. Additionally, with the advent of new game mechanics and genre breaking game play, learning to play this new game style becomes a major concern for designers. Players are fickle and easily distracted. They are also easily bored resulting in their abandoning playing the game. In this chapter, the focus is on the initial stages of the UX of games; the first time someone learns how to play the game. The players at the initial stages of the game need to learn the tools of the game in order to perceive that they have the possibility to master the game. While they are learning these tools, the players must be sufficiently motivated, whether it is through game play challenge, story, emotional connection with the character, pressure from their peers, or all of these. The game needs to unfold for the user in a way that he or she understands well enough to continue to explore the game, without giving away too much, while motivating the player to investigate and continue to play further. This concept is called Game Approachability academically and in some industry circles, Game Accessibility. In this chapter, we will use the terms Game Approachability and Approachability interchangeably (Desurvire 2007; Desurvire and Wiberg 2007, 2008, 2009).

With the strong emphasis continuing to be expected on inexperienced players, the concept of Game Approachability is fast becoming as crucial an aspect of gaming fun and entertainment as "engagement" has been historically. Casual, or inexperienced gamers, as their name implies, frequently lack extensive prior game play experience. The casual game player's more occasional or periodic exposure to games in contrast to their hardcore counterparts often means that casual gamers require more guidance playing video games. This in turn suggests a challenge to support the casual gamer in getting started with game play without divulging the secrets of the game itself—that is, to provide the tools to play games so casual game players have the potential to be confident in their mastering of the game as well. Therefore, in order to better meet the needs of casual gamers now being included in the mix of targeted people for whom games are designed requires specific methodology and approaches in game design.

There are currently no standardized normative lists or set of principles for creating useful and well-designed tutorials or first learning levels in games. Typically, game designers create the first level and tutorials last, basing them on how the game has developed. Further, the designs are poorly conceptualized because of scheduling practices that put them at the end of an already rushed design schedule. Even if there is enough time, designers have no clear guidelines or principles and there are also prolonged feedback loops between designers and the results of user research making it too late to make substantial changes for ideal designs for fun and learning.

The goal of having GAP is in having a list of guidelines that create both a common language, and to identify the details of what causes improved approachability. Similar to what was found with Nielsen's productivity software heuristics, the GAP heuristics can potentially allow a deeper analysis of a game as opposed to best guessing (Desurvire 1994). These offer game user researchers and game designers a better understanding of what is required in order to promote better approachability, and further, what underlying elements in the game that are already promoting good approachability.

As GAP was developed, we sought guidance when it comes to how people learn. In order to find this guidance in learning, we looked at research from the pedagogical field. There is a substantial body of research from interactive learning found in learning theories in psychology and education. (cf. Bandura 1994, 1977; Bruer 2000; Gee 2003, 2005) The principles for game approachability were developed from and subsequently validated by the research findings in these fields as well as good game design principles. This chapter will cover the purpose of the most related work in these fields in order to show how the theoretical ground of the GAP list was developed.

The objective of this chapter is to present the findings reached in the development of an inspection method for evaluating and improving the level of, what is called, Game Approachability (GAP). This term is explained as the level of helpfulness in a computer game for new and inexperienced players to be able to initiate and continue to play the game. This issue is highly relevant for the game industry. A large number of inexperienced gamers need to be enticed into exploring and entering into gaming. In order to get these new player groups to experience gaming as fun, entertaining and enjoyable, they will need a gentle push over the threshold into the game. Hence, the problem is to help new players just enough without giving away too much of the plot.

8.2   Game Approachability

Inexperienced gamers are likely to start and continue to play games if these games are more easily approachable. That is, the game needs a high level of game approachability. So far, research on game approachability has been formed from educational research, and includes aspects such as social learning theory, self-efficacy and cognitive learning theory. There are many systems and artifacts where approachability is highlighted as central, for example, online learning, productivity software and hardware. However, games have not been one of them. We need to ask ourselves how approachability research can apply to games and what needs to be revised and redesigned in concepts and methods? How will these methods help designers include better approachability into their games? In the following section, some related work is revealed in order to contextualize the work presented in this paper.

8.2.1   *Learning as a Means to Approachability*

There is no global theory of learning. Learning can be understood in numerous ways. However, some learning theories include the potential of having a high level of applicability to game design. Theories of learning often highlight aspects such as motivation, helping behaviors, ensuring the tools become second nature and engagement that are central for gaming. While these ideas have been applied in educational settings to improve student learning, they can also provide a starting point for describing how game design can improve the accessibility of games for casual gamers.

Some applicable theories are: (1) Social Learning Theory, (cf. Bandura 1977), which emphasizes the importance of observation and modeling in the learning process; (2) Cognitive Learning Theory, (cf. Bruer 2000), which emphasizes the active construction of knowledge and is most commonly associated with the ideas of Piaget; (3) Self-Efficacy is another term used in education and learning (Ormond 1999; Bandura 1994) and refers to people's beliefs about their own capabilities, or their beliefs about their ability to reach a goal; (4) John Paul Gee's research in the current educational field actually uses good game design to develop principles for designing educational materials and curriculum that are both motivating and fun for students (Gee 2003, 2005). The following are a subset of the elements identified by Gee that are applicable to accessibility: (1) Identity, (2) Co-Design, (3) Customization, (4) Manipulation and Perception, (5) Information On Demand And In Time, (6) Sandbox and (7) System Thinking (for a more thorough description of the points discussed above see earlier publications. cf. Desurvire et al. 2007, 2009).

With the knowledge that there are Usability and game design principles, there is a need to identify and utilize Approachability principles in order to round out the gaming UX for use as both evaluation and design purposes. There is a need, therefore, to identify and validate the Approachability principles for games.

8.3 Design of the Study: Comparison of Empirical Usability Evaluation and Heuristic Evaluation by GAP

The most common way of identifying the areas of games that need to be improved is through User Testing. User Testing has been found to be quite successful in improving the design of games. The need to design games in a way that makes them more accessible to casual gamers has also added the need to define and utilize a set of principles for conceptualizing the design as well as to utilize usability research to refine the design.

The learning of skills and techniques in a video game is similar to the way that people learn anything else. It follows therefore that what is needed is to consider theories of learning when determining how to design games in such a way that players learn the needed skills while they are also having fun. In previous research, a set of principles and heuristics were developed that describe the types of activities necessary to promote learning within a game. These heuristics are intended to support User Testing by focusing on issues of accessibility within a game when evaluating and when doing User Testing as a checklist to refine the design. In addition, and most importantly, the accessibility principles can be used to design a good tutorial from the onset of game design. In many cases, the lack of accessibility results in the failure of a game resulting occasionally in the failure of studios that would otherwise have produced good and successful games.

The current study compares the results from User Testing as a benchmark of all usability methods with an evaluation performed using the Approachability principles to identify what types of issues each method found in the same games. Did both User Testing and the Heuristic Evaluation identify the same issues in the games? Did one method find more accessibility issues or playability and usability issues than the other? How do the different methods complement each other?

8.3.1 The Games

This study includes data from four games to identify the differences and similarities between a Heuristic Evaluation based on Game Approachability Principles (GAP) and User Testing. In order to obtain a breadth of popular game styles and consoles we studied two games that were Shooter and Strategy games developed so that both were played on an Xbox 360 console. The other two games were racing games still in the development stage, one that was played using a Nintendo Wii and one that was played using a Playstation3[1]. The beginning, learning stage, of the games were studied, since it is their goal to provide easy access to learning how to play the game, while having fun and most importantly, excited and addicted to continuing to play.

---

[1] The names of the games cannot be revealed due to confidentiality agreements

8.3.2   Heuristic Evaluation Based on GAP

The principles in the GAP list were developed from previous research and based on current literature in relation to learning (Bandura 1977, 1994; Gee 2003, 2005; Ormond 1999). Usability/Playability evaluation was performed using the Heuristic Evaluation, focusing on how each accessibility heuristic was supported or violated and then defined the issue. Another Usability/Playability researcher performed User Testing in a one-on-one think aloud method, identifying any Usability/Playability and Approachability issues. The following is the list of GAP utilized in both methods of evaluation.

The GAP List[2]
1. Practice
2. Demonstration of Type
3. Demonstration of Action
4. Self-Efficacy (reinforcement and encouragement)
5. Scaffolding (Failure prevention where help is at first general then more specific as needed.)
6. Sandbox (Gee: In control: co-identify, manipulation, perception).
7. Playability Based Heuristics (PLAY) (This comprises areas including categories of Game Game Mechanics, Game Immersion and Game Play) (Desurvire and Wiberg 2009).
8. Coolness and Entertainment
9. Information On Demand and In Time
10. Knowledge Transfer and Acquisition
11. Self Mastery (Development of self Mastery is summative based on the other heuristics).

8.3.3   Empirical Usability Evaluation

After Heuristic Evaluation and Empirical Usability/Playability laboratory testing were completed with the four games, the results were compared. Heuristic Evaluation was analyzed first, followed by the empirical User Testing sessions. During the empirical usability evaluation of the four games, 32 players engaged in usability/ playability sessions. For one game, eight players were observed, for another game twelve players were observed, and for two of the games six players were observed.[3] The majority of the players were male, with only two players being female. All were between the ages of eight and thirty-five. Forty-nine percent of the players were considered casual players, 25 % were considered moderate players and the rest were considered hardcore players. Each session was organized as a one-on-one think

---

[2] This is the GAP list of major categories, the full list of GAP is available upon request.

[3] Uneven sample sizes was necessary due to the needs of the game development and were accounted for in the analysis, since this is formative research a small sample size is typical.

aloud evaluation session, in an environment similar to the one where they would actually play the game. Participants were given instructions to begin the game, and asked to think "out loud" during the session, except when it interrupted their game play. They were asked several probing questions while using the game prototype. The players were then thanked, debriefed and asked to fill out a satisfaction questionnaire. The evaluator recorded a log of the players' actions, comments, failures, missteps, and then coded each of these as a positive player experience or a negative player experience. A positive experience was defined as anything that increased their pleasure, immersion, and/or the challenge of the game. A negative experience was defined as any situation where the player was bored, frustrated or wanted to quit the game. The probing questions and the players' comments were used to verify any assumptions made by the evaluator. GAP was utilized during the sessions by the evaluator as a checklist to assist in identifying and categorizing accessibility issues observed. After the sessions were complete, any issues that were considered hindrances to learning how to play the game and having fun, were identified, analyzed and documented.

8.3.4 Comparison of Results

After both the Heuristic Evaluation and the User Testing were completed, the results were compared to identify what types of issues each method found in the same games. The issues found for each evaluation were categorized either as an accessibility/approachability issue or as a playability/usability issue. As noted earlier, the terms accessibility and approachability are used interchangeably depending upon which of two communities one inhabits. In academia, the term accessibility would be associated with disabilities of one kind or another and therefore the use of the term approachability. The gaming community is more familiar with the term accessibility. The accessibility issues were then categorized as one or more of the accessibility heuristics. The accessibility issues in the games were compared to see what issues the Heuristic Evaluation found that usability did not, what issues User Testing found that the Heuristic Evaluation did not, and what issues both methods found. In addition, the Heuristic Evaluation and the User Testing results were compared to determine the number of accessibility issues identified in each as well as the overall number of issues found by both methods. Lastly, the descriptions of the issues identified by both methods were compared to determine any similarities or differences in the granularity of each method's description of the issues.

8.4 Results of the Heuristic Evaluation by GAP Heuristic Counts

The Heuristic Evaluation identified a higher percentage of accessibility issues as well as more types of accessibility issues than the User Testing, while the User Testing found more issues relating to playability/usability. For the four games, the Heuristic Evaluation identified 90 issues, 47% or 43 issues relating to accessibility and 52% or 27, which were issues of playability/usability (see Table 8.1). The User Testing found 207 issues in total, 11%, or 22 issues relating to accessibility and 89% or 185 that were issues of playability/ usability. In addition, the Heuristic Evaluation found more types of accessibility issues than in the usability study. The issues found in the Heuristic Evaluation incorporated ideas across six categories of accessibility heuristics as compared to four categories in the usability study.

The following quotes and screen shots provide examples for the types of accessibility issues found in only the User Testing, only in the Heuristic Evaluation, and those shared in both the User Testing and the Heuristic Evaluation.

8.4.1 Examples of Approachability Found In Data

GAP as Heuristic Evaluation not Found in User Testing The GAP principle of Amount and Type of Demonstration occurred twice in the Heuristic Evaluation and not at all in the User Testing. An example of this Amount and Type of Demonstration was identified in the Shooter game, where the player was unable to win against the Artificial Intelligence (AI) opponent, even when not making any mistakes. The

Table 8.1 Accessibility heuristics identified

Principle	User testing	Heuristic evaluation
Practice	–	5
Demonstration of Type	–	2
Demonstration of Actions	2	7
Self Efficacy	–	3
Sandbox	–	9
Information Presented in Time	1	–
Scaffolding	1	–
Prior Knowledge	–	–
PLAY	17	12
Entertainment & Coolness	–	–
Self Mastery	–	–
Total	22	43

Fig. 8.1 GAP: Self efficacy found in heuristic evaluation in racing game

players did not recognize they could get extra points by doing combination moves, required in order to win, as these were not obvious from playing the game. Having AI Non-Playing Characters doing these moves would demonstrate to the player that this is both possible and an option. Furthermore, demonstrating the controller buttons and thumbsticks using a controller image, and an increased health meter would demonstrate exactly how to do this. User Testing did not find this GAP principle.

Finding that Self-Efficacy was a violated GAP principle found via Heuristic Evaluation, but not User Testing has implications for using GAP in design. Since this is an issue that was found when called out by using GAP as a checklist in the Heuristic Evaluation, but not found in User Testing alludes to it being a more subtle issue not easily discovered from players' comments and from observing their experience. Self- Efficacy was found to be violated, for example, when the evaluator determined the players would be expected to know how to perform several button combinations, along with timing in competing against some challenging AI opponents in a Shooter game. In the Racing game (see Fig. 8.1), the evaluator determined the players would not know certain moves, such as a special 180 that would help them beat the AI opponents. Without these moves, they would be unlikely to continue to try to win without considerable motivation to continue. They would likely not feel confident they could continue and that would undoubtedly cause the players to feel incapable of making it through the first level. The rest of the levels would therefore be too difficult. There is a considerable likelihood this player would be one to drop out of playing this game. Increasing Self-Efficacy would give the players confidence that they would be able to continue and be successful. This would require giving the player some of the basic GAP principles, such as Demonstration, Practice, Reinforcement, Scaffolding and Sandbox. The specifics would depend on the type of issue identified. In this case, the player needed to have the fighting techniques Demonstrated, then have a chance to Practice, be given Reinforcement (positive feedback), and Scaffolding help if they could not kill all the opponents before the end of the level, since the first level needs to be a successful experience.

Fig. 8.2 GAP: Gee: Sandbox without consequence; lack of sandbox in shooter game

This has implications for initial concept design, since the designers could plan for Self-Efficacy and have the design refined based on real user testing (User Testing).

The GAP Gee (Identify, Co-Design, Customization, Manipulation, Information On Demand and in Time, Sandbox) was found in Heuristic Evaluation, but not with the User Testing. Predicting the users playing the beginning learning levels, it was identified that there was the need for the GAP Gee: Sandbox Without Consequence. In the Shooter game, players were taught how to use a combination of buttons for attacking their enemies. They were taught three new moves, and then were required to use these attacks in game play. Due to the Heuristic Evaluation, players would need to practice any new moves successfully, and would otherwise likely lose their characters' lives. Many players would not have enough time to play and master the new skills without consequences, as per the approachability principle Gee: Sandbox without consequence. When the players have the time to practice, they can combine the new skills in an open play format without the risk of losing. When they have learned these skills via the Sandbox, the players would continue to first level with preparation, and thus be able to fairly defend themselves (see Fig. 8.2).

The GAP Heuristic Evaluation assisted the evaluator to notice and design for the consequence of not having enough practice, via a Sandbox. Thus, adding a Sandbox.

GAP Found in User Testing not Found in GAP Heuristic Evaluation User Testing found issues related to GAP Scaffolding, not found in the GAP Heuristic Evaluation. The GAP Scaffolding was found to be missing when the player was supposed to cut some chains down from a fort in order to release a bridge; the player was stuck (see Fig. 8.3). They did not know what to do in this learning level and could not continue the game. Had this occurred in real life, the player would likely quit

Fig. 8.3 Example of GAP, scaffolding needed in shooter game, via *User Testing*

the game. Scaffolding was violated and had it been added, would have assisted the player in continuing the game. Scaffolding would be useful because if the player still did not understand after being offered a small parcel of assistance, other and more varied parcels would be offered. User Testing offered this insight, since the players were stuck without this information.

Issues that were found only in User Testing and not in the GAP Heuristic Evaluation, were more GAP—HEP and PLAY guidelines. Since User Testing has the advantage of real players, thinking aloud their experiences in real-time, the evaluator had the advantage of players' comments of their experience, "I think the tutorial is way too long. I want to be playing the game, but instead I'm doing the tutorial. I thought the stuff in the beginning was useful, but now it just seems like too much and I am not having that much fun".

This led to the identification of the GAP—HEP and PLAY, where the guidelines spells out the players are having a fun and successful experience in the first 10–20 min. The Heuristic Evaluation did not find this. Ideally, the key for the tutorial based on GAP, is a design where the player is learning the tools while this learning is masked by their having fun through game play challenge and story motivation. This has implications for designing using GAP as a checklist of the conceptual tutorial design. However, seeing where the actual users are having a fun and successful experience seems to only be validated with real players; otherwise, it is simply a guess.

Information On Demand and In Time in System Thinking, from GAP was one that was found from User Testing in the Shooter game, but not in the Heuristic Evaluation. When there were instructions offered in both text and audio, the evaluator observed players that still missed this information. They were onto another area of the game. Since players missed the necessary information when it was presented, they then did not have the ability to repeat the instructions to learn what they had missed. As one player said, "the instructions need to be clearer and you should have

Fig. 8.4 GAP information on demand and in time, system thinking in shooter game

the ability to repeat instructions. It just seems like they tell you the instructions once and if you miss it you are lost. (see Fig. 8.4) In addition, this instruction was teaching a skill that would be required for later play in the game. In other words, System Thinking meant what the player learned would have consequences to the players' game tools later in the game. If there were repeatable and plausible instructions, the player would then have the ability to receive the instruction when they needed it, rather than when it was offered. And later on when the player may need the instruction again, they could locate this assistance. In this Shooter game, the objectives text actually disappeared after the instruction was given. It would be better for the text to stay on the screen until the players were successful and well onto the next area of the game. Having this list accessible at all times, via a button leading to a table of contents help screen, for example, would allow the players access later in the game if they should forget. Alternatively or in addition, employing the basic GAP such as Demonstration, Practice, and Sandbox would help reinforce this new skill for later use (System Thinking). This GAP was missed in the Heuristic Evaluation, as it was likely the evaluator could not predict that the skill had not been taught and offered On Demand and In Time. This is a good example of while the designers can make their best guess, User Testing will validate this principle. The GAP offered a structure for the evaluators to categorize what was missing, and it will lead to potential solutions.

This explanation provides implications for both design and evaluation, since GAP can offer designers the conscious design principle that information ideally is taught On Demand and In Time for skills required to play the game (System Thinking), and refined via User Testing. Heuristic Evaluation would identify this as a potential issue, but could only be validated with real representative players.

8.4.1.1 GAP Found in Both User Testing and Heuristic Evaluation

From both the GAP Heuristic Evaluation and User Testing, the GAP—HEP and PLAY were both found. There were many issues found in both methods, (seventeen in User Testing and twelve in Heuristic Evaluation). This is not surprising, since HEP and PLAY issues are related to fun and playability. These do not directly have anything to do with learning and approachability, but learning must be fun and successful. These are issues that are the focus of game usability/playability, which both methods are focused upon. The difference is that Heuristic Evaluation can identify these issues, but User Testing validates these with real players. The violated issues that were identified under GAP—HEP and PLAY in both User Testing and Heuristic Evaluation in the games were the following:

a. The first 10–20 min of play was fun and successful.
b. Players should not experience being penalized repetitively or for the same failure.
c. Varying activities and pacing during the game in order to minimize fatigue or boredom.
d. The game provides clear goals; overriding goals are presented early and short-term goals throughout game play.
e. The skills needed to attain goals were taught early enough to play or use later, or right before the new skill was needed.
f. The game gave rewards that immersed the player more deeply in the game by increasing their capabilities or capacity to do things in the game.

8.4.2 Level of Detail

In addition to differences in the number of accessibility/playability issues identified by each method, there was also a difference in the level of detail that each method provided concerning the identified issues. The User Testing referred more to specific areas of the games where problems occurred, providing a count of the number of players that had difficulty at certain areas of the game, as well as quotes from players that indicated frustration. Conversely, the Heuristic Evaluation identified areas where a player was not given the means to master a skill-set, whether by motivation to follow through or by the actual teaching given and practicing allowed. This evaluation then indicated other areas in the game that might give players trouble since they had not learned the needed skill. This is most likely a result of User Testing describing problems as they are seen while Heuristic Evaluations are predicting problems players are likely to have. The high number of HEP and PLAY issues identified by User Testing may also be a result of this difference. (see Table 8.1) For User Testing, each area that a player had difficulty in was identified as an issue, such as unclear goals, and thus each separate area would be counted as an issue. For the Heuristic Evaluation, the problem was counted once but then noted that players would continue to have problems with a certain skill-set because it had not been learned at the time the designers intended.

8.5 Conclusion

Our results indicated that the usability one-on-one testing and the GAP Heuristic Evaluation of the games provided information that supplemented each other. The GAP principles were useful in evaluating the game design and offering suggestions to the designers based on the principles and the associated issues found. GAP provides a structure for organizing approachability issues, so that designers can have an understanding of what is lacking, and thus what is necessary to create an optimal learning level that is also fun. The GAP Heuristic Evaluation alone provided more information about game approachability while the User Testing provided more information about playability/usability of the games. GAP with User Testing can be perhaps best thought of a way to validate and refine assumptions made in the initial GAP Heuristic Evaluation, with real players. This was evident especially with the GAP Scaffolding and Information on Demand and in Time. GAP used for Heuristic Evaluation, is likely to provide more approachability issues, since that is the focus of the evaluation, and whereas, the User Testing focuses on not just approachability, but usability/playability issues that may supersede the approachability focus. Alternatively, the User Testing is able to provide a level of detail that is not possible in the Heuristic Evaluation, such as specific quotes from the players that validate real experience, rather than predicted experience. It is important to note that the evaluation is performed with live players, and as we know, human behavior can never be accurately predicted. More importantly for approachability, GAP offers the promise and ability to be proactive when used by the developers in creating a design that includes these principles prior to the design being set. This in fact may be one of the most valuable uses of GAP, since the conceptual design sets the foundation. If a design is used based on GAP, then it provides a built-in structure for learning while having fun. Heuristic Evaluation, using the same language and structure in GAP allows a refinement, and User Testing with GAP uses a finer level of evaluation since real users are involved.

Further, since GAP is a novel approach to User Testing, evaluators may be more likely to focus on more traditional usability issues, as opposed to approachability ones. With more practice and experience with GAP, evaluators are likely to uncover more issues upon further use, when testing real players. There is evidence evaluators go deeper with their evaluation and analysis of the player experience than they would without GAP. Still, Heuristic Evaluation, used as an adjunct and alternative inspection method, allows a way to uncover some issues that may be similar to evaluating real users, and some that are beyond what is found with real users. GAP also would be a viable structure for game designers to utilize for conceptualizing and setting a good new player experience design, that is based in what we know about how humans learn and also have fun.

In summary, the suggested best use of GAP and User Testing is to utilize GAP as a checklist as a way to design and refine a good tutorial and entry game level. The User Testing can then be utilized to refine the design, and GAP as a Heuristic Evaluation can be used as an adjunct to User Testing between research iterations.

Thus, taken together, both methods of research can help make video games more accessible to casual players. The GAP list offers a checklist for the conceptual design for Approachability while Usability/Playability one-on-one evaluation offers both validation, and correction to the design for approachability

8.6   Future Work

The GAP checklist has already been utilized for conceptual design as well as with evaluation of many games from notable companies worldwide, and student games, resulting in new player experiences that are improved, some to the extent of creating higher conversion rates and increased continuing play. This is a win for both the game companies and the players. In addition, GAP has been used by many students at USC's Interactive Media and Games Department game design projects, as well as User Behavioristics Research, Inc. game client games, including those that have some of the largest group of game subscribers. Utilizing other research methods, such as the Think Aloud, as a refinement of the conceptual design and subsequent design for approachability has been found to be important in evaluation, validation and refinement of the design with real users (for which there has to date found to be *no substitute*), since we learn about the "what caused this problem" which leads to potential design solutions and from the real users. In the process of using GAP on game tutorials and first design levels, we have found them to be a good foundation for both designing and evaluation. This may in part be due to the structured manner of having to think in a full dimensional way, as well as including the guidelines' playability and how-to-learn principles. We believe that for each type of genre, there may be particular issues that go beyond the foundation of high standard game access. There may have additional issues with for example, multiplayer, mobile, VR or augmented reality platforms. In addition, different styles of games where fun may not be the intent, such as serious games.

To summarize, PLAY and GAP are heuristics that are meant to be solely guidelines, not rules, and that are generalizable. Like all guidelines, these are meant to be broken and only used to provide a way to evaluate and analyze the player experience in a deeper way. We want these Heuristics available to provide a way for Designers and Evaluators to gain a deeper insight for creating a good player experience, where everyone, including the players themselves, benefit.

References

Bandura A (1977) Social learning theory. General Learning, New York

Bandura A (1994) Self-efficacy. In: Ramachaudran VS (ed) Encyclopedia of human behavior, vol 4. Academic, New York, pp 71–81

Bruer J (2000) Schools for thought. MIT, Cambridge

Benyon D, Turner P, Turner S (2005) Designing interactive systems. People, Activities, Contexts, Technologies

Csikszentmihalyi M (2008) Flow: the psychology of optimal experience. Harper Perennial Modern Classics, UK

Desurvire H (1994) Faster cheaper!! are usability inspection methods as effective as empirical testing? In: Nielsen J, Mack R (eds) Usability inspection methods. J. Wiley and Sons, New York, pp 173–202

Desurvire H (2007) List of core and approachability principles for good game design (LA CHI Association Meeting Presentation)

Desurvire H, Chen B (2006) 48 differences between good and bad video games: game playability principles (PLAY) for designing highly ranked video games

Desurvire H, Wiberg C (2007) Master of the game. In the proceedings of the CMID'07 The first international conference on cross-media interaction design, held in Hemavan Sweden, April 2007

Desurvire H, Wiberg C (2008) Master of the Game: Assessing Approachability in Future Game Design In the proceedings of CHI 2008 (http://publik.tuwien.ad.at/files/PubDat_167638.pdf (Page 3177)), Florence, Italy, April, 2008

Desurvire H, Wiberg C (2009) Game usability heuristics (PLAY) for evaluating and designing better games: the next iteration. HCI conference, San Diego

Desurvire H, Caplan M, Toth J (2004) Using heuristics to improve the playability of games. CHI conference, Vienna

Desurvire H, Jegers K, Wiberg C (2007) Evaluating fun and entertainment: developing a conceptual framework design of evaluation methods. Presented at the workshop 'HCI and New Media Arts: Methodology and Evaluation' at the CHI 2007 conference, San Jose CA, USA, April

Desurvire H, Wiberg C (2009) Game usability heuristics (PLAY) for evaluating and designing better games: the next iteration. HCI Conference, 2009, San Diego, California USA

Federoff M (2002) Heuristics and usability guidelines for the creation and evaluation of FUN in video games. Thesis at the University Graduate School of Indiana University, Dec. 2002 (melissafederoff@yahoo.com)

Federoff M (2003) User testing for games: getting better data earlier. Game Developer Magazine (June 2003), pp. 35–40

Forlizzi J, Battarbee K (2004) Understanding experience in interactive systems. Proceedings of DIS2004, Cambridge, USA

Gee JP (2003) What video games have to teach us about learning and literacy. Palgrave Macmillan, New York

Gee JP (2005) Learning by design: games as learning machines: Interactive Educational Multimedia 8: (15–23)

Hassenzahl M, Tractinsky N (2006) User experience—a research agenda. Behav Inf Technol 25(2):99–97

Hassenzahl M, Law E, Hvannberg ET (2006). User experience—towards a unified view. The 2nd COST294-MAUSE International Open Workshop held in conjunction with NordiChi, Oct, 14, 2006, Oslo, Norway.

Jegers K (2007) Pervasive game flow: Understanding player enjoyment in pervasive gaming. J Comp Entertainment (CIE), ACM

Korhonen H, Elina M (2006) Koivisto: playability heuristics for mobile games. Mobile HCI 2006: 9–16

Malone TW (1982) Heuristics for designing enjoyable user interfaces: lessons from computer games. In: Thomas JC, Schneider ML (eds) Human factors in computing systems. Ablex Publishing Corporation, Norwood

McCarthy J, Wright PC (2004) Technology as experience. MIT Press, Cambridge

Nielsen J (1993) Usability engineering. Morgan Kaufmann Inc, San Francisco

Ormond JE (1999) Human learning, 3rd ed. Prentice-Hall, Upper Saddle River

Pagulayan R, Keeker K, Fuller T, Wixon D, Romero R (2003) User-centered design in games (revision). In: Jacko J, Sears A (eds) Handbook for human-computer interaction in interactive systems. Lawrence Erlbaum Associates, Inc, Mahwah

Sweetser P, Wyeth P (2005) GameFlow: a model for evaluating player enjoyment in games. J Comp Entertainment (CIE), 3(3). ACM

Vanderheiden G (2003) Interaction for diverse users. In: Jacko JA, Sears A (eds) The human-computer interaction handbook. Fundamentals, evolving technologies and emerging applications. L. Erlbaum Associates Inc., Hillsdale, pp 397–400

Wiberg C (2003) A measure of fun: extending the concept of web usability. PhD Thesis. Dept of informatics, Umeå University.

Yee N (2007) Motivations of play in online games. CyberPsychol Behav 9:772–775

Heather Desurvire Principal of User Behavioristics Research, Inc. is one of the foremost specialists on Game User Research; Faculty in the Interactive Media and Games Department, School of Cinematic Arts, University of Southern California (USC), Los Angeles, California. Her original research on game user research for fun, approachability, accessibility, immersion and more, have assisted the industry in identifying how to create better games, including several professional conferences, as of this date (e.g., CHI 04', 06', 08', HCI 09' CHI 12', FDG 12' CHI 13', CHI 14'). She is on the board of directors of the newly formed SIG GUR (Game User Research). Her published work on usability methodologies has been presented at several conferences including CHI, HCI, and is published in Jakob Nielsen's seminal book on Usability Inspection Methods (1992). As a practitioner, Ms. Desurvire's clients benefit from her wealth of knowledge and depth of experience with creating optimal user and gamer experiences. She has worked with many top Fortune 100 companies such as Microsoft, United Airlines, Citibank, Federal Reserve, and top game publishers including Disney Interactive, Blizzard, Caesars Interactive, Electronic Arts, THQ, LucasArts, Sega, Nickelodeon, as well as many more.

Charlotte Wiberg Assistant Professor in Informatics, at Umeå University, Sweden. Dr. Wiberg specializes in evaluation methods for evaluating fun and entertainment in digital media and Information Technology. Her work focuses on games, web sites, and other experience related applications. In her earlier work, she conducted evaluations using traditional usability methods on entertainment IT and she proposed revision of the methods according to results in order to evaluate fun. Wiberg has conducted usability design—as a researcher and practitioner—for Vodafone, Swedish National TV (SVT), TeliaSonera, Coke Zero, Le Meridien to mention some.

Chapter 9
A Heuristic Framework for Evaluating User Experience in Games

Christina Hochleitner, Wolfgang Hochleitner, Cornelia Graf and Manfred Tscheligi

Abstract This book chapter describes an approach of evaluating user experience in video games by using heuristics. We provide a short overview of video games and explain the concept of user-centred design for games. Furthermore we describe the history of heuristics for video games and the role of user experience of games in general. Based on our previous work and experience we propose a revised framework consisting of two sets of heuristics (game play/game story, virtual interface) to detect the most critical issues in games. To assess its applicability to measure user experience factors we compare the results of expert evaluations of six current games with the user experience-based ratings of various game reviews. Our findings indicate a correlation between the extent to which our framework is satisfied and the game's average rating.

9.1 Introduction

The computer games industry has remarkably increased in importance over the last years (ESA 2011). The numbers of units sold climb up steadily and video games have changed from being a product for a small minority to a widely used and accepted medium. The expanding game market also opens the door for a series of research-related activities. Especially the term *user experience* (UX) has become increasingly important. Researchers and human-computer interaction (HCI) experts

C. Hochleitner (✉) · M. Tscheligi
Innovation Systems Department, Business Unit Technology Experience,
AIT Austrian Institute of Technology, Vienna, Austria
e-mail: Christina.Hochleitner@ait.ac.at

W. Hochleitner
Playful Interactive Environments, University of Applied Sciences Upper Austria, Hagenberg, Austria

C. Graf
Center for Usability Research and Engineering, Vienna, Austria

M. Tscheligi
Center for Human-Computer Interaction, Christian Doppler Laboratory "Contextual Interfaces",
Department of Computer Sciences, University of Salzburg, Salzburg, Austria

© Springer International Publishing Switzerland 2015
R. Bernhaupt (ed.), *Game User Experience Evaluation,*
Human-Computer Interaction Series, DOI 10.1007/978-3-319-15985-0_9

187

want to find out how computer gamers experience the game situation (cf. Clarke and Duimering 2006) to create more compelling and immersive game environments, and the industry is interested in finding ways to measure UX and to interpret the collected data (e.g. to acquire new target groups). The evaluation of the user's experience and the closely connected user-centred development of video games have been addressed in numerous publications (cf. Marsh et al. 2005; Bostan and Marsh 2010). Several researchers have designed methods to evaluate video games by adopting techniques from the usability field such as usability tests and heuristic evaluations. In recent years, sets of heuristics for the evaluation of video games have been proposed, all treating overlapping subject areas but diverse in detail and quality of description (cf. Federoff 2002; Desurvire et al. 2004; Korhonen and Koivisto 2006; Schaffer 2007; Pinelle et al. 2008a, b; Bernhaupt et al. 2007, 2008; Desurvire and Wiberg 2009; Livingston et al. 2010).

An approach similar to the one used in this chapter was presented by Febretti and Garzotto (2009). They conducted a study for evaluating engagement, usability and playability, all UX factors, but they did not focus on the overall UX of a game, which is the main aspect of our work.

As part of our research we are interested in reliable and cost-efficient methods to measure and predict the UX of games. An area where this approach is expected to be widely beneficial is the sector of so-called *indie games*—games that try to be innovative and provide new experiences for the player on the one hand and that are developed by smaller companies with little budget for expensive user and play testing on the other hand (Gril 2008). Within the last years we have investigated several different sets of heuristics including various aspects and oriented at different goals. Based on our experience in heuristic evaluations and games we have categorized 49 heuristics into 12 categories that, from our point of view, contain the most important factors for both, the system's usability, as well as the perceived UX. To validate our approach to heuristics and prove their connection to UX, we have conducted an evaluation of six games and related the obtained results to common game review reports.

9.1.1 Overview

Only few approaches are currently linking the results of heuristic evaluation methods to UX. Especially in the field of computer games, where the experience is the leading factor, different aspects can be evaluated using heuristics. Therefore, we put the main focus of this chapter on the assessability of a game's UX through the use of heuristics. We provide an overview of previously available heuristics and introduce categorized heuristics based on available literature, as well as our personal experience in the field of video games. To evaluate the applicability of our heuristics to UX ratings, we conduct heuristic evaluations of several games and compare the resulting data to UX-based game reviews. Finally we critically assess our method and offer improvements and future perspectives. We deliver a complete and updated framework usable for evaluating the usability and UX of games and provide proof for the connection between the developed heuristics and the game's UX.

9.2   Video Game and Game Genres

Before discussing heuristics for video games, we want to get a clear understanding of the terminology *video game*. Esposito provides an interesting definition (Esposito 2005):

"A videogame is a game which we play thanks to an audiovisual apparatus and which can be based on a story".

Esposito's definition contains four important elements that classify a video game: *game, play, audiovisual apparatus,* and *story*. These elements are derived from literature such as Huizinga (1950), Caillois (1961) and Zimmerman (2004).

We second this definition and want to point out the need to clearly distinguish games from productivity applications as done in Pagulayan et al. (2003). Finally, to avoid misunderstandings about the term itself we consider video games as an umbrella term for all electronic games, independent of their platform (computer, console, arcade, etc.). Still, there is need to put games into certain categories to be able to unite titles of similar type.

There are many different distinctions available, some more common than others. Wolf defined a set of 41 genres in (Wolf 2001), being sometimes too specific (e.g. when defining Diagnostic Cartridges as a genre). Ye proposes to adapt the genre term and certain genre conventions from movies to games, but does not give a clear genre definition himself (Ye 2004). A common and well established genre definition has been created by the NPD group and is mentioned amongst others in Pagulayan et al. (2003) and used by ESA (2011) for their market statistics. This classification contains 11 well known and well established (super-) genres such as role-playing game (RPG), action or shooters and abstains from introducing fine-grained subcategories. We propose the use of these genres in order to be able to classify games in accordance with the market/industry later on and focus mainly on computer based (PC) video games for the subject of this chapter.

9.3   User-Centred Design in Games

User-centred design is a design philosophy, which describes a prototype-driven software development process, where the user is integrated during the design and development process. The approach consists of several stages that are iteratively executed: requirements analysis, user analysis, prototyping and evaluation. User-centred design is specified in EN ISO 9241-210—Human Centred Design Processes for Interactive Systems (ISO 9241-210 2010). This approach is also used for game design as described by Fullerton et al. (2004). It contains three distinct development phases: conceptualization, prototyping and playtesting. The first phase typically involves the complete planning, such as identification of goals, challenges, rules, controls, mechanics, skill levels, rewards, story and the like (Pagulayan et al. 2003). These specifications are done by game designers and are put on record in game design documents.

The second phase—prototyping—is used to quickly generate playable content. This version of the game is in no way final but can be efficiently used to do play testing, thus giving players an opportunity to play the game, test its game mechanics and provide feedback on their UX (Fullerton et al. 2004). Measurable attributes are, for example, the overall quality (commonly denoted as fun), the ease of use or the balancing of challenge and pace (Pagulayan et al. 2003).

To gather results for these variables a range of usability methods can be applied during playtesting. Pagulayan et al. propose structured usability tests (cf. Dumas and Redish 1999) and rapid iterative testing and evaluation (RITE, cf. Medlock et al. 2002) as two applicable methods. They also propose additional evaluation methods, such as prototyping, empirical guideline documents or heuristics (Pagulayan et al 2003). We believe that especially heuristics can be a fast and cost-efficient, but still effective and accurate evaluation method for UX in games. Therefore we will present our own set of heuristics in Chap. 5 and verify them by conducting an expert evaluation. Before that we will give a short introduction to heuristic evaluation as an expert-based usability approach.

9.3.1 Heuristic Evaluation

Heuristic evaluation is one of the so-called expert-based usability inspection methods (Nielsen and Mack 1994). It is an efficient analytical and low-cost usability method to be applied repeatedly during a development process, starting at the very beginning of a project design circle (Nielsen and Mack 1994). In general, heuristics can be considered as rules of thumb that describe the affordances of the users to a particular system. The formulation of heuristics is more universally than the one of usability guidelines (Koeffel 2007). The heuristics should provide enough information to enable the evaluator to judge all possible problems of a system (Sarodnick and Brau 2006). During a traditional user-interface evaluation three to five experts (in the field of the application, usability or both) inspect a system according to recognized and established usability principles (i.e. the heuristics). The number of detected usability issues increases significantly with the first three evaluators and the most problems are expected to be discovered employing three to five experts (Nielsen and Mack 1994). Heuristics allow for an evaluation of systems in a very early stage of the design process (e.g. paper mock-ups). Although numerous heuristics are available for the evaluation of video games (see following section), no particular work on how to evaluate UX through the application of heuristics has been introduced.

9.4   History of Heuristics for Video Games

In the following a brief overview of the history of heuristics for video games will be presented, starting with Malone who was the first one to introduce the idea of using heuristics to evaluate games (Malone 1980, 1982). His heuristics mainly focused on educational games, not possessing the graphical, acoustic and computational possibilities that current video games offer. Malone categorized his heuristics into challenge, fantasy and curiosity.

Although Malone has introduced his heuristics as early as 1980, this method was only adopted by a wider audience with Jakob Nielsen's ten heuristics that he introduced in 1994 (Nielsen 1994). Since then these ten heuristics are the mostly referenced set of heuristics and frequently used for different kinds of applications. Originally they have been developed for traditional interfaces, nevertheless they are also (to a certain extent) applicable to several other areas, such as video games. Federoff assessed the applicability of these heuristics to this area (Federoff 2002). She discovered their usefulness and developed a set of 40 heuristics that was partially based on Nielsen's heuristics. For a better overview and easier assignment of single problems to heuristics she categorized them into game interface, game mechanics and game play. In our opinion the heuristics published by Federoff sometimes do not cover the entire extent of facets offered by video games, especially when considering the capabilities of state of the art video games. Furthermore they appear to concentrate on role playing games and are therefore not applicable to all possible game genres.

In 2004 Desurvire et al. (2004) released a new set of verified heuristics, called HEP (heuristic evaluation of playability), which were based on the heuristics introduced by Federoff. In contrast to Federoff's approach, these heuristics were categorized into the four sections game story, game play, game mechanics and game usability. Through further evaluations these heuristics have proven to be effective. The categorisation of heuristics for video games into game play, game story, game mechanics and game usability has been taken into account when formulating our framework. Still, we think that the heuristics by Desurvire et al. do not consider the important impact of challenge onto the user's experience. The evaluation of mobile games has also been of interest to researchers. In 2006 Nokia released a framework for the evaluation of the playability of mobile games (Korhonen and Koivisto 2006). Their framework is split into modules containing heuristics for game play, game usability and mobility. The modules do not have to be evaluated at the same time and the modules concerning game play and game usability should be able to be applied to other kinds of games, not only mobile games.

In April 2007 Schaffer released a white paper introducing a new version of heuristics for video games (Schaffer 2007). According to his opinion, the heuristics introduced so far were too vague, difficult to realize, more suitable to post-mortem reviews and not applicable during the design process. He provides a set of detailed heuristics with graphical examples for each heuristic, which eases the evaluation significantly, especially when it is not conducted by an expert in the field of computer games.

Pinelle et al. introduced a set of heuristics based on game reviews in 2008 (Pinelle et al. 2008a). For their work five researchers reviewed 108 game reviews of the Gamespot[1]-website and categorized the found issues into 12 different problem categories. They subsequently generated ten final heuristics out of these categories. According to Pinelle et al. this approach offers the possibility to evaluate a game's usability without reviewing unnecessary technical issues and issues related to entertainment. In a follow-up work Pinelle et al. extended their research by taking genres into account. They grouped the analysed games into 6 major genres and assigned the found problems to their 12 categories. Through this they were able to determine that the frequency of certain problems occurring is dependent on the genre (Pinelle et al. 2008b).

A further development and refinement of the HEP heuristics (Desurvire et al. 2004) was presented in form of the Heuristics of Playability (PLAY) (Desurvire and Wiberg 2009). The set consists of three categories, namely game play, coolness/entertainment/humor/emotional immersion and usability & game mechanics. The PLAY heuristics were tested by 54 gamers and overall the heuristics were found useful. Based on the findings of Pinelle et al., Livingston et al. created a heuristic evaluation technique they call "Critic Proofing" in 2010. Through the application of a genre rating they were able to create prioritized severity ratings in order to help developers focus on the most important issues for their genre first (Livingston et al. 2010).

Korhonen et al. (2009) compared the HEP heuristics (Desurvire et al. 2004) with the playability heuristics for Mobile Games (Korhonen and Koivisto 2006) and assessed their strengths and weaknesses. Overall the game evaluators liked the heuristic evaluation method but their results also indicated that the heuristics needed further improvements before they could be widely adopted. In 2011 Korhonen (2011) conducted a study where 36 novice evaluators evaluated a mobile game using two different sets of heuristics; the first one based on Pinelle et al. (2008a), the second based on Korhonen and Koivisto (2006). The evaluators also analysed and described the problems found. The study results showed that the heuristic set had to cover the main aspects of playability to guarantee its usefulness.

9.5 User Experience of Games

Within recent years UX has become a well-established concept within the community focusing on HCI. According to Hassenzahl and Tractinsky (2006) this is the counter-reaction to the more dominant task and work related usability paradigm. Still, this is not a completely new concept. The American philosopher and psychologist John Dewey described experiences to be "*not mere feelings; they are*

---

[1] http://www.GameSpot.com.

characteristics of situations themselves, which include natural events, human affairs, feelings, etc." as early as 1934 (Dewey 1934).

Nevertheless, a clear definition and founded understanding of this term has long been missing (Law et al. 2008). According to Law et al. the main problem is that UX treats non-utilitarian aspects of interactions between humans and machines. This means that UX mainly focuses on affect and sensation—two very subjective impressions. It encompasses areas from traditional usability to beauty, hedonic, affective or experimental aspects of technology use (Forlizzi and Battarbee 2004). Hassenzahl and Law, one of the leading researchers in the field of UX, define it as "*a momentary, primarily evaluative feeling (good-bad) while interacting with a product or service*" (Hassenzahl 2008). Therefore UX is designing for joy and fun instead of designing for the absence of pain (Hassenzahl and Tractinsky 2006). Thus the community has recently undertaken measures to better understand the meaning of UX and to find a unified definition through different conferences, workshops (Law et al. 2008; Roto and Kaasinen 2008; Roto et al. 2011), forums and the like. Especially the MAUSE COST Action 294[2] has aimed for finding a definition and measurement of UX. Law et al. performed a survey among 275 participants from the fields of industry and research to gather the community's understanding of the term UX. The study showed that UX was seen as something dynamic, context-dependent and subjective (Law et al. 2009).

In 2010 ISO defined UX as "*a person's perceptions and responses that result from the use or anticipated use of a product, system or service*" (ISO 9241-210 2010). Law sees this definition as a starting point for discussion but also states that it is too imprecise and abstract. Finding a final definition might be an ostensible task (Law 2011).

9.5.1   Measuring User Experience in Games

According to literature, UX in games can be measured using the following qualitative and quantitative methods (Federoff 2002; Desurvire et al. 2004; Sweetser and Wyeth 2005; Hazlett 2006; Koivisto and Korhonen 2006; Mandryk and Atkins 2007; Nacke et al. 2010): psycho-physiological measurements, physiological measurements, expert evaluation (heuristics, etc.), subjective, self-reported measures and usability tests. Fierley and Engl discussed how common UX research methods such as thinking aloud can be used in the context of gaming. Furthermore they presented approaches for adapting common methods for measuring UX in games (Fierley and Engl 2010). Similar to this Bernhaupt and Linard presented how UX evaluation should be adopted to the area of multi-modal interaction in games (Bernhaupt and Linard 2010). A collection of UX factors as well as evaluation methods is provided in Bernhaupt (2010).

---

[2] http://www.cost294.org/.

Integral factors of UX are the state of flow and immersion defining the level of enjoyment and fun (IJsselsteijn et al. 2007). The measurement of the state of flow through different methods is one of the major topics of UX in games and by many seen as the optimal experience when playing games (cf. Sweetser and Wyeth 2005). According to Hassenzahl the concept of flow is very close to the idea of UX and describes flow as *"a positive experience caused by an optimal balance of challenges and skills in a goal-oriented environment"* (Hassenzahl 2008). The concept of flow was first introduced in Csikszentmihalyi (1975) and further refined to fit to video games and player enjoyment by Cowley et al. (2008) and Sweetser and Wyeth (2005). Whereas Cowley et al. introduce a framework to map flow to the game play, Sweetser and Wyeth try to integrate heuristics into a model to help design and evaluate enjoyment in games. They found out that there is a certain overlap of the heuristics investigated and the concept of flow.

Another concept that is tightly linked to UX is immersion. One definition of immersion and its stages was proposed by Brown and Cairns (2004). Through a semi-structured interview with seven gamers they were able to distinguish immersion into three phases: engagement, engrossment and total immersion. Engagement is the first stage of immersion. According to Brown and Cairns the players have to be interested in the game to reach this state. When the user continues to play a game after the stage of engagement she will reach engrossment. When engrossed in a game, the player's emotions are directly affected by the game. Total immersion is the most immersed a user can get. She will be completely involved in the game and experience absolute presence, where only the game and the emotions produced by the game matter. In a follow-up work Cheng and Cairns have further investigated the different stages of immersion (Cheng and Cairns 2005). They tested a game with changing graphics and behaviour on 14 different users. Through this experiment Cheng and Cairns found out that when a user is immersed in a game, she would oversee usability issues and even not notice changes in the game's behaviour.

Our work is influenced by the approach described in Sweetser and Wyeth (2005) to integrate common known heuristics into the eight steps of flow as proposed by Csikszentmihalyi. Nevertheless, we will not try to measure UX through the factor flow. Instead we will provide a set of heuristics that is independent of the flow approach and will target usability and UX of the evaluated games. A detailed overview of this process will be given in Sect. 9.6.

9.6 Overview and Review of Existing Video Game Heuristics and Their Impact on User Experience

As introduced in Sect. 9.3 and further discussed in Sect. 9.4, heuristics can be a valuable method in video game design. In this section we want to present a modular framework which is based on our previous work (Koeffel 2007; Koeffel et al. 2009) and current literature. The framework consists of the sections game play/game story and virtual interface. The section game play/game story contains heuristics regarding these very topics. In the section about the virtual interface heuristics concerning the displayed virtual interface that the player interacts with are presented. The heuristics treating game play/game story and the virtual interface are shown in Table 9.1.

9.6.1 Video Game Heuristics

In our previous work (Koeffel et al. 2009) we collected a literature-based set of 29 heuristics derived from research by Nielsen and Molich (1990), Federoff (2002), Desurvire et al. (2004), Sweetser and Wyeth (2005), Korhonen and Koivisto (2006), Röcker and Haar (2006), Schaffer (2007) and Pinelle et al. (2008a).

The major part of these heuristics was similar to the approach introduced in Sweetser and Wyeth (2005). It was their main goal to establish a method to measure the state of flow that a game offers to the player. Moreover, they put usability on a level with UX, which has proven to be a different concept (see Sect. 9.4). Furthermore they only applied their heuristics to the area of real-time strategy games, whereas we sought to generate a set of heuristics that was applicable to multiple game genres.

Our research showed that in the literature many heuristics focused either on usability (e.g. Pinelle et al. 2008a) or on playability, fun and enjoyment (e.g. Sweetser and Wyeth 2005)—factors closely connected to UX. We therefore want to create a more holistic set of heuristics that does not solely concentrate on either UX or usability. Moreover, we want to focus on all aspects offered by video games, especially as occurring problems have an impact onto the UX, and the quality of a game can hardly be determined by usability only.

We previously established a connection between a game's perceived UX and the use of the previous iteration of our heuristics (Koeffel et al. 2009). Nevertheless, through further research and the application of these heuristics we encountered inconsistencies within them. One of the more frequent issues was in their discriminatory power. When categorizing issues, it was at times difficult to assign them to only one heuristic. Since some heuristics were kept very general, their quintessence would apply to multiple issues, e.g. *"The player should be able to identify game elements [...]"* and *"The menu should be intuitive and the meanings obvious [...]"* could both apply to a badly readable help text. In other words, in some cases up to five heuristics would be assigned to one issue. Thus, we saw the need for heuristics that are easier to distinguish, more autonomous and moreover, easy to apply.

We also intended to address the inclusion of different genres into our new set of heuristics. The 12 problem categories established in Pinelle et al. (2008a) and the large number of evaluated games have been used in Pinelle et al. (2008b) to generate genre-dependent profiles. This data was used by Livingston et al. to derive a formula for a genre-weighted severity rating (Livingston et al. 2010). While we support the process of generating a genre coefficient that is taken into account when determining the severity of issues, it is limited to the data compiled by Pinelle et al.

Table 9.1 Revised heuristics concerning game play/game story and virtual interface

	No.	Heuristic
Game play/ game story	*O1*	*Goals*
	1.1	Overall goal: The player is presented clear goals (e.g. overriding goals) early enough or is able to create her own goals and is able to understand and identify them
	1.2	Short-time goals: There can be multiple goals on each level (short-term and long-term goals), so that there are more strategies to win. Furthermore the player knows how to reach the goal without getting stuck
	O2	*Motivation*
	2.1	The player is receiving meaningful rewards. The acquisition of skills (personal and in-game skills) can also be a reward
	2.2	The game does not stagnate and the player feels the progress
	2.3	The game and the outcome are perceived as being fair
	2.4	The game itself is replayable and the player enjoys playing it
	2.5	The game play does not require the player to fulfil boring tasks
	2.6	Challenges are positive game experiences and encourage the user to continue playing
	2.7	The first-time experience is encouraging
	O3	*Challenge*
	3.1	The game is paced to apply pressure to but does not frustrate the player
	3.2	Challenge, strategy and pace are in balance
	3.3	The artificial intelligence is reasonable, visible to the player, consistent with the player's expectations and yet unpredictable
	3.4	There are variable difficulty levels for a greater challenge
	3.5	The challenge of the game is adapted to the acquired skills. The difficulty level varies so the player experiences greater challenges as she develops mastery
	3.6	Challenging tasks are not required to be completed more than once (e.g. when dying after completing a hard task)
	3.7	The game is easy to learn, but hard to master
	O4	*Learning*
	4.1	The player is given space to make mistakes, but the failure conditions must be understandable
	4.2	The learning curve is shortened. The user's expectations are met and the player has enough information to get immediately started (or at least after reading the instruction once)
	4.3	General help displaying the game's fundamentals exists and is a meaningful addition to the game and provides useful assistance before and during the game
	4.4	Tutorials and adjustable levels are able to involve the player quickly (learning) and provided upon request throughout the entire game
	O5	*Control*
	5.1	The player feels that she is in control. That includes the control over the character as well as the impact onto the game world. It is clear what's happening in the game

Table 9.1 (continued)

	No.	Heuristic
	5.2	The player can impact the game world and make changes
	5.3	The player is able to skip non-playable and repeating content if not required by the game play
	5.4	The game mechanics feel natural and have correct weight and momentum. Furthermore they are appropriate for the situation the player is facing
	5.5	The player is able to save the game in different states (applies to non arcade-like games) and is able to easily turn the game off and on
	5.6	The player is able to respond to threats and opportunities
	O6	*Consistency*
	6.1	Changes the player makes to the game world are persistent and noticeable
	6.2	The game is consistent and responds to the user's action in a predictable manner. This includes consistency between the game elements and the overarching settings as well as the story
	O7	*Game story*
	7.1	The meaningful game story supports the game play and is discovered as part of the game play
	7.2	The story suspends disbelief and is perceived as a single vision, i.e. the story is planned through to the end
	7.3	The game emotionally transports the player into a level of personal involvement (e.g. scare, threat, thrill, reward, punishment)
Virtual interface	*O8*	*Feedback*
	8.1	The acoustic and visual effects arouse interest and provide meaningful feedback at the right time
	8.2	Feedback creates a challenging and exciting interaction and involves the player by creating emotions
	8.3	The feedback is given immediately to the player's action
	8.4	The player is able to identify game elements such as avatars, enemies, obstacles, power ups, threats or opportunities (orthogonal unit differentiation)
	8.5	The player knows where she is on the mini-map if there is one and does not have to memorize the level design
	8.6	The player does not have to memorize resources like bullets, life, score, points and ammunition
	O9	*Visual appearance*
	9.1	In-game objects are standing out (contrast, texture, colour, brightness), even for players with bad eyesight or colour blindness and cannot easily be misinterpreted
	9.2	The objects look like what they are for (affordance)
	10	*Interaction*
	10.1	Input methods are easy to manage and have an appropriate level of sensitivity and responsiveness
	10.2	Alternative methods of interaction are available and intuitive. When existing interaction methods are employed, they are adhering to standards

Table 9.1 (continued)

No.	Heuristic
10.3	The first player action is obvious and results in immediate positive feedback
11	*Customization*
11.1	The game allows for an appropriate level of customization concerning different aspects (e.g. audio and video settings, etc.)
11.2	The input methods allow customization concerning the mappings. The customization is persistent
12	*Menu and interface elements (HUD)*
12.1	The interface is consistent in control, colour, typography and dialog design (e.g. large blocks of text are avoided, no abbreviations) and as non-intrusive as possible
12.2	The menu is intuitive and the meanings are obvious and perceived as a part of the game
12.3	The visual representation (i.e. the view) allows the user to have a clear, unobstructed view of the area and of all visual information that is tied to the location
12.4	Relevant information is displayed and the critical information stands out. Irrelevant information is left out. The user is provided enough information to recognize her status and to make proper decisions
12.5	If standard interface elements are used (buttons, scroll bars, pop-up menus), they are adhering to common game interface design guidelines

and therefore their 12 problem categories. Although we see the inclusion of genre-specific aspects as a valuable part in a heuristic evaluation, we chose not to adhere to Pinelle et al.'s categories and rather define our own (thereby knowingly forfeiting the possibility to resort to their genre-data) since we found their categories not exhaustive.

Table 9.1 contains the final 49 heuristics concerning game play/game story and virtual interface. They have been grouped into 12 categories for easier application. When an issue is found the reviewer can at first choose the appropriate category and proceed to assign a heuristic from the remaining subset.

As mentioned before, these heuristics are based on our previous 29 heuristics (Koeffel et al. 2009). While some heuristics remained the same, we split or rephrased those that had proven to be too unspecific or ambiguous. The introduced categories can further help choosing the right heuristic.

The categories were chosen to cover the most important aspects of video games in terms of game play/game story and virtual interface. The *goals* cover the game's overall objective as well as short term goals to be completed by the player. *Motivation* contains important aspects to cause the player to continue playing, such as rewards, fairness or the avoidance of completing mundane tasks. The *challenge* created by the game addresses issues connected to pacing, difficulty and player skills. As the game's acceptance is also connected to the player's learning curve, *learning* contains aspects related to help, tutorials and error conditions. Possibilities to influence the game world as well as being able to perform desired actions at any given time (e.g. saving or quitting) are part of the *control* category. Making changes that last and predictable responses by the game are covered by *consistency*. Emotional involvement and narratives are part of the *game story*.

The virtual interface needs to provide meaningful and timely *feedback*. This concerns acoustic and visual feedback, the possibility to identify game elements and the player's location within the game. The assessment of the *visual appearance* of in-game objects and their purposes must be possible for the player. The quality of the game's input methods is covered by the category *interaction*. The possibility to adapt the game to the player's needs and desires is part of the *customization*. Finally, *menu and interface elements* addresses all components provided by the heads up display (HUD) and the game's menu.

Our assumption is that a game that is enjoyable to play has, to a large extent, be free of usability issues that keep the user from enjoying a game. Especially the heuristics targeting game play/game story deem appropriate not only for classical usability issues (missing feedback, etc.), but also to issues connected to enjoyment and fun of a game (challenge, fairness, etc.).

In order to be able to estimate the UX through heuristics, we have set up a methodology to prove this concept (see following section). Our approach states that the overall UX of video games can be determined by conducting an expert-based evaluation of the game in question, using the heuristics shown above. The more heuristics are met, the higher the overall UX is, the more heuristics point to flaws in the game, the worse the UX is.

9.6.2 Heuristic Approach to User Experience

In the previous sections we linked heuristic evaluations to UX and used a similar approach for the newly developed heuristics. This was done, on the one hand, to evaluate the usefulness of the newly developed set of heuristics and on the other hand, to prove the applicability of these heuristics to the measurement of UX. We decided to focus our research on the field of indie games, since a low-cost evaluation method seems appropriate and could be a valuable tool for a part of the game industry that is not supported by big companies and/or large budgets. In his work Larsen states that common game reviews are to a major part based on the subjective evaluation of a game's UX from the game reviewer's point of view (Larsen 2008). Game reviewers have been unwittingly evaluating UX of games for nearly two decades.

Following this idea, we chose to evaluate a number of computer games using our 49 heuristics and compare the results to common game reviews. Therefore, we are able to compare the heuristics—primarily designed to detect usability issues—with UX oriented game reviews. In order to be able to make a quantitative statement we tried to establish a connection between the number of problems found through the heuristic evaluation and the numerical rating obtained from several different game reviews. The process of our evaluation was designed as a heuristic evaluation for video games. To obtain meaningful results, three evaluators conducted the study. All three of them were experienced in the fields of computer games and usability, with two being usability experts with gaming experience and third one vice versa. Two female and one male researcher were selected. Since gaming habits and preferences could influence the outcome, one evaluator can be considered as a so-called core-gamer who frequently plays games of different genres. The second evaluator was rather a representative of the casual gaming scene with experience in different genres (among them also core-games) while experience and preferences of the third evaluator where situated somewhere between those two extremes. For the evaluation we decided to choose games from different genres in the field of indie games in order to avoid biasing towards one genre, as experienced in some of our analysed work (cf. Federoff 2002; Sweetser and Wyeth 2005). Furthermore, the chosen games had to be rather recent ones to exhaust all current technical possibilities. Therefore the following games have been selected:

- *Adventures*: Machinarium (Amanita Design)[3], Gemini Rue (Wadjet Eye Games)[4], The Tiny Bang Story (Colibri Games)[5]
- *Casual*: Rhythm Zone (Sonic Boom Games)[6], Fortix 2 (Nemesys Games)[7]
- *Action*: Drug Wars (Paleo Entertainment)[8]

The games were chosen due to the broad range of their Metacritic.com[9] ratings. The best game was rated with 85 %, the worst with 35 %. Even though, three games are classified as Adventure games, they show considerable differences in their core game mechanics. Furthermore, the reviewers had no prior experiences with the games to avoid biasing.

We defined our evaluation protocol in the following way: Each evaluator obtained a list with the according heuristics and an evaluation report for the found usability issues. Previous to the evaluation the reviewers met and previewed the heuristics in order to get familiar with them and to avoid misapprehensions. All three reviewers evaluated each single game by playing it for exactly 30 minutes. Issues found while playing were noted in the evaluation report. For the assessment of the games, two different ratings were applied: a Nielsen severity scale and a point-scale ranking (to enable a better comparison to the game-review site).

First the researchers reviewed each game after playing it, using the heuristics to rank the found issues according to Nielsen and Mack's severity scale (Nielsen and Mack 1994), which led to the number of total usability issues found per game as displayed in Table 9.2.

---

[3] http://machinarium.net/demo/.

[4] http://wadjeteyegames.com/gemini-rue.html.

[5] http://www.colibrigames.com/.

[6] http://www.sonicboomgames.com/.

[7] http://www.fortix2.com/.

[8] http://www.paleoent.com/.

[9] http://www.metacritic.com/.

Table 9.2 The results of the evaluation ranked according to points obtained, issues found and compared to the results of Metacritic.com

Rank	Ranking according to found issues	Ranking according to points	Metacritic.com ranking
1	Machinarium (27)	Fortix 2 (75.09%)	Machinarium (85%)
2	Tiny Bang Story (27)	Machinarium (65.07%)	Gemini Rue (82%)
3	Fortix 2 (33)	Tiny Bang Story (65.02%)	Fortix 2 (73%)
4	Gemini Rue (34)	Gemini Rue (60.37%)	Tiny Bang Story (65%)
5	Rhythm Zone (35)	Rhythm Zone (50.87%)	Rhythm Zone (44%)
6	Drug Wars (49)	Drug Wars (44.39%)	Drug Wars (35%)

1. Not a usability problem at all
2. Cosmetic problem only: It does not have a profound impact onto the game
3. Minor problem: It has a slight impact onto the game and influences the experience a bit
4. Major problem: This problem has a severe impact onto the game and negatively influences the user experience
5. Usability catastrophe: This problem has to be fixed in order to allow for a decent user experience

Second, the evaluators assigned a score from 0 to 4 (0 being worst, 4 being best) to every single heuristic to determine how well the game fulfilled each of them. The problems and their severity, which were found during the rating according to the above mentioned scale, helped to determine which heuristics were the least satisfied ones. The achieved score was then converted into a percentage scale indicating to which degree the game complied with the heuristics (100% would mean the achievement of maximum points for each heuristic).

9.7   Results

To compare the results of the expert-based heuristic evaluation, we chose to select at least 10 game reviews (on average 20) for each game to avoid biasing of the single reviewers and therefore guarantee a more objective rating. Metacritic.com exactly fulfils these requirements by accumulating scores from different reviewing sites and calculating a weighted average. Their score reaches from 0 to 100 and can therefore be seen as a percentage rating, which is very common among reviewing sites. The results of our study can be seen in Table 9.2.

In order to assess the linear relationship between the results of our evaluation and the Metacritic.com scores, we calculated the Pearson product-moment correlation coefficient (PPMCC, r) after ensuring a normal distribution of our calculated data (Kolmogorov–Smirnov test). The resulting coefficients, as well as the respective coefficient of determination (R^2) are shown in Table 9.3.

Table 9.3 r and R^2 show medium to high relationships between game play, virtual interface and average point score and the Metacritic.com rating as well as the number of issues found and the Metacritic.com rating

Correlation	r	R^2
Gameplay point score × Metacritic.com rating	0.793	63%
Virtual interface point score × Metacritic.com rating	0.647	42%
Overall point score × Metacritic.com rating	0.782	62%
Number of Issues found × Metacritic.com rating	−0.733	54%

The PPMCC denotes the strength of a linear relationship ($-1 < r < 1$). A positive value means a positive linear relationship and vice versa. In the case of the Metacritic.com score and our heuristic point score a high linear relationship exists. This means that a higher conformance to the heuristics results in a higher Metacritic.com score. The same applies to the sub-parts of our heuristic framework (game play/game story and virtual interface). A high but negative linear relationship exists for the number of issues found and the Metacritic.com score: the fewer issues are found, the higher the resulting Metacritic.com score.

9.8 Discussion and Future Work

In a nutshell, the results presented in the previous section demonstrate that the UX measured through heuristic evaluations is reflected by the Metacritic.com rating. This tendency shows the connection between heuristic evaluations and UX. In relation to the results from Metacritic.com we can state that the more usability issues are found during a heuristic evaluation, the worse the UX is. The fact that the ranking according to points is not as high as the ranking according to Metacritic.com can be caused by the fact that our heuristics focus on usability issues that might not be detected during a game review or that might not be weighted that dramatically. Nevertheless, to further prove this concept, more extensive evaluations, involving a higher number of games that belong to several different genres other than the ones tested so far need to be conducted. This could also add up to a genre specific analysis in the form of Pinelle et al. (2008b). An additional outcome of such tests could also be a definitive number of heuristics, which have to be fulfilled in order to grant an optimized UX.

We do, however, acknowledge that we use a quantitative score from the reviews and not the qualitative data represented by the actual content of the review. Such a score cannot represent the written review in its entirety and is therefore less accurate. Still, using the review score allows us to draw the conclusion that the UX of a game is worse the less it adheres to the heuristics.

Our experience gathered as part of the evaluations has indicated that an evaluation period of 30 minutes, although helpful in assessing the first impression and critical issues of a game, does not suffice to judge all aspects of the game in question. Thus, overarching goals or the quality of the game story throughout the game cannot be completely assessed. Therefore it will be necessary in our future work to prolong the time played or even complete the game.

Summary

The present chapter has introduced a possibility to evaluate the overall UX of video games using heuristic evaluation. The topic of UX has significantly gained in importance in the HCI community and research. The experience a user perceives when playing a computer game has been one of the central issues of many recent publications. Although being a subjective impression, researchers seek to objectively evaluate and properly describe it (cf. Phillips 2006).

Therefore we have analysed and reviewed the most common heuristics for video games and built a framework upon our findings. This framework consists of 49 heuristics, categorized into the parts game play/game story and virtual interface.

We used our framework to conduct an expert-based heuristic evaluation of six different video games to determine weaknesses and problems. We then attempted to prove that heuristics can be used to measure the level of UX by comparing the results of our study with accumulated reviews from several different gaming sites. Since theses reviews focus on explaining how the UX of a game was perceived by the author we see it as a legitimate description of UX for a game. Our results indicate a direct correlation between the outcome of the heuristic evaluation and the level of UX as indicated by an average rating score (Metacritic.com).

References

Bernhaupt R (2010) Evaluating user experience in games: concepts and methods, 1st edn. Springer, London

Bernhaupt R, Linard N (2010) UX evaluation for multimodal interaction in games, workshop during EICS 2010, online. http://research.edm.uhasselt.be/~craymaekers/deng-ve/

Bernhaupt R, Eckschlager M, Tscheligi M (2007) Methods for evaluating games—how to measure usability and user experience in games? Proceedings of the international conference on advances in computer entertainment technology (Salzburg, Austria, June 13–15, 2007). ACE'07, vol. 203. ACM, New York, pp 309–310

Bernhaupt R, Ijsselsteijn W, Mueller F, Tscheligi M, Wixon D (2008) Evaluating user experiences in games. Extended abstracts on human factors in computing systems (Florence, Italy, April 05–10, 2008). CHI'08. ACM, New York, pp 3905–3908

Bostan B, Marsh T (2010) The 'interactive' of interactive storytelling: customizing the gaming experience. In: Yang HS, Malaka R, Hoshino J, Han JH (eds) Proceedings of the 9th international conference on entertainment computing (ICEC'10). Springer-Verlag, Berlin, pp 472–475

Brown E, Cairns P (2004) A grounded investigation of game immersion. Extended abstracts on human factors in computing systems (Vienna, Austria, April 24–29, 2004). CHI'04. ACM, New York, pp 1297–1300

Caillois R (1961) Man, play, and games. University of Illinois Press

Cheng K, Cairns PA (2005) Behaviour, realism and immersion in games. Extended abstracts on human factors in computing systems (Portland, OR, USA, April 02–07, 2005). CHI'05. ACM, New York, pp 1272–1275

Clarke D, Duimering PR (2006) How computer gamers experience the game situation: a behavioral study. Comput Entertain 4(3):1–23

Cowley B, Charles D, Black M, Hickey R (2008) Toward an understanding of flow in videogames. Comput Entertain 6(2):1–27

Csikszentmihalyi M (1975) Beyond boredom and anxiety. Jossey-Bass, San Francisco

Desurvire H, Wiberg C (2009) Game usability heuristics (PLAY) for evaluating and designing better games: the next iteration. In: Ozok AA, Zaphiris P (eds) Proceedings of the 3rd international conference on online communities and social computing (OCSC'09). Springer-Verlag, Berlin, pp 557–566

Desurvire H, Caplan M, Toth JA (2004) Using heuristics to evaluate the playability of games. In: Extended abstracts on human factors in computing systems (Vienna, Austria, April 24–29, 2004). CHI'04. ACM, New York, pp 1509–1512

Dewey J (1934) Art as experience. Minton, Balch, New York

Dumas J, Redish J (1999) A practical guide to usability testing. Intellect Books, Exeter

ESA (2011) Essential facts about the computer and videogame industry, 2011 sales, demographic and usage data. Entertainment Software Association. http://www.theesa.com/facts/pdfs/ESA_EF_2011.pdf. Accessed 27 April 2012

Esposito N (2005) A short and simple definition of what a videogame Is. Proceedings of DiGRA 2005 conference: changing views—worlds in play (Vancouver, British Columbia, Canada, June 16–20, 2005). DiGRA'05. University of Vancouver, BC

Febretti A, Garzotto F (2009) Usability, playability, and long-term engagement in computer games. CHI EA'09. ACM, New York, pp 4063–4068

Federoff MA (2002) Heuristics and usability guidelines for the creation and evaluation of fun in videogames. Master's thesis, Department of Telecommunications, Indiana University

Fierley R, Engl S (2010) User experience methods and games: lessons learned. BCS'10. British Computer Society, Swinton, pp 204–210

Forlizzi J, Battarbee K (2004) Understanding experience in interactive systems. Proceedings of the 5th conference on designing interactive systems: processes, practices, methods, and techniques (Cambridge, MA, USA, August 01–04, 2004). DIS'04. ACM, New York, pp 261–268

Fullerton T, Swain C, Hoffman S (2004) Game design workshop: designing, prototyping, and playtesting games. CMP Books, San Francisco

Gril J (2008) The state of indie gaming, Gamasutra. http://www.gamasutra.com/view/feature/3640/the_state_of_indie_gaming.php. Accessed 27 April 2012

Hassenzahl M (2008) User experience (UX): towards an experiential perspective on product quality, keynote IHM. http://www.uni-landau.de/hassenzahl/pdfs/hassenzahl-ihm08.pdf. Accessed 07 December 2008

Hassenzahl M, Tractinsky N (2006) User experience—a research agenda. Behav Inf Technol 25(2):91–97

Hazlett RL (2006) Measuring emotional valence during interactive experiences: boys at videogame play. Proceedings of the SIGCHI conference on human factors in computing systems (Montréal, Québec, Canada, April 22–27, 2006). CHI'06. ACM, New York, pp 1023–1026

Huizinga J (1950) Homo Ludens: A study of the play-element in culture. Beacon Press, Boston

IJsselsteijn WA, de Kort YAW, Poels K, Jurgelionis A, Belotti F (2007) Characterising and measuring user experiences. Proceedings of the international conference on advances in computer entertainment technology (Salzburg, Austria, June 13–15, 2007). ACE'07, vol 203. ACM, New York

ISO 9241-210 (2010) Ergonomics of human-system interaction—Part 210: human-centred design for interactive systems. International Organization for Standardization, Geneva. http://www.iso.org/iso/iso_catalogue/catalogue_tc/catalogue_detail.htm?csnumber=52075. Accessed 27 April 2012

Koeffel C (2007) Heuristics for tabletop games. Master's thesis, Department of Digital Media, Upper Austria University of Applied Sciences Hagenberg

Koeffel C, Hochleitner W, Leitner J, Haller M, Geven A, Tscheligi M (2009) Using heuristics to evaluate the overall user experience of video games and advanced interaction games. In: Bernhaupt R (ed) Evaluating user experience in games. Springer, London, pp 233–256

Korhonen H (2011) The explanatory power of playability heuristics. In: Romão T, Correia N, Inami M, Kato H, Prada R, Terada T, Dias E, Chambel T (eds) ACE'11. ACM, New York, Article 40, 8 p

Korhonen H, Koivisto EMI (2006) Playability heuristics for mobile games. MobileHCI'06. ACM, New York, pp 9–16

Korhonen H, Paavilainen J, Saarenpää H (2009) Expert review method in game evaluations: comparison of two playability heuristic sets. MindTrek'09. ACM, New York, pp 74–81

Larsen JM (2008) Evaluating user experience—how game reviewers do it. Evaluating user experiences in games, workshop at the 2008 conference on human factors in computing systems (Florence, Italy, April 05–10, 2008). CHI'08

Law E (2011) The measurability and predictability of user experience. Proceedings of the 3rd ACM SIGCHI symposium on engineering interactive computing systems (EICS'11). ACM, New York, pp 1–10

Law E, Roto V, Vermeeren AP, Kort J, Hassenzahl M (2008) Towards a shared definition of user experience. CHI'08 extended abstracts on human factors in computing systems (Florence, Italy, April 05–10, 2008). CHI'08. ACM, New York, pp 2395–2398

Law E, Roto V, Hassenzahl M, Vermeeren AP, Kort J (2009) Understanding, scoping and defining user experience: a survey approach. Proceedings of the 27th international conference on human factors in computing systems (CHI'09). ACM, New York, pp 719–728

Livingston IJ, Mandryk RL, Stanley KG (2010) Critic-proofing: how using critic reviews and game genres can refine heuristic evaluations. Proceedings of the international academic conference on the future of game design and technology (Futureplay'10). ACM, New York, pp 48–55

Malone TW (1980) What makes things fun to learn? Heuristics for designing instructional computer games. Proceedings of the 3rd ACM SIGSMALL symposium and the first SIGPC symposium on small systems (Palo Alto, CA, September 18–19, 1980). SIGSMALL '80. ACM, New York, pp 162–169

Malone TW (1982) Heuristics for designing enjoyable user interfaces: lessons from computer games. Proceedings of the 1982 conference on human factors in computing systems (Gaithersburg, Maryland, United States, March 15–17, 1982). ACM, New York, pp 63–68

Mandryk RL, Atkins MS (2007) A fuzzy physiological approach for continuously modeling emotion during interaction with play technologies. Int J Hum-Comput Stud 65(4):329–347

Marsh T, Yang K, Shahabi C, Wong WL, Nocera L, Carriazo E, Varma A, Yoon H, Kyriakakis C (2005) Automating the detection of breaks in continuous user experience with computer games. Extended abstracts on human factors in computing systems (Portland, OR, USA, April 02–07, 2005). CHI'05. ACM, New York, pp 1629–1632

Medlock MC, Wixon D, Terrano M, Romero R, Fulton B (2002) Using the RITE Method to improve products: a definition and a case study. Usability Professionals Assoc., Orlando

Nacke LE, Drachen A, Goebel S (2010) Methods for evaluating gameplay experience in a serious gaming context. Int J Comput Sci Sport 9(2):1–12. (International Association of Computer Science in Sports)

Nielsen J (1994) Usability engineering. Morgan Kaufmann, San Francisco

Nielsen J, Mack RL (1994) Usability inspection methods. Wiley, New York

Nielsen J, Molich R (1990) Heuristic evaluation of user interfaces. Proceedings of the SIGCHI conference on human factors in computing systems: empowering people (Seattle, Washington, United States, April 01–05, 1990). CHI'90. ACM, New York, pp 249–256

Pagulayan RJ, Keeker K, Wixon D, Romero R, Fuller T (2003) User-centered design in games. In: Jacko J, Sears A (eds) Handbook for human-computer interaction in interactive systems. Lawrence Erlbaum, Mahwah

Phillips B (2006) Talking about games experiences: a view from the trenches. Interactions 13(5):22–23

Pinelle D, Wong N, Stach T (2008a) Heuristic evaluation for games: usability principles for video-game design. Proceeding of the twenty-sixth annual SIGCHI conference on human factors in computing systems (Florence, Italy, April 05–10, 2008). CHI'08. ACM, New York, pp 1453–1462

Pinelle D, Wong N, Stach T (2008b) Using genres to customize usability evaluations of video games. Proceedings of the 2008 conference on future play: research, play, share (Future Play'08). ACM, New York, pp 129–136

Röcker C, Haar M (2006) Exploring the usability of videogame heuristics for pervasive game development in smart home environments. Proceedings of the third international workshop on pervasive gaming applications—PerGames 2006 (Dublin, Ireland, May 7–10, 2006). Springer-Verlag, Heidelberg, pp 199–206

Roto V, Kaasinen E (2008) The second international workshop on mobile internet user experience. Proceedings of the 10th international conference on human computer interaction with mobile devices and services (Amsterdam, The Netherlands, September 02–05, 2008). MobileHCI'08. ACM, New York, pp 571–573

Roto V, Vermeeren A, Väänänen-Vainio-Mattila K, Law E (2011) User experience evaluation—which method to choose? Proceedings of the 13th IFIP TC 13 international conference on Human-computer interaction—Volume Part IV (INTERACT'11), Pedro Campos, Nuno Nunes, Nicholas Graham, Joaquim Jorge, and Philippe Palanque (eds.), Vol. Part IV. Springer-Verlag, Berlin, Heidelberg, pp 714–715

Sarodnick F, Brau H (2006) Methoden der Usability Evaluation, Wissenschaftliche Grundlagen und praktische Anwendung. Hans Huber, Bern

Schaffer N (2007) Heuristics for usability in games. Technical report, Rensselaer Polytechnic Institute. http://friendlymedia.sbrl.rpi.edu/heuristics.pdf. Accessed 07 December 2008

Sweetser P, Wyeth P (2005) GameFlow: a model for evaluating player enjoyment in games. Comput Entertain 3(3):3–3

Wolf MJP (2001) The medium of the videogame. University of Texas Press, Austin

Ye Z (2004) Genres as a tool for understanding and analyzing user experience in games. Extended abstracts on human factors in computing systems (Vienna, Austria, April 24–29, 2004). CHI'04. ACM, New York, pp 773–774

Zimmerman E (2004) Narrative, interactivity, play, and games. In: Wardrip-Fruin N, Harrigan P (eds) First person. MIT Press, Cambridge

Part IV
Game Specific Approaches

Chapter 10
Enabling Co-Located Physical Social Play: A Framework for Design and Evaluation

Elena Márquez Segura and Katherine Isbister

Abstract During the last decade, we have witnessed an increased interest in social play in digital games. With this comes an urge to understand better how to design and evaluate for this new form of play. In this chapter, we encapsulate best practices for game design and evaluation, grounded in other game researchers' work, as well as our own research and practice. We focus on a sub-area of social games that has experienced great growth and has attracted general interest in research and in practice. It is also the area that has driven our own research: co-located, physical, and social play that is technology supported. In this overview, we provide a sense of the challenges and opportunities involved when designing for this particular area, using good empirical grounding and presenting a framework in the form of lenses through which to think about the design of co-located physical social games.

10.1 Introduction

Before 2000, the majority of digital games designed were for individual play (Costikyan 2002; Zagal et al. 2000). The internet era made networked gaming possible, and the smartphone era has made this even easier. Developing games meant to be played together has become a very popular and lucrative pursuit for game developers. For example, in 2009 Farmville was launched. At its peak this game had 80 million average monthly users, and this success led to tremendous growth in the online social game category as a whole. Advances in sensor technology have allowed game developers to instrument the body in new ways, allowing people to play using physical movement, and leading to the broad adoption of movement-based game input devices. In 2010, Microsoft released the Kinect, a movement-gaming platform, which was ideally suited to social play in the living room. The Kinect has sold more

E. Márquez Segura (✉)
Department of Informatics and Media, Uppsala University, Box 513, 751 20 Uppsala, Sweden
e-mail: elena.marquez@im.uu.se

K. Isbister
New York University, 2 Metrotech Center, Office 874, Brooklyn, NY 11201, USA
e-mail: katherine.isbister@nyu.edu

© Springer International Publishing Switzerland 2015
R. Bernhaupt (ed.), *Game User Experience Evaluation*,
Human-Computer Interaction Series, DOI 10.1007/978-3-319-15985-0_10

than 24 million units since that time. At this time all three major game consoles have movement devices available for purchase, and some of the most successful games for these platforms have been movement based games (e.g. Just Dance which was the 9th best seller among all console games in April 2012). Also, during the last decade, the top selling video games are or at least have included a multi-player modality (ESA 2014). Game consoles are no longer the province of the young boys in a household; they are considered gathering points for the whole family (Voida and Greenberg 2009). In a prior overview (Isbister 2010), Isbister pointed out that 59 % of gamers surveyed reported playing games with others, either in-person or online (ESA 2008). This number increased to 62 % in 2012 (ESA 2014).

Since 2008, smartphones (primarily iOS and Android) have forced a dramatic shift in the handheld gaming environment, taking over territory once held by Nintendo's handheld gaming devices (see Andrew 2011). With their ready connectivity, smartphones allow for social gameplay in wide ranging contexts. Finally, device makers have begun to create custom platforms for co-located social play (such as the Sifteo platform, or the Oriboo, one of our exemplars in this chapter), expanding the possibility space for supporting social play in everyday contexts. With this tremendous growth of social gameplay, there has been a pressing need to better understand how to effectively support design and evaluation, as well as to encapsulate best practices from broadly released social games toward better future design.

Since the last review (Isbister 2010), we have witnessed the emergence of new modalities of interaction and genres of social games, too broad to be represented in a single chapter. Hence, we chose to focus on a sub-area of social games that has driven our own research, and that has been one of the growth areas: co-located, physical social play. We will use this as a lens through which to offer insights and recommendations about the design and evaluation of games for social play in general.

10.2 The Emergence of Physical Social Play

Although play has always had a strong social component, the start of the digital era in computer games focused on solo play, perhaps because of the difficulty of designing technologically-supported group play (Costikyan 2002; Zagal et al. 2000). Games designed for solo play immersed the player in a virtual world that was reactive and engaging, created through the use of sophisticated graphics, sound, and simulated physics.

The internet allowed game developers to add network-supported multi-player games, providing opportunities for players to act together in gameplay (what Stenros et al. 2009 call 'social play') and also to engage in side conversation about what they were doing (what Stenros et al. 2009 call 'sociability'). There has been extensive writing about the nuances of the social experience of this sort of play (e.g. Taylor 2006), and how to design for it (e.g. Salen and Zimmerman 2003; Bell 2012), and comprehensive coverage of this domain is beyond the scope of the chapter.

Household game consoles always offered a form of co-located social play, through the use of multiple controllers for multi-player gaming. However, the popularity of physical co-located social play began with the introduction of the Wii console in 2006, and since then gaming platforms have increasingly included technologies for instrumenting the player's moving body, allowing for more physical activity during play. Wireless and embedded technologies have allowed the digitalization of physical objects, which has led to the creation of interactive toys with interesting input/output mappings that can support open physical play (Bekker et al. 2010). In our everyday lives, there is an ever greater saturation of technologies–laptop computers, tablets, smartphones–which has shifted how people relate to and interact with these devices. We are now far more likely to expect and even invite physical and social playfulness into our interactions with technology in our daily routine (Fernaeus 2012).

Researchers have invested considerable design and development effort into better understanding how to design physical experiences with technology to enhance bodily awareness (Khut 2007, 2006; Loke and Khut 2011; Loke et al. 2012; Simbelis and Höök 2013), engage the emotions (Paiva et al. 2003; Lindström et al. 2006; Höök 2008; Stahl et al. 2009; Isbister 2011) and create social experiences (Lindley et al. 2008; Isbister et al. 2011a, b).

Of course physical social play has always been an important human activity (Huizinga 1955; Wilson 2012). We believe this category of play has been emphasized in digital practice lately because of the transformation and extension possible due to broad distribution of sensing and mobile technologies. Researchers are hard at work trying to understand how to design enhancement of and affordances for situated play using augmenting technology (Jakobs et al. 1996, 1997; Magerkurth et al. 2004; De Kort and Ijsselsteijn 2008; Márquez Segura et al. 2013; Márquez Segura 2013).

At this point in digital game history, we have created a hybrid and portable physical and digital 'magic circle' of play (Huizinga 1955). Although the magic circle has always had a strong notion of space, it is now that digital gaming has moved outside stationary computers and screens that it has regained its physical and social importance in digital gaming, moving away from its initial strong static component forced by those stationary platforms. This offers new challenges as well as opportunities for design (Márquez Segura 2013; Isbister 2012; Mueller and Isbister 2014).

In this chapter, we present the possibilities and challenges that this hybrid sphere provides in terms of designing and evaluating physical and co-located play. Developers have traditionally focused on evaluating play in terms of balancing elements within the game, instead of focusing on the social and physical component of play (Isbister 2010). The addition of technologies that allow for physical interaction further complicates design and evaluation–how can we measure the impact of physical movement on social play? What are best practices for prototyping technologically augmented physical play? We will propose a framework for designing and evaluating social play, with a strong focus on the co-located physical experience. This is based on our experience designing for physical and social play (Isbister 2011; Isbister 2012; Márquez Segura et al. 2013; Márquez Segura 2013). We identify the design materials this hybrid sphere offers, and provide design principles based on our own practice and research.

10.3   Related Work

There is no agreed-upon framework for designing and evaluating technology-supported co-located and physical social play, but there has been considerable work done in elucidating some of the design and evaluation challenges toward finding helpful common ground among practitioners. In this section we give a brief overview of this work.

10.3.1   Designing Co-Located Social and Physical Play

In the past decade, there has been quite a bit of research done in the space of social and physical play. It is already known how movements add to the scene in the form of socio-emotional responses. Movement influences the energy level of the players (Isbister et al. 2011b), increases their arousal (Isbister et al. 2011a) and engagement (Bianchi-Berthouze et al. 2007; Lindley et al. 2008), and also shapes social interaction (Lindley et al. 2008; Isbister et al. 2011a).

Many of the positive effects that social play brings to the scene are similar to the effects that physical play brings, such as higher engagement, arousal, and positive emotions (Ravaja et al. 2006; Mandryk et al. 2006).

Social play adds to experience compared to solo play (Gajadhar et al. 2008; Voida and Greenberg 2009). For many players, one of the main reasons for console gaming is the social interaction that co-located play affords (Voida and Greenberg 2009). The level of presence of other players and spectators influences gameplay and the game experience. Gajadhar et al. (2008) found out that co-presence had a positive impact in affect, and perceived competence, tension and hostility in the game, compared to game settings in which you play against a computer or against a mediated other.

Even in solo play, the fact that play evolves in a setting with co-located others adds to the experience (Carr et al. 2004). Studying solo play, Carr et al. (2004) stumbled upon many instances of social interaction, which points to the interactivity that happens in hybrids forms of solo play, i.e. when the player is surrounded by others. Even in these cases of solo play, the social element becomes one of the major reasons why the game is worth playing.

Many scholars have brought forward the importance of the socio-spatial setting in shaping a situated experience (Jakobs et al. 1996, 1997; Magerkurth et al. 2004; Manstead 2005; De Kort and Ijsselsteijn 2008). Playing with others in a shared environment has an effect on performance since the actions of the players are visible to others (Jakobs et al. 1996; De Kort and Ijsselsteijn 2008) –there can be negative effects of this also, such as social pressure and shame, or evaluation apprehension (De Kort and Ijsselsteijn 2008).

De Kort and Ijsselsteijn (2008) highlight how in co-located settings people's behaviors are influenced by different elements, such as the game characteristics, the social affordances of the interface (i.e. the characteristics of the interface regarding visibility, types of controls, etc., which provide –or not– the players with a shared frame of reference), and finally, some spatial characteristics regarding the distribution and orientation of the players and other physical object in the shared physical space where play takes place. In this chapter, we are elaborating on some elements of the socio-spatial setting as a design material and a lens to evaluate social and physical play.

Despite all this work in the area of social play in the hybrid physical and digital world, we lack of a common framework for design and evaluating in this field, with only a few noteworthy attempts.

Magerkurth et al. (2004) propose a framework and software architecture for designing hybrid games in the form of tabletop-like augmented games in which the virtual domain is augmented with elements of the social and physical domain, whose emphasis enriches game experiences. With this approach, Magerkurth et al. (2004) claims back the importance of what traditionally happens in the social and physical spheres of board games, which they consider in the design of their augmented games. Yet, this framework is targeted more towards hybrid digital and physical board-like games, and does not fully support games in which the focus in on movement-based interaction, like dance games.

Specifically for movement-based interaction, Loke and Robertson (2013) suggest a method drawing upon the first-person perspective that is based on somaesthetics (Shusterman 2008) and somatic practices. This methodology focuses on technology-supported movement activities and proposes methods and tools for three elements that feature movement-based interaction: the mover, the observer, and the machine. The mover deals with the felt experience of the moving body, from a first-person perspective of attending to the movement; the observer deals with the perspective of a spectator observing the mover and includes tools for describing and documenting movements (Laban movement analysis, spatial movement schemas, etc.); the machine deals with the technology that supports the physical experience, focusing on the mapping of inputs/outputs and how the technology makes sense of the moving body.

This method is very interesting in that it brings forwards the importance of the felt experience of physical play, and attempts to draw upon this experience to design the technology that supports the activity. However, it misses much of the social element, except for considering external and passive observers (Márquez Segura 2013).

Dealing more with the situated physical and social context of play, we have Mueller et al.'s framework for designing and analyzing exertion games (Fig. 10.1). This framework deals with how *"the body responds, moves, senses, and relates to other bodies"* (Mueller et al. 2010), offering suggestions on how to design the technology to support a social and physical activity. The framework involves a multi-layered perspective of the player:

The *responding body* and the *moving body* deal with the first-person perspective. The former, in terms of the internal physiological state, and its changes over time and interaction. It uses body biodata such as electrodermal activity, or heart rate. The latter refers to the position of the body, focusing on the position of the parts of the body in relation to one another (proprioceptive skills). The *sensing body* deals

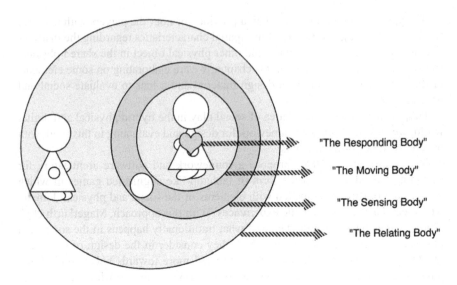

Fig. 10.1 Figure included in Márquez Segura 2013, from Mueller et al. 2010

with an exteroceptive perspective of the moving body, focusing on how the body senses and moves in the physical space. This layer covers the objects, tools, and technology, as well as the environment where the activity unfolds. Finally, the *relating body*, which relates to the social aspect of the bodily experience, i.e. how the participants' bodies relate to one another, mediated and supported by the technology (Márquez Segura 2013).

Mueller et al., extend the first person perspectives typical of somaesthetics and somatic practices to consider also the environment and the social aspect of play.

Márquez Segura argues that all these layers are not separate constructs and they affect one another. In this chapter we propose addressing the moving body by the systematic design of key elements in several of these layers and their interrelationship to aim toward a rich social and physical experience. We mainly opt for designing the *relating* and the *sensing* body layer, which in turn influence the *moving body* and the *responding body*.

10.3.2 Evaluating Co-Located Social and Physical Play

As was pointed out in a prior review (Isbister 2010), evaluation of social play adds a layer of complexity to the game user research process. Developers note the importance of early and frequent prototyping and testing to help reduce risk (Koivisto and Suomela 2007). The many frameworks and perspectives outlined in the design section above can be used as guiding values for evaluation of a game's success in accomplishing design aims, and for helping to scope and refine the evolution of prototypes as development advances.

The prior review recommends taking care to provide an ecologically valid context for play–is the group of a similar composition to those that may occur 'in the wild'? Is the play context similar to the contexts where play will take place outside the lab? In it Isbister also points out that players have less attention available for giving 'think-aloud' style feedback to the evaluator, and may not want to share all of their feelings and insights in front of the other gamers if the social play is co-located. In effect, players are having an individual play experience, and also having a social experience that goes along with play. This experience includes both *social play* and *sociability* (Stenros 2009). Interrupting all this with questions is likely to have a detrimental impact on the experience and on the validity of any data that might be collected about the experience. Asking questions of the whole group at natural break-points in play can result in social biases in response (individual players saying what they think the others want to hear). Separating people to answer questions individually can disrupt the social flow of the session. Effective social play test sessions in commercial game development settings (Tisserand 2010) tend to consist of a combination of video recording and screen capture during active play sessions, brief group interviews during breaks and longer ones after play, and individual questionnaires for players to get at their own feelings and insights about the play experience. It can be challenging to do adequate analysis of what is seen in the video records, to give timely turn-around to developers.

10.4 Framing Examples: Yamove and Oriboo

To present and elucidate the points in our design and evaluation framework, we are using games that we've developed for social, physical, and co-located play. In this section, we briefly describe the games, so that the reader has a basic understanding of their design.

10.4.1 Yamove

Yamove is a dance battle game, created at the NYU-Poly Game Innovation Lab, with some initial support from Yahoo Research (Fig. 10.2). Yamove was an IndieCade Finalist in 2012 and was a featured game at the 2012 NYU No Quarter exhibition. It has also been featured at the World Science Festival and at IndieCade East.

The game is played by two teams of two dancers. Each dancer puts an iPod touch device on her wrist, using a special holster (see Fig. 10.2). The teams take turns for brief rounds of play. During a round, a dance pair performs moves that they improvised together. They can do anything so long as they do it in synch. The game uses the on-board accelerometer in the iPod touch and compares the signal from the two dancers. They are scored on synchrony, as well as on how much they move (intensity) and on whether they mix their moves so they are not doing the same thing all the time (creativity). The highest possible score is 100, and is a weighted calculation

Fig. 10.2 Yamove, a dance battle game that uses synchronized dancing as its core mechanic

based on all three factors. The two teams take turns through 3 rounds of play, and the team with the highest average score from the three rounds wins.

In contrast to many commercial dance games (such as Dance Central and Just Dance), Yamove allows players to improvise with one another to make up moves, and puts the attention of spectators and dancers on the dancers themselves (see Fig. 10.3, Isbister 2012). The game was created with a focus on the core mechanic

Fig. 10.3 Yamove puts the attention on the dancers instead of on the shared screen

of synchronized movement, which has been found to build trust and connection between people (Valdesolo and Desteno 2011).

Yamove is hosted by an MC who calls out feedback to the dancers during a round. This person may also be providing the dance music, or there may be a DJ as well. Players get feedback about their performance during the round from the MC, but there is also a large display showing how the pair is doing, which is useful to those who are watching the round. The iPod touch devices also show the end score on their screens after a round. For more about the game, see (http://gil.poly.edu/research/yamove).

10.4.2 Oriboo

The Oriboo is a mobile game platform (Fig. 10.4) for movement-based interaction (http://oriboo.com/) designed as a dance companion by Jin Moen (Moen 2006 and 2007) and recently commercialized by the company Movinto Fun (http://www.movintofun.com/). The device looks like a small ball with eyes (LEDs) on the forefront and a small display for navigation through different games at the back. The Oriboo can move along a leash that the player holds at its ends. Feedback is provided by means of sound, light (eyes), its movement along the leash, and its small display. The device has an accelerometer inside for feedback on the users' movements. The Oriboo was originally conceived to encourage and support whole body interaction, and to foster a user's exploration of her movements and the space around her (for more design details, see Márquez Segura et al. 2013; Moen 2006, 2007).

With this interactive concept, Moen and her company Movinto Fun received grants from several entities, such as VINNOVA (Swedish Governmental Agency for Innovation Systems, http://www.vinnova.se/en/), and the EU MEDIA Program (http://ec.europa.eu/culture/media/index_en.htm). With their first product, the Oriboo, the company Movinto Fun has received different awards, like the IT entrepreneur of the year.

When Márquez Segura et al. started researching the Oriboo and designing games for it, there were several games already implemented, from which only one targeted dance-based interaction: "Dance it" (Márquez Segura et al. 2013). In this game, the Oriboo guides the player through a limited repertoire of eight simple movements (tug up, down, forwards, right, left, spin, jump, and twist). The players score every time they perform these movements accurately enough and at the right moment.

Fig. 10.4 Two Oriboo devices

Fig. 10.5 Early games with the Oriboo were designed in a way that led to artifact-focused interaction, instead of focusing on the social and physical context around

"Dance it" had some interaction issues due to the limitations of the sensing mechanisms implemented in the device, and its game design. This constrained both the movements allowed in the game, reducing them to a small set of simple movements, and also the posture of the player. This result is not aligned with the initial design criteria for the Oriboo, i.e. encouraging the user to move freely (Márquez Segura et al. 2013). Also, Tholander and Johansson 2010a, b) highlighted the fact that the device required too much artifact-focused interaction due to the dominance of the visual means to provide feedback and the outcome of the game (see Fig. 10.5). Therefore, the player focused too much on the small screen rather on her movements and what surrounded her -the physical space, and other players.

The Oriboo's makers asked Márquez Segura and colleagues to create multiplayer games for children for future versions of the Oriboo (which would have radio communication to allow this modality) that would not constrain the user to a small set of movements and a specific posture. Also, Márquez Segura et al. wanted to avoid the dominance of the screen for feedback to avoid this artefact-focused interaction (Márquez Segura et al. 2013, Márquez Segura 2013). This chapter does not elaborate on the design process of the different games created for the Oriboo, nor delve into details about the different games designed (see Márquez Segura et al. 2011, 2013; Márquez Segura et al. 2013). Instead, the focus is on introducing elements that has worked well in these various games, to illustrate the design principles and framework presented in this chapter.

10.5 Framework for Designing and Evaluating Co-Located Physical Social Play

10.5.1 Make Good Use of all of the Design Material at Hand–Technology, People, Setting

We find it helpful to consider not just the technology, but also the social and spatial context for play–these elements together comprise the design material that one works with to create the play experience, and should be considered as a whole during the design process (Márquez Segura et al. 2013; Márquez Segura 2013).

Technology

A game like Yamove includes several technologies–iPod touch devices, wireless network, large shared screen, server, an iPad to drive the play rounds, and a music and microphone set-up. This diverse set of technologies work together to enable the player experience as a whole. The iPod touch devices track player movement, the network shares this data to the game server, the large display allows spectators to see how the players are doing, and the microphone and iPad enable the MC to drive the turn-taking at the heart of the game, and give the dancers real-time feedback. This configuration of technologies was honed through much trial and error, with extensive cycles of prototyping and playtesting.

In the case of the Oriboo, the technology platform was a gating factor for creating the games. The designers' task became to make the most of this technology's capacity to enhance player social and physical experience. The team needed to engage the technology in depth, in terms of what sort of experience it could really provide to players and then carefully design to play to its strengths. For example the Oriboo leash, with two straps similar to that used in the Wii remote control, affords holding it in a specific way, which is precisely the way in which the player needs to hold the Oriboo to perform the movements in "Dance it" so that they are recognized. This is making the most of the system. In contrast, the game "Dance it" provided feedback mainly by using the Oriboo's small display, which caused overly artifact-focused interactions (Fig. 10.5; Tholander and Johansson 2010a).

We believe it is important to consider technology fully in service of the end player experience–to avoid the dominance of the technology and artefact-focused interaction (Tholander and Johansson 2010a). If we look at traditional folk or playground games, we see that the attention of players is not constantly taken up by the play technologies such as balls, bats, bases, and scoreboards. Instead, those artifacts serve as props in a game in which much of the player attention is focused on one another and the play environment. The nuances of interaction among players are a vital component to the fun of this kind of social play. We believe strongly that this is one key pillar in supporting social play with technology–we must not lose the joy of co-participation and co-action and the focus on one another. As Waern puts it (2009), the game should be technology-supported not technology-sustained, meaning that the technology is but one of many parts of the game, responsible only for part of the game, instead of the game sustaining the whole activity like in technology-sustained games (Waern 2009; Márquez Segura et al. 2013; Márquez Segura 2013).

One way to do this is to reintroduce human roles into the adjudication and management of the game, as is done in non-digital games. In Yamove, for example, the MC gives the players feedback on how they are doing, and also manages the rounds of the game using an iPad. This allows for more adaptive and custom pacing of the experience, as well as greater focus on the humans who are playing the game. In the Oriboo design exercises, the team designed games in which the outcome came from another player, (e.g. games "The Blind Mirror ") instead from the device (like in "Dance it" or "Join My Move"), or games in which the goal was set socially (e.g. "Make My Sound").

This approach to the use of technology also allows the designer more space to consider the sensing capacities and limitations of any given device, and to design an experience that makes the most of the machine's ability to sense and respond. This may mean limiting how players can move so that sensors can recognize the movement, but it may also mean instead doing things like asking players to judge the success of more complex competitions, and enter these judgments into the scoring system.

Márquez Segura et al. (2013) found the adaptation of Loke et al. (2007) of the Benford et al. (2005) framework for designing with sensors very helpful (see Fig. 10.6). This model differentiates between the movements a player can perform, the movements that can be recognized by the sensing mechanisms, and the movements allowed by a game. Using this model, the design team set up their goal of extending the movements allowed by the game to cover as much as possible of the movements the player can do. This is done in the Oriboo case without modifying the sensing capabilities of the device, but using instead different tricks, such as designing games that would not use sensing data at all in which the device would have other roles (e.g. pacing the game, distributing roles among the players, …) and the players would take over the role of controlling the rules or outcome of the game, or using other kind of mappings of movements and output.

For example, the game "Make My Sound" worked particularly well in supporting and encouraging the players' exploration of movements and the space, by the use of a different movement mapping that bridged the sensing limitations of the technology (Fig. 10.7). In the game, we mapped three different music loops with three different types of movements: jerky robotic-like movements, slow and fluent movements, and shaky and energetic movements. These kind of movements were easily recognized by the accelerometer inside the Oriboo's body. This way of providing feedback, mainly by means of sound instead its original dominant visual channel (small screen), eased the artifact-focused interaction issue, allowing the players to connect more with their movements, the space around them, and with one another. Some children reported using others' movements to give them hints about how "to sound" like them. Some others, said using the devices' music loops

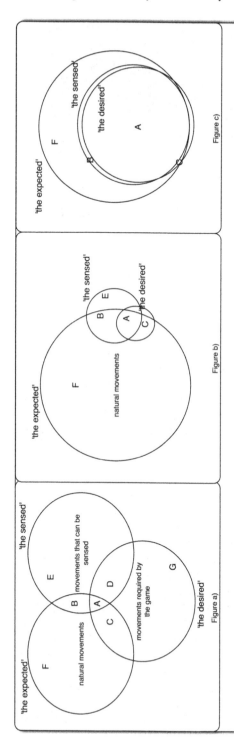

Figure a)

Figure b)

Figure c)

A: Free and expressive movements that are sensed by the accelerometer and are desired by the application. In 'Dance it' (Fig. b)), the repertoire of movements. Our design goal is to make this set as big as possible (Fig. c)).

B: Free and expressive movements that are sensed by the accelerometer but subvert the game etiquette. in 'Dance it' (Fig. b)), performing a movement that is registered as correct but that is not what the BodyBug required (e.g. a tug left could be mistaken for a counter clock spin). We would like to minimize this set (Fig. c)).

C: Free and expressive movements that can't be sensed by the device even being within its required movements. Bugs in the current game. In 'Dance It' (Fig. b)), problems in the movement recognition (e.g. when a player does a movement required by the BodyBug, but it is not recognized by the system). We would like to minimize this set (Fig. c)).

D: Movements that can be sensed and the game requires, but are not naturally carried out.

E: Movements that can be sensed but are not naturally carried out and the game does not require. Usually noise of the data.

F: Free and expressive movements that can't be detected, nor are required by the game. The aim of the BodyBug should be to make this subset as small as possible, by designing 'the desired' so that it covers as much as possible of 'the expected' (Fig. c)). This does not happen in reality (Fig b)).

G: Movements required by the game that are unnatural for the user and can't be sensed.

Fig. 10.6 a) The sensed, expected, and desired framework original from Benford et al. 2005; b) Benford's framework adapted to reflect the way the original games in the Oriboo made use of the movements of the player; c) Benford's framework adapted to reflect our team's design goal.
Note: The Oriboo is referred in this picture as the BodyBug, the name of early prototypes of the Oriboo, used prior to its commercialization.

Fig. 10.7 "Make my sound" players

for feedback on their movements, and some others mentioned they were just trying different movements until they got "the right sound".

> "*I listened to the music*", "*I looked at the others*", "*I just shook it!*" –quotes from post-game interviews (Márquez Segura et al. 2013).

The sensing limitations of the device were also bridged by games that would not rely on sensing data at all, like "The Blind Mirror". In this game, the device was used to mark time slots indicating turns for the players. At each player's turn, they would have to perform a movement of their choice. They would also need to remember everyone else's movements. At the end of the round, the Oriboo would pick "a leader", to whom the rest would have to perform the movement this leader had performed before. The outcome of the game was provided by this leader, who would choose the player who best and fastest performed the movement. We succeeded in re-directing the players' attention to their movements, the space, and others' movements, lessening the artifact-focused issue commented above. We also managed to cater for a wider variety of movements allowed in the game compared to "Dance it". However, the youngest children (aged around 8) reported they would prefer the Oriboo rather than another player to "judge" their movements. They reported this preference despite being aware that the device made more mistakes in judging them than the leader (Márquez Segura et al. 2013).

Another way to make sure that the technology stays in service of the social fun, is to make careful and judicial use of technological feedback systems to support appropriate social engagement. Social play in a co-located setting normally involves players and spectators, whose roles are fluidly interchanged as people move in and out of gameplay (Reeves et al. 2005; Reeves 2011). Well-designed games support this interchange by giving spectators a window into understanding the game, while providing players with suitable feedback, given their focus on the play at hand (Mueller and Isbister 2014). Game designers can make artful use of feedback systems to create interesting mixes of visible and hidden. Reeves et al. (2005) characterize interfaces in terms of how their manipulations and effects are visible to a spectator. The interfaces can be *secretive* if both the manipulations and effects are not visible for an outsider; *expressive* if both are visible; *magical* if the effects are visible, but the manipulations are not; and *suspenseful* if the manipulations are visible, but the effects are not.

Typical secretive interfaces are often hand-held devices, like the mobile phone. Szentgyorgyi et al. (2008) show how the use of the Nintendo DS creates around the person who operates the device a private game sphere, which is result of this interface being secretive. This happens in spite of the fact that play happens in a co-located multi-player setting with a more or less "face-to-face" configuration of players. The reason for this lies in the fact that the small screen of the hand-held device does not provide a shared frame of reference for the players and the audience present during play.

The Oriboo device is similar to hand-held devices in that small gestures like button pressing are missed by an audience, and big gestures are not. Also, the effects of the manipulations are mainly provided by the visual channel (eyes of the Oriboo, and small display), which makes it difficult for an audience to follow, especially when the Oriboo is being moved around; an spectator needs to fix her eyes onto the eyes of the Oriboo (the small screen is out of an spectator's reach) and follow the feedback while the player is moving the device up and down. This relates to the concept of sensory affordances (design attributes that help to sense something, like a font size that makes a label readable, Hartson 2003) from a third person perspective. Feedback from small items leads to a third-person artefact-focused interaction, in which the spectator focuses too much on e.g. the Oriboo's eyes, instead of on the player who is moving, on her moves, on the space around her, etc.

If we want to design for an easy understanding of the effects of player movements on game state, we should design a shared frame of reference that can be easily accessed by all players. For example, Yamove has a large, shared screen (See Figs. 10.2 and 10.3) that supports spectators' understanding what is happening to the score as players dance. Very little information is shown on the private displays of the iPod touch for each player, because players are too busy to stop to look at the screen, in any case.

It is important to note that we made the decision with Yamove to show relatively simple play data, and also, we positioned the competing teams facing one another. We took both these steps to minimize the amount of time players and spectators spent staring at the common screen. This is the balance necessary when making use of technology to heighten and augment a social experience without overpowering it (Mueller and Isbister 2014).

Socio-Spatial Setting

The arrangement and composition of a group playing the game, and the space in which the game is played, can also be considered part of the material of design alongside the technologies for play (De Kort and Ijsselsteijn 2008; Márquez Segura et al. 2013; Márquez Segura 2013). Is the game taking place in a living room in front of a large screen on a shared console? This tends to facilitate certain kinds of play and performance and not others–for example, there is only so much space in front of the console in the average living room, which delimits how many people can play at once. Yamove was designed for a party or festival setting, in which we were able to set up a dance floor of some sort, a large screen, and an MC/DJ area, and so is not optimized for a living room. Does the game require players to move through the space in novel ways (like Wilson's J.S. Joust, which has players holding Sony Move controllers run about to avoid one another)? Does the game make use of particular characteristics of a space (such as physical structures or hiding places)? All of these factors influence design.

Games themselves regulate social engagement through the ways in which they structure participation. In Fig. 10.8, we can see different configurations (Márquez Segura 2013, based on the player interaction patterns by Avedon 1971, and Fullerton et al. 2008). These can be useful in combination with a consideration of the spatial contexts players are likely to encounter, in helping you to make good design decisions to facilitate social physical play.

In designing the games for the Oriboo, we realized that the organization of players in space was an important factor that we considered alongside the game goals and roles (see Márquez Segura 2013). We made use of many of the configurations of player interaction patterns in Fig. 10.8. In the game "Dance it" we used a socio-spatial arrangement of "aggregate single players vs. device". In "The Mirror", we used the configuration of "aggregate inter individual". In "The Bomb", "The Blind Mirror", and "Join My Move", we used the form of "multilateral competition" (see Fig. 10.9).

10.5.2 Design to Embrace Player Influence and Impact

When designing for social play, our focus is on the social and physical interaction that emerges when players engage with our games. For this, we need to design games that can be easily owned and appropriated by the player to their liking. In this design situation, the designer faces a second-order design problem in which emergent play is targeted, but cannot be designed directly (Salen and Zimmerman 2003). The role of the designer becomes therefore that of creating this magic circle that invites and facilitates the player to safely engage in the game and craft their play at their like.

Consider Yamove, for example. We realized during our playtesting and iteration that players must bring a dance-ready, festive attitude to the game for it to succeed. When we tested the game without the right cues and ambience, players engaged in less enjoyable and sometimes counterproductive play (for example, getting into calisthenics competitions–see Fig. 10.10). An essential part of the Yamove set-up is great music, the re-creation of a dance floor feeling (with space set out and ideally, appropriate lighting), and the participation of an energetic and amiable MC who keeps the game flowing. These non-digital factors help the players to get into the frame of mind that drives the game to flow well, and that welcomes spectators into playing the game without too much social anxiety.

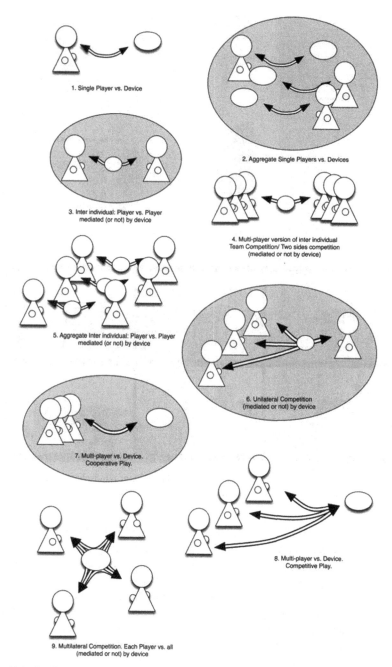

Fig. 10.8 Configurations of social play from Márquez Segura 2013, based on the player interaction patterns by Avedon 1971; Fullerton et al. 2008

Fig. 10.9 Players in a 'multilateral competition' style of play, during the game "Join My Move"

Fig. 10.10 Without the elements that help create a dance party atmosphere, Yamove players can end up creating less fun play experiences for themselves, such as engaging in calisthenics competitions

As a designer, you can create a circle of play in which the different design materials are arranged in a way that invites the player to engage, and fosters play. A way of encouraging players to engage is to let your design remain open to their exploration, manipulation, interpretation, and appropriation. Gaver (2011) calls these designs *self-effacing*—the ambiguity of purpose of the design encourages the user to engage in a wide- ranging conversation with it. Games that target self-effacing play do not necessarily implement pre-defined and concrete functions or goals, but they support a self-motivated and explorative form of play in which the players can themselves set goals, rules, and purposes. Yamove works in this way by enabling improvisation of moves that players perform. The team can choose any move they like, and often do (see http://www.youtube.com/watch?v=N5igt11X6Bg for a range of moves performed by players at Indiecade 2012). The broad terrain of possible moves invites more creative participation.

Fig. 10.11 Oriboo game "The Mirror"

For the Oriboo game "Make My Sound", we discarded a goal and performance-oriented game design in favor of providing a context for explorative behavior. Three sound loops were associated to three different movement qualities and the children were let to explore the sounds and the movements that triggered those sounds on their own (Márquez Segura et al. 2013). Goals in this context emerged when children tried to sound like someone, or trigger specific sounds, or move and sound unlike no one in the group. Therefore in "Make My Sound", the players create their own goals if any, they explore together beyond the question of "what is this" (device), to wonder "how does this work" and "what can I do with this".

However, leaving designs extremely open and ambiguous is not the only possible approach to foster play. Many of our games have a designed formal structure (with rules, goals, conflict, means, game mechanics) that drives and guides play. This structure is rigid enough to drive play in interesting directions, but flexible enough so that players can bend it, twist it, and shape it to fit their like, and emergent play can rise (Isbister 2012; Márquez Segura 2013).

One way to do this is lo leave some of the formal elements that shape our game structure up to the players. For example, with the Oriboo, we played a game called "The Mirror" (Fig. 10.11). Children were paired, one in the role of "the leader", performing movements at her will; the other one in the role of "the follower", mimicking the leader's movements. We played the game with different variations, with and without music/Oriboo/beeps for timing (Márquez Segura et al. 2013). In this game, we designed the core mechanics (making up moves—the leader-, and repeating moves -the follower), and the means and rules (for example, holding the Oriboo while dancing, or moving in turns marked by the Oriboo). Apart from this, the difficulty, the goal, and tone of the game were decided by the players. For example, it was up to the players (the leader) to decide how complex the movements were, or at what pace they were performed, or how many variations of moves to perform.

The players also negotiated whether they mirrored one another real time or with a small delay, or taking turns. Likewise, they decided whether to perform original movements or movements learnt from choreographies of their own or copied from official musical clips. They would even decide the tone of the game, whether to make it a competition by the leader challenging the follower with difficult moves, or a collaborative activity, by the leader making tricks to ease the mimicking, such as repeating sequences of movements that they anchored to key points in the music, or using symmetric movements (repeating movements to the left and the right), or using turn-taking.

To design for the player impact in the game, not only we need to design a flexible structure of play, but we need to communicate this flexibility to the players, so that they feel it is ok to bend this structure, that they can take over some roles of the game, that they change roles if they want to … that they own the game. With Yamove, we used the MC role as a prompt to remind players they can improvise anything they would like. The MC can also suggest some easy moves to begin with if a team is feeling shy or stymied about where to start.

Wilson (2012) advocates providing space for players by leaving the game incomplete or broken through intentionally not implementing some parts or functionalities of the game so that players need to step in and handle these parts. In his game B.U.T.T.O.N. (Wilson 2011), players need to press a button of a controller placed far from the starting position, in a certain manner (e.g. hop toward the controller). However, the game cannot actually sense whether a player jumps or not. Thus the players have to police one another's actions.

This is an interesting approach for hybrid physical and digital games that focuses on the activity that happens in the physical sphere. Independently of how accurate and sophisticated the sensing technology is, "*Only we ourselves, the human players, are able to referee what happens in front of the screen, out in the physical world*" (Wilson 2011).

In another of the Oriboo games, "The Bomb", we let the children in control of the rules and outcome. In this game, the children were placed in a circle, each with an Oriboo (Márquez Segura et al. 2013). They were told there was an imaginary bomb about to explode, which they had to pass around using the Oriboo. A contextual sound in the background was pacing the game, providing clues about when the bomb would explode (increasing frequency sound, and a final explosion sound). In this game, we saw the festive context that happened with children trying to influence the outcome of the game by "cheating". For example, a child tried to hold the bomb until it was about to explode, to pass it at the very end and make it go off in the hands of another child. However, he miscalculated the timing and the rest of the players 'punished' him by returning the bomb back to him until it exploded. This brought about much laughter and excitement. One of the reasons why we think this game worked better than "The Blind Mirror" for the youngest children is that there is no "right"/"wrong" movement in "The Bomb" (like there is in "The Blind Mirror"), but smart moves in the form of strategies to influence the game.

In order for the players to start tweaking a game, they need to understand the structure of the games, its rules, and its goals, so that they can figure out how to modify this to their service. This relates to Piaget's model (Piaget 1999) of how children learn to play games. They usually pass through different phases. First, they need to learn the rules and the formal structure of the game. Rules are designed for the sake of making a kind of activity possible (Suits 1978). Therefore, in order to play a game, the players need to agree to adhere to the written rules of the game, as well as their own "house" rules. Then, and once they are comfortable with the game structure and rules, players might start to see how the rules can be changed and adapted so to change the activity. At this point is when players might decide to do so in order to support a certain kind of activity they want to engage in.

A way to empower players to influence the game, by owning it, and changing its structure, is to create a straightforward structure so that players pass quickly from the initial phase of grasping and understanding the game to the phase of thinking of how they can influence the game.

Another way to go about this is to provide familiar elements in our games. As we mentioned before, players enter in the magic circle of play when they feel safe and comfortable with the game and with the people with whom they play. A previous relationship usually helps for establishing this bond of trust essential for play, but when playtesting games, many times you have players who do not know each other. How do you get around this issue?

The designer can present a context of play familiar to the players, which increases the chances they step easily in the game (De Koven 2011). However, many times game designers strive for novelty in their designs. In such cases, we can always use some conventions and elements in the game to extend a common basis of familiarity, such as concepts of playing fair, and usual game mechanics like taking turns (De Koven 2011). When the players recognize such elements, they may feel more in control of the game, and it is easier to establish a common ground among the players.

Both in Yamove and in many games for the Oriboo, we work with an element that is very familiar to all the players: mirroring. Copying another person's movements is used by people in an everyday basis, conscious or unconsciously (Kavanagh et al. 2011); it is a tool people use to learn, to express (e.g. empathy, like/dislike), etc. Mimicking is also quite contagious, and the disposition to imitate a physical move appears a quasi-irresistible drive, like when someone yawns or smiles, or starts running (Caillois 2001). A side benefit of this technique is the fact that emotions tend to be contagious as well—and so excited movement begets more excitement, for example (Hatfield et al. 1994).

In the game "The Mirror", we saw how movements performed by a pair of children dancing transcended the local sphere where they were first performed, and pairs of children located far from the mentioned pair copied their movements. This was due to the fact that the children were arranged in a spatial organization in which they had visibility over the group's movements (there was a big mirror in one of the walls which allowed this, see Fig. 10.11). Yamove players were also often seen making use of moves they have seen others had performed before, with a good scoring result. We can take advantage of the visibility of other players to engage players in social learning (Bandura 1977) to help scaffold participation in and mastery of the game. This also allows us to build complexity of the game over time, building upon the shared knowledge of the players of the prior moves and techniques.

10.5.3   Encourage and Protect the 'We' in Social Play

When designing for social play, it is important that players understand that the most important element in play is the 'we'—the collective experience of fun—rather than the individual's score or mastery of the game's mechanics. The designer can choose to emphasize this through design choices that get away from the typical emphasis on individual achievements, performance, and accuracy of movements. Yamove, for example, has at its heart cooperative play between a pair of dancers. The pair receives a joint score, so there is no such thing as the ability to discern which individual has best mastery of the game.

Another way of letting the player know that the structure of the game can be twisted to maximize social pleasure and engagement is by inviting the player to not take the game seriously. Wilson refers to unachievement to foreground the focus on designing a festive context of play in which what is more fun in the game is the meta-game, the social interchange between the players, instead of accurate performance (Wilson 2011). Unachievement is closely related to broken games, in which the game does not implement all the usual functionalities and does not cater for rewarding accurate performance. Take as an example the game B.U.T.T.O.N. in which the rules are not controlled by the game. In this game, not only the system does not ensure the fulfillment of the rules, it even encourages the players to cheat. The actual game turns to be the meta-game in which the players "compete" to make the most smart cheat, trick, or improvised move to have control over the controller. The fun comes in hand of the festive context around cheating.

Both in Yamove and in the Oriboo case studies we designed for festive contexts, putting forward the social context in which play takes place. Like B.U.T.T.O.N., we are dealing with games in the hybrid physical and digital world. In contrast with augmented reality games, our games, like B.U.T.T.O.N, err on the side of less intervention from the technology and more social input, toward bringing players back to the physical space inhabited by moving bodies and people who interact with each other.

The game "Make My Sound" does not encourage cheating, since there is no winning condition implemented. However, with our game design we wanted to lessen the importance of "performing well" in favor of and a festive context that opens up for exploration. In the game "The Blind Mirror", we actually left the players to take control over the rules and outcome of the game. The youngest children appreciated more when the assess of movements came from "an objective" external device rather than from the subjective evaluation of another player.

Broken games like B.U.T.T.O.N. stand in opposition to many current movement-based commercial games, in which the focus is put on implementing sophisticated sensing mechanisms and technologies, which try to make sense of what happens in the physical scene to provide feedback and an outcome for the game. Although this design strategy can work in certain contexts, such as a commercial game console with robust sensors, it does not work for limited sensing platforms. And there are negative side effect when constraining game design to what the technology can sense, such as the restrictions imposed to the moving body (Benford et al. 2005; Márquez Segura et al. 2013; Mueller and Isbister 2014).

Moreover, the fun of a movement game, even for high accuracy game platforms, is not determined only by the extent to which the movements of the players can be recognized. Simon (2009) highlights how sometimes players prefer a festive context over "performing well", even when the latter is rewarded and not the former. Simon illustrated this with his studies about Wii players. He realized how many times players opted for performing with "gestural excess", i.e. with big and exaggerated gestures, for the sake of doing them, even if they couldn't be accommodated by the game platform (Simon 2009).

In most of the games in the Oriboo, we give a step forwards and specifically target Simon's gestural excess with games that reward movement exploration (e.g. "Make My Sound") and creativity and elaborated movements (e.g. "The Blind Mirror"). Yamove rewards movement excess through the core mechanic of simply using the accelerometer data from any movement at all from the player.

When players understand that they can influence the game, they can start thinking of ways of doing so, in order to make the most of the game and of themselves. De Koven refers to the concept of the "well-played game" when describing games that become excellent just because how they are played (De Koven 2002). In such games, the players reach a common understanding not only about the rules, but about what they are looking for in the game, what they want to take from it, how the want to engage, etc. It means having a deep understanding of the participants of the activity, and their abilities and capabilities and their likes. This leads to the players working to *co-liberate* one another (De Koven 2011). De Koven refers to this concept of *co-liberation* as an ideal experience in which the players take the most not only of the game, but of them engaged in the game. Co-liberation, like the concept of *flow* in game design (Csikszentmihalyi 2009), refers to an optimal experience that requires balance. However, while in *flow* the balance is between challenge and one's ability to fulfill that challenge, in a well-played or co-liberating game, the tension lies in the "me" and the "we" in "us playing". Collaboration is drawn as a zone between these two concepts: too much towards "me" means the player feeling isolated, too self-conscious, alienated; too close to "we" might mean losing identity and becoming too much immersed in what the group wants (De Koven 2011).

In our games, we saw examples of players collaborating with one another. One cannot play Yamove without collaborating. In the Oriboo game "The Mirror", we played a version of the game with music, which happened to be a bit too high paced for the children to cope with mirroring. This resulted in interesting dynamics in which the leader would turn to tricks to ease the mimicking, such as repeating sequences of movements that they anchored to key points in the music, or using symmetric movements (repeating movements to the left and the right), or using turn-taking.

Finally, to protect the 'we' in social play, we need to provide the players with a safe space in which they can reveal themselves and act without fear. For this, we need to design the boundaries of the magic circle of play, like the rules of the game, which *"determine what 'holds' in the temporary world circumscribed by play"* (Huizinga 1955, p. 11).

However, the rules that hold this magic are not only the formal rules that we can design; they also comprise the implicit rules or rules of etiquette. In order to safely engage in the magic circle of play, the participants need to understand and agree upon the rules. The formal rules of the game can be outlined by the game designer. What happens with the implicit ones? They can be left for the players to agree on their own, although, depending on the situation, the game designer may want to make these rules explicit (e.g. if one of these implicit rules are thought at risk due to the background or age of the players).

This actually happened to us in a group version of "The Mirror", called "The Creative Ring" in which the children were placed in a circle, each sharing an end of the leash of the Oriboo with the person next to them. A player would start with a movement that had to be passed around the circle, like a wave. They players could decide to pass the movement around or "break" the wave by passing back a different movement. In the youngest group, a child decided to hint a hit to the following player with the Oriboo they were sharing, and this player in turn decided to continue to hit the following person. The children starting hitting each other laughing, but the hits increased in strength and we had to stop the dynamic by explicitly stating that hitting was not allowed in the game.

However, rules do not guarantee that players will feel safe within the circle of play. Players also need to feel safe with one another to engage in social play (Salen and Zimmerman 2003). The pre-existing relationships players have when entering the game are important for shaping their roles in the game, their communication, expression, and also this feeling of safety. However, many times, players engage in play without knowing each other. In this case, how do we design for a safe feeling among strangers?

As designers, we can influence the tone and atmosphere of the game with our design materials, and with the formal elements of the game. Before, we mentioned how we can present a game that encourages players to not take it seriously. Another way of influencing a casual atmosphere in the game is to de-emphasize achievements, as we mentioned before. Another way is to use the technique of defamiliarization, used by designers designing systems for the moving body (Wilde et al. 2011). This technique encourages the making of something extra ordinary out of what is ordinary. Wilde et al. 2008 uses this technique in her hipDisks or hipdiskettes (Wilde et al. 2008), with wearable systems that reward the participants when making "the embarrassing" or "the strange", i.e. moving in exaggerated ways.

In the game "The Mirror", we saw how the Oriboo helped defamiliarize the children's movements, since when playing the game with the device, they expanded their movement repertoire and even the space they used for moving, their kinesphere. We also saw how the Oriboo provided the players with an excuse to explore movements out of their usual repertoires. Sometimes these movements fell into what could be considered "embarrasing". For example, a girl made a very girlish

Fig. 10.12 B-boy and b-girl trying out the Yamove sensing devices on their ankles

movement so that to the follower, a boy, had to repeat it. The boy carried out the movement without much trouble, which brought about a lot of laughter.

Players of Yamove tend to improvise wilder and wilder moves as they get comfortable with the system, to test the boundaries of the sensors and to find the 'sweet spot' of creativity and intensity while staying in synch. Figure 10.12 shows some b-boy/girl style dancers who tried out the game in the lab, who strapped the iPod touches to their ankles to see how that could work.

Finally, the way you present the game or activity also influences the way the participants take it up. For example, games from the New Games Foundation welcome players like this:

> *"Welcome to New Games, where all ages find fun and no one gets left out"* (http://inew-games.com/). The New Games movement embodies a unique attitude towards play that de-emphasize the extreme features in competitive games and foregrounds interactive cooperative games that can be played for anyone, independently of background, gender, age. Despite some games mechanics include competition, the point is always to play and have fun together instead of to play against or beat one another. In the book The New Games Book by The New Games Foundation present their games under this motto: *"Play Hard, Play Fair, Nobody Hurt."* (Fluegelman et al. 1976; DeKoven 2011). As we mentioned earlier in this section, Yamove benefits from the party atmosphere that we always set up as part of the game context. Thinking about the ways that you frame and shape first exposure to a game during a play session can have a profound effect on how comfortable and engaged players will be.

10.6   Recommendations for Optimal Process

10.6.1   Design

To design good social physical movement games, it is important to observe how play emerges, unfolds, and evolves from the situations that we create. Early explorations with players through techniques such as bodystorming (Oulasvirta et al. 2003; Schleicher et al. 2010; Márquez Segura et al. 2013, Márquez Segura 2013), and frequent prototyping and testing are a vital part of the design process. Designers should be prepared to take advantage of any serendipitous realizations that emerge during the process of this playtesting, and allow time for these kinds of changes in the development process.

The design materials (technology and socio-spatial context) can be used as lenses with which to look at play (Márquez Segura et al. 2013; Márquez Segura 2013). How do players use and move in the space? How are they using the technology, what distribution of roles work for different game experiences, etc. Analyzing this lets the designer gather interesting insights that can be used in design iteration.

When designing for social play, it is important to foreground designing for a context in which the players can safely engage with one another and with the game, appropriating it to their liking. For this, the designer needs to empower the players and give them strategies for owning and adapting the game to suit the kind of activity in which they want to engage.

Above all, designers should keep in mind the end effects they hope to create among players, and hold the results of their iterations to these end experience standards (Mueller and Isbister 2014). This may require extensive redevelopment and, where possible, revisiting of the technological components involved and the tuning of how they are used, in order to reach a final optimal play experience.

10.6.2   Evaluation

Social play that involves physical movement adds the challenge of interpreting and understanding players' physical expressivity and interaction (Isbister 2012). Social physical play that takes place across wide-ranging terrain (such as is the case with augmented reality games in which players might move through city streets) gives the evaluator even more of a headache in following players and transcribing information about play without disturbing the experience. Games that take place across social networks on mobiles or the internet require creativity on the part of the experimenter in setting up ecologically valid studies of how a game works across a social group, and in sampling the right mix of players with varying skill and interest levels, who are also in a social network with one another. Even constructing playtests for co-located social game play requires careful thought about what sorts of social groupings to bring into the lab and how best to recruit them, and the arrangement of the appropriate physical setting and ambience.

In short, evaluation of social gameplay requires careful attention to process, and typically requires a mixed-methods data collection and analysis approach to truly test whether the impacts upon players that the designers wish for are being achieved. It's important to devise an evaluation plan and to budget for the time and expenses involved in doing iterative testing as the design process takes place. There is extant published advice on game user research that should be used to help guide this process (e.g. this volume; Isbister and Schaffer 2008). It's often the case that co-located social games require a great deal more effort put into creating the right social atmosphere to ensure external validity of the test results. Make sure to factor this into the workflow for evaluation.

10.7 Conclusions and Future Work

Social play continues to be a burgeoning area of game development, with a need for better techniques and standards for both the design and evaluation processes. We hope this chapter has provided the reader with a sense of the challenges involved, and that it has also given some good grounding and a practical framework for thinking about the design and evaluation of social play, through the lens of our work on co-located physical social games.

The authors are particularly interested in the evolution of better tools to support social game design and evaluation–methods and means for rapid prototyping and sharing of experiences, and less laborious techniques than video coding and interview transcription for understanding the nuances of the social impact of a game. We plan to continue future research in these areas, and welcome reader feedback and leads about promising work in these domains.

References

Andrew K, (2011) Rise of iOS and Android halves Nintendo DS game revenue in US in 2 years. Pocket Gamer website, http://www.pocketgamer.biz/r/PG.Biz/Flurry/feature.asp?c=35150. Accessed 29 March 2015

Avedon E, (1971) The study of games, chapter. The structural elements of games. Wiley, New York

Bandura A, (1977) Social learning theory. Prentice Hall, Englewood Cliffs

Bekker T, Sturm J, Eggen B (2010) Designing playful interactions for social interaction and physical play. Pers Ubiquit Comput 14(5):385–396

Bell C (2012) Designing for friendship: shaping player relationships with rules and freedom. GDC 2012 talk, accessible in GDC vault. http://gdcvault.com/play/1015706/Designing-for-Friendship-Shaping-Player. Accessed 29 March 2015

Benford S, Achnädelbach H, Koleva B, Anastasi R, Greenhalgh C, Rodden T, Jonathan G, Ghali A, Pridmore T, Gaver B, Boucher A, Walker B, Pennington S, Schmidt A, Gellersen H (2005) Expected, sensed, and desired: a framework for designing sensing-based interaction. ACM Trans Comput-Hum Interact 12(1):3–30

Bianchi-Berthouze N, Kim WW, Patel D (2007) Does body movement engage you more in digital game play? and why? Proceedings of the 2nd international conference on affective computing and intelligent interaction, ACII '07. Springer-Verlag, Berlin, pp 102–113

Caillois R (2001) Man, play and games. University of Illinois Press, Champaign

Carr D, Sachott G, Burn A, Buckingham D (2004) Doing game studies: a multimethod approach to the study of textuality, interactivity, and narrative space. Media Int Aust Inc Culture Policy 110:12

Costikyan (2002) I Have No Words & I Must Design: Toward a Critical Vocabulary for Games. In Proceedings of Computer Games and Digital Cultures Conference, ed. Frans Mäyrä. Tampere University Press

Csikszentmihalyi M 2009. Flow. HarperCollins, New York

De Kort YAW, Ijsselsteijn WA (2008) People, places, and play: player experience in a socio-spatial context. Comput Entertain 6(2). doi:10.1145/1371216.1371221

DeKoven B. (2002) The well-played game: a playful path to wholeness. iUniverse, Bloomington

DeKoven B (2011) On coliberation: exploring the experience of having fun together [Internet]. Version 1. Bernie DeKoven's Blog. http://berniedekoven.wordpress.com/article/on-coliberation-2hzxx66zkihpf-8/. Accessed 25 Sep 2011

ESA Entertainment Software Association (2008) Essential facts about the computer and video game industry. http://www.theesa.com/facts/pdfs/ESA_EF_2008.pdf. Accessed 17 July 2008

ESA. Entertainment Software Association (2014) Essential facts about the computer and video game industry. http://www.theesa.com/wp-content/uploads/2014/10/ESA_EF_2014.pdf. Accessed 29 March 2015

Fernaeus (2012) How do you design for the joy of movements. In Fernaeus Y, Holopainen J, Höök K, Ivarsson K, Karlsson A, Lindley S, Norlin C (eds) Plei-Plei. PPP Company Ltd., Hong Kong. http://plei-plei.info/thoughts/many-ways-of-moving-bodies/. Accessed 29 March 2015

Fluegelman A, Tembeck S (1976) The new games book. Play hard, play fair, nobody hurt. A Headlands Press Book, Dolphin/Doubleday

Fullerton T, Swain C, Hoffman S (2008) Game design workshop: a playcentric approach to creating innovative games. Gama Network Series. Elsevier Morgan Kaufmann, San Francisco

Gajadhar B, de Kort Y, IJsselsteijn W (2008) Influence of social setting on player experience of digital games. In CHI '08 extended abstracts on human factors in computing systems, CHI EA '08, pp 3099–3104. ACM, New York

Gaver B (2011) Designing for homo Ludens, still. In: Binder T, Löwgren J, Malmborg L (eds) (Re)searching the digital bauhaus. Springer, London, pp 163–178. http://www.gold.ac.uk/media/46gaver-ludens-still.pdf

Hartson HR (2003) Cognitive, physical, sensory, and functional affordances in interaction design. Behav Inf Technol 22:315–338

Hatfield E, Cacioppo JT, Rapson RL (1994) Emotional contagion. Cambridge University Press, Paris

Höök K (2008) Affective loop experiences—what are they? In: Proceedings of the 3rd international conference on Persuasive Technology, PERSUASIVE '08. Springer-Verlag, Berlin, pp 1–12

Huizinga J (1955) Homo Ludens: a study of the play-element in culture. Beacon paperbacks. Beacon Press, New York

Isbister K (2010) Enabling social play: a framework for design and evaluation. In: Bernhaupt R (ed) Evaluating user experience in games: concepts and methods. Springer, London, pp 11–22

Isbister K (2011, September/October) Emotion and motion: games as inspiration for shaping the future of interface. Interactions 18(5):24–27

Isbister K (2012) How to stop being a buzzkill: designing yamove!, A mobile tech mash-up to truly augment social play. Keynote presentation, abstract included in Proceedings of MobileHCI 2012, San Francisco

Isbister K, Schaffer N (2008) Game usability: advice from the experts for advancing the player experience. Morgan Kaufmann, San Francisco

Isbister K, Schwekendiek U, Frye J (2011a) Wriggle: an exploration of emotional and social effects of movement. work in progress presented at CHI 2011. (Short paper included in Conference Proceedings)

Isbister R, Schwekendiek U, Hayward E, Lidasan J (2011b) Is more movement better? A controlled comparison of movement-based games. Poster presented at Foundations of Digital Gaming 2011, Bordeaux (Short paper included in Conference Proceedings)

Jakobs E, Manstead A, Fischer A (1996) Social context and the experience of emotion. J Nonverbal Behav 20(2):123–142

Jakobs E, Fischer AH, Manstead AS (1997) Emotional experience as a function of social context: the role of the other. J Nonverbal Behav 21(2):103–130

Kavanagh LC, Suhler CL, Churchland PS, Winkielman P (2011) When it's an error to mirror: the surprising reputational costs of mimicry. Psychol Sci 22(10):1274–6

Koivisto EMI, Suomela R (2007) Using prototypes in early pervasive game development. In: Proceedings of Sandbox Symposium 2007, San Diego, CA, pp 149–156. August 4–5

Khut GP (2006) Engage: interaction, arts & audience experience, chapter interactive art as embodied enquiry: working with audience experience. Creativity and Cognition Studios Press, University of Technology, Sidney

Khut GP (2007) Cardiomorphologies: an inner journey through art. IEEE MultiMedia 14(4):5–7

Lindley SE, Le Couteur J, Berthouze NL (2008) Stirring up experience through movement in game play: effects on engagement and social behaviour. In: Proceedings of the SIGCHI Conference on Human Factors in Computing Systems, CHI '08. ACM, New York, pp 511–514

Lindström M, Ståhl A, Höök K, Sundström P, Laaksolathi J, Combetto M, Taylor A, Bresin R (2006) Affective diary: designing for bodily expressiveness and selfreflection. In: CHI '06 Extended Abstracts on Human Factors in Computing Systems, CHI EA '06. ACM, New York, pp 1037–1042

Loke L, Khut G (2011) Surging verticality: an experience of balance. In: Proceedings of the fifth international conference on Tangible, embedded, and embodied interaction, TEI '11. ACM, New York, pp 237–240

Loke L, Robertson T (2013) Moving and making strange: An embodied approach to movement-based interaction design. ACM Trans Comput-Hum Interact 20(1):7:1–7:25

Loke L, Larssen AT, Robertson T, Edwards J (2007, December) Understanding movement for interaction design: frameworks and approaches. Pers Ubiquit Comput 11(8):691–701

Loke L, Khut GP, Kocaballi AB (2012) Bodily experience and imagination: designing ritual interactions for participatory live-art contexts. In: Proceedings of the Designing Interactive Systems Conference, DIS '12. ACM, New York, pp 779–788

Magerkurth C, Engelke T, Memisoglu M (2004) Augmenting the virtual domain with physical and social elements: towards a paradigm shift in computer entertainment technology. Adv Comput Entertain Technol 2(4):12

Mandryk RL, Inkpen KM, Calvert TW (2006) Using psychophysiological techniques to measure user experience with entertainment technologies. Behav Informat Technol 25(2):141–158

Manstead T (2005) The social dimension of emotion. Psychologist 18(8):484–487

Márquez Segura E (2013) Body games: designing for movement-based play in co-located social settings. Licentiate thesis dissertation. Department of Computer and Systems Sciences, Stockholm University, Stockholm

Márquez Segura E, Johansson C, Moen J, Waern A (2011) Bodies, boogies, bugs and buddies—shall we play? In: Yi-Luen Do E, Gross MD, Oakley I (eds) Work-in-progress workshop proceedings on tangible, embedded and embodied interaction, TEI '11. ACM SIGCHI, pp 115–120

Márquez Segura E, Waern A, Moen J, Johansson C (2013) The design space of body games: technological, physical, and social design. In: Proceedings of CHI'13. ACM, New York, pp 3365–3374

Moen J (2006) KinAesthetic Movement Interaction. Designing for the Pleasure of Motion. PhD thesis, KTH

Moen J (2007) From hand-held to body-worn: embodied experiences of the design and use of a wearable movement-based interaction concept. In: Proceedings of the 1st international conference on Tangible and Embedded Interaction, TEI '07. ACM, New York, pp 251–258

Mueller F, Givvs MR, Frank V (2010) Towards understanding how to design for social play in exertion games. J Personal Ubiquitous Comput 14(5):417–424. Springer Publisher

Mueller FF, Isbister K (2014) Movement-based game guidelines. In: Proceedings of CHI 2014. Toronto, pp 2191–2200

Oulasvirta A, Kurvinen E, Kankainen T (2003) Understanding contexts by being there: case studies in bodystorming. Pers Ubiquit Comput 7:125–134. doi:10.1007/s00779-003-0238-7

Paiva A, Chaves R, Piedade M, Bullock A, Andersson G, Höök K (2003) Sentoy: a tangible interface to control the emotions of a synthetic character. In: Proceedings of the second international joint conference on Autonomous agents and multiagent systems, AAMAS'03. ACM, New York, pp 1088–1089

Piaget J (1999) The moral judgment of the child. Developmental psychology: Routledge. Routledge, New York

Ravaja N, Saari T, Turpeinen M, Laarni J, Salminen M, Kivikangas M (2006) Spatial presence and emotions during video game playing: does it matter with whom you play? Presence 15(4):381–392

Reeves S (2011) Designing interfaces in public settings: understanding the role of the spectator in human-computer interaction. Springer

Reeves S, Benford S, O'Malley C, Fraser M (2005) Designing the spectator experience. In: Proceedings of the SIGCHI Conference on Human Factors in Computing Systems (CHI '05). ACM, New York, pp 741–750

Salen K, Zimmerman E (2003) Rules of play: game design fundamentals. MIT Press, Cambridge

Schleicher D, Jones P, Kachur O (2010) Bodystorming as embodied designing. Interactions 17(6):47–51

Shusterman R (2008) Body consciousness: a philosophy of mindfulness and somaesthetics. Cambridge University Press, Cambridge

Simon B (2009) Wii are out of control: Bodies, game screens and the production of gestural excess. Loading 3(4)

Simbelis V, Höök K (2013) Metaphone: an artistic exploration of biofeedback and machine aesthetics. In: CHI '13 Extended abstracts on human factors in computing systems, CHI EA '13. ACM, New York, pp 2995–2998

Ståhl A, Höök K, Svensson M, Taylor AS, Combetto M (2009) Experiencing the affective diary. Personal Ubiquitous Comput 13(5):365–378

Stenros J, Paavilainen J, Mäyrä F (2009) The many faces of sociability and social play in games. In: Proceedings of the 13th International MindTrek Conference: everyday life in the Ubiquitous Era, MindTrek '09. ACM, New York, pp 82–89

Suits B (1978) The grasshopper: games, life and utopia. Broadview encore editions. Broadview Press, Printed in Canada

Szentgyorgyi C, Terry M, Lank E (2008) Renegade gaming: practices surrounding social use of the Nintendo DS handheld gaming system. CHI 2008 Proceedings, pp 1463–1472

Taylor TL (2006) Play between worlds: exploring online game culture. MIT Press, Cambridge

Tholander J, Johansson C (2010a) Bodies, boards, clubs and bugs: a study of bodily engaging artifacts. In: Proceedings of the 28th of the international conference extended abstracts on Human factors in computing systems, CHI EA '10. ACM, New York, pp 4045–4050

Tholander J, Johansson C (2010b) Design qualities for whole body interaction: learning from golf, skateboarding and bodybugging. In: Proceedings of the 6th Nordic Conference on Human-Computer Interaction: Extending Boundaries, NordiCHI' 10. ACM, New York, pp 493–502

Tisserand D (2010) PlayStation: evolving user testing to social, casual and portable gaming. Presentation at GDC 2010. In: GDC vault. http://www.gdcvault.com/play/1012600/PlayStation__Evolving_User_Testing_to_Social,_Casual_and_Portable_Gaming?sid=1012600. Accessed 29 March 2015

Valdesolo P, DeSteno D (2011) Synchrony and the social tuning of compassion. Emotion 11(2):262–266. doi:10.1037/a0021302

Voida A, Greenberg S (2009) Wii all play: the console game as a computational meeting place. In: Proceedings of the SIGCHI Conference on Human Factors in Computing Systems, CHI '09. ACM, New York, pp 1559–1568

Waern A (2009) Information technology in pervasive games pervasive games: theory and design. In: Morgan Kaufmann Game Design Books. Morgan Kaufmann Publishers/Elsevier, Burlington

Wilde D (2008) The hipdiskettes: learning (through) wearables. In: Proceedings of the 20th Australasian COnputer-Human Interaction Conference, OZCHI '08. ACM

Wilde D, Schiphorst T, Klooster S (2011) Move to design/design to move: a conversation about designing for the body. Interactions 18(4):22–27

Wilson D (2011) Brutally unfair tactics totally ok now: on self-effacing games and unachievements. Game Stud 11(1). http://gamestudies.org/1101/articles/wilson. Accessed 29 March 2015

Wilson D (2012) Designing for the pleasures of disputation-or-how to make friends by trying to kick them! Ph.D. dissertation. http://doougle.net/phd/Designing_for_the_Pleasures_of_Disputation.pdf. Accessed 29 March 2015

Zagal JP, Nussbaum M, Rosas R (2000) A model to support the design of multiplayer games. Presence: teleoper. Virtual Environ 9(5):448–462

Chapter 11
Evaluating Exertion Games

Florian Mueller and Nadia Bianchi-Berthouze

Abstract Games that demand exertion of the players through bodily movements have experienced commercial success and have been attributed with many physical, mental and social benefits, thus changing the way we play computer games. However, there is a lack of understanding of how to evaluate such exertion games, mainly because although the games' facilitated bodily movements are believed to be responsible for the generated user experiences, they are not considered in traditional evaluation methods that primarily assume keyboard and gamepad-style input devices. We do not believe there is a generic approach to evaluating exertion games, and therefore offer an overview of our mixed experiences in using various methods to guide the reader for future evaluations in this domain. We support the presented methods with data from case studies we undertook in order to illustrate their use and what kinds of results to expect. By identifying remaining issues in regards to evaluation methods for exertion games, we aim to provide an informed way forward for research in this area. With our work, we hope to contribute towards the advancement of such games, fostering their many benefits towards a more positive user experience.

11.1 Introduction

Many years into the history of games, gamers have seen the emergence of a new gaming genre that has been labeled exergaming or exertion games, which describes the emerging computer game titles that combine exerting bodily movements with computer gaming. Inspired by the early successes of arcade systems such as Dance Dance Revolution, computer game companies became excited about the potential of embracing physical activities in their games, and the Nintendo Wii, Sony's PlayStation Move and Microsoft's Xbox Kinect emerged. Exer-

F. Mueller (✉)
Exertion Games Lab, RMIT University, Melbourne, Australia
e-mail: floyd@floydmueller.com

N. Bianchi-Berthouze
UCLIC University College London, MPEB Gower Street, London, WC 1 6BT, UK
e-mail: n.berthouze@ucl.ac.uk

© Springer International Publishing Switzerland 2015
R. Bernhaupt (ed.), *Game User Experience Evaluation,*
Human-Computer Interaction Series, DOI 10.1007/978-3-319-15985-0_11

tion games, defined as computer games that require intense physical effort from their players (Mueller et al. 2003), are believed to be able to work against the prevailing computer gaming image of facilitating the modern world's sedentary lifestyles. The use of the Wiimote and the Wii Fit by gamers to address their personal weight goals has made worldwide headlines (DeLorenzo 2007) and influenced game companies to release more interactive fitness games. Clinicians have discovered the potential of such games to address the obesity epidemic and are conducting studies to test these games' effectiveness in motivating users, especially children and teenagers, to incorporate more physical exercise into their daily lives by engaging them through exertion gameplay (Graves et al. 2007). They have also discovered the use of exertion games for rehabilitation purposes to make traditionally repetitive boring exercise tasks more fun (LeBlanc 2008, Powell 2008). These exertion games are also attracting new audiences that have previously not been catered for, offering a transition in the user experience from "highscore-chasing" gaming to "party-fun", especially Nintendo Wii's bowling seems to be attractive to seniors, who organize championships in their nursing homes (Clark 2008). This new trend in gaming might ultimately challenge our understanding of the previously distinct terms of computer game, sports and exercise: the Dance Dance Revolution game, a computer game that requires exhausting jumping on dance pads, has been recognized as an official dance sport in Finland (Well-being Field Report nd..), and "Sports over a Distance" applications have enabled sportive exercise between geographically distant locations (Mueller et al. 2007). Several research studies have added weight to anecdotally reported physical, mental and social health benefits (Lieberman 2006; Graves et al. 2007; Wakkary et al. 2008; Bianchi-Berthouze 2013; Eriksson et al. 2007), and their proliferation appears to contribute to an understanding that these exertion games have the ability to introduce a new era in the history of computer gaming that changes the perspective for players, developers, and even spectators in regards to how we see computer gaming.

Being able to understand what makes players engage in such exertion games could result in improved experiences (Bianchi-Berthouze 2013), but also increased energy expenditure, and hence enhanced fitness (Bogost 2005), resulting in a healthier population that also benefits from mental and social benefits facilitated by these games. Studies on recreational physical activity (Wankel 1985) for non-athletes have indeed shown that flow, i.e. a form of optimal experience (Csikszentmihalyi 1990) is an important and relevant factor in maintaining the level of motivation high and reducing drop-out. However, what is lacking is an in-depth understanding of how such games should be evaluated to improve the user experience (Hoysniemi 2006). Traditional approaches to evaluating the user experience in games can fall short in providing a complete story of the user experience when it comes to exertion: exertion games offer opportunities that mouse and gamepad-controlled games lack, and not considering the unique aspects of exertion in such games might result in evaluation work that does not provide a complete picture of the user experience, ultimately failing in contributing towards the advancement of such games. In order to contribute to the success of exertion games, researchers and practitioners need to have an understanding of the opportunities but also challenges that arise when evaluating user experiences in exertion games. The purpose of this chapter is to contribute to this understanding.

We first provide a review of the literature that investigates the relation between body movement and affective experience. We then report on the lesson learnt from our work. We do not believe there is a generic approach to evaluating exertion games, and therefore offer an overview of our experiences in using various methods in order to provide the reader with a personal account that can serve as guide for future evaluations in this domain. We detail specific aspects user experience researchers and practitioners might encounter based on our results of evaluating exertion games using a range of methods. Our stories are based on over seven years experience in designing, developing and evaluating exertion games, and we refer back when appropriate to our original work to offer the reader concrete examples, supplemented with empirical evaluation data, to offer insights into our work. The aim is to provide the interested practitioner with guidance based on completed evaluation tasks of exertion games, supplemented with some practical examples of "lessons-learned". Furthermore, we hope our work can provide researchers with inspiration for further investigations into this area, by contributing to an understanding of how to approach the task of evaluating such games. We conclude by suggesting a research agenda for future work on the topic of evaluating the user experience of exertion games and provide an outlook on what challenges lie ahead. With our work, we hope to contribute towards the advancement of such games, fostering their many benefits.

11.2 Exertion Games and Affective Experience

As many of our approaches to evaluating exertion games refer to body movements and how they affect and are affected by the players' affective experiences, we begin by providing a brief overview of the literature that explores the relationship between body movement and affective experience. We then report on the lesson learnt from our work.

Studies in embodied cognition have increasingly provided evidences for the double role of body movements: body movements do not only represent a window on what a person feels, but they also affect a person's cognitive and affective processes. Studies done by (Laird 1974; Riskind and Gotay1982; Stepper and Strack 1993) have shown that people who were asked to assume a certain posture (e.g. slumped vs. upright) reported a perception of themselves and of their own performances that reflected the valence of the postural stance. Other studies, e.g. by (Wells and Petty 1980; Cacioppo et al. 1993; Chandler and Schwarz 2009) have shown that this effect goes beyond affecting self–perception. These studies showed that when people evaluate products while performing unrelated movements that are generally associated with a particular emotional valence (e.g., head nodding vs. head shaking), the valence of those movements bias the evaluation of the product.

Given the evidence for a relationship between body movement and cognitive and affective processes, researchers have been investigating the biological and neurological explanations of this relationship (Neumann et al 2000; Niedenthal et al 2005). They suggest that these effects are due to the fact that certain postures or movements activate the brain approach-avoidance mechanisms that then bias the processing of any incoming information. Carney et al. (2010) show evidences that posture affects the levels of hormones that control people's tolerance of risk. They found that posing in high power displays vs. low power displays produces an increase in testosterone and a decrease in cortisol and an increased feeling of power and tolerance to risk. Cole and Montero (2007) also proposed the term affective proprioception and discussed the possible neurological basis and evolutionary origin for the existence of a dedicated connection between proprioceptive system and brain area involved in the affective processing of stimuli that is akin to that of the tactile system. According to this perspective, the qualities of the body movement (e.g., fluidity, harmony) itself would trigger an affective experience.

Given these evidences, it seems highly likely that body movement in games has a role not only to facilitate the control of the game, but also to modulate how a person feels and experiences the events of the game. Recent works in HCI have investigated the interrelationship between body movement and game experience. Some of our work (Bianchi-Berthouze 2013) investigated through various studies how body movements that were imposed on players in exertion games produced changes in the emotional, social and role-play experience of the player. Her framework extends current engagement models presented in the game literature (e.g., Brown and Cairns 2004; Ermi et al. 2005; Yannakakis and Hallam 2008) by exploring the role of proprioceptive feedback. In her paper, she identifies five categories of body movements that steer and affect the player's experience: movements necessary to play the game, movements facilitating the control of the game, movements related to the role-play the game offers, affective body expressions and social gestures. Building on the evidences provided earlier, these studies show that, through proprioceptive feedback, each category of movements play a key role in shifting the engagement experience away from a pure hard-fun type (Lazzaro 2004), where the players' motivations are mainly to win and challenge themselves, to an experience that grounds its pleasure in taking up the role-play that the game offers.

Further studies investigated more in-depth how the quality of body movement required to play the game affects the emotional states of the player. Melzer et al. (2010) found that playing a Nintendo Wii game (Manhunt 2) that encouraged rapid aggressive gestures led to higher negative affect than when players played the same game using a standard controller. Isbister et al. (Isbister 2010; Isbister and Dimauro 2010; Isbister et al. 2011) found that increased amount of vigorous movement was statistically correlated with reported increase of arousal. They also found evidence of increased social connectedness as in Bianchi-Berthouze (2013).

Some authors have investigated how people engage their body movements according to the motivation they have to play the game. Pasch et al. (2009) showed that when the motivation for playing is to win the game, experienced players make an efficient use of their body movements in order abide to the control rule of the game. When instead their motivation is to relax, the body movement becomes an object of experience in itself (in line with Cole and Montero (2007)'s idea of affective proprioception) even if this may lead to a lower score. Nijhar et al. (2012) investigated further this question by providing quantitative evidence of such difference. Combined, these studies point to the importance of considering the affective user experience in exertion games during the evaluation task. In the next section, we describe how we used this in various approaches in our own work to advance the knowledge of evaluating exertion games.

11.3 Approach

All these studies point to the importance of defining new methods to investigate user experience in game

Prior work has acknowledged that the evaluation of exertion games can benefit from methods that consider and accommodate the unique characteristics of exertion games in their evaluation task design (Hoysniemi 2006). However, there is a limited understanding of what opportunities exist for the design of evaluation tasks and what shortcomings need to be considered when evaluating user experiences in such games. This lack of a comprehensive understanding of the challenges exertion brings to the evaluation process can hinder the advancement of these games and therefore limit the benefits they can offer to their users. Our work addresses this shortcoming by exploring how the user experience in exertion games can be evaluated based on our experiences of evaluating these games and informed by our results. Our approach begins with detailing our evaluation experiences of a diverse set of existing commercial and prototypal gaming systems. Based on the game under investigation, we have chosen different evaluation approaches, which we subsequently improved and refined. We highlight personal experiences we gained from evaluating these games and provide insights into the shortcomings of some of the methods we used, a summary of which is given in Table 11.1. We also describe opportunities for further research that arose out of particular instances. Furthermore, we provide an opinioned commentary that is aimed at giving the reader a critical view of what to expect in their evaluation tasks when faced with an exertion game. By also describing our results, we hope to offer guidance when there is a need to choose between several methods.

We acknowledge that our approach cannot and is not intended to result in a comprehensive list of all available methods nor describe every aspect specific to exertion games. However, with our approach, we aim to focus on providing an experienced-based account of what opportunities lie ahead in this exciting new field. We believe our experiences on this topic will give the reader an extensive, although not comprehensive, view from various perspectives, contributing to an understanding that can inspire and guide future investigations.

11.4 Evaluating User Experience Post-Playing

We begin by describing evaluation methods that are based on the belief that the game experience can be (self-)assessed after it has occurred, for example a popular approach is to use interviews with participants immediately after playing. Such approaches have the advantage that they leave the experience un-altered, as they separate the experience from the evaluation process. Next, we discuss the use of interviews, as they are often used in non-exertion games also and are a familiar evaluation tool, however, we focus on what purpose they serve in contributing to our understanding of exertion games.

11.4.1 Interviews

For most of our experiments, we conducted semi-structured interviews with the participants after the gaming action. We have also videotaped these interviews, and we now describe our experiences with this method based on one particular case study. We selected this case study as it offered some unique insights into the social aspects of exertion games, as the players were geographically distant, connected only over

Table 11.1 Summary of case studies, outcomes and challenges in evaluating post-playing and in-place user experience

Case studies	Approaches	Outcomes	Challenges
Table tennis for three: single condition	Semi structured interviews, observations and coding of video data	Exertion facilitates social play in and outside gameplay, e.g. fosters the recollection of the experience through kinesthetic stimulation	a) How to define coding systems b) How to overcome that re-enacting might bring players to reinterpret their experience?
Breakout for two: exertion vs. non-exertion condition	Prisoner dilemma and questionnaires	Exertion stimulates competition, connectedness	Measures overcome the limitations of self reports, but are not as 'direct'
Donkey Konga: exertion vs. non-exertion conditions	Quantitative comparison of verbal and non-verbal behavior	Exertion facilitates empathic behavior in cooperative games: increase social interaction and emotional experience	How to define coding systems that produce high inter-rater reliability?
Guitar hero: exertion vs. non-exertion conditions	Quantitative analysis of movement by motion capture system	fantasy role-taking experience. Amount of movement of the player correlates with engagement	The automatic analysis of complex movements (e.g., pointing, shrugging) is technically challenging

a computer network. We present a collocated exertion game study that also included interviews further below, but report on a different method there.

Case study: Table Tennis for Three We have conducted semi-structured interviews in an attempt to qualitatively analyze the social play in Table Tennis for Three. Table Tennis for Three is an exertion game that was inspired by table tennis, but can be played by three geographically distant participants. It uses a real bat and ball on a modified table tennis table that detects the ball's impact in order to modify virtual game content, projected onto the playing surface, and augmented with a videoconferencing component to support a social aspect amongst the participants. A detailed description of the system can be read here (Mueller and Gibbs 2007a; Mueller and Gibbs 2007b) and the evaluation process is described here (Mueller and Gibbs 2007b). After having played the game, the participants were interviewed in one room together. The video recordings of the interviews were coded using qualitative analysis software. This approach revealed an interesting aspect specific to exertion games, which we aim to sensitize other researchers to, as it might affect the evaluation process. However, we begin by describing the study design.

Experimental Setup 42 participants were recruited and asked in the advertising material to organize themselves preferably in teams of three. If they were unable to do so, we matched them up randomly with other participants in order to have always three people participating at the same time. We had one last minute cancellation; in this case we replaced the third player with a participant that had played previously, hence we report on 41 distinct participants. The participants were between 21 and 55 years old (arithmetic mean 32 years), whereas 27 were male and 14 female. After each group of three participants played for at least 30 min, they were brought together into the same room after the game, where we conducted semi-structured interviews with all three of them together. The interviews lasted from 20 to 60 min and included open-ended questions about their experience and their interactions with the other players. We took notes during the interviews as well as videotaped each session. We analyzed the video data using a coding process based on grounded theory (Strauss and Corbin 1998) with the help of a database for all the video data. An iterative coding process was used to identify important themes and ideas. We also used the notes and created affinity diagrams to further refine our concepts.

The joyful atmosphere of the exertion game carried over to the interviews, which appeared to be facilitated by the use of bodily actions during the interviews as exhibited as part of the gameplay. For example, players used movements not only in relation to play directly, such as throwing their hands in the air to indicate they won. A player jokingly made a fist to the other players; another participant put her tongue out. Players often applauded others on their performance, and the joyful atmosphere seemed to have carried over into the interviews. Players used their bodies to retell their experiences, and the video recordings were viable tools in capturing this retelling. For example, one team patted on each other's shoulders and slapped each other comradely several times during the interview. Another team initiated a group hug.

In addition to the theoretical concepts we identified as part of the investigation of Table Tennis for Three, we found the aspect of bodily movements facilitated by the exertion game that carried over to a retelling in the interviews particularly intriguing for an understanding of user experiences in games. Such a retelling is an element of metagaming, a social play phenomenon that refers to the relationship of a game to elements outside of the game. One way that metagaming occurs "during a game other than the game itself … are social factors such as competition and camaraderie" (Salen and Zimmerman 2003). The participants in Table Tennis for Three used this to turn the interview into a metagaming event by verbally and non-verbally commenting on the other players' performance and turning the post-game into a social spectacle. The retelling of what happened in a game is an important part of a "lived experience" (McCarthy and Wright 2004). Players predominantly used their exertion skills in the games, so they drew on these skills again during the reliving of the experience. This reliving of a "pleasurable kinesthetic stimulation" has been suggested to re-trigger the associated pleasurable emotions (Iso-Ahola and Hatfield 1986). Re-enacting the exertion movements can also support the player's cognitive processes, helping them to remember certain parts of the game (Lindley and Monk 2008). Players gave further meaning to these exertion actions by sharing them with others, the opportunity for metagaming provided by the interview task therefore contributed towards a meaningful social play experience. In contrast, the exertion actions supporting metagaming are missing in keyboard and gamepad-controlled computer games, and the players have to rely on their cognitive skills to remember their experiences and associated affective responses. Furthermore, Moen (2006) believes that movement literacy can be improved by physically exploring movement, as our players did during gameplay, but also by verbally reflecting on it, which they did through the interviews. This suggests that the interview task might have contributed to the participants' movement literacy.

Our observations during post-game interviews suggest implications for evaluation methods used in exertion games. Researchers need to be aware that retelling, in particular as part of metagaming, is an important aspect of the user experience, and players will use opportunities to enable such an experience. We believe user experience researchers should be aware of such effects in order to be able to consider them in their experimental designs and be sensitive towards them during the interview process. If the game to be investigated features exertion actions, researchers should anticipate that bodily movements will play a role in the interview process as well. Any capturing should accommodate for this: we valued the use of video, as a traditional audio-only recording and analysis would have neglected the bodily actions we observed that revealed valuable insights into the game experience.

11.4.2 Prisoner-Dilemma Task

We now report on our findings on a distributed soccer-like game called Breakout for Two (Mueller et al. 2003) that allows two participants to engage in a ball sports activity although being apart. In the accompanied study, we were interested in understanding if the required exertion to play the game has an effect on the sense of connectedness between the participants, and hence compared the exertion game with a similar game that is played with a keyboard. We present an element of a larger evaluation study: a Prisoner's Dilemma task.

Measuring social effects between participants based on short periods of gaming activity can be difficult, as many outside factors such as personality types and situational context can affect social behavior. Social interaction is one aspect of it, but even measuring this is not trivial: humans use many cues to express social needs, and a comprehensive account of all social elements within human communication is an almost insurmountable task. The Breakout for Two study consequently focused on investigating whether the system could facilitate a sense of trust between the participants. This sense of trust was probed with a variation of a Prisoner's Dilemma task (Palameta and Brown 1999). A between-subjects experimental design tested the effects of the exertion game on performance in the Prisoner's Dilemma task in comparison with a non-exertion version of the game. There are many interpretations and alteration of the traditional Prisoner's Dilemma task, however, they mostly follow the same principle. The variation used in the study requires to make a decision based on another person's decision, however, their decision is not accessible when the decision needs to be made, because the participants cannot communicate during the process. Such a task is a commonly used measure of trust and cooperation, and multi-round Prisoners' Dilemma tasks have been successfully used to assess levels of trust established between participants in remote locations (Zheng et al. 2001 2002, Rocco 1998).

Case study: Breakout for Two Facilitating exertion as part of a gaming experience is believed to positively influence social factors between the participants. The case study of Breakout for Two was designed to investigate if the positive effects on sociality transfer to mediated communication scenarios, in other words: does the addition of an exertion interface still facilitate social benefits even if the players can only interact with one another over a videoconference? The research answered this by presenting a study that allowed distributed players to exert themselves with a physical ball that was the interface to a shared virtual game: the players had to kick the ball at certain targets before the other player did, and these targets were interconnected over the network. The players could comment on each other's play and see their progress through an integrated large-scale videoconference. The winner was the player who hit the ball the hardest and most accurately, thereby scoring the most points.

Experimental Setup 56 volunteers were recruited through flyers and email postings at local universities, sports clubs and youth hostels. The average age of the participants was 26, the youngest being 17 and the oldest 44. 34 volunteers were asked to play the physical game and 22 played the non-exertion, keyboard-controlled game. 77% of the participants were male in the exertion group, 64% in the non-exertion group. This equal distribution was not deliberate, but opportune. After the participants played Breakout for Two, they were escorted to a different area where they could not see nor hear each other. They were faced with written instructions, which explained that their task was to choose if they wanted to put a big X on the back of a sheet of paper or not. If both of the players chose not to put anything down, they would both receive an additional 5 € to their payment, in order to ponder their choice seriously. If only one of them would mark an X, this person would receive an additional 10 €, but if both of them would draw an X, they would receive nothing.

Analysis and Discussion   In the exertion group, 15 players put an X on the back of their sheet (44 %). This comprises 11 pairs where only one person put an X down (resulting in this person receiving an extra 10 €), 2 teams where both participants wrote an X (resulting in no extra payment), and 4 teams where both players left the page blank (resulting in an extra 5 € for each of them). In the non-exertion group, only 5 players put down an X (23 %). In each case, their partner left the page blank, resulting in an extra 10 Euros payment for the first player. Six pairs put nothing down, receiving an additional 5 € each and no team had an X on both sheets.

We expected that the participants in the exertion condition would be more likely to cooperate in the Prisoner's Dilemma task than their non-exertion counterparts, based on the higher levels of connectedness that were recorded in the questionnaire survey and interviews within the same setup (Mueller 2002). It seems plausible to anticipate that participants who play a team sport are more likely to cooperate in a Prisoner's Dilemma task. After all, a correlation between sport and trust has been previously studied (Clark and Gronbegh 1987). However, the results showed that players were *less* likely to cooperate if they participated in the exertion game.

Further investigations with larger user numbers are necessary to shed light on this surprising result; however, we have a hunch about what have caused the players' reactions. We believe it could be speculated that the exertion component increased the competitive aspect of the game. The game in both conditions was identical in terms of its competitive element, however, investing bodily actions might have triggered the participants to "take it more seriously" and value the competitive aspect higher. In order to strengthen this claim, we would like to draw attention to the element of competition in traditional exertion sports games: most sports are of a competitive nature, and almost all organized sports have provisions such as overtime or penalty shootouts to determine a winner, if not at the end of a game, at least at the end of the season. It seems competition and exertion can go hand in hand, however, this does not imply that physical games cannot foster non-competition: collaborative physical games experienced a high in the 70s as the New Games movement, and augmented derivatives exist (Lantz 2006), however, these games have slowly faded and lack the widespread success of competitive sports.

Reflecting upon the pervasive role of competition in traditional exertion sports, it could be hypothesized that the introduction of exertion activity in a game context amplifies any competitive element. This is underlined by anecdotal incidents observed during gameplay, in which some participants appear to become "more into it" and were more eager to win once they have achieved a certain level of exertion. This would extend the findings that exertion can amplify competition by a virtual gameplay component. However, further empirical research is needed to investigate whether augmented exertion can amplify any competitive aspect in games.

We are aware that a Prisoner's Dilemma task does not measure user experience in games per se. However, our investigation demonstrates that using such a task to test for social effects as an outcome of exertion gaming has its caveats. In particular, it leads to the speculation that exertion can amplify competitive notions developed during gameplay. If further research confirms this assumption, this can have implications on how to evaluate competitive games in which the bodies are involved, whether the evaluation includes a Prisoner's Dilemma or any other task, as the investigated concept, here trust, might be skewed by the altered competitiveness that the exertion aspect facilitated.

11.4.3 Questionnaire

Finally, we conclude this section by discussing the use of questionnaires to gather data for evaluation purposes since this approach is a common practice, and has been increasingly used for an understanding of games as well. As part of our research we have also used questionnaires and have acquired experience from using established questions, but also developed our own set of questions to gather data depending on the context, research question and study design we faced. Although questionnaires may seem to be a generic tool for evaluating user experience, and its use for exertion games might not appear to require any specific attention, we have observed that using questionnaires within the context of exertion games can pose some interesting caveats that we believe researchers should be aware of in order to account for them in their evaluation designs.

One aspect that makes the use of questionnaires particular in the context of exertion games is related but not identical to the critique of using questionnaires for games in general. The use of questionnaires for evaluating user experience has been criticized for its inadequacy of capturing a user state during the game, as players answer questions regarding their experience after they have played the game, 'outside' their immediate engagement with it. The participants need to divert their focus of attention to the evaluation task, away from the experience; the same experience they are now asked to self-assess. This criticism is common amongst questionnaire approaches, whether the game facilitates exertion or not. However, if the players exerted themselves as part of the gameplay, several factors influence their answers in ways different to a keyboard or gamepad experience: firstly, as exertion games are believed to facilitate more emotional play (Bianchi-Berthouze et al. 2007), these affective states could influence the assessment players give, in particular if the questions are asked immediately after the game. We acknowledge that these altered emotional states could be a desired effect of the game, worth capturing in the evaluation process; however, we want to point out that researchers should be aware that the emotional change could occur from the game content, but also from the physical exertion the game facilitates, which might have different implications for the analysis. Secondly, a possibly lower recovery curve from a heightened state of arousal based on exertion might affect a comparison with non-exertion game data. To explain: the emotions facilitated by the involvement of the body interact with the physiological functions of the body in a bidirectional relationship, and it has been suggested that this relationship can affect the emotional engagement with the game for longer than in a traditional non-exertion game, in which the engagement is mainly regulated by cognitive functions (Lehrer 2006). This prolonged engagement with the game is not limited to emotional aspects; for example, in our investigations of Breakout for Two (Mueller et al. 2003), we have observed that players needed a break to physically recover from the activity before they were able to fill out a questionnaire. This suggests that the exertion aspect can affect the time between the game experience and answering questions, possibly altering the recall ability of participants. Furthermore, research has shown that cognitive functions are improved after exercise (Ratey 2008), which might also impact upon how the participants answer, independent from the experience under investigation. These potential effects do not eradicate the use of questionnaires as evaluation method for exertion games, but researchers might benefit from being aware of these potential influences in order to address them in their evaluation design.

11.5 Evaluating User Experience In-Place

In the previous sections, we have focused on methods that rely on data gathered after the gaming action. We are now describing our experiences with directly observing exertion actions while they are taking place. We focus on how the analysis of participants' non-verbal behavior can give insights into their experience, in particular, we describe how it helped us to quantify and reason about the effect of a game's design on social and emotional experience.

11.6 Coding Body Movement

Case study: Donkey Konga We carried out a study to investigate how the use of larger body movement game controllers would change the way players engage in a game (Lindley et al. 2008). An experiment was thus designed to observe and compare the behavior of players playing the same game but using different types of controllers: controllers that require only finger movement to control the game and controllers that require larger body movement.

Experimental Setup Levels of engagement and the degree of emotional and social interaction between players were explored in a game of Donkey Konga (Lindley et al. 2008). The input devices were bongos and a standard dual-pad controller. When bongos were used players were encouraged to tap the bongos and clap their hands in time with the music; when the dual-pad controller was used these actions were performed through button presses using fingers and thumbs. We are aware that playing augmented bongos does not necessarily result in intense physical exhaustion, however, the involved body movements and their reliance on rhythmic coordinated kinesthetic actions have many characteristics similar to sportive behavior and have been previously compared to exertion games (Bogost 2005), and hence the results should be able to contribute to an understanding of exertion games.

Ten pairs of participants were asked to play in both conditions, and the order of the two conditions was counterbalanced across the pairs. Being all beginners, the players played in two-player cooperative mode ('Duet') at the easiest skill setting. The playing sessions were videotaped and an existing engagement questionnaire (Chen et al. 2005) was used. The scores for the participants in each pair were summed. To measure the emotional and social engagement of the participants, their verbal and non-verbal behaviors were coded using the Autism Diagnostic Observation Schedule (Lord et al. 2000). We found this scheme particularly useful, however, other researchers seem to prefer Laban's notations, especially when concerned with dance-like movements (Loke et al. 2007). The length of time that each participant spent producing speech and other utterances was measured. Non-verbal behaviors were also classified according to two categories: Instrumental gestures were defined as those in which the action conveyed a clear meaning or directed attention (e.g., pointing, shrugging, and nods of the head); empathic gestures were defined as those in which the action was emotive (e.g., placing the hands to the mouth in shock). These gestures were selected as they indicate the players' social and emotional involvement.

Analysis and Discussion To understand the magnitude of the effect the body movements has on the players, a statistical analysis of the non-verbal and verbal behaviors was performed. Prior to this, scores on the game were compared across the two conditions to ensure that possible effects were not due to variations in performance. A Wilcoxon's two-tailed matched-pairs signed-ranks test showed that the type of controller had no significant effect on performance ($Z = -0.889$, $p = 0.414$). All further differences were evaluated for statistical significance using Wilcoxon's one-tailed matched-pairs signed-ranks tests, with the pair as the sampling unit. The participants produced more speech ($Z = -1.478$, $p = 0.08$) and significantly more other utterances ($Z = -2.599$, $p < 0.01$) when using the bongos. Participants also made significantly more instrumental ($Z = -1.895$, $p < 0.05$) and empathic ($Z = -2.5273$, $p < 0.01$) gestures when using the bongos rather than the wireless controller, lending further weight to the idea that there was more social interaction in this condition. The participants rated themselves as experiencing a significantly higher level of engagement ($Z = 2.803$, $p < 0.01$) when using the bongos (mean $= 248.80$, max score $= 336$, std. dev. $= 23.03$) rather than the wireless controller (mean $= 198.50$, max score $= 336$, std. dev. $= 25.33$).

This study has contributed to an understanding of the quality of engagement in the game. Whereas the engagement questionnaire informed us of a statistically significant higher level of engagement in the bongo condition, the players' behavior informed us that the dynamics of the experience differed between the two conditions, an important implication for our understanding of how to evaluate such games. As shown by the number of instrumental gestures and utterances, players in the bongo condition were socially more interactive. It is important to note that the increased number of gestures cannot simply be accounted for by the fact that players have their hands free. They still need to use them to control the game (i.e., clapping and tapping). The fact that the number of emotional expressions (e.g., dancing) and empathic gestures was statistically higher in the bongo condition compared with the traditional controller condition suggests that playing the bongos facilitated more emotional and social experiences. We believe our results can inform the choice of future evaluations, because they shed light on characteristics unique to exertion. For example, other measuring techniques, such as biosensors, might have captured emotional engagement and increased physical activity, however, we believe it is unlikely that they would have detected how the social and emotional interaction between players unfolded, a very important information for usability purposes. Whilst Mueller et al. (Mueller et al. 2003) have proposed that arousal associated with physical movement might support social interaction, Mandryk and Inkpen (Mandryk and Inkpen 2004) have shown that the presence of a friend results in higher engagement. Lindley and Monk (Lindley and Monk 2008) have argued further that social behavior and experience are intertwined to the extent that measures of conversation can be used to tap into unfolding experience. By affording realistic movements, the bongos may have facilitated a willing suspension of disbelief during gameplay, and their flexibility may have promoted enjoyment by encouraging clapping and dancing.

11.6.1 Automatically Coding Body Movement

In the previous section, we have shown how the statistical analysis of non-verbal and verbal behavior enabled us to investigate the effect that changes to a game's interface may have on the emotional and social experience of the player. In this section, we discuss how this approach can be improved: we describe how such an analysis could be facilitated by using a motion capture system to obtain a more objective analysis of the movements and to reduce the amount of time necessary to analyze the captured video footage. To our knowledge, this was the first time such a device has been used to evaluate exertion gaming experiences. With the Microsoft Xbox Kinect, measuring body movement becomes even more feasible and hence a source of information that should be considered.

Case Study: Guitar Hero Here, we present a study in which movement actions captured by using an exoskeleton were quantitatively analyzed to understand the relation between movement and the level and quality of player engagement.

Experimental Setup Participants were asked to play Guitar Hero, a guitar simulation game for Sony's PlayStation (Hero 2015). This game sees the player perform a song by pressing in sequence a number of color-coded buttons on a guitar-shaped controller. Twenty players were randomly assigned to two different playing conditions. In one condition (called D hereafter), the guitar-shaped controller was used as a dual-pad controller, i.e., the participants were taught all of those features that are controlled solely with the hands (i.e., fret buttons, strut bar and whammy bar). In the second condition (called G hereafter), the participants were informed that to gain "star power" they could make use of a tilt sensor in the neck of the guitar, i.e. by raising the guitar upward. The participants were fitted with a lightweight exoskeleton so as to provide angular measurements for each of the upper-body joints. In addition, a video camera was placed in front of them to record their body movements during play. After playing two rock songs (for about 10 min) at the beginner level, the player's engagement level was assessed using the previously mentioned engagement questionnaire.

The engagement scores were analyzed using a t-test revealing that the G condition returned significantly higher engagement scores ($t = 5.123$, $p < .001$) thus suggesting that body movement imposed in the G condition affected the player's engagement level. To further clarify this finding, we correlated the engagement scores with the amount of motion measured with the motion capture system. We identified a negative correlation in the D condition and a positive correlation in the G condition.

Analysis and Discussion The results seem to indicate that the amount of movement could be a measure of engagement, at least for certain types of movement-based games. However, the amount of movement alone is not sufficient as specific types of movements, e.g. fidgeting, could be an indication of boredom as reported in (Bianchi-Berthouze et al. 2006). By analyzing the video footage of this experiment, we observed that in condition G, players displayed more, even if briefly, guitar-like player movements (e.g., dancing) showing a tendency to take over the role-play offered by the game (e.g., being a rock-star). They also showed expressions of higher levels of arousal and positive experience, such as expressions of excitement. In condition D, players seemed more driven by a desire to win the game (hard fun), leading to an increased focus on the display and to emotional expressions of frustration when a mistake was made. They displayed more still behavior and some rhythm-keeping foot behavior that may have facilitated control of the game. The amount of movement that possibly contributed to a different type of engagement could be identified in more positive emotional expressions and movements that reflect the role the player assumes in the game. Even though in this study we were yet unable to automatically perform such an analysis, new tools for gesture and affective movements detection are becoming available, and a motion capture system could facilitate the capturing of these different types of behaviors automatically. Berthouze and colleagues (Bianchi-Berthouze and Kleinsmith 2003; Kleinsmith et al. 2011; Savva et al. 2012) proposed a low-level description of body posture and movement that enable the mapping of bodily expressions into emotion categories or emotion dimensions. By using low-level descriptions of posture, motion capture, and connectionist or statistical modeling techniques to these descriptions, they have suggested that mapping models can easily be adapted to detect different types of expressions irrespective of the context in which these expressions are displayed. Using this approach, they explored whether the style of play of the players could be a factor affecting the players' experience.

Although this study has only shown the use of simple measures of movement, the use of a motion capture system paves the way for more complex analyses of bodily movement. Furthermore, it might enhance our understanding of how the type of movements that the game either imposes or affords can affect the strategies adopted by players and hence the emotional and social experience. The use of an exoskeleton could in fact facilitate the analysis of movement strategies (e.g., smooth and long movement vs. jerky and fast movement) (Pasch et al. 2009) and help produce movement measures that can be indicators of user experience. This approach is thus promising as it offers a more objective way to measure movement. The use of motion capture devices to measure non-verbal behavior is increasingly becoming available but given the challenge gesture recognition technology still faces when dealing with unpredictable scenarios whereby the set of movements and gestures cannot be predefined, we believe this approach still needs to be used in connection with other measures such as video analysis when the meaning of movement needs to be interpreted.

11.7 Other Approaches of Evaluating Exertion Games

Other researchers have also been concerned with investigating user experience when evaluating interactive technology that involves exertion. However, most of the work evolved from a physiological perspective, primarily concerned with the physical health outcomes that result from participating in such experiences. When applied to gaming applications, these investigations mainly focus on any physical health effects that the game can facilitate, for example whether an exertion game can lead to weight loss (Graves et al. 2007, Tan et al. 2002). In order to shed light on the contribution the game makes to a physiological benefit, the exertion level of the player has been measured. We now describe a few approaches that are derived from these studies, but have potential to be useful and practical for evaluating user experience. Although mostly new to the context of games, we believe they hold promise for exertion games due to their special characteristics. The following outline is by no means comprehensive, but should give the reader a starting point. We believe future investigations will shed light on our understanding of such approaches in the context of games, in particular when combined with more traditional methods.

11.7.1 Physiological Measurements

So far, we have highlighted how our work suggests that movement and engagement can be intertwined in exertion games. However, capturing objective movement might only tell one story: different people exert themselves differently when performing the same physical movement, depending on their fitness level and bodily capabilities. Physiological measurements could create a more objective measure as to how much exertion players invested into the game, possibly contributing to a more complete understanding of engagement and user experience. One cost-effective way of measuring a participant's exertion intensity is to use a heart rate monitor. Heart rate monitors are widely available, and a few models allow interfacing with a PC for subsequent analysis. Athletes and hobby sportspeople often use heart rate monitors in their training, hence study subjects can often already be familiar with such devices and knowledge about their advantages and shortcomings is widely available. Human-computer interaction research has previously used heart rate monitors not only for measuring, but also for controlling games (Nenonen et al. 2007; Mandryk et al. 2006), furthering acceptance in the community through its pervasive use. Heart rate monitors are also small, lightweight and battery powered, making them suitable for mobile use (Mueller et al. 2007). They can provide physiological user data for little cost and are easy to administer, however, the type of exertion activity that is involved during the gameplay can determine its utility, as heart rate monitors are best utilized in aerobic activities. It should also be noted that a player's heart rate could be affected by other factors outside the game environment. Hart gives a few examples: outside temperature, too much clothing or caffeine drinking can affect heart rate data (Hart 2003). If such data is not useable, researchers have suggested to use performance measurements to evaluate exertion activities, for example through measurement devices in the participants' shoes or by using GPS data to track a player's movements (Mueller et al. 2007). Yannakakis and Hallam (2008) proposes a method based on heart monitoring and skin conductance measurements that allow to separate fun from exertion activity and provide a better measure of the player's experience. We believe these approaches can, if supplemented with body data from the user, give insights into the energy expenditure during gameplay, contributing to a wider picture of game experience.

11.7.2 Borg's Perceived Exertion Scale

Another way of measuring a participant's exertion level is by using Borg's scale (Borg 1998), which aims to acquire the rate of perceived physical exertion by the participant. It is a simple scale, requiring no technical equipment, which was designed for athletes and sports coaches to be used to assess the intensity of training and competition. The Borg scale, or often referred to as 'Rating of Perceived Exertion', is presented to the participant in form of a chart. The participant then has to select how hard she/he feels she/he is working by giving a rating such as "Light" or "Maximal". The original scale has 21 points of exertion, but variations with less points exist (Hart 2003). The Borg scale has the advantage that it is easy to administer and understand by participants. It has also been demonstrated that the scale correlates well with more reliable indicators of exercise intensity such as blood lactate, VO2, ventilation and respiration rates, and it is also not affected by the environmental factors associated with skewed heart rate monitor data (see above). The results are subjective, however, and the players need to give their rating during or right after the exertion activity. For example, asking a subject during a treadmill-based game to rate their exertion level seems doable, however, chasing a player on a football pitch to acquire an intensity rating might seem impractical.

It should be noted, however, that such a focus on the outcome of the game experience, whether through heart rate monitors or Borg's scale, might aid in offering recommendations as to which exertion games support the most intense workout, however, they fall short in contributing to an understanding of whether and how the game facilitates an intrinsic motivation for the participants to play in the first place. Hence we believe such approaches should not be used exclusively, but rather complement the methods we described in more detail above. By doing so, they might be able to contribute to a more complete story of the user experience in exertion games.

11.7.3 Evaluating Exertion Games Based on User Groups

We also would like to point the reader to the work by Hoysniemi (Hoysniemi 2006), who describes the design and evaluation of physically interactive games she has been involved in designing herself. The author argues that different user groups can benefit from different evaluation methods, and that the unique characteristics of exertion games demand a critical reflection on which method to choose. Next to interviews and questionnaires, she has used observational as well as Wizard-of-Oz and peer tutoring methods to evaluate exertion games. Similar to Loke et al. (Loke et al. 2007), she has also attempted to describe the bodily movements exhibited in a game using dance-derived movement analysis. She selected specific methods depending on the user group, children, dancers or martial art athletes, and argues that each has potential for unique insights.

11.7.4 Evaluating Using Blogs

As users have appropriated exertion games for their personal weight loss goals, it might be possible to use their self-reported progress reports to evaluate such games: for example, upon its release the Nintendo Wii inspired many avid gamers who described themselves as reluctant exercisers to use the accompanied exertion games to increase their energy expenditure through gaming. Many of these gamers reported their progress in blogs (see for example (DeLorenzo 2007)), and used the social support they gained from comments and page-view statistics as motivational tools. Although this data needs to be trusted, the sheer amount of user data and availability could make such an approach an intriguing tool to evaluate games in terms of their effectiveness to reduce players' waistlines, but also to investigate any long-term effects to engage players, based on their dedication to report about it.

11.8 Future Challenges

relationship could be a view from the opposite direction: by examining the exertion component, researchers might be able to infer affective aspects from the gaming experience. This appears to be a valid approach, as bodily expressions are an important index of emotional experience. For example, past research has shown that body movement and posture can be an important modality in the human judgment of behavioral displays including affective states and moods (Argyle 1988; Bernhardt and Robinson 2008). Although most work in this area has focused on facial expressions (Ambady and Rosenthal 1992; Ekman and Rosenberg 2005), studies embraced a more body-centric approach and found that the perception of emotion is often biased towards the emotion expressed by the body (Meeren et al. 2005), meaning the inference of affective states through body posture in exertion games could yield improved results compared to facial-expression approaches. It should be noted, however, that unlike the recognition of facial expressions, which has been generally based on quantitative models that map pattern of muscle activation into emotions (e.g., (Ekman and Rosenberg 2005)), recognition of bodily expressions of emotions has long been mostly qualitative. Recent advances make the process of identifying emotions from basic movement and posture units more objective and measurable. For example Berthouze et al. (Bianchi-Berthouze and Kleinsmith 2003; De Silva and Bianchi-Berthouze 2004) proposed a general description of posture based on angles and distances between body joints to support the mapping of body postures into emotions. Although such approaches might suffer from the general limitations of any automatic recognition systems, their ability to mature through a demand of supporting the creation of technology that can adapt to the affective states of the user can make them a powerful new avenue for evaluation.

11.9 Final Thoughts

We have described our work on the topic of evaluating user experiences of exertion games. We do not believe there is a generic approach to evaluating exertion games, and therefore we offered a diverse set of observations with the intention to contribute towards an understanding of this new emerging area from varied viewpoints. By supporting our experience reports with concrete data from case studies, we hope to be able to provide the reader with practical guidance on what kind of effects one can expect that are unique to evaluating exertion games. Our aim was to provide a lively account in order to inspire researchers to further investigations into this area, and present them with opportunities for future work encouraged by our results.

We have presented methods known from traditional evaluation tasks, and described their different use in an exertion game setup. We found that whether asking a participant interview or questionnaire-style questions, any post-experience evaluation should take into account that the player will be exhausted after the game. The exertion activity demanded the investment of physical effort, and players can be expected to be out of breath, tired and in an altered emotional state. This altered state can show in many ways, and although mostly beneficial when it comes to the well-being of the player, that it can also affect the evaluation task, an issue we believe researchers should be aware of in future studies. Evaluators should also be aware that motivation to play these exertion games can not only be facilitated through the gameplay, but also by an intrinsic drive to improve one's health: many players have subscribed to a weight-loss goal, and use their game as a more "fun" way to achieve this goal, instead of exercising in a traditional gym. The user experience might be affected if such an internal motivation is dampened by the weight scale not responding in the expected direction: it could be that the game facilitated increased energy-expenditure, however, environmental factors outside the magic circle of the game (Salen and Zimmerman 2003) might have caused a weight gain. Gyms that use such exertion games to combine the advantages of engaging gameplay with the social aspects of working out in a dedicated space exist (XRtainment 2012), and evaluating exertion games in such contexts offers opportunities to understand these games from a holistic view on health and social aspects. Measuring physiological or bodily performance data might not only enhance our understanding of physical health implications, it might also supplement results from other methods to help paint a more complete picture of the user experience. Making such data available to the user, for example through displaying the heart rate, could also contribute to the experience itself, as the users' intrinsic motivation might benefit from an immediate feedback showing the game 'works' for their goals.

Using the body's actions to not only facilitate, but also understand affective experience is an exciting area. Technological advances contribute towards rapid evolvement of this field. Using the interrelationship between affect and body movements for evaluation purposes might provide new opportunities for understanding how exertion games engage players, but also be used in other areas of human-computer interaction to create more affective-aware technology. Combining some of the other methods with their individual advantages will also contribute to being able to tell a story that gives justice to the many benefits exertion can offer to its players. By learning from past experiences and appreciating perspectives from various research views, an understanding of exertion games will unfold that, in turn, can offer an exciting new outlook on how we play and interact with technology. We hope with our work, we have contributed towards such advancement, and we were able to excite other researchers to explore this emerging new field further.

Acknowledgments Some of the case studies presented in this paper have been supported by the Marie Curie International Re-Integration Grant "AffectME" (MIRG-CT-2006-046434). The authors also wish to acknowledge the role of Media Lab Europe and the MIT Media Lab in supporting initial work on Breakout for Two, together with Stefan Agamanolis, Rosalind Picard and Ted Selker. Thanks also to the University of Melbourne and CSIRO Collaborative Research Support Scheme in supporting initial development work on Table Tennis for Three. Florian 'Floyd' Mueller's contribution to the initial edition of this chapter was produced during his time at the University of Melbourne, and he thanks the people in the Interaction Design Group for their support. Special thanks to Martin R. Gibbs and Frank Vetere at the University of Melbourne.

References

Ambady N, Rosenthal R (1992) Thin slices of expressive behavior as predictors of interpersonal consequences: a meta-analysis. Psychol Bull 111:256–274

Argyle M (1988) Bodily Communication. Routledge

Bernhardt D, Robinson P (2008) Interactive control of music using emotional body expressions. In CHI'08 Extended Abstracts on Human Factors in Computing Systems (pp. 3117–3122). ACM

Bianchi-Berthouze N (2013) Understanding the role of body movement in player engagement. Hum–Comput Interact 28(1):40–75

Bianchi-Berthouze N, Kleinsmith A (2003) A categorical approach to affective gesture recognition. Connect Sci 15:259–269

Bianchi-Berthouze N, Cairns P, Cox A, Jennett C, Kim WW (2006) On posture as a modality for expressing and recognizing emotions. Workshop on the role of emotion in HCI, HCI 2006

Bianchi-Berthouze N, Kim WW, Patel D (2007) Does body movement engage you more in digital game play? and Why? In: Affective computing and intelligent interaction (pp. 102–113). Springer Berlin Heidelberg

Bogost I (2005) The rhetoric of exergaming. Digital arts and cultures (DAC) Conference. Denmark

Borg G (1998) Borg's perceived exertion and pain scales. Human Kinetics, Champaign

Brown E, Cairns P (2004) A grounded investigation of game immersion. In: CHI'04 extended abstracts on Human factors in computing systems (pp. 1297–1300). ACM

Cacioppo JT, Priester JR, Berntson GG (1993) Rudimentary determination of attitudes: II. Arm flexion and extension have differential effects on attitudes. J Pers Soc Psychol 65:5–17

Carney DR, Cuddy AJC, Yap AJ (2010) Power posing: Brief nonverbal displays affect neuroendocrine levels and risk tolerance. Psychol Sci 21(10):1363–1368

Chandler J, Schwarz N (2009) How extending your middle finger affects your perception of others: learned movements influence concept accessibility. J Exp Soc Psychol 45(1):123–128

Chen M, Kolko B, Cuddihy E, Medina E (2005) Modelling and measuring engagement in computer games. In: DIGRA Conference 2005

Clark R (2008) Seniors trump barriers in Wii bowling tourney. <http://www.nj.com/sunbeam/index.ssf?/base/news-4/1222587621327110.xml&coll=9>. Accessed 1 Feb 2012

Clark M, Gronbegh E (1987) The effect of age, sex and participation in age group athletics on the development of trust in children. Int J Sport Psychol 18:181–187

Cole J, Montero B (2007) Affective proprioception. Janus Head 9(2):299–317

Csikszentmihalyi M (1990) Flow: the psychology of optimal performance. Harper and Row, New York

De Silva PR, Bianchi-Berthouze N (2004) Modeling human affective postures: an information theoretic characterization of posture features. Comput Anim Virtual Worlds 15:269–276

DeLorenzo M (2007) Wii sports experiment. <http://wiinintendo.net/2007/01/15/wii-sports-experiment-results/>. Accessed 1 Apr 2015

Ekman P, Rosenberg EL (2005) What the face reveals: basic and applied studies of spontaneous expression using the facial action coding system (FACS). Oxford University, USA

Eriksson E, Hansen T, Lykke-Olesen A (2007) Movement-based interaction in camera spaces: a conceptual framework. Pers Ubiquit Comput 11:621–632

Ermi L, Mäyrä F (2005). Fundamental components of the gameplay experience: analysing immersion. In: Castell S, Jenson J (eds) Proceedings of the DiGRA conference changing views: worlds in play, pp. 15–27

Graves L, Stratton G, Ridgers ND, Cable NT (2007) Comparison of energy expenditure in adolescents when playing new generation and sedentary computer games: cross sectional study. BMJ 335:1282–1284

Hart M (2003) Borg scale gets 'thumbs up'. <http://www.torq.ltd.uk/pfm_disp.asp?newsid=18>. Accessed 1 Feb 2012

Hero G (2015) Guitar hero. <http://guitarhero.com>. Accessed 1 Apr 2015

Hoysniemi J (2006) Design and evaluation of physically interactive games. PhD thesis. University of Tampere

Isbister K (2010). Enabling social play: a framework for design and evaluation. In: Bernhaupt R (ed) Evaluating user experiences in games: concepts and methods, 1st edn. Springer

Isbister K, Dimauro C (2010) Waggling the form baton: analyzing body-movement-based design patterns in nintendo wii games, toward innovation of new possibilities for social and emotional experience. In: Whole Body Interaction, D. England (ed). Springer

Isbister K, Schwekendiek U, Frye J (2011). Wriggle: an exploration of emotional and social effects of movement. Proceeding of the twenty-sixth annual SIGCHI conference on Human factors in computing systems, 1885–1890.

Iso-Ahola SE, Hatfield BD (1986) Psychology of sports: a social psychological approach, Wm. C. Brown, Dubuque

Kirsh D, Maglio PP (1984) On distinguish epistemic from pragmatic action. Cognit Sci 18:513–549

Kleinsmith A, Bianchi-Berthouze N, Steed A (2011). Automatic recognition of non-acted affective postures. IEEE Trans on Syst, Man, and Cybernet Part B 41(4):1027–1038

Laird JD (1974) Self-attribution of emotion: the effects of expressive behavior on the quality of emotional experience. J Pers Soc Psychol 29(4):475–486

Lantz F (2006) Big games and the porous border between the real and the mediated. <http://www.vodafone.com/flash/receiver/16/articles/indexinner07.html>. Accessed 1 Feb 2012

Lazzaro N (2004). Why we play games: four keys to more emotion without story. Technical report, XEO Design Inc., 2004

LeBlanc C (2008) Nintendo Wii Fits in Neurorehabilitation. http://www.healthcarereview.com/2008/10/nintendo-wii-fits-in-neurorehabilitation/. Accessed 1 Apr 2015

Lehrer J (2006) How the Nintendo Wii will get you emotionally invested in video games. Seedmagazine.com. Brain & Behavior. <http://www.seedmagazine.com/news/2006/11/a_console_to_make_you_wiip.php>. Accessed 1 Apr 2015

Lieberman DA (2006) Dance games and other exergames: what the research says. <http://www.comm.ucsb.edu/faculty/lieberman/exergames.htm>. Accessed 1 Feb 2012

Lindley SE, Monk AF (2008) Social enjoyment with electronic photograph displays: awareness and control. Int J Hum Comput Stud 66:587–604

Lindley SE, Le Couteur J, Berthouze NL (2008) Stirring up experience through movement in game play: effects on engagement and social behaviour. Proceeding of the twenty-sixth annual SIGCHI conference on Human factors in computing systems. Florence. ACM, Italy

Loke L, Larssen A, Robertson T, Edwards J (2007) Understanding movement for interaction design: frameworks and approaches. Pers Ubiquit Comput 11:691–701

Lord C, Risi S, Lambrecht L, Cook EH, Leventhal BL, DiLavore PC, Pickles A, Rutter M (2000) The autism diagnostic observation schedule-generic: a standard measure of social and communication deficits associated with the spectrum of autism. J Autism Dev Disord 30:205–223

Maglio, P. P, Wenger MJ, Copeland AM (2008) Evidence for the role of self-priming in epistemic action: expertise and the effective use of memory. Acta Psychol 127(1):72–88

Mandryk RL, Inkpen KM (2004) Physiological indicators for the evaluation of co-located collaborative play. ACM, New York

Mandryk R, Atkins S, Inkpen K (2006) A continuous and objective evaluation of emotional experience with interactive play environments. CHI '06: Proceedings of the SIGCHI Conference on Human Factors in Computing Systems. ACM Press

McCarthy J, Wright P (2004) Technology as experience. The MIT Press

Meeren HKM, van Heijnsbergen C, de Gelder B (2005) Rapid perceptual integration of facial expression and emotional body language. Proc Natl Acad Sci 102:16518–16523

Melzer A, Derks I, Heydekorn J, Steffgen G (2010) Click or strike: realistic versus standard game controls in violent video games and their effects on aggression. In: Yang HS, Malaka R, Hoshino J, Han JH (eds) International Conference, ICEC 2010. Springer, Berlin

Moen J (2006) KinAesthetic movement interaction: designing for the pleasure of motion. KTH, Numerical Analysis and Computer Science, Stockholm

Mueller F (2002) Exertion interfaces: sports over a distance for social bonding and fun. Massachusetts Institute of Technology

Mueller F, Gibbs M (2007a) A physical three-way interactive game based on table tennis. Proceedings of the 4th Australasian conference on Interactive entertainment. Melbourne, Australia, RMIT University

Mueller F, Gibbs M (2007b) Evaluating a distributed physical leisure game for three players. Conference of the computer-human interaction special interest group (CHISIG) of Australia on Computer-human interaction: OzCHI'07. Adelaide, Australia, ACM

Mueller F, Agamanolis S, Picard R (2003) Exertion interfaces: sports over a distance for social bonding and fun. Proceedings of the SIGCHI conference on Human factors in computing systems. Ft. Lauderdale, Florida, USA, ACM

Mueller F, Stevens G, Thorogood A, O'Brien S, Wulf V (2007) Sports over a distance. Pers Ubiquit Comput 11:633–645

Nenonen V, Lindblad A, Häkkinen V, Laitinen T, Jouhtio M, Hämäläinen P (2007) Using heart rate to control an interactive game. Proceedings of the SIGCHI conference on Human factors in computing systems. ACM Press, New York

Neumann R, Strack F (2000) Approach and avoidance: the influence of proprioceptive and exteroceptive cues on encoding of affective information. J Pers Soc Psychol 79(1):39–48

Niedenthal PM, Barsalou LW, Winkielman P, Krauth-Gruber S, Ric F (2005) Embodiment in attitudes, social perception, and emotion. Pers Soc Psychol Rev 9(3):184–211

Nijhar J, Bianchi-Berthouze N, Boguslawski G (2012). Does movement recognition precision affect the player experience in exertion games? International Conference on Intelligent Technologies for interactive entertainment

Palameta B, Brown WM (1999) Human cooperation is more than by-product mutualism. Anim Behav 57:1–3

Pasch M, Berthouze N, van Dijk EMAG, Nijholt A (2008) Motivations, strategies, and movement patterns of video gamers playing nintendo wii boxing. Facial and Bodily Expressions for Control and Adaptation of Games (ECAG 2008). Amsterdam, the Netherlands

Pasch M, Bianchi-Berthouze N, van Dijk B, Nijholt A (2009) Movement-based sports video games: investigating motivation and gaming experience. Entertain Comput 9(2):169–180

Powell W (2008) Virtually walking? Developing exertion interfaces for locomotor rehabilitation. CHI 2008. Workshop submission to "Exertion Interfaces"

Ratey J (2008) Spark: the revolutionary new science of exercise and the brain. Little, Brown and Company, Boston

Riskind JH, Gotay CC (1982) Physical posture: could it have regulatory or feedback effects on motivation and emotion? Motiv Emotion 6(3):273–298

Rocco E (1998) Trust breaks down in electronic contexts but can be repaired by some initial face-to-face contact. ACM/Addison-Wesley Publishing Co, New York

Salen K, Zimmerman E (2003) Rules of play: game design fundamentals. The MIT Press, Cambridge

Savva N, Bianchi-Berthouze N (2012). Automatic recognition of affective body movement in a video game scenario. International Conference on Intelligent Technologies for interactive entertainment

Stepper S, Strack F (1993) Proprioceptive determinants of emotional and nonemotional feelings. J Pers Soc Psychol 64:211–220

Strauss A, Corbin J (1998) Basics of qualitative research: techniques and procedures for developing grounded theory. SAGE Publications, Washington DC

Tan B, Aziz AR, Chua K, Teh KC (2002) Aerobic demands of the dance simulation game. Int J Sports Med 23:125–129

Wakkary R, Hatala M, Jiang Y, Droumeva M, Hosseini M (2008) Making sense of group interaction in an ambient intelligent environment for physical play. Proceedings of the 2nd international conference on tangible and embedded interaction. Bonn, Germany, ACM

Wankel LM (1985) Personal and situational factors affecting exercise involvement: the importance of enjoyment. Res Q Exerc Sport 56:275–282

Well-being Feild Report (2012) <http://nsg.jyu.fi/index.php/Well-being_Field_Report>. Accessed 1 Feb 2012

Wells GL, Petty RE (1980) The effects of overt head movements on persuasion: compatibility and incompatibility of responses. Basic Appl Soc Psychol 1:219–230

XRtainment (2012) XRtainment - Where working out is all play! <http://www.xrtainmentzone.com/>. Accessed 1 Feb 2012

Yannakakis GN, Hallam J (2008) Entertainment modeling through physiology in physical play. Int J Hum Comput Stud 66(10):741–755

Zheng J, Bos N, Olson JS, Olson GM (2001) Trust without touch: jump-start trust with social chat. ACM, New York

Zheng J, Veinott E, Bos N, Olson JS, Olson GM (2002) Trust without touch: jumpstarting long-distance trust with initial social activities. ACM, New York

Chapter 12
Beyond the Gamepad: HCI and Game Controller Design and Evaluation

Michael Brown, Aidan Kehoe, Jurek Kirakowski and Ian Pitt

Abstract In recent years there has been an increasing amount of computer game focused HCI research, but the impact of controller-related issues on user experience remains relatively unexplored. In this chapter we highlight the limitations of current practices with respect to designing support for both standard and innovative controllers in games. We proceed to explore the use of McNamara and Kirakowski's (Interactions 13(6):26–28, 2006) theoretical framework of interaction in order to better design and evaluate controller usage in games. Finally, we will present the findings of a case study applying this model to the evaluation and comparison of three different game control techniques: gamepad, keyboard and force feedback steering wheel. This study highlights not only the need for greater understanding of user experience with game controllers, but also the need for parallel research of both functionality and usability in order to understand the interaction as a whole.

12.1 Introduction

Over its brief history, human-computer interaction (HCI) has developed a multitude of techniques for measuring and evaluating user experience with technology (Kirakowski and Corbet 1993; Nielsen 1993; Rubin 1994; ISO 1998a; Brown 2008).

M. Brown (✉)
Horizon Digital Economy Research, University of Nottingham, Nottingham, UK
e-mail: michael.brown@nottingham.ac.uk

A. Kehoe
Logitech, Cork, Ireland
e-mail: akehoe@logitech.com

J. Kirakowski
People and Technology Research Group, Department of Applied Psychology,
University College Cork, Cork, Ireland
e-mail: jkz@ucc.ie

I. Pitt
IDEAS Research Group, Department of Computer Science, University College Cork,
Cork, Ireland
e-mail: i.pitt@cs.ucc.ie

© Springer International Publishing Switzerland 2015
R. Bernhaupt (ed.), *Game User Experience Evaluation,*
Human-Computer Interaction Series, DOI 10.1007/978-3-319-15985-0_12

263

Many of the design considerations and usability issues that arise in game software are significantly different from those encountered in other software genres. For example, a game that allows a player to complete quests quickly and easily might score highly with respect to ISO 9241-11 (1998b) software efficiency and effectiveness measures; but it would probably rate very low with respect to user satisfaction because of the lack of challenge. As a result, in recent years we have seen the emergence of HCI research focused on computer games, addressing the unique challenges that this area presents (Desurvivre et al. 2004; Federoff 2002; Jørgensen 2004; Kavakli and Thone 2002).

The visual and audio presentation capabilities of gaming platforms have increased dramatically over the last twenty years, and much of the associated research has focused on these aspects of games. However, the game controller, and how that controller is supported in the game, can have a significant impact on the player's gaming experience. Mastery of the control system is an important part of most games (Johnson and Wiles 2003). In order to have an enjoyable gameplay experience it is important that players feel a sense of control over the game interface and the associated game controls.

In this chapter we describe how McNamara and Kirakowski's (2006) theoretical framework for understanding interactions with technology can be applied to the evaluation of controllers in games. Using this model as a guide, a user study was performed to explore the use of a range of game controllers in terms of functionality, usability and user experience. The framework is described in section three, below. The results of this study are presented and discussed in Sect. 4.

12.2   The Evolution of Game Controllers

As far back as the 1950s, general purpose computing platforms have been used for the development and playing of computer games. The pre-existing input and output capabilities of the computing platforms were leveraged for game play purposes. For example, in 1961, the initial implementations of the "Spacewar!" game, running on the DEC PDP-1, used the test-word toggle switches for player input (Graetz 1981).

However, even in those early game environments the opportunities for specialized game controllers were recognized. The location of the toggle switches on the DEC PDP-1 (c. 1960), relative to the visual display, gave one of the players the advantage of being able to see the display more easily. To overcome this problem a dedicated control box incorporating these switches was constructed. In addition to implementing the required switch functionality, the control box configuration also utilized more natural and intuitive mappings for the controls, e.g., the rotation switch was configured so that moving the switch to the right resulted in the craft being rotated to the right; a lever-style control could be moved to accelerate the craft. Graetz, one of the "Spacewar!" developers, stated that the new control mechanism "improved ones playing skills considerably, making the game even more fun" (Graetz 1981).

Over the past decades, the improvements in processor speeds and storage have been matched by developments in the field of input and output devices. During this time, the evolution of game software and game controllers has been inextricably linked. Games have influenced the design of game controllers, and game controllers have influenced the design of games (Cummings 2007). Many games, especially those played on general purpose computing platforms, have been designed to use the pre-existing control methods for the platform. However, the development of new generations of dedicated gaming platforms, and sometimes specific games, has often incorporated innovation in the area of game controllers.

12.2.1 Standard Game Controllers

The majority of games have been designed to operate with standardised (or de facto standardised) platform-specific controllers, e.g., each game console has an associated standardized first-party controller. Today most games running on consoles support the standard console controller; most games running on personal computers support input via the keyboard and mouse; mobile phone games are played using the standard phone controls; and the recent proliferation of devices incorporating a touch screen have also supported that interaction method in games. Thus, the majority of games are designed to incorporate support for existing control methods.

Much of the innovation in the area of game controllers has been associated with dedicated gaming platforms. There are a number of popular-press books that document the development of the console games industry and technology (Sheff 1993; Kent 2001; Forster 2005). Throughout this almost 40-year development of game consoles, newer generations of consoles were typically accompanied by some degree of development and innovation in the associated game controller. In many cases the level of controller innovation for a new console was relatively minor, and in some cases there was significant change and innovation, e.g., Nintendo Wii Remote, Nintendo Entertainment System gamepad, etc.

Controllers for dedicated gaming platforms have traditionally been very tightly integrated with the console system electronics, supporting firmware/software and games. Through the 1970s and early 1980s, players used a variety of controls (switches, dials, sliders) that were an integral part of the console itself, e.g., Magnavox Odyssey 100–500 series, Coleco Telstar series, etc. From the early 1980s onwards it became increasingly common for the controllers to be distinct separate physical entities (usually gamepads or joysticks) that were connected to the game console through a cable, or in more recent systems, a wireless link.

Each of today's game consoles has a "standard" controller that was designed with the capabilities of its console in mind, and is tightly coupled to that system. A "standard" controller, with support implemented in games in a uniform manner, can help ensure a consistent interface for the user while playing games on that platform. Most games take a conservative approach and adhere to the recommended controller guidelines for their target platforms. The widespread use of standard controllers, together with the use of common control mechanisms within many game genres results in controls being one of the most difficult areas in which to innovate within a game (Rabin 2005).

12.2.2 Focus on Innovative Game Controllers

While uniformity of game controller support can be beneficial, it can also be very limiting for both the game designer and the player (Rabin 2005). Even in the early years of game console systems, when the console and game controls were part of the same mechanical enclosure, there were attempts to make controllers that were targeted towards a particular game or genre of game, e.g., Atari Stunt Cycle (Atari Inc. 1977) and steering wheel controller. These types of developments mirror what was also happening in the arcade machine arena, i.e., the use of dedicated controllers for flying games, racing games, etc.

In recent years an increasing number of games have added support for new and innovative controllers in their games. Incorporating support for innovative controllers in games offers opportunities for a game to distinguish itself in the market place (Kane 2005; Marshall et al. 2006). Custom controllers, designed to operate with specific games, offer possibilities to enhance the user experience in games by enabling interaction styles that are not possible using standard controllers, as described above.

While designing and implementing a custom controller offers opportunities to greatly enhance a game, it also introduces significant additional work, more project schedule risk, and probably an increased retail price for the game-plus-controller bundle. However, apart from platform-specific checklists, the advice available to guide designers and developers considering new or innovative controllers is very limited. Support for innovative controllers must be carefully planned and designed, and their performance evaluated. Problems associated with developing and implementing support for custom controllers have been listed in the post-mortem reports which are published on a monthly basis in Game Developer magazine (Game Developer Magazine 2008). For example: Guitar Hero in Feb06 edition; Metal Gear Solid in May06 edition and Tony Hawk in Jan07 edition.

More recently, the development of gesture-based interaction games using technologies, such as Microsoft Kinect, Nintendo Wii and PlayStation Move have resulted in additional challenges as developers try to enhance the player's experience (Dourish 2001; Van Beurde 2011).

12.3 Evaluating Game Controllers: Experience, Usability and Functionality

As with all technology, the interaction between humans and game controllers is multifaceted and complex. This section describes McNamara and Kirakowski's (2006) theoretical framework for understanding interactions with technology and discusses the implications of applying this model to game controllers.

Fig. 12.1 Components of technology usage, from McNamara and Kirakowski (2006)

12.3.1   Introduction to the Components of Human Computer Interaction

Recent developments in HCI have highlighted the importance of focusing on user experience in the design of technology. This need for high quality user experience is especially important for computer games, as their primary function is to entertain. This revelation has lead to some theoretical difficulties, as the concept of user experience does not easily fit into the traditional HCI fields of usability and ergonomics. In order to fully understand interactions with technology, we must understand the various components of the interactions and how these components impact on each other.

McNamara and Kirakowski (2006) propose a three factor model for understanding the interactions between humans and technology, represented in Fig. 12.1. This theoretical framework presents three separate but co-dependent components of human-computer interaction. 'Functionality' describes the technology side of the interaction, focusing on the technological possibilities of the interaction. Conversely, 'experience' describes the purely human side of the interaction. This factor looks at how the interaction impacts on the person involved by asking questions such as: do they enjoy the interaction? does it make them happy? etc. Finally, 'usability' looks at the dynamics of the interaction itself, is it efficient, effective and satisfying? They propose that in order to fully understand an interaction we must study each of these three components.

12.3.2   Functionality and Game Controllers

This aspect describes the purely technology-based part of the interaction. Key questions in this area are: 'does it work?' and 'what does it do?'. This is the one aspect of the interaction that is relatively independent of both environment and user.

Looking at game controllers, it becomes clear that the primary function is to facilitate user interaction with computer game software. Traditionally controllers only supported a one-way interaction from the user to the game, with audio visual devices providing feedback from the game to the user. However, the recent development of in-controller feedback means that the interaction with game controllers is now bi-directional. For example: haptic gamepads; steering wheels and speakers integrated in the WiiMote. These developments mean that, when considering game controller functionality, we must consider the range of input and feedback that a given control method can provide.

In some cases, controllers may not have the required number of controls to allow the player to invoke all the game commands. For example, flight simulator games typically support a larger number of game commands (often more than 30) than there are physical controls on a low-end joystick. In this case the player must select a subset of the game commands to be assigned to their joystick controls, and the remaining commands can be invoked via the keyboard (or perhaps not used at all by the player).

Another important issue of game controller functionality is the level of support for the controller in a given game. A controller with a wide range of possible inputs and outputs is of little benefit if game software does not support it. Assessing controller functionality in isolation from software is fairly straightforward, as the range and sensitivity of various inputs and outputs can be easily tested. However relating this to in-game functionality is a more complex issue, as the range and sensitivity of a controller may not be supported or necessary for a given game.

12.3.3 Usability and Game Controllers

A classic description of usability is "The extent to which a product can be used by specified users to achieve specified goals with effectiveness, efficiency and satisfaction in a specified context of use" (ISO 1998a). This definition highlights four core concepts central to interaction: effectiveness, efficiency, satisfaction and context of use. Each of these concepts is important when discussing game controller design.

Effectiveness describes the ability of the user to complete specific tasks with the technology. This goes further than basic functionality, as not only must the technology have the potential to perform tasks, the user must also be able to operate the technology sufficiently to actually complete these tasks. The importance of effectiveness in game controller design is obvious: if users can not use a controller to perform game tasks, they will be unable to interact with the game in any meaningful way.

The importance of efficiency in game controller design is a more complex issue. Efficiency considers the resources that must be expended by the user to complete tasks. These resources can be mental effort, physical effort or time. In terms of computer games this is closely linked to concept of difficulty: i.e., if a game requires a large amount of resources (time, skill, mental effort etc.), then it is described as difficult and, conversely, if it requires few resources it is described as easy. This might seem to be of limited importance when discussing game controllers, as the main focus of games is to enjoy playing them, not to effectively complete tasks. However, as Csikszentmihalyi (1975) reports, completing tasks that are easy can become boring and tasks that are difficult can become frustrating. This need for balance of effectiveness presents a dilemma in game controller design.

The concept of satisfaction deals with how the interaction impacts the user; are they free from discomfort and do they have a positive attitude towards the interactions? Once again the importance of this concept to game controller design is fairly obvious, as playing computer games is an entertainment-driven activity, and the interaction should be satisfying. Unlike efficiency, effectiveness and context of use, satisfaction is purely subjective. While the other core concepts of usability can to some degree be directly observed, satisfaction must be assessed solely on the basis of user feedback. This can cause problems in game controller design, as variables such as context of use can influence user report and distort findings.

Context of use is unlike the other concepts discussed as it is not a vital part of usability, but is a factor that must be considered when studying efficiency, effectiveness and satisfaction. Basically, context of use describes the situation in which an interaction is happening (Bevan and MacLeod 1993). It is important to consider that this refers not only to the physical environment, but also to individual differences and the social environment in which the interaction is taking place. While this concept is vital when studying all forms of technology, it is especially important when working with control devices because, as interaction facilitation devices, they introduce additional complexity that must be considered. The device a controller is being used to control has a huge influence on the usability of the interaction. In terms of game controllers, this means both the hardware (PC or console) and software (the specific game) must be considered in design.

12.3.4 Experience and Game Controllers

This final aspect of interaction design is perhaps the most recent to be explored. Experience refers to the psychological and social impact technology has on users. While this is related to the usability concept of satisfaction, it has a much wider scope, looking at interaction in a much broader sense than merely task completion. When studying experience, concepts external to the interaction must be considered; for example aesthetics, marketing, social impact, attachment and mood can all affect users' experience of interacting with technology.

Once again, the nature of game controllers as intermediary devices can make studying this aspect of user interaction difficult. In addition to the social, psychological and environment factors that must be considered when looking at experience of any technology, the hardware and software that is being controlled may also impact on user experience with game controllers. Little research or theory exists relating to user experience with game controllers, making it impossible to predict what factors are key to users experiences in this area. However, the tools needed to explore this area do already exist; qualitative psychological methods such as critical incidents technique, semi-structured interview, grounded theory, content analysis and ethnography have been use to evaluate experience in a wide range of fields (McCarthy and Wright 2004) and their flexible nature means they can be easily applied to the study of game controllers.

12.3.5 *Evaluation and Design of Game Controllers*

This section discusses the impact of the McNamara and Kirakowski framework on research and design in this field. First, current literature is explored, and then the implications for design are discussed.

Looking at recent research into controllers in general reveals that a significant number of research papers have explored the performance of pointing devices (including mice, touch-pads and trackballs), keyboards in traditional desktop/laptop computing scenarios, and keypads usage on handheld devices (Card et al. 1978; MacKenzie 1992; Silfverberg et al. 2000). In recent years, HCI researchers have also explored a variety of increasingly popular interaction methods including gesture, touch, haptics and styluses (Dennerlein et al. 2000; Forlines et al. 2007, Albinsson and Zhai 2003). Most of this work has been concerned with the effectiveness and efficiency of the input methods, but user satisfaction has also been considered (Brewster et al. 2007; ISO 1998b).

Despite the fact that game control has been highlighted by many studies as an important aspect of game design (Federoff 2002; Johnson and Wiles 2003; Desurvivre et al. 2004; Adams 2005; Hoysniemi 2006; Pinelle et al. 2008; Falstein and Barwood 2008) little research has been conducted that focuses on game controllers. Some work has studied the development of input devices and how they affect user performance (Cheema and LaViola 2011; Gerling et al. 2011; Klochek and MacKenzie 2006; Pagulayan et al. 2003; Kavakli and Thone 2002); however the effects of game controllers on user experience has yet to be explored in detail. According to McNamara and Kirakowski's (2006) model, we will not be able to fully understand the interaction involved with game controllers until it has been studied in terms of functionality, usability and user experience.

Current game controller design practice continues this pattern, with an emphasis on the functionality aspects but little attention paid to usability, still less to user experience. For example: the game-play and console compliance checking activities incorporate evaluation of controller support. The associated checklists typically contain very specific advice with respect to assignment of functionality to buttons. Apart from this very platform-specific advice, the guidelines and heuristics related to support of standard controllers are very limited.

The next question that must be answered is how adopting this model impacts game controller design? Currently, little research exists to help focus game controller evaluation on the aspects of game controllers that have the greatest effect on user interaction. This lack of focus leaves controller designers with two choices when it comes to evaluation: either perform a broad range of evaluations to ensure that all aspects of the controller are examined, or perform a few tests and hope that most of the important issues are found. Neither of these are ideal solutions, as the first is costly to perform and it may be even more costly to correct all the issues found, and the second is likely to miss key issues and produce a poor product. The McNamara and Kirakowski (2006) model highlights the distinct components of the interaction, allowing designers to perform fewer evaluations but still investigate each of the components of the interaction. Ensuring that controller functionality, usability and user experience are all evaluated means that all the vital aspects of the controller can be assessed without performing a huge range of evaluations.

12.4 Case Study

In order to further explore this area, a case study was designed to evaluate both standard and innovative computer game controllers usages in a game. This study focused on control of racing games and evaluated keyboard and mouse, standard gamepad and force feedback steering wheel control methods with respect to each aspect of user interaction, as described by McNamara and Kirakowski (2006). This study is designed in order to highlight the benefits of evaluating user experience, within the context of a multi-component game controller evaluation.

12.4.1 Justification

In order to fully explore the interaction between user and game controller, each controller was assessed in terms of functionality, usability and user experience. Measuring each of these components measures brings with it unique challenges.

12.4.1.1 Functionality

Functionality describes the purely technology based part of the interaction. Since this component is relatively independent of both environment and user, it can be measured by an inspection of the technical limitations of each game controller This inspection was done by comparison of the quantity and range of outputs produced by each controller relative to possible inputs recognised by the game. In addition to this, the use of inputs was measured with custom logging software.

12.4.1.2 Usability

This quality is dependent not only on the user, but also the environment in which the interaction takes place. Each aspect of usability as described by the ISO (1998b) was measured independently. Efficiency was measured in terms of mental effort required to use the controllers: the lower the mental effort required, the more efficient the interaction with the controller. Mental effort was measured using the self-report Subjective Mental Effort Questionnaire (Arnold 1999). Effectiveness was measured via lap time. The faster users can complete a lap using a controller, the more effective the interaction, as fast lap completion is the primary task in racing games. Satisfaction was measured via the Consumer Product Questionnaire (CPQ) (McNamara 2006), a standardized measure for evaluating user satisfaction with electronic consumer products.

12.4.1.3 Experience

As this aspect is purely subjective in nature, it can be difficult to measure and is dependent on a huge range of psychological and social factors external to the interaction itself, including aesthetics, advertising and social desirability (McCarthy and Wright, 2004). Critical Incidents Technique (CIT) (Flanagan 1954) was used to collect qualitative data describing user experience. This method involves asking each user to report his/her three most positive and three most negative experiences with the controller in an open ended questionnaire. This method was chosen for two key reasons. Firstly, as a post game play measure, it will not interfere with the game play experience itself. Many during-play methods such as talk out loud, can alter the experience of game play and reduce the validity of any findings. Secondly, CIT is open-ended and does not require a knowledge base in the area being explored. This is important, as a lack of previous research in this area means that other researcher-lead methods are not appropriate. In addition to the CIT evaluation, each subject was asked to report his/her preference between the controllers on a set of three two-way controller preference scales (ranging from "much preferred controller A" to "much preferred controller B").

12.4.2 Methodology

A total of twelve subjects took part in this study. Gender balance was reasonably equal with five female and seven male subjects. The mean age of the participants was 24.6, with ages ranging from 19 to 30. Participants were also asked if they drive regularly as this may give them an advantage with the steering wheel controller; five responded that they did. They were also asked if he/she had any experience of racing games; all except subject 1 responded that he/she had little or none.

The test system was a HP Compaq dc7800p running Windows XP. The following three controllers were evaluated in the study:

Keyboard Dell USB keyboard.

Gamepad The Logitech Dual Action is a USB gamepad, with two mini-joysticks (similar to those commonly used on game consoles) and 12 digital buttons.

Steering Wheel The Logitech MOMO Racing is a USB force feedback device, with an analog steering wheel, analog accelerator and brake pedals, and 10 digital buttons.

A single game was used in the study, Colin McRae Rally DiRT (Codemasters 2007). In order to minimize the impact of game specific artifacts on the evaluation, a number of the game settings were fixed. The same difficulty level (amateur), control assignment, view (behind the car), car (Subaru Impreza) and track (Avelsbachring) was used for all subjects.

This study used a repeated measures type design with each subject taking part in every condition. The independent variable was the type of control method used and was operationalised in three conditions: Gamepad, Keyboard and Force Feedback Steering wheel.

In order to reduce confounding variables between conditions, a number of controls were used. The order of conditions was counterbalanced in order to counteract any effects due to learning. Each condition used the same software and hardware, except for the control method, so reducing the effect these may have on the evaluation.

12.4.2.1 Procedure

After completing a short demographic questionnaire, the subjects were introduced to the game and the first control method they would use. They were then asked to play the game until they felt comfortable with the control method. How long this step took was left to the participants' discretion and varied from 5 to 20 min. Then the participant performed two timed laps of the test track. Once they had done this the participant was asked to complete the CPQ, SMEQ, and CIT questionnaires. This procedure was repeated for each control method.

12.4.3 Results

12.4.3.1 Functionality

When comparing the controllers in terms of functionality, there are two issues to be considered. Firstly, are all the game commands supported by the controller? And secondly, the issue of exactly how the control is supported. The DiRT game has only a small set of commands. In addition to steer, accelerate and brake, a small number of extra commands are also supported (change camera, handbrake, look left/right/back, gear up/down). Even though the use of all the game commands was not examined in the study, the various controllers had sufficient controls for all of these game commands to be assigned, i.e., 100% of the game commands can be assigned to the controllers.

Both the gamepad and steering wheel support analog steering. However, as Table 12.1 highlights, their response characteristics are very different, with the wheel being several times more precise in terms of angular resolution. This data show that in terms of functionality in the context of this game, the steering wheel is the superior control method, with the widest range of motion and sensitivity. Conversely, the keyboard has the poorest functionality, only accommodating binary input for both steering and acceleration.

Table 12.1 Functional differences between gamepad and wheel controllers

Control parameter	Gamepad	Wheel
Physical range (approx.)	25	240
Analog counts	255	1024
Deadzone	Yes (center)	No
Angular resolution (approx.)	Less than 10.2	4.3

12.4.3.2 Usability

The usability of each game controller was measured in terms of effectiveness, efficiency and user satisfaction.

Table 12.2 shows the results for each component of the usability analysis of the three controllers. It indicates poorer performance for the steering wheel compared to the other two control methods in terms of both completion time and SMEQ (low values of SMEQ indicate mental effort required). Gamepad and Keyboard results for these two measures appear to be much closer. In terms of CPQ results, the Keyboard reports an extremely low result for satisfaction, with the Gamepad and Steering Wheel performing slightly better (50 % on the CPQ is an average device score, according to the CPQ database). A series of one way repeated measures ANOVAs were used to determine the statistical significance of these results. ANOVA was used as it is a robust method of difference testing and performing multiple t-tests would increase the likelihood of a type II error. For this exploratory study an alpha level of 0.05 was used.

Table 12.3 shows that the ANOVA results indicate significant results at an alpha level of 0.05 for completion time and SMEQ scores. Results for CPQ scores show the data approaches significance, but fails to reject the null hypothesis at a 0.05 alpha level. In order to further investigate the differences a post hoc STEP analysis was performed on each of the significant ANOVA results.

Table 12.4 shows the probability values for the STEP analysis of the completion time data and reveals significant differences between Gamepad and Wheel, and

Table 12.2 Means scores on usability measures

Controller type	Completion time	SMEQ score	CPQ score (%)
Steering wheel	04:39	72.92	20.83
Gamepad	02:59	34.42	15.08
Keyboard	03:13	42.58	6.25

Table 12.3 ANOVA results for usability measures

	Completion time	SMEQ score	CPQ score
F value	5.876	7.258	3.268
Degrees of freedom	10	10	10
P	0.021	0.011	0.081

Table 12.4 *P*-values for STEP analysis of completion time ANOVA

Completion time	Steering wheel	Gamepad	Keyboard
Steering wheel	–	0.014	0.027
Gamepad	–	–	0.4
Keyboard	–	–	–

Table 12.5 *P* values for STEP analysis of SMEQ ANOVA

SMEQ results	Steering wheel	Gamepad	Keyboard
Steering wheel	–	0.014	0.027
Gamepad	–	–	0.4
Keyboard	–	–	–

Keyboard and Wheel. This shows that the steering wheel performed significantly worse than the other two methods in terms of effectiveness.

Table 12.5 reveals similar results for the STEP analysis of the SMEQ data. Significances were found between Steering wheel and Gamepad, and between steering wheel and keyboard. This shows that the steering wheel also performed significantly worse than the other control methods in terms of efficiency.

In summary, the usability data collected shows an interesting trend in terms of the steering wheel. This controller scored significantly worse than both of the other control methods in terms of efficiency and effectiveness (as measured by Completion Time and SMEQ), but scored the highest in the measure of user satisfaction. This set of results suggests that while the steering wheel was not an effective or efficient controller, the participants enjoyed using it. Keyboard data shows the opposite trend, with good efficiency and effectiveness scores, but the poorest satisfaction results. Finally the Gamepad performed the best of three controllers in terms of usability, producing the best lap times, the lowest SMEQ scores and a reasonable score in the CPQ, compared to the other controllers. It is also worth noting that all three control systems performed poorly in terms of user satisfaction, with means scores ranging from 6.25 to 20.83 %. The lack of statistical significance may be due to a 'floor' effect, i.e., the CPQ scores could hardly get much worse.

12.4.3.3 User Experience

The data collected to measure user experience took two forms: user preference was gauged and secondly CIT was used to report user attitudes towards the devices.

Table 12.6 presents the mean user preference scores and shows a preference towards the gamepad compared to the other two controllers, and a preference for the keyboard over the steering wheel. In order to test the significance of these results, one-way repeated measures ANOVA was performed at alpha level 0.05, producing an F value of 3.015 with 10 degrees of freedom. This falls outside the critical region and so does not show statistical significance.

As the CIT produces quantitative data, a more detailed analysis is required. The responses for each game controller were formed into categories using Content

Table 12.6 User preferences scores on a 1–5 scale

User preference	Keyboard-gamepad	Keyboard-steering wheel	Steering wheel-gamepad
Mean	4	2.5	3.92
Std dev.	1.28	1.57	1.44

Table 12.7 Content analysis of steering wheel comments

Steering wheel-categories	Positive comments	Negative comments	Total
Sensitivity	3	9	12
Feedback	7	4	11
Easy to pick up	7	4	11
Realism	9	2	11
Physical characteristics	4	3	7
Learning potential	1	3	4
Miscellaneous	0	1	1
Total	31	26	57

Analysis. This method involved grouping the comments collect into categories, based on the content of those categories, in order to identify the key areas of the users' experience with the game controllers.

Table 12.7 shows the results of the content analysis of the steering wheel comments. This table highlights *Sensitivity, Feedback, Easy to pick up* and *Realism* as the most reported aspects of users experience with this device.

The *Sensitivity* comments highlight the high sensitivity of left/right steering using the wheel. For example:

> ... impressive accuracy while playing. (Subject 1, positive)
> Controller is very sensitive to movement, it takes a while to judge accurately how much force is required. (Subject 7, negative)
> Hard to control. The steering was highly sensitive. (Subject 11, negative)

While the majority of these comments are negative, showing frustration at the highly sensitive controls, three of the subjects listed this as a positive feature that actually enhanced their game play experience.

Comments in the *Feedback* category discuss the force feedback produced when using the steering wheel. For example:

> The motion of the wheel when on rough terrain (vibration) added to the experience of crashing. (Subject 6, positive)
> The vibrations of the wheel were a nice effect in making it seem like you were really on the terrain, like the grass. (Subject 12, positive)
> The motion/vibration of the wheel often made turning the wheel very difficult—it moved a lot less smoothly (Subject 6, negative).

Again the comments in this category are both positive and negative. The positive comments show an appreciation of the fun and realism that force feedbacks adds to the interaction, while the negative comments mention situations where it got in

Table 12.8 Content analysis of keyboard comments

Keyboard/categories	Positive comments	Negative comments	Total
Ease of use	10	3	13
sensitivity	3	8	11
Physical characteristics	5	6	11
Realism	0	3	3
Comfort	0	2	2
Feedback	0	2	2
Familiarity	2	0	2
Total	20	24	44

the way of playing the game. This shows the care with which innovative controller features should be applied so that they add to the game experience without getting in the way of the basic features of the game, in this example steering.

The *Easy to pick up* comments mention instances where this control system was or wasn't easy to pick up and use. Some subjects found the familiar steering wheel and pedals provided an intuitive control system, but for others the reproduction of driving conditions was not accurate enough to make it easy to pick up. For example:

Using a steering wheel is quite intuitive; it's obvious how it works. (Subject 6, positive)
The accelerator and brake pedals were awkward to use at first and I never really got comfortable with them. (Subject 3, negative)

The *Realism* category produced the most positive comments for the steering wheel, with only two negative comments from eleven. These comments mainly praise the realism of this control method and two of the comments call for even more realism. For example:

The wheel combined with the pedals made it seem like a very realistic driving system. (Subject 6, positive)
"Steering wheel only had half turn each way rather than the 1.5 as I am used to when driving." (Subject 8, negative)

Table 12.8 shows the results of the content analysis of the keyboard comments. It is worth noting that this is the only control method that received more negative comments than positive ones. The categories that contain the most comments and are the focus of the evaluation are *Ease of Use, Sensitivity* and *Physical Characteristics*.

The *Ease of Use* category contains comments discussing how easy the keyboard was to use. Most of these are positive comments focusing on the simplicity of the interface, but some mention the limited control that is afforded by keyboard control. For example:

Actions didn't translate well to game. Even though controls are simple, car was difficult to control and judge. (Subject 7, negative).

The category containing the most negative remarks was *Sensitivity*, and contained comments relating to the binary nature of the keyboard input. A few comments

Table 12.9 Content analysis of gamepad comments

Gamepad-categories	Positive comments	Negative comments	Total
Comfort	8	2	10
Learnable	4	3	7
Sensitivity	3	4	7
Personal preference	2	5	7
Ease of use	6	1	7
Feedback	0	3	3
Realism	1	1	2
Misc	2	0	2
Total	26	19	45

praised this as easy to use, while most of them criticised the lack of sensitivity. For example:

> Easier to make incremental adjustments during steering. (Subject 2, positive)
> Breaking was instantaneous, I had no control over slowing down, it was stop or nothing. (Subject 3, negative)

Comments in the *Physical Characteristics* category discuss the implication of the physical layout of the keyboard, either praising the localised controls or criticising it for being cramped. For example:

> Small choice space-i.e. arrow keys within easy range of fingers. (Subject 2, positive)
> "Spacing of input keys is a small bit cramped." (Subject 9, Negative)

Table 12.9 shows the results of the content analysis of the gamepad comments and reveals that the comments in this category are more evenly spread across the categories produced; this suggests that there were not any aspects of the interaction that were experienced by all the users. The categories that contain the most comments are *Comfort, Learnable, Sensitivity, Personal Preference* and *Ease of Use*.

Comfort is the largest category produced and contains the most positive comments. These comments simply talk about how comfortable the gamepad is. For example:

> Very comfortable. I could hold it all day long. (Subject 3, positive)
> Makes my thumb sore after playing for a while. (Subject 1, negative)

Comments in the *Learnable* category talk about how easy or difficult it is to get used to using the gamepad controller. For example:

> Very familiar. I knew exactly how it worked within very little time. (Subject 3, positive).
> Maybe if someone used this for the very first time it would be difficult to figure out. (Subject 7, negative).

It is interesting to note that while several users mention this method is easy to learn, none talk about how intuitive it is, as they did with both the steering wheel and the keyboard. This may suggest that it may be familiarity with this device rather than an intuitive interface that makes learning easier.

The Sensitivity comments highlight the positive and negative effects of steering, acceleration and break sensitivity. For example:

Natural feeling, right sensitivity. (Subject 1, Positive)
The acceleration and brakes didn't seem to work well together. It was hard to brake slightly; you had to come to a complete stop. (Subject 11, negative)

Comments in the *Personal Preference* category discuss issues relating to control assignment setting in the game. Most of these comments are negative, perhaps representing the fact that the participants were not allowed to alter these settings during the study. For example:

Would have preferred to accelerate on the 'trigger' buttons. (Subject 2, negative)
The button for the break should be to the right side, not above the accelerator. (Subject 8, negative)

The *Ease of Use* category contains comments relating the simplicity (or lack of) using this control method. Most of these comments are positive with only a single comment stating that this device is difficult to use. For example:

Very easy to use. Actions were displayed accurately in the game. It was easy to judge how much movement/force was required. (Subject 7, positive)
The joystick seems sometimes a little bit difficult to use. (Subject 5, negative)

In addition to highlighting some of the key issues in game controller user experience, this data has revealed an interesting trend, the mixture of positive and negative comments throughout the categories relating to all three control methods. The vast majority of categories discovered contain both positive and negative comments; this trend highlights the importance of individual differences when analyzing game controllers. What some users may see as a positive feature or aspect of a game controller, others may view in an extremely negative light. For example, when discussing the binary nature of the keyboard, one subject found it much easier to steer with, while another found the lack of sensitivity frustrating.

Easier to make incremental adjustments during steering. (Subject 2, keyboard, positive)
Very difficult to control the strength of the control/action by simply pressing one key. (Subject 4, keyboard, negative)

12.4.4 Combining the Results

While each of the evaluations produced interesting results, a more complete picture can be gained by looking at a combination of all three measures. While a complete analysis of all the data collected falls outside the scope of this chapter, this section highlights a single issue that was reported by several of the analysis methods and explores it in more detail.

The issue of controller sensitivity is one that seems to have an impact on all three components of the interaction. The user experience analysis highlighted controller sensitivity as an important aspect of experience for each of the control methods. Categories within each analysis revealed each control method's advantages and disadvantages in terms of sensitivity. The results suggest that this aspect of the interaction was the most influential when using the steering wheel, as nine comments mentioned sensitivity as a problem. However, in terms of functionality the steering wheel is clearly superior, being sensitive to small gradations in terms of steering, acceleration and braking.

To examine this in more detail, an analysis of the data collected by the logging software for subject 1 (the subject with the best laps times using the wheel) and subject 5 (a subject with close to average lap times with the wheel) was conducted.

Figure 12.2 shows the reports captured by the logging software for subjects 1 and 5, while using the gamepad and steering wheel to control the steering axis while driving the two timed laps of the track. The chart is a frequency distribution of the range of controller reports. Both controllers report a different range of values in response to movement. In order to display them all on the same X-axis scale the data from both controllers has been normalized; −1000 is the controller axis at the extreme left; +1000 is the controller axis at the extreme right; 0 is the center position for the controller. The Y-axis represents the total number of reports of a given value.

The bias of data towards the left hand side of the chart is a result of the track being driven in an anti-clockwise direction. As can be seen in Fig. 12.2, the profile of reports generated by both subject 1 and subject 5 while using the gamepad is very similar. The distribution of the data shows that little of the analog capability of the mini-joystick on the gamepad is being used. Most of the reports are either close to the axis centre (mini-joystick is moved to the centre 'deadzone') or at the limit of the device range, i.e., the gamepad mini-joystick is essentially being used as a digital control in a manner similar to the keyboard.

The profiles of reports generated by both subjects while using the steering wheel are obviously different. The increased number of wheel reports for Player 5 versus

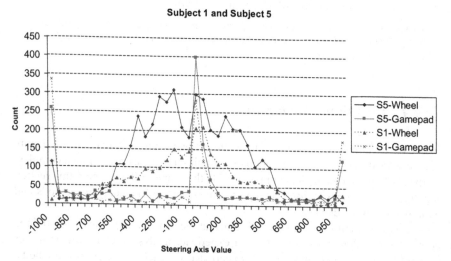

Fig. 12.2 Device steering reports for subjects 1 and 5

Player 1 is a reflection of the fact that Player 5 took more time to complete the two laps while using the wheel, and thus generated more reports. In contrast to the gamepad data, the analog capability of the wheel is being utilized. The graph for Player 1, who had the fastest drive time for the wheel, shows a concentration of reports about the centre position of the wheel. In contrast, the graph for Player 5 shows a wider distribution of data, as he/she struggled to control the vehicle using the wheel, i.e., significant over steering.

This suggests that, although a more sensitive control method is a useful tool for a more skilled user, it is of little benefit to those of less skill. As few of the participants had much experience with steering wheels in games; this could explain the negative comments regarding the steering wheel, as they found it frustrating to use without the time to master. The distraction caused by this unfamiliar sensitivity could also go some way towards explaining the poor usability scores reported for the steering wheel. The analog nature of the brakes and pedals on the steering wheel controller allows the player to perform a variety of real-world rally driving techniques in a game, such as the "heel-and-toe" and "left foot braking". However, none of the subjects in the study used these techniques.

This example highlights the main advantage of using this multi-component analysis: the ability to fully explore an issue that has been highlighted by one of the methods and find its root cause. While a traditional usability or user experience evaluation would probably discover that sensitivity is a key issue for these control devices, they would not be able to explore this issue in its entirety, as this multi-component evaluation has.

12.4.5 Critique

When considering the results of this study, there are several possible short weaknesses that must be considered. The most obvious of these is the range of methods used. While this allows a great deal of data to be collected for each component of the interaction, it also means that compromises have to be made when assessing each component. For example: when exploring used experience, McCarthy and Wright (2004) suggest evaluations in the field, but the present study used a laboratory environment so that usability evaluations could be performed simultaneously. The lab was set up to closely resemble a home environment, but it is impossible to recreate the exact conditions of a field study.

Another factor that must be considered is the inexperienced participants. Only one of the twelve subjects reported having regularly played racing games, and none of them had more than a few hours of experience with steering wheel controllers. The results must be interpreted with this in mind, and may not be generalisable to more experienced gamers.

12.4.6   Conclusions

The steering wheel is an attractive device which supports all the functions needed by the game commands, and therefore may be a selling point for the game. In the hands of an inexperienced user, however, it will lead to poor game performance. Nonetheless, at least initially, users will feel satisfied with it.

Although the gamepad comes out above the steering wheel and the keyboard on usability performance measures, the keyboard has the advantage that it is regarded as very easy to learn. "Experience" and "usability" in this case seem to be telling different stories. Which should the game designer go for if there is a choice to be made? If there is a tradeoff between the keyboard and the gamepad, the designer may well choose to not support the gamepad if user experience is the key issue.

The issue of controller sensitivity shows the complexity involved in understanding a small aspect of user experience with game controllers. It highlights not only the need for greater understanding of user experience with game controllers, but also the need for parallel research of both functionality and usability in order to understand the interaction as a whole.

Overall, all three of the devices studied were able to support the game command functions, and the steering wheel was also able to transmit extra output using haptic feedback. Thus we may infer that for the game and devices studied, the game controller was working at 100%. However, the devices differed in the way the user interacted with them in the game. This study shows that the method of user interaction is actually an important aspect of game play, and how one may be able to assess its impact in a simple and direct laboratory evaluation. With experienced facilitators, a study such as this need not take more than two elapsed days.

In terms of game controller user experience, several issues where highlighted that appear to be important for all of the controllers evaluated. These include: Sensitivity; Ease of Use; Realism and Comfort. This information represents an initial baseline of game controller user experience, which can be further explored with future research.

12.5   Discussion

Much of on-going game-play testing that is performed as a regular part of the development process is accomplished using informal techniques. Such informal evaluation could also be complemented by more a structured evaluation of controller support, as outlined in the user study. It is relatively quick and easy to perform, and could be especially useful during the early stages of development to benchmark controller support.

12.5.1 *Implications and Recommendations*

Between discussion and the case study presented here, the advantages and disadvantages of a multi-method evaluation have been highlighted. The main advantage shown is the ability to identify the root cause of the issues discovered in any of the evaluations. The main disadvantage is that when performing a range of evaluations simultaneously, compromises such as the use of a laboratory setting, must be made.

In terms of practical implications; these finding suggest that a multi-component model such as this could be useful within a game development process, where it is important not only to highlight issues, but also discover their root causes and fix them. However, the compromises that must made in the evaluation process means that focused user experience evaluations may be more appropriate in academic setting, where understanding of the intricacies of an issue are more important.

12.5.2 *Future Research*

In terms of user experience, the case study presented has laid the ground work for exploring how game controller effect user experience. Having discovered some of the key issues in this area, the next step is to explore these issues in more detail with more in depth data collection and analysis, such as interview and grounded theory.

This user study was deliberately constrained in that it only explored the initial stages of game play for each of the controllers in a single game. However, with extended game play, the players will become more familiar with both the game and the controllers. As a result, longitudinal studies would be required to explore the issues that arise in the context of longer game play durations over an extended period of time. The same techniques applied in this user study could also be applied in the context of longitudinal studies, and the data then analyzed to explore change over time.

The data collected in the study consists of both data collect during game play (with logging software), and data collected afterwards as subjects complete questionnaires. The data collected during game play in the study was limited to the reports generated by the game controllers. It would be useful to complement this in-game data with biometric and video capture data (with emphasis on facial expressions and body movement). This could perhaps allow better interpretation of the in-game reports, and complement the information collected post game play in the questionnaires.

Future studies should seek to elaborate on the effects of functionality on usability and experience. For instance, where possible, to observe the effects on game players in setups where the game controls, controllers, and support devices offer different levels of functionality as defined in this paper.

Acknowledgements This work was supported by RCUK through the Horizon Digital Economy Research grant (EP/G065802/1).

References

Adams E (2005) Bad game designer, no twinkie! VI. Gamasutra designer's notebook. http://www.gamasutra.com/features/20050603/adams_01.shtml. Accessed 23 Aug 2008

Albinsson P, Zhai S (2003) High precision touch screen interaction. Proceedings of the SIGCHI on human factors in computing systems. ACM, New York, pp 105–112

Arnold A (1999) Mental effort and evaluation of user interfaces: a questionnaire approach. Proceedings of the 8th International conference on human-computer interact.. ACM, New York, pp 1003–1007

Atari Stunt Cycle {computer software} (1977) Atari Inc. http://en.wikipedia.org/wiki/Stunt_Cycle

Bevan N, Mcleod M (1993) Usability measurement in context. Behav Inform Technol 13:132–145

Brewster S, Faraz C, Brown L (2007) Tactile feedback for mobile interactions. SIGCHI conference on human factors in computing systems CHI 2007. ACM, New York, pp 159–162

Brown M (2008) Evaluating computer game usability: developing heuristics based on user experience. Proceedings IHCI conference. University College Cork, Ireland, pp 16–21

Card S, English W, Burr BJ (1978) Evaluation of mouse, rate-controlled isometric joystick, step keys, and text keys for text selection on a CRT. Ergonomics 21:601–613

Cheema S, LaViola J (2011) Wizard of Wii: toward understanding player experience in first person games with 3D gestures, Proceedings of the sixth international conference on the foundations of digital games, pp 265–267 (June 2011)

Colin McRae: Dirt {computer software} (2007) Codemasters

Csikszentmihalyi M (1975) Beyond boredom and anxiety. Jossey-Bass, London

Cummings A (2007) The evolution of game controllers and control schemes and their effect on their games. Proceedings of the 17th annual university of Southampton multimedia systems conference

Dennerlein J, Martin D, Hasser C (2000) Force-feedback improves performance for steering and combined steering-targeting tasks. CHI Letters, vol. 2, 1st edn. ACM, New York, pp 423–429

Desurvivre H, Caplan M, Toth JA (2004) Using heuristics to evaluate the playability of games. Extended abstracts, conference on human factors in computing systems. ACM Press, pp 1509–1512

Dourish P (2001) Where the action is: the foundations of embodied interaction. MIT, Cambridge

Falstein N, Barwood H (2008) The 400 Project. http://theinspiracy.com/400_project.htm. Accessed 6 Nov 2008

Federoff M (2002) Heuristics and usability guidelines for the creation and evaluation of fun in video games. Thesis. Indian University

Flanagan JC (1954) The critical incident technique. Psychol Bull 51(4):327–358

Forlines C, Wigdor D, Shen C, Balakrishnan R (2007) Direct-touch vs. mouse input for tabletop displays. Proceedings of the SIGCHI conference on human factors in computing systems. ACM, New York, pp 647–656

Forster W (2005) The encyclopedia of game machines—consoles, handheld and home computers 1972–2005. Hagen Schmid, Berlin

Game Developer Magazine (2008) http://www.gdmag.com/homepage.htm. Accessed 8 Nov 2008

Gerling KM, Klauser M, Niesenhaus J (2011) Measuring the impact of game controllers on player experience in FPS games. MindTrek 2011. Tampere, Finland

Graetz JM (1981) The origin of spacewar. Creative computing, August 1981. http://www.atarimagazines.com/. Accessed 12 Nov 2008

Hoysniemi J (2006) International survey on the dance dance revolution game. Computer entertainment 4(2): 8

ISO (1998a) 9241 Ergonomic requirements for office work with visual display terminals (VDTs)—part 9—requirements for non-keyboard input devices (ISO 9241-9)

ISO (1998b) 9241 Ergonomic requirements for office work with visual display terminals (VDTs)—part 11—guidance on usability (ISO 9241-11)

Johnson D, Wiles J (2003) Effective affective user interface design in games. Ergonomics 46(13/14):1332–1345

Jorgensen AH (2004) Marrying HCI/Usability and computer games: a preliminary look. Proceedings of the 3rd Nordic Conference in HCI, pp 393–396.

Kane C (2005) Beyond the gamepad http://www.gamasutra.com/features/20050819/kane_pfv.htm. Accessed 20 Oct 2008

Kavakli M, Thone J (2002) A usability study of input devices on measuring user performance in computer games. Proceeding of the first international conference on information technology and applications 2002, pp 291–295

Kent LS (2001) The ultimate history of video games: from Pong to Pokémon. The story behind the craze that touched our lives and changed the world. Three Rivers Press. New Jersey

Kirakowski J, Corbet M (1993) SUMI: the software usability measurement inventory. Br J Educ Technol 24(3):210–212

Klochek C, MacKenzie IS (2006) Performance measures of game controllers in a three-dimensional environment. Proceedings graphics interface, vol. 137, pp 73–79

MacKenzie S (1992) Fitts' law as a research and design tool in human-computer interaction. Hum Comput Interact 7:91–139

Marshall D, Ward T, McLoone S (2006) From chasing dots to reading minds: the past, present, and future of video game interaction. Crossroads 13(2):10

McCarthy J, Wright P (2004) Technology as experience. The MIT, London

McNamara N (2006). Measuring user satisfaction with consumer electronic products. Doctoral thesis. University College Cork, Ireland

McNamara N, Kirakowski J (2006) Functionality, usability, and user experience: three areas of concern. Interactions 13(6):26–28

Nielsen J (1993) Usability engineering. Academic Inc, Oxford

Pagulayan RJ, Keeker K, Wixon D, Romero RL, Fuller T (2003) User-centered design in games. In: Jacko JA, Sears A The human-computer interaction handbook: fundamentals, evolving technologies and emerging applications (Human factors and ergonomics). L. Erlbaum Associates. Hillsdale, pp 883–906

Pinelle D, Wong N, Stach T (2008) Heuristic evaluation for games: usability principles for video game design. ACM SIG CHI '08, pp 1453–1462

Rabin I (2005) Introduction to game development. Charles River Media, Boston p 125

Rubin J (1994) Handbook of usability testing. Wiley, West Sussex

Sheff D (1993) Game over—how Nintendo zapped an American industry, captured your dollars, and enslaved your children. Random House, New York

Silfverberg M, MacKenzie IS, Korhonen P (2000) Predicting text entry speed on mobile phones. Proceedings of the SIGCHI conference on human factors in computing systems. CHI '00. ACM, New York, pp 9–16.

Van Beurden MHPH, IJsselsteijn WA, de Kort, YAW (2011) User experience of gesture-based interfaces: a comparison with traditional interaction methods on pragmatic and hedonic qualities, workshop of gesture in embodied communication and human-computer interaction Athens, Greece, pp 121–124.

Printed in the United States
By Bookmasters